DOING BUSINESS IN THE MIDDLE EAST

The Middle East has for a long time been at the centre of global trade as well as political interest. Demographic and social change shifts in global economic power, rapid urbanisation, climate change and resource scarcity, and significant technological development make this region both complex and hugely important.

Doing Business in the Middle East highlights both the opportunities and constraints confronting foreign investors in the region and proposes strategies on how best to overcome them. The book explores the existing and emerging political and legal frameworks, sociocultural patterns, national infrastructures, regulatory environment, conflict resolution and how to negotiate in the Middle East. It also provides useful insights into how to approach advertising and marketing, promotion and distribution, and also at the strategies for investing in the region and appropriate modes of entry. With a number of features such as case studies, examples of effective and ineffective practices, clear takeaways, and a note on a future agenda on each given topic, this book is highly practical.

Based on robust research, this comprehensive guide to doing business in the Middle East is an ideal reference tool for potential foreign investors, those who are already doing business or intend to do so in the region, and for a range of business and policy decision-makers. The book is also suitable for students and researchers in the fields of international management and business, international and strategic HRM, cross-cultural management, and business communication.

Pawan Budhwar is the 50th Anniversary Professor of International HRM, Head of Aston Business School, and an Associate Pro-Vice Chancellor International (India) at Aston University, UK.

Vijay Pereira is Full Professor of International and Strategic Human Capital Management and Department Chair of People and Organizations department at NEOMA Business School, France.

DOING BUSINESS IN THE MIDDLE EAST

A Research-Based Practitioners' Guide

Edited by Pawan Budhwar and Vijay Pereira

LONDON AND NEW YORK

Designed cover image: Hasan Zaidi

First published 2023
by Routledge
4 Park Square, Milton Park, Abingdon, Oxon OX14 4RN

and by Routledge
605 Third Avenue, New York, NY 10158

Routledge is an imprint of the Taylor & Francis Group, an informa business

© 2023 selection and editorial matter, Pawan Budhwar and Vijay Pereira; individual chapters, the contributors

The right of Pawan Budhwar and Vijay Pereira to be identified as the authors of the editorial material, and of the authors for their individual chapters, has been asserted in accordance with sections 77 and 78 of the Copyright, Designs and Patents Act 1988.

All rights reserved. No part of this book may be reprinted or reproduced or utilised in any form or by any electronic, mechanical, or other means, now known or hereafter invented, including photocopying and recording, or in any information storage or retrieval system, without permission in writing from the publishers.

Trademark notice: Product or corporate names may be trademarks or registered trademarks, and are used only for identification and explanation without intent to infringe.

British Library Cataloguing-in-Publication Data
A catalogue record for this book is available from the British Library

ISBN: 978-0-367-43782-4 (hbk)
ISBN: 978-0-367-43785-5 (pbk)
ISBN: 978-1-003-00576-6 (ebk)

DOI: 10.4324/9781003005766

Typeset in Bembo
by SPi Technologies India Pvt Ltd (Straive)

To Laxmi and Gaurav for their continued support and love (PB).

To Veronica, Anisha and Amelia, for their patience, support and love, as always, but especially during our five-year stint, as expatriates in the Middle East (VP).

To those who have interest in doing business in the Middle East region.

CONTENTS

List of Figures	*x*
List of Tables	*xi*
Contributors	*xiii*
Preface	*xvi*

PART I
The Middle East Business Context   1

1. The Middle East Context: An Introduction   3
   Pawan Budhwar and Vijay Pereira

2. Economic Environment in the Middle East: Facts and Initiatives   10
   Dimitrios Reppas and Yama Temouri

3. The Political Environment in the Middle East:
   A Comparative Analysis of the UAE, Egypt, and Iraq   23
   Abdul-Nasser El-Kassar, Sophie Lythreatis and Tamirace Fakhoury

4. Changing Legal Framework of the GCC Countries   38
   T.P. Ghosh

5. Wasta in the Middle East: A Corruption or an Opportunity   62
   Mohammad Ta'amnha, Susan Sayce and Olga Tregaskis

PART II
Conducting Business in the Middle East   **83**

6   Entry Modes to Middle East-GCC Markets:
      The Case of the UAE   85
      Vijay Pereira, Bhaskar Dasgupta, Daicy Vaz and
      Glenn Muschert

7   Employment Relations in the Middle East and
      North Africa (MENA)   98
      Mike Leat and Ghada El-Kot

8   Banking and Financial Institutions in the Gulf
      Cooperation Council Region   116
      Vikash Ramiah, Vijay Pereira, Bhaskar Dasgupta,
      Alex Frino and Huy Pham

9   Accounting and Taxation Systems in the Middle East   131
      Peter Rampling and Albert Wijeweera

10 Managing Human Resources in the Middle East   146
      Pawan Budhwar, Vijay Pereira and Mohammed Aboramadan

11 Conflict Management and Negotiation in the Middle
      Eastern Workplace   161
      Gita Bajaj and Ahmad Said Al-Shuabi

12 Performance Management in the Middle East   176
      Shahina Javad

13 Expatriate Management in the Middle East   191
      Prerna Kumari

PART III
Emerging Themes   **207**

14 Gender Issues at the Workforce in the Middle East   209
      Maryam Aldossari and Sara Chaudhry

15 Innovation: The Unconventional Gateway to the Middle East 222
    Yassir Nasief and Abdulrahman Basahal

16 Government e-Services and Reputation: Case of UAE 235
    Fatima Al Ali, Melodena Stephens and Vijay Pereira

Index 253

FIGURES

4.1	State of Oil Dependency in GCC Countries: Average of 2012–2018	41
5.1	Measurement Model for Wasta Scale	76
8.1	Financial Crises in the GCC	127
15.1	GII 2021 Rankings Overall and by Pillar, Egypt	226
15.2	GII 2021 Rankings Overall and by Pillar, Saudi Arabia	228
15.3	GII 2021 Rankings Overall and by Pillar, UAE	230
16.1	Innovation in Digital Economy and Public Sector Response – Timeline and Key Events	236
16.2	Global Cross-border Flows 2005–2015 (bandwidth)	238
16.3	Happiness Meter Dashboard	246

TABLES

2.1	GDP Per Capita (in US Dollars) for Selected Countries in the Middle East for 1990–2020	11
2.2	Contribution (as value added, % GDP) of Four Major Economic Sectors for the Year 2020	13
2.3	Unemployment Rates (%) for Selected Countries in the Middle East for the Years 2010 and 2021	13
2.4	Regulatory Quality for Selected Countries in the Middle East for the Years 2010, 2015, and 2020	17
4.1	Foreign Direct Investment, Net Inflows (in US$ million)	40
4.2	Non-oil GDP as % of GDP in GCC Countries	41
4.3	Minimum Capital Requirement in LLC and Private Joint Stock Company Structure in the GCC	48
4.4	Key Reforms in the Legal Framework of GCC Countries	53
4.5	Positive and Negative Lists for 100% FDI participation in GCC Countries	56
4.6	Indicators of State of Oil Dependency in the GCC Countries	59
5.1	Bribery and Wasta Rates Based on People Who Received These Services from Government Departments	63
5.2	Items for Wasta Scale	74
8.1	Central Banks Operating in the GCC	121
8.2	Different Types of Financial Institutions in Bahrain as of July 2020	123
8.3	Different Types of Financial Institutions in the UAE as of July 2020	123
8.4	Different Types of Financial Institutions in Saudi Arabia as of July 2020	124

8.5	Different Types of Financial Institutions in Kuwait and Oman as of July 2020	125
9.1	The Middle Eastern and North African Countries	132
9.2	The Middle East vs Global Comparison for Tax Rates and Compliance	134
11.1	Legislative Systems in the GCC Countries	164
12.1	Factors and Sub-factors Influencing Performance Management in the Middle East	177
13.1	Resources for Evaluating Sociocultural Context	203
13.2	Resources for Evaluating Economic Context	204
13.3	Resources for Evaluating Political Context	205
14.1	Female Education and Labour Market Participation Rates	210
15.1	Egypt's Innovation Ecosystem	227
15.2	Saudi Arabia's Innovation Ecosystem	229
15.3	UAE's Innovation Ecosystem	231

CONTRIBUTORS

Mohammed Aboramadan is an Assistant Professor, School of Economics, Administration, and Public Policy, Doha Institute for Graduate Studies, Doha, Qatar.

Fatima Al Ali is at the Department of Business Administration, University of Wollongong, Dubai, UAE.

Maryam Aldossari is a Senior Lecturer of HRM at Royal Holloway, University of London, UK.

Ahmad Said Al-Shuabi is an Assistant Professor of HRM at IMT Business School, Dubai, UAE.

Gita Bajaj is a Professor of OB & HRM at IMT Business School, Dubai, UAE.

Abdulrahman Basahal is an Assistant Professor in the Faculty of Economics and Administration at King Abdulaziz University, Riyad, Saudi Arabia.

Pawan Budhwar is the 50th Anniversary Professor of International HRM and Head of Aston Business School, Birmingham UK.

Sara Chaudhry is a Senior Lecturer, Department of Management, Birkbeck, University of London, UK.

Bhaskar Dasgupta is an Associate Director – Market Development, Financial Services Regulatory Authority, ADGM, Abu Dhabi, UAE.

Abdul-Nasser El-Kassar is an Associate Professor of Quantitative Methods, Lebanese American University, Beirut, Lebanon.

Ghada El-Kot is a Professor in Human Resources & Organizational Behavior, Graduate School of Business and Deputy President for Strategic Affairs, Arab Academy for Science & Technology & Maritime Transport, Egypt.

Tamirace Fakhoury is an Associate Professor of Political Science and International Affairs and the Director of the Institute for Social Justice and Conflict Resolution at the Lebanese American University, Beirut, Lebanon.

Alex Frino is a Professor of Financial Economics, Senior Deputy Vice-Chancellor (Innovation, Enterprise and External Relations), University of Wollongong, New South Wales, Australia.

T.P. Ghosh is a Professor of Accounting and Finance at IMT Dubai, UAE.

Shahina Javad is an Associate Professor in OB & HRM at IMT Dubai, UAE.

Prerna Kumari is a Doctoral Researcher at Abu Dhabi University, UAE.

Mike Leat is an Honorary Research Fellow at Plymouth Business School, Plymouth, UK.

Sophie Lythreatis is a Lecturer in Business Analytics, School of Management, University of Bristol, Bristol, UK.

Glenn Muschert is a Professor in the Department of Humanities and Social Sciences at Khalifa University, Abu Dhabi, UAE.

Yassir Nasief is CEO Palm Ventures and VP Baseqat Consulting, Riyadh, Saudi Arabia.

Vijay Pereira is a Professor of Strategic and International Human Capital Development and Head of People and Organization Department, NEOMA Business School, Reims, France.

Huy Pham is a Senior Lecturer in Finance at **RMIT** University in Vietnam.

Vikash Ramiah is an Associate Professor and Director of Research, Faculty of Business, University of Wollongong, Dubai, UAE.

Peter Rampling HDR Supervisor, School of Business, Excelsia College, New South Wales Australia.

Dimitrios Reppas is an Assistant Professor of Economics in the Department of Humanities and Social Sciences at Khalifa University, Abu Dhabi, UAE.

Susan Sayce is an Associate Professor at Norwich Business School, University of East Anglia, Norwich, UK.

Melodena Stephens is a Professor of Innovation Management at Mohammed Bin Rashid School of Government, Dubai, UAE

Mohammad Ta'amnha is a Faculty at German-Jordanian University, Jordan.

Yama Temouri is an Associate Professor in the Department of Humanities and Social Sciences at Khalifa University, Abu Dhabi, UAE.

Olga Tregaskis is a Professor of International HRM and Head of Norwich Business School, University of East Anglia, Norwich, UK.

Daicy Vaz is a Doctoral Researcher at NEOMA Business School, Reims France.

Albert Wijeweera is an Associate Professor, Department of HSS, College of Arts & Sciences, Khalifa University, Abu Dhabi, UAE.

PREFACE

Increasingly more and more countries in the Middle East continue to become important from a business perspective due to a variety of reasons, including a rapid growth in population and its spending power. As a result, the region is witnessing a significant growth in foreign direct investment, an increase in the number of business start-ups, incentives offered to foreign businesses to operate there, rapid developments with infrastructure to support the growth of businesses, low operating costs and high return, amongst others. Accordingly, there is a strong interest from foreign businesses to set up their operations in the Middle East. Due to a variety of factors such as massive sociocultural, politico-legal and economic diversity between different countries in the region, lack of reliable information for international managers on how to successfully operate in the region, the ongoing stereotypes and myths about the area, and regular regional disturbances, foreign firms planning to enter the markets in the region may find it very confusing, uncertain and even intimidating when they start their operations in the Middle East. Through this important book, we attempt to provide 'ready to use' information and tips for international managers to effectively deal with the challenges they may experience when they start operations in the region. Thus, the objective of this book is to provide the reader with an understanding of the dynamics of doing business in the Middle East. It should also enable the reader to understand in a better way the 'context-specific' issues and, possibly, ways forward on the same in order to operate successfully in the region.

To achieve our objective, we invited all contributions around a set framework. It included the aims of the chapter, why such a chapter is important for foreign investors/organisations/managers, coverage of the core topic of the chapter, key challenges for the given theme(s) and a sensible way forward. Each chapter also includes a short case study(ies), clear takeaway(s) for international managers and links to key resources. We believe the book consolidates, through a single source, key research-based input on the dynamics of doing business in the Middle East and in particular questions pertaining to the *'what'*, *'why'* and *'how'* of operating in the region. All the chapters in this volume are original contributions to the field and were specially commissioned for the handbook.

We would like to thank all those who have helped us in various ways to make this project a success. Our special thanks to all the contributors and colleagues at Routledge – Sophie Peoples, Rebecca Marsh and Terry Clague, who helped us to complete this work.

Pawan Budhwar
Aston Business School, UK
Vijay Pereira
NEOMA Business School, France

PART I
The Middle East Business Context

1
THE MIDDLE EAST CONTEXT
An Introduction

Pawan Budhwar and Vijay Pereira

The Middle East Context

The term Middle East is defined as a cultural area, which does not have clear borders and a variety of terms have been used to denote the region. These include the 'Middle East', 'Near-East', 'Middle East–North Africa (MENA)', 'Southwest Asia', 'Greater Middle East', 'Levant', 'Arabian-peninsula' or the 'Arab World' in a very general sense by both academics and policymakers (see Budhwar and Mellahi, 2016). A limited version of the region includes the Gulf state countries of Kuwait, Saudi Arabia, Bahrain, Qatar, the United Arab Emirates, Oman, as well as Iran, Iraq and the Levant region. In some cases, the region extends to countries in North Africa, with a clear connection to and the use of Arabic language, which includes the countries Tunisia to the west and Eritrea, Djibouti and Somalia to the south-east (see Britannica.com, 2022). For this volume, we use the last interpretation of the Middle East.

Expectedly, there are a few commonalities between the countries in the region; nevertheless, each nation has its own historical evolution and development, and a unique set of socio-economic features, which are an outcome of the interplay between sociocultural institutions, historical developments, demographic variables and political relations and systems core to themselves. Moreover, each of the countries in the region is at a different stage of industrialisation and economic and political development (Budhwar et al., 2021). Such contextual complexities should be kept in mind while operating in the region.

The Middle East is the birthplace of three main monolithic religions – Islam (followed by approximately 95% of the total population, out of which 85% are Sunnis and remaining Shias), Judaism and Christianity. It is also home to some of the oldest civilisations of the world, including Phoenicia, Babylon and Egyptian. The population of the Middle East in 2021 was around 472 million, representing

DOI: 10.4324/9781003005766-2

about 6% of the total world population (World Bank, https://data.worldbank.org/indicator/SP.POP.TOTL?locations=ZQ), with Iran, Turkey, Iraq, Saudi Arabia and Yemen, respectively, being the most populous countries. The region also hosts around 65% of the world's known oil reserves. However, until the discovery of oil in the 1960s and 1970s, the region had the lowest levels of economic development in the world (Budhwar et al., 2019). The economic growth of the majority of the countries in the region has been flat. Through the sharp increase in oil prices since the Russian invasion of Ukraine in early 2022, the GDP growth of the Middle East now stands at 5.2% (ICAEW, 2022).

The Middle East then has a history of erratic economic growth which can be attributed to a combination of factors such as the so-called 'curse of natural-resource abundance' (over-dominance of the oil sector in oil-rich countries), structural imbalances, deficient political systems and political reforms, underdeveloped financial markets and slow integration into the global economy. These factors are compounded by a dominant and inefficient public sector where the bulk of locals gain employment, linked to growing unemployment, lack of creation of employable skills, underutilisation of skilled women, dated and inefficient government systems in the region to conditions of war and conflict and mass migration (see Budhwar and Mellahi, 2016; Budhwar et al., 2021).

The developments over the last decade or so in the region (such as the Arab Spring and the toppling down of governments in many countries in the region, amongst others) resulted in regional (and, to some extent, global) disturbances. These were witnessed in the form of deaths of hundreds of thousands and mass migration from the region – mainly from Syria both into adjoining countries and Europe (for details The Guardian, 2022). Such developments have serious implications for foreign direct investment (FDI) in the region, and due to serious concerns for security, a large number of multinationals pulled out of the disturbed parts of the Middle East, leaving a significant vacuum for economic growth. Nevertheless, many are now regularly entering the Middle East markets, with countries like Saudi Arabia, the UAE, Qatar, Israel and Oman in particular expected to lead on inward FDI (Patton, 2022).

Due to the above-highlighted developments, the business context of the Middle East continues to evolve rapidly, and foreign investors and international managers are regularly looking for information. This can help them to smoothly access the regional markets (e.g., by selecting ideal local partners); develop a good idea about the cultural nuances, cultural diversity, approach to effective communication, decision-making and related dos and don'ts of doing business; help to deal with conflicts and negotiate complex deals. Additionally, it helps to understand the global contemporary issues for the region such as disruption caused by the COVID-19 pandemic and the emerging post-pandemic ways of doing business; security issues; move towards renewable energy and the impact of the new global tax accord signed by Saudi Arabia, the UAE, Qatar, Bahrain and Oman (the last event resulted in multinationals requiring to pay a minimum of 15% corporate income tax for profits to the corporations with an annual revenue upwards of 750 million euros).

Looking at the various emphasis on economic development in different countries (e.g., Saudi Vision 2030, Dubai Industrial Strategy 2030, Qatar National Vision 2030, Oman Vision 2040, Bahrain Economic Vision 2030), which, amongst many other things, is setting out both the roadmaps for development and to serve as a tool for its measurement (for details see Mogielnicki, 2022), are pushing countries in the region to pursue Industry 4.0, which now seems to have moved beyond political rhetoric (for details see ISI Consultants, 2022; PWC, 2022).

Evidence also suggests that most countries in the Middle East are now emphasising both human resource and organisational development. In particular, the oil-rich countries have been making serious efforts to reduce their dependence on this depleting natural resource and develop other sectors, which need skilled human resources. Similarly, many countries in the region have been emphasising the development of 'locals' and reducing the number of 'foreigners' due to the pressure of rapidly growing populations and to provide jobs to their natives as part of their nationalisation programmes (i.e., to reserve jobs for locals) such as Saudi Arabia. However, there are serious concerns related to employable skills and the mind-set of the locals who do not prefer to work in the private sector and on lower-level positions (for details see Budhwar and Mellahi, 2016).

To summarise, the Middle East region is now continuously in the news and is of interest to most nations of the world for a variety of economic, political, demographic challenges, migration, supply of oil, ongoing conflicts and security-related reasons. There is also a drive by most countries in the region to further assimilate into the global economy. The latest attempt was the hosting of the Dubai expo by the UAE (albeit delayed and held in 2021, because of the COVID-19 pandemic situation in 2020). Nevertheless, a number of macro-level phenomena unique to the region (presented above) are creating challenges in this regard. Such developments have serious implications for foreign firms to successfully operate in the region. This book provides useful insights in this regard.

Topics Covered in the Book

The 16 chapters in this volume are covered under three broad themes of business context, conducting business – a functional perspective, and emerging themes. In order to achieve consistency and a comprehensive picture of each contextual scenario, we asked all the contributors to write along and coordinate with specific themes. These included the aims of the chapter, why such a chapter is important for foreign investors/organisations/managers, coverage of the core topic of the chapter, key challenges for the given theme(s) and a sensible way forward. Each chapter also includes a short case study(ies), a clear takeaway for international managers and links to key resources. Such features will help interested stakeholders gain useful insights from this book.

In Chapter 2, Reppas and Temouri cover the topic of economic environment and focus on themes of economic development strategies and economic challenges found in the Middle East region. Specifically, they provide a snapshot of the countries' current economic situation, in terms of their GDP per capita, GDP by sector and unemployment. They also discuss dimensions of economic development, particularly the ease of doing business. Some of the region's dominant economic characteristics include labour market imperfections, the lack of investments in education and human capital and the role of State interventions to control local markets. The chapter also gives a special emphasis on the GCC countries' initiatives to move away from oil-based economic dependence.

In contrast to Chapter 2, El-Kassar, Lythreatis and Fakhoury in Chapter 3 analyse the political environment of the Middle East. In particular, they provide a comparative analysis of three very different Middle Eastern countries (i.e., the UAE, Egypt and Iraq) with the aim of discussing relevant information on host country factors that influence inward FDI. The nations that constitute this strategic region are known to share some similarities in values, societal culture and religion, and also possess unique characteristics that contribute to the ease or hindrance of conducting business within their boundaries. The chapter explores political details and business specifics of each country in the interest of unveiling business opportunities. The chosen countries represent three different case studies as they highlight disparities in the Middle East and operate in different political environments. Due to the prevalence of different political systems, resulting in different diverse decision-making by the governments, the countries also display distinct rules and regulations, with varying imposed taxes, to operate a business. Such information should be helpful for foreign operators in the region.

Sticking to the theme of external environment, Ghosh, in Chapter 4, analyses the changing legal framework in GCC (Gulf Cooperation Council) countries. In particular, he focuses on reforms in the legal and administrative framework in the chosen countries, their diversification strategies and liberalisation of the FDI law, changes in the commercial company law and its impact on FDI. Ghosh further emphasises the need to improve the corporate governance mechanisms in firms operating in the Middle East region. The chapter also presents a summary of key regulatory reforms and their impact on inward FDI.

Continuing with the business context theme of the Middle East, in Chapter 5, Ta'amnha, Sayce and Tregaskis present the construct of 'wasta' – a social relational form of capital mechanism which is dominant in the Arabic business setting, particularly in facilitating business transactions and other social activities, though it is considered in many cases resulting in corruption. The authors present a practical instrument that can be used to not only understand the core aspects of wasta, but also to measure it. They support this by providing findings of an empirical study with professionals who work in the IT sector in Jordan. Their findings reveal an increase in the usage of Wasta due to the pressures created by the COVID-19 pandemic. The chapter presents a 14-item 'wasta legitimacy scale' (WLS), which is developed around the dimensions of pragmatic legitimacy, normative legitimacy and cultural-cognitive legitimacy. This scale is helpful to understand the cross-cultural issues around the practice of wasta.

The focus of Chapter 6 by Pereira, Dasgupta, Vaz and Muschert is on entry modes to Middle-East-GCC markets. The authors caution foreign investors to carefully analyse the weak political, commercial and institutional environments of the Middle East in order to minimise substantial risks when deciding to invest in the region. They use the case of UAE to highlight how to identify, pre-empt, mitigate and manage risks while entering the Middle East markets via planned actions and while developing their internationalisation strategies.

In Chapter 7, Leat and El-Kot detail the employment relations scenario in the Middle East. Their presentation includes an analysis on labour markets and regulation, religious and cultural contexts, management in practice and collective employee relations. They conclude the chapter by drawing key observations regarding the current state of collective employee relations in the region which is an outcome of a complex mix of sociocultural, economic-politico and legal aspects of the Middle East.

Chapter 8, by Ramiah, Pereira, Dasgupta, Frino and Pham, provides useful insights into the background and mode of operandi of the banking and financial institutions in the GCC region. Utilising the patchy information available on the core topics of this chapter, the authors present the features of the banking regulatory framework prevalent in the GCC, the variety of different national legal systems and financial institutions existing in these nations, the similarities and differences in their roles of Central Banks and the reasons for which the region is vulnerable to crises. Like other chapters, this also provides a set of useful takeaways for decision-makers.

Rampling and Wijeweera, in Chapter 9, present an overview of the region's dominant accounting and taxation systems and the challenges foreign investors and multi-national companies (MNCs) may experience in adapting to these systems. The authors make a number of useful recommendations on how foreign investors may best approach accounting and taxation practices in the MENA region. The religious and cultural contexts of accounting and taxation systems in the MENA region are a pervasive theme throughout this chapter and reflect the vital role these play in determining how modern accounting and taxation standards both derive and manifest in the regional economies.

In Chapter 10, Budhwar, Pereira and Mohammed focus on the various aspects of managing human resources in the Middle East. The chapter provides useful insights into the present state of HRM (human resource management) practices, the forces contributing to the development of specific approaches to managing human resources, and highlights the HR challenges and how to tackle the same. Such information should assist HR practitioners operating in the region to generate context-relevant HRM policies and practices.

Chapter 11 is dedicated to conflict management and negotiations in the Middle East. Bajaj and Al-Shuabi highlight the usefulness of understanding the interests, desires, resources, influences and the working and decision-making styles of the people in the Middle East region, in order to deal with conflicts and conduct effective business negotiations. They present about how to identify the interests and aspirations of the interdependent entities, namely, employees, employers (companies) and governments and explain what empowers and challenges different entities during conflict and negotiation. Their analysis also reveals the nuances involved in how the Arabs resolve conflict and how non-Arabs can relate to their style. The authors make a number of useful recommendations regarding the approaches for effectively managing conflict in the Middle East.

Chapter 12 details various aspects of performance management in the Middle East. Javad provides an overview of the major factors that influence performance management practices, uses of performance appraisals in the Middle Eastern context and the key features of performance management systems in Middle East–based organisations. Via her analysis, the author highlights the key determinants of performance appraisals and performance management in the region. Such information should be helpful for foreign investors, line managers and human resource professionals for designing and administering effective performance management systems.

Kumari, in Chapter 13, deals with the topic of expatriate management. This chapter provides information regarding how to facilitate expatriate management, what challenges decision-makers will experience while dealing with expatriates in the region and how best to tackle the same. Furthermore, she provides useful advice on how managers and expatriates aim to achieve success in the Middle East region.

Chapter 14, by Aldossari and Chaudhry, examines the gender issues in the workplace in the Middle East. This chapter begins by highlighting the overarching trends in terms of women's employment in the Middle East, which is followed by a discussion of the social-institutional norms and cultural restrictions that impact women's employment in the Middle East. It also highlights the institutionalised gender inequalities, and the dynamic creation and interaction of visible and invisible inequalities, vis-à-vis organisational policies and practices. The authors also provide an overview of the current structural and institutional changes that are influencing women's employment in Saudi Arabia as an example. Finally, the chapter concludes with some recommendations that address these existing inequalities at the meso/organisational level of analysis.

Nasief and Basahal, in Chapter 15, reveal the key developments taking place within the broad topic of innovation in the Middle East. The authors use examples of Saudi Arabia, the UAE and Egypt to explore the rapidly emerging innovation systems in the region along with the creation of new knowledge in the form of patents. The chapter analyses the topics of technology transfer and innovation and how the three countries score on the global innovation index. The analysis also provides a clear takeaway for international managers interested in pursuing innovation in their organisations in the Middle East.

Building on the topic of innovation, the last chapter (Chapter 16) by Ali, Stephens and Pereira is dedicated to highlighting the e-services being pursued by the government of the UAE and its impact on the reputation of both the organisations and the country. The analysis reveals how the COVID-19 pandemic acted as a tipping point, pushing governments to digitalise faster, whether it was the adoption of health care, education, remote working or virtual courts. The authors further reveal how the UAE e-governance is utilising the ICT and other web-based technologies to improve efficiency in delivering and accessing government services for all kinds of stakeholders in government-to-citizen (G2C), government-to-government (G2G) and government-to-business (G2B) relations. The UAE case is being used by other countries in the region as a benchmark to develop their own e-governance mechanisms. The takeaway from this chapter should help international firms operating in the Middle East to build their own e-governance ecosystems suitable for operating in the region.

Useful Websites

World Bank: http://www.worldbank.org/en/region/mena

GCC: http://www.worldbank.org/en/country/gcc

Middle East Media Research Institute: http://www.memri.org

Middle East Institute: http://www.mei.edu

References

Britannica (2022) http://www.britannica.com/place/Middle-East

Budhwar, P. and Mellahi, K. (2016) (Eds) *Handbook of Human Resource Management in the Middle East.* Cheltenham: Edward Elgar.

Budhwar, P., Pereira, V., Mellahi, K., and Singh, S. K. (2019) The state of HRM in the Middle East: Challenges and future research agenda. *Asia Pacific Journal of Management*, 36(4), 905–933.

Budhwar, P., Pereira, V., Temouri, Y. and Do, H. (2021) International business research and scholarship in the middle east: Developments and future directions. *International Studies of Management & Organization*, 51(3): 185–200.

ICAEW (2022) Economic update: Middle East. https://www.icaew.com/technical/economy/economic-insight/economic-insight-middle-east#:~:text=Consequently%2C%20our%202022%20GDP%20growth,expansion%20of%202.9%25%20in%202021 (accessed on 23 July 2022).

ISI Consultants (2022) 5 key international business trends for Middle East Africa 2022. https://www.isi-consultants.com/insights/vz837psrjppdbpfywhhx8p40i07paa (accessed on 23 July 2022).

Mogielnicki, R. (2022) Competing economic visions in the Gulf. *The Cairo Review of Global Affairs*. https://www.thecairoreview.com/essays/competing-economic-visions-in-the-gulf/ (accessed on 23 July 2022).

Patton, C. (2022) Five Middle Eastern countries for investors to watch in 2022. https://www.investmentmonitor.ai/analysis/five-middle-eastern-countries-investors-2022 (accessed on 23 July 2022).

PWC (2022) Five GCC economic themes to watch for in 2022. https://www.pwc.com/m1/en/blog/five-economic-themes-to-watch-for-2022-in-gcc.html (accessed on 23 July 2022).

The Guardian (2022) Arab and Middle East unrest. https://www.theguardian.com/world/arab-and-middle-east-protests (accessed on 23 July 2022).

2
ECONOMIC ENVIRONMENT IN THE MIDDLE EAST

Facts and Initiatives

Dimitrios Reppas and Yama Temouri

Introduction

The literature on the economic environment in the Middle East has grown significantly over the last two decades. For instance, the World Bank, the IMF, and the OECD have all undertaken several studies over the last few years to describe the development experiences of countries in this region. The UNDP has also launched, since 2002, the Arab Human Development Report series which analyzes the dynamics of human capital (social, economic, and political trends) in the Arab region.[1]

Overall, countries in the Middle East have been quite heterogeneous in terms of their populations, land sizes, natural resource endowments, as well as in terms of their investments in technology and human capital. Therefore, it is no surprise that countries in this region have experienced varying degrees of economic development. This chapter summarizes the related economic themes, development strategies, and economic challenges found in the Middle East area. More specifically, we first provide a snapshot of the countries' current economic situation, in terms of their GDP per capita, GDP by sector, and unemployment. We then briefly turn into some other dimensions of economic development, particularly the ease of doing business. Some of the region's dominant economic characteristics are labor market imperfections (due to gender bias); the lack of investments in education and human capital; and the role of State interventions to control local markets. Regarding the latter and more generally in terms of State intervention (i.e., government functioning, political participation, pluralism, and civil rights), it seems that the majority of the MENA countries ranks under authoritarian and hybrid regimes, rather than under flawed democracies or full democracies (The Economist's Intelligence Unit's Index of Democracy, 2021[2]). It is important to emphasize that this chapter does not aim to provide an in-depth description of any single country's economic environment in the Middle East; nevertheless, emphasis is given on the GCC countries overall and their key initiatives to move away from oil-based economic dependence. Therefore, readers, wishing to examine in more detail the region's economic realities or/and get a country-by-country analysis should refer to the detailed reports available by the previously mentioned global organizations.

The rest of the chapter is structured as follows. We first outline key aggregate developments for GDP per capita across GCC countries and sectors of the economy and unemployment trends. We then discuss the progress toward economic diversification and ease of doing business in the GCC region. We conclude with various recommendations that the region can undertake in the future in order to overcome economic challenges in the quest to develop their countries more sustainably.

GDP per Capita

Economists use GDP per capita as a rough measure of economic development. Table 2.1 presents GDP per capita (in 2015 US dollars) for selected countries in the Middle East, over the period 1990–2020. In general, an increasing trend of GDP per capita over time is associated with higher standards of living in a country. Also, using GDP as a measure of a country's standards of living has drawbacks, as it ignores, for instance, household production, underground economic activities, leisure, and negative externalities (Acemoglu, Laibson and List, 2016). The latter may be significant for oil-rich countries, and therefore if not internalized, GDP tends to overestimate social welfare.

TABLE 2.1 GDP Per Capita (in US Dollars) for Selected Countries in the Middle East for 1990–2020

	1990	2000	2011	2015	2020
Bahrain	18,160	23,243	20,774	22,634	19,514
Egypt	2,051	2,610	3,472	3,562	4,028
Iran	3,333	3,888	5,409	4,904	4,883
Iraq	3,559	4,337	4,218	4,688	4,247
Israel	—	28,747	33,678	35,808	37,481
Jordan	3,252	3,587	4,521	4,164	4,029
Kuwait	—	29,951	33,166	29,869	24,429
Lebanon	3,538	6,728	8,773	7,663	5,382
Oman	16,187	20,624	19,868	18,444	15,743
Qatar	—	56,865	65,129	63,039	56,026
Saudi Arabia	17,453	17,690	19,813	20,627	18,691
Syria	933	1,254	1,659	916	—
Turkey	5,354	6,543	9,299	11,006	12,038
UAE	66,023	60,716	33,246	38,663	37,497
Yemen	2,042	2,383	2,311	1,601	—

Source: The World Bank https://data.worldbank.org/indicator/NY.GDP.PCAP.CD.

Table 2.1 reveals that several of these Middle East countries have not experienced a significant increase in their per capita income, over the period 1990–2020. The corresponding mean annual growth rate (over this time) in the GDP per capita for most of these countries is estimated to be around 1%, except for Turkey, Egypt and Israel, whose annual growth rates are around 2.5%. Moreover, the growth in the GDP per capita for Egypt, Turkey (as well as Jordan and Lebanon) has not been driven by higher labor productivity, but by population increases (Schiffbauer et al., 2015; World Bank, 2016).

One of the main reasons behind the economic underperformance in the Middle East is the lack of governments' transparency in data collection, particularly at the micro-business level (Arezki et al., 2020) and at the micro-level household surveys with income inequality (Alvaredo, Assouad and Piketty, 2018). Arezki et al. (2020), for instance, estimate that the observed decline in MENA's transparency between 2005 and 2018 has been associated with a loss of the region's income per capita, ranging from 7% to 14%. Transparency, in general, affects economic development through the following path: reliable data assist policymakers in undertaking the right economic reforms; these government findings/policies can then be disputed by researchers; and independent media can finally communicate information to the public with a view to having citizens participating in the policy debate. In the Middle East, the observed limited ability of the research community, media, and citizens to obtain credible information at the macro as well as micro-level seems to be an important obstacle for establishing effective structural economic reforms.

The main recommendation for foreign firms attracted to the region or international managers already invested in the GCC is to realize the significant differences of growth rates of GDP per capita coupled with realistic expectation about future trends. This also means that, in the absence of more detailed data about GDP per capita growth rates, foreign firms and international managers should invest in additional analysis about economic developments in different parts of a particular country, prior to investing and locating their operations in the GCC.

GDP Across Sectors of the Economy

Table 2.2 presents, for selected countries in the Middle East, the contribution (as value added, percent of GDP, for the year 2020) of four broad economic sectors, as per the United Nations System of National Accounts, i.e., agriculture (including forestry and fishing), industry (including construction), manufacturing, and services. For most of these countries' economies, agriculture and manufacturing seem to be much less important than the other two sectors. Furthermore, no major structural changes can be detected in the composition of these countries' economies for the period 2006–2015 (Pelzman, 2018, p. 29).

Unemployment

Table 2.3 presents unemployment rates for selected countries in the Middle East, for the years 2010 and for 2021. Unemployment for the Arab Gulf countries

TABLE 2.2 Contribution (as value added, % GDP) of Four Major Economic Sectors for the Year 2020

	Agriculture	Industry	Manufacturing	Services
Bahrain	0.3	40.3	18.1	56.7
Egypt	11.6	32	16.4	51.8
Israel	1.2	18.6	11.3	71.4
Iraq	5.9	41.1	3	54.3
Jordan	5.2	23.9	17.3	61.6
Lebanon	3.0	6.9	3.1	87.2
Oman	2.6	47.5	8	54.7
Qatar	0.3	52.3	7.9	52.7
Saudi Arabia	2.6	41.4	13	56.2
Turkey	6.7	28	19.1	54.2
UAE	0.9	40.9	9.7	58.2
Yemen	5	35.6	—	16.8

Source: The World Bank:
For Agriculture: https://data.worldbank.org/indicator/NV.AGR.TOTL.KD?name_desc=true
For Industry: https://data.worldbank.org/indicator/NV.IND.TOTL.ZS?name_desc=true
For Manufacturing: https://data.worldbank.org/indicator/NV.IND.MANF.ZS?name_desc=true
For Services: https://data.worldbank.org/indicator/NV.SRV.TOTL.ZS

TABLE 2.3 Unemployment Rates (%) for Selected Countries in the Middle East for the Years 2010 and 2021

	2010	2021
Bahrain	1.1	1.9
Egypt	8.8	9.3
Iraq	8.3	14.2
Israel	8.5	5
Jordan	12.5	19.3
Kuwait	1.8	3.7
Lebanon	6.8	14.5
Oman	4	3.1
Qatar	0.4	0.3
Saudi Arabia	5.6	7.4
Syria	8.6	10.6
Turkey	10.7	13.4
UAE	2.5	3.4
Yemen	12.8	13.6

Source: International Labor Organization (https://ilostat.ilo.org/data/).

(particularly Bahrain, Kuwait, Qatar, the UAE, and Saudi Arabia) has been much lower compared to middle- and lower-income countries of the region. In fact, the former countries have acted as a "relief" for the unemployed youth of Egypt, Yemen, Syria, Jordan, and Lebanon (UNDP, 2019, p. 13).

What is striking in the Arab Middle East countries is that the percentage of unemployed young people (i.e., aged 15–29) is at around 30%, which is twice the world's average (of 14%) (UNDP, 2016, p. 26). Moreover, the age structure in the region is quite different from that of several other countries, in the sense that Middle Eastern countries have a relatively larger proportion of their population below 30 years old and a smaller proportion (than other countries) above 65 years old. In other words, countries in the Middle East have a unique opportunity to develop, due to their large percentage of population falling in the most economically productive phase. This is an opportunity they need to seize soon.

Regarding unemployment, female labor force participation is extremely low in the region. Except for the UAE, Qatar, Kuwait, and Bahrain (in which around 40–55% of the female population participated in the 2021 labor force), female labor force participation in the remaining countries of this region has remained very low, at around 10–30% in 2021 (for instance, it was only 13.5% in Jordan and 15.4% in Egypt).[3] Countries in the Middle East (particularly Syria, Egypt, Saudi Arabia, and Iran) have one of the highest gender biases in employment in the world. For instance, the employment to population ratio of the female youth in the Arab States was 4.8, and for its male youth was 36.7, for 2019; while these numbers for Europe were 35.7 (for female youth) and 38.8 (for male youth) (ILO, 2020, p. 27). Data for the UAE labor market also reveal that the unemployment rate among women, was four times higher than for males (5.9% versus 1.3%) in 2018 (World Bank, 2020a). Moreover, Arab women's income is only 21% of Arab men's (while globally, women's income is 57% of men's) (UNDP, 2019).

The main reason behind this limited participation of Arab women in the labor force seems to be the nature of families in the region, characterized as *"patriarchal …with women having been marginalized for several decades …*and where *societies and laws do not entirely embrace the concept of equality"* (UNDP, 2016, p. 30). Arab countries, in general, need to address problems related to the modern notion of citizenship (i.e., the provision of political, economic, and cultural rights) and embrace pluralism and diversity (UNDP, 2019). This finding, nevertheless, may not be consistent with the initiatives of the leaders of some Arab countries (e.g., the UAE), where the value of women in the economy is acknowledged and their governments have enabled rapid changes in the economic and social landscape over the last decade or so.

As in the case of data for GDP, information about unemployment in the region can be obscure or difficult to get (for instance, Oman, Saudi Arabia, the UAE, and Qatar are unclear whether they follow the International Labor Organization definitions for employment and unemployment). Countries in the Middle East need to conduct surveys at the firm and household level; harmonize their various definitions with international standards; digitize data; and enable public access to the survey data (Arezki et al., 2020).

The economic system is captured not only through measures of GDP or unemployment, but also through other variables, whose levels are expected to improve as incomes rise. Such variables include educational and health services, gender equality, the state of the country's legal system, government corruption, environmental sustainability, etc. For instance, the United Nations has constructed a broader measure, the *Human Development Index*, which combines GDP, life expectancy, health, and education.[4] Unfortunately, in the Arab countries, only about 43% of the 97 world-level indicators necessary for monitoring the UN's Sustainable Development Goals seem to be available (UNDP, 2019).

Our recommendation for foreign firms attracted to the region or international managers already invested in the GCC is to realize the opportunity that a pool of large youth unemployment as well as underutilized female participation in the labor market brings. However, the segment of the long-term unemployed would be more difficult to integrate by firms. Therefore, in the short term the expectation would be that firms need to invest more in training and firms need to realize that the reliance on government schemes and benefits emanating from any government labor market programs would be much more longer-term expectations. Moreover, foreign firms and international managers should invest in additional analysis about labor market indicators and private versus public sector competition for workers in different parts of a particular country prior to investing and locating their operations in the GCC.

In the rest of this chapter, we briefly present some of the economic reforms undertaken in the region, by focusing on the GCC countries, their initiatives to move away from oil-based economic dependence, and by summarizing some of their progress in terms of encouraging private sector activities.

Progress Toward Economic Diversification and Ease of Doing Business in the GCC Region

The Arab model of economic development from the 1950s onward has been based on having a strong central State, setting economic priorities, and providing limited political and social rights in exchange for material benefits, such as employment and energy subsidies (UNDP, 2019). In other words, over the past decades, particularly the oil-dependent countries were able to finance strong redistributive social welfare programs (through national resource rents) and, therefore, significantly raise their social and economic indicators. In the 1980s and 1990s, countries in the Middle East started implementing structural economic reforms (such as trade liberalization) with a view to setting the foundations for a market-based economy. Nevertheless, the implementation of these reforms has largely been incomplete. That is, the past gains in human development and the transformations in the Arab countries (of the 1980s and the 1990s) into a market economy have rarely translated into gains in productivity and growth, because these countries' development model "trapped human capital in unproductive public sector jobs … and also gave economic advantages to companies and individuals closely linked to decision makers, i.e., it reinforced structural alliances among political and economic elites" (UNDP, 2016, p. 20).

Data regarding the size of the public sector in the Middle East reveal that it employs between 20 and 30% of all workers; while total government spending in Oman, Iraq, Kuwait, and Saudi Arabia was around 40% of each country's 2018 GDP, and around 30% for Lebanon, Bahrain, Egypt, Qatar, and Jordan (UNDP, 2019).

Moreover, the young Arabs seem to prefer government jobs to private sector employment, due to their lifelong security. As a result, data for the 2018 UAE labor market reveal an occupational segmentation for nationals (World Bank, 2020a).

Overall, several economies in the Middle East are characterized by the absence of markets (as conventionally understood). Instead, there is a strong reliance on State planning, *who pursue goals potentially incompatible with growth...such as providing benefits to political supporters ... and not liberalizing and democratizing the indigenous economy* (Pelzman, 2018, pp. 30–31)....That is, *local government officials pass laws which prolong the life of the least efficient units ... and industrialization policies in these countries have not led to the adoption of technology* (Pelzman, 2018, pp. 81–2). In short, corruption in the Arab world has been strengthening an exclusionist economic model and has harmed the process of economic development (UNDP, 2016, p. 21).

Corruption in the Middle East has not only made foreign direct investments less attractive in the region but has also marginalized (socioeconomically) parts of the population. The outcome of such policies (of economic and social injustices) for several decades eventually resulted in the wave of protests of 2011, widely referred to as the "Arab Spring." Following the 2011 uprising, the IMF acknowledged that undertaking macroeconomic reforms (for achieving countries' fiscal discipline) should be assessed along with the needs of poor people (IMF, 2014).

Largely, the Arab Spring proved insufficient to generate enough market reforms in the Middle East (UNDP, 2016); for instance, the region continues to suffer from high restrictions on movements of goods (World Bank, 2020b). Nevertheless, the GCC economies (particularly the UAE) have been able to implement more structural reforms than the rest of the countries, and therefore attract foreign investments, expatriate workers, embrace Fintech, improve their business environments, and gradually diversify their economies away from oil (World Bank, 2019). Next we outline the progress achieved in the GCC countries toward diversification and some of the improvements recorded in the business environment.[5]

Table 2.4 presents the Regulatory Quality Indicator (RQI) for selected countries in the Middle East, for the years 2010, 2015, and 2020. The RQI captures the perceptions of a country's citizens for its government's ability to implement policies favoring the development of the private sector. Numbers in this table provide each country's score on the aggregate indicator in units of standard normal distribution. Countries with positive values are Bahrain, Israel, Jordan, Oman, Qatar, Turkey, and the UAE (therefore, these countries seem to have undertaken efforts which limit State intervention and create more favorable market conditions); while Egypt, Iran, Iraq, and Yemen have negative values (therefore, the State in these countries seems to be controlling economic activities tightly).

Bahrain is the most diversified of all GCC economies (about 82% of its 2018 GDP was attributed to its non-oil sector; while, in the year 2000, its non-oil sector accounted only for 44% of its GDP). The UAE follows (with 70% of its 2018 GDP coming from the non-oil sector); Oman (with 59%), Saudi Arabia (with 57%); Qatar (with 53%); and the least diversified of the GCC countries is Kuwait (slightly more than half of its 2018 GDP was attributed to the oil sector)

TABLE 2.4 Regulatory Quality for Selected Countries in the Middle East for the Years 2010, 2015, and 2020

	2010	2015	2020
Bahrain	0.732	0.828	0.63
Egypt	−0.157	−0.796	−0.69
Iran	−1.695	−1.280	−1.46
Iraq	−1.051	−1.233	−1.38
Israel	1.225	1.270	1.24
Jordan	0.230	0.048	0.23
Lebanon	0.078	−0.277	−0.63
Oman	0.458	0.582	0.46
Qatar	0.606	0.692	0.85
Saudi Arabia	0.183	0.030	0.26
Turkey	0.311	0.330	−0.01
UAE	0.336	1.133	1.08
Yemen	−0.596	−1.101	−1.8

Source: For 2010 and 2015, Pelzman, 2018, p. 9 (modified Table 1.5); for 2020 see https://www.theglobaleconomy.com/rankings/wb_regulatory_quality/

(World Bank, 2019). Moreover, the non-oil sub-sectors of Finance, Insurance, Real Estate, Transportation, and Communication (especially in Saudi Arabia, Qatar, and Bahrain) have been responsible for the modest average (i.e., across all GCC countries) growth rate (of 0.8% in GDP) observed over the last two years (i.e., from 2018 to 2019). The diversification of Bahrain's economy is expected to continue due to its growth in manufacturing and infrastructure; while in Oman, diversification will be driven mainly by investments in transportation, logistics, and tourism; and in the UAE, a significant boost in tourism is expected due to Dubai's Expo 2020[6] (World Bank, 2019). For instance, Bloomberg recorded a significant expansion in the UAE non-oil business activity, just one month after the expo's official opening[7]. The UAE has also taken the lead in terms of diversifying its economy through investments in the renewable sector: the UAE accounts for about 70% of the GCC's renewable energy capacity; while Saudi Arabia and Kuwait follow with about 17% and 10% only respectively (World Bank, 2019). Moreover, the UAE has set the most ambitious (of all GCC countries) renewable energy target by aiming to increase its share of renewable energy sources to 44% of its power generation, by the year 2050 (UAE, 2017).

In the future, GCC countries need to continue their economic diversification by aligning their strategies with local and global environmental objectives. All GCC countries face considerable environmental problems, such as poor air quality (due to their operating power, chemical, and desalination plants and due to their transportation infrastructure); coastal degradation (due to oil spills and brine from desalination units); water scarcity (due to unsustainable agricultural practices); and waste management issues (due to their rapid urbanization, which is above 80% in the GCC countries, World Bank, 2020b). In the past, GCC countries had followed a more "traditional" diversification strategy, which enabled them to decrease their dependence on hydrocarbons, but it still focused on energy-intensive heavy industries (such as the manufacturing of cement, metals, and other construction materials, and the production of products closely related to hydrocarbons, i.e., petrochemicals, plastics, refinery products). In the future, GCC countries need to intensify their investments in the renewable energy sector and in carbon capture and storage.

The overall ability of GCC countries to invest in renewable energy projects depends crucially on their governments' decisions not only to reduce subsidies for fossil fuels (toward industrial users and energy plants) but also to change their publics' perceptions of having very low domestic energy prices. For instance, data on energy subsidies for the year 2017 reveal that Saudi Arabia and Kuwait continue to subsidize energy at around 5% of their GDP, which is almost ten times more than the rest of the world (UNDP, 2019, p. 9). Furthermore, GCC governments may want to send clear signals to foreign investors that they are indeed pursuing an environmentally sustainable (rather than the "traditional") approach to diversification, by setting business environments which attract innovative knowledge-intensive and low-carbon private firms.

The main recommendation for foreign firms attracted to the region or international managers already invested in the GCC is to understand each country's strategy and plan for diversification in the future and compare the rhetoric with what has been achieved so far, particularly with regard to the industry that a firm is operating in. This is crucial as the gap between "traditional" versus more innovative and low-carbon private firms is significant in many Middle East countries. As the governments are playing a large role in their economies, focusing on their support and policy implementation is a must prior to entry as well as post-entry.

Significant steps toward changing the business and investment environment have already been taken. For instance, Saudi Arabia featured as the world's most improved country in the World Bank's 2020 "Doing Business Report" (it was ranked 62nd worldwide, according to the Ease of Doing Business Index, from 92nd on the previous report); while Bahrain and Kuwait were among the top ten global improvers (for instance, Bahrain featured in the 2020 Report at the 43rd place worldwide and moved up 19 places compared to the previous report). Among all MENA countries, the UAE is still the highest ranked, at number 16 worldwide (World Bank, 2020c).

But except for some of the GCC countries (including Oman, which ranked 68 worldwide in terms of the Ease of Doing Business Index), the performance of the remaining of the Middle East countries (in terms of encouraging private sector activities) is rather disappointing. For instance, Egypt ranked 114 relative to the world, Iran 127, Lebanon 143, Iraq 172, and Yemen 187 (World Bank, 2020c).

In general, the Ease of Doing Business Index is constructed on several variables, such as the number of procedures required to register a business (most of the countries in the Middle East require around 7 interactions with government agencies to issue business licenses); the number of days required to start a business

Economic Environment in the Middle East **19**

(Oman, Qatar, Turkey, Bahrain, and the UAE, require about 7 or 8 days; while Saudi Arabia, Kuwait, Iraq, and Yemen around 20–40 days); the cost of business startup procedures (expressed as a percentage of the country's per capita Gross National Income; this was, in 2016, around 1% for Bahrain, around 3% for Kuwait, around 6% for Qatar, around 13% for the UAE, around 16% for Turkey, around 4% for Saudi Arabia and Oman, around 22% for Jordan, and 52% for Iraq); the Ease of getting Credit; the protection of minority investors from conflicts of interests; the amount of taxes and mandatory contributions that need to be paid within a year; the time and cost of exporting and importing goods (in terms of document compliance and border compliance); the time and cost of resolving commercial disputes through courts; etc. For a more detailed assessment of the Middle East countries regarding other aspects of facilitating business activities (for details see the World Bank's 2020 Doing Business Report, World Bank, 2020c).

Economic growth in the Middle East for the near future (i.e., for 2020–2021) is subject to significant uncertainties due to the recent dual and related shocks of the COVID-19 pandemic and of the collapsing oil prices of April 2020. The COVID-19 pandemic quickly spread in the Middle East (with Iran probably being hit the hardest[8]) and resulted in a slowdown of economic activities: "social distancing" practices and the restrictions on business activities have decreased domestic consumption and investments, while major travel restrictions were being introduced worldwide (affecting therefore countries of the Middle East, such as Jordan, Egypt, and Turkey, who are relying on tourism). The overall decrease in the demand for oil worldwide resulted in the oil price collapse of April 2020.[9] The UAE economy, although relatively diversified compared to its GCC neighbors, remains dependent on regional oil-driven liquidity and is still vulnerable to crashes in oil prices (World Bank, 2020a). For instance, the UAE's non-oil GDP contracted by 6.2% in 2020; the country's population decreased by 2.3% (the first decline after 20 years), due to the departure of many expatriates; and additional government structural reform efforts are required to ensure higher productivity (IMF, 2022).

Despite these short-term uncertainties due to the recent pandemic, long-term economic diversification in the Middle East requires not only (as mentioned earlier) the alignment of the countries' strategies with the global environmental objectives, but also additional educational reforms, with a view to expanding these countries' workforce and improving the employability of women. Economists have shown that productivity (and therefore economic development) depends crucially on the level of education attainment. Investments in human capital, nevertheless, vary across countries of the Middle East: the UAE, Qatar, Kuwait, Saudi Arabia, and Bahrain are ranked as countries with very high Human Development Index in education (for the period 2005–2015); Oman, Iran, Turkey, Lebanon, and Jordan are considered as countries with high HDI in education; Egypt and Iraq with medium HDI; while Yemen and Syria with low HDI (Pelzman, 2018, pp. 42–45). Overall, the educational system in the Middle East is largely seen as a credential, i.e., as a ticket for public sector employment. Countries in the Middle East need to reform their education systems so that they provide skills which enable young people to get employed across different sectors or/and across places, i.e., make them more mobile (World Bank, 2020b).

The main recommendation for foreign firms attracted to the region or international managers already operating in the GCC is to incorporate and follow over time indices such as the Ease of Doing Business Index for each country. Although such indices give an overall impression of countries, they are nevertheless important as they capture different dynamics which are reflected in countries going up or down the rankings. The Ease of Doing Business Index should be complemented with other indices that firms in different sectors may find more appropriate, such as the ones that we outlined above on GDP and the labor market. Other indices would be trade-related indices, financial market indices, and more detailed institutional quality indices.

Conclusions

Overall, countries in the Middle East have experienced different degrees of economic growth, depending on their natural resource endowments (i.e., being oil-rich countries, or not), and the tolerance of their government institutions toward market reforms and trade. Some of the current unifying themes and initiatives which need to be undertaken in the future in the region are: (a) reduce their dependence, particularly the GCC countries, on natural resources, i.e., continue the diversification away from oil and gas production and instead target non-oil sectors (such as transportations and logistics infrastructure); (b) integrate environmental sustainability into their economic diversification strategies (e.g., proceed with scaling up investments in carbon capture and storage, particularly the GCC countries; implement renewable energy projects to mitigate the impacts of climate change; and build capacity for environmental research, in order to deal with their pressing environmental issues, such as water scarcity, waste management, and air pollution); (c) make more investments in human capital by reforming their educational systems, undertaking more R&D, and encouraging innovation; (d) utilize their demographic comparative advantage, i.e., the fact that a very large percentage of the Arab region's population is below 30 years of age; they should therefore introduce institutions/reforms which will make their rapidly increasing (in numbers) labor force more mobile and technologically competitive; (e) acknowledge the role of women in their economies (i.e., increase their female labor force participation rates); (f) abandon the State-led development model dominated by the public sector and by a reliance on social connections/family ties for the distribution of jobs (i.e., acknowledge that economic productivity requires meritocracy); (g) expand trade possibilities by participating in the global economy and embracing globalization; and (h) rely on evidence-based decision-making by standardizing monitoring protocols and by providing more reliable data on economic variables and indicators that will enable credible economic analysis and effective policymaking in the region.

Foreign firms are advised to explore differences and keep an eye on how able and successful each government in the GCC is to implement and improve according to the areas (a)–(h) that we outlined above. Each of these areas presents economic benefits to the countries as well as foreign firms that invest in those host countries. The challenge for foreign firms is to find host countries that are suitable for their expansion or relocation strategies in their particular industries as well as formulating a strategy to communicate and collaborate with regional/national governments in order to highlight the needs and support mechanism they need from them.

Notes

1 https://arab-hdr.org/
2 Available from: https://www.economist.com/graphic-detail/2021/02/02/global-democracy-has-a-very-bad-year.
3 Labor force participation estimates, for 2021, are available from the International Labor Organization: https://ilostat.ilo.org/data/.
4 Information about the HDI is available from: https://hdr.undp.org/en/content/human-development-index-hdi.
5 We omit the growth of financial services in the region because financial reforms are the topic of another chapter of this edited volume.
6 Dubai's Expo 2020 was postponed for October 2021 due to the global coronavirus pandemic.
7 https://www.bloomberg.com/news/articles/2021-11-03/uae-business-activity-quickens-as-dubai-expo-spurs-tourism.
8 Iran has more than 6.8M reported cases and more than 134K deaths, as of February 2022 (https://www.worldometers.info/coronavirus/#countries).
9 The latter was triggered not only by the low demand for oil, but also by Russia's and Saudi Arabia's decisions to unilaterally boost their oil productions.

References

Acemoglu, D., Laibson, D. and List, J. (2016) *Economics*. London: Pearson.
Alvaredo, F., Assouad, L. and Piketty, T. (2018) *Measuring inequality in the Middle East 1990–2016: The World's Most Unequal Region?* WID (World Inequality Database) world working paper No 2017/15, Paris. https://wid.world/document/alvaredoassouadpiketty-middleeast-widworldwp201715/
Arezki, Rabah, Lederman, Daniel, Abou Harb, Amani, El-Mallakh, Nelly, Fan, Rachel Yuting, Islam, Asif, Nguyen, Ha and Zouaidi, Marwane. (2020) *Middle East and North Africa Economic Update, April 2020: How Transparency Can Help the Middle East and North Africa*. Washington, DC: World Bank. https://openknowledge.worldbank.org/handle/10986/33475
ILO. (2020) *Global Employment Trends for Youth 2020: Technology and the Future of Jobs* Geneva: International Labour Office. https://www.ilo.org/global/publications/books/WCMS_737648/lang--en/index.htm
IMF. (2014) *Toward New Horizons: Arab Economic Transformation Amid Political Transitions*. Washington, DC. https://www.imf.org/external/pubs/ft/dp/2014/1401mcd.pdf
IMF. (2022) *United Arab Emirates IMF Country Report No.22/51*. Washington, DC. https://www.imf.org/en/Publications/CR/Issues/2022/02/17/United-Arab-Emirates-Selected-Issues-513270

Pelzman, Joseph. (2018) *The Economics of the Middle East and North Africa (MENA)*. 2nd Edition. New Jersey: World Scientific.

Schiffbauer, Marc, Sy, Abdoulaye, Hussain, Sahar, Sahnoun, Hania and Keefer, Philip. (2015) *Jobs or Privileges: Unleashing the Employment Potential of the Middle East and North Africa*. MENA Development Report; Washington, DC: World Bank. https://openknowledge.worldbank.org/handle/10986/20591

UAE. (2017) *Energy Strategy 2050*. Ministry of Energy and Industry, United Arab Emirates.

UNDP. (2016) *Youth and the Prospects for Human Development in a Changing Reality*. Arab Human Development Report, United Nations Development Program. https://hdr.undp.org/content/arab-human-development-report-2016-youth-and-prospects-human-development-changing-reality

UNDP. (2019) *Leaving No One Behind: Towards Inclusive Citizenship in Arab Countries*. Arab Human Development Report Research Paper, United Nations Development Program. https://www.arabdevelopmentportal.com/publication/leaving-no-one-behind-towards-inclusive-citizenship-arab-countries

World Bank. (2016) *What's Holding Back the Private Sector in MENA?: Lessons from the Enterprise Survey*. Washington, DC: European Bank for Reconstruction and Development; European Investment Bank; World Bank Group. https://openknowledge.worldbank.org/handle/10986/24738

World Bank. (2019) *Gulf Economic Update: Economic Diversification for a Sustainable and Resilient GCC*. December 2019. https://www.worldbank.org/en/country/gcc/publication/gulf-economic-monitor-december-2019

World Bank. (2020a). *United Arab Emirates Economic Update April 2020*. http://pubdocs.worldbank.org/en/879771554825521024/mpo-are.pdf

World Bank. (2020b) *Convergence: Five Critical Steps toward Integrating Lagging and Leading Areas in the Middle East and North Africa. Overview*. Washington, DC. https://openknowledge.worldbank.org/handle/10986/33187

World Bank. (2020c) *Doing Business 2020. Comparing Business Regulation in 190 Economies*. Washington, DC. https://openknowledge.worldbank.org/handle/10986/32436

3
THE POLITICAL ENVIRONMENT IN THE MIDDLE EAST

A Comparative Analysis of the UAE, Egypt, and Iraq

Abdul-Nasser El-Kassar, Sophie Lythreatis and Tamirace Fakhoury

Introduction

The Middle East has been referred to as the birthplace of civilization and is distinguished by its momentous history. The region is a natural land that connects three continents and contains ample natural resources. Its crucial location and assets have been points of interest for many parts of the world that have made establishing strong connections in the region a priority (Donboli and Kashefi, 2005). Nevertheless, the Middle East has an identity that is linked to ongoing conflicts and wars. There is no doubt that it is a powerful region in international economics and political affairs (Khakhar and Rammal, 2013). Over the years, the countries within the Middle East have demonstrated varying growth potential and outcomes. Some countries have received more foreign direct investment (FDI) that has created job opportunities and enhanced their economy, than others, and why this is the case has been a fundamental question in international business (Contractor et al., 2020). The difference in attracting FDI is exhibited through three different levels in the Middle East: countries that have displayed rapid change success stories (such as Qatar), countries whose growth remains promising (such as Morocco), and countries that seem to indicate a state of enduring confinement to internal and external disputes (like Libya).

This chapter covers a comparative analysis of three very different Middle Eastern countries with the aim of discussing relevant information of host country factors that influence inward FDI. Although the nations that constitute this strategic region are known to share some similarities in values, societal culture, and religion, each country possesses unique characteristics that contribute to the ease or hindrance of conducting business within its boundaries (Lythreatis et al., 2019). In fact, the Arab world has been recognized for its heterogeneity, thus, it is essential to excavate political details and business specifics of each individual country in the interest of

DOI: 10.4324/9781003005766-4

unveiling business opportunities. Doing so for all countries is beyond the scope of this chapter and to provide a flavor about the political environment in the Middle East, we provide a comparative analysis of three very different countries. The three countries are the United Arab Emirates (UAE), Egypt, and Iraq. These countries represent three different case studies as they highlight disparities in the Middle East and operate in different political environments. Because of different politics, hence different decision-making by the governments, the countries also display distinct rules and regulations, with varying imposed taxes, to operate a business. A comparative analysis of these three countries is novel to the existing literature. Additionally, a lot of the available literature that compares Middle Eastern nations is dated and does not cover the ongoing changes in the socio-economic and political conditions in the area. Understanding the current separate environments will allow the evaluation of business prosperity in each country. Such information should be very helpful for foreign operators in the region.

Among the chosen three countries, the UAE has the highest inward FDI ($13.8 billion), followed by Egypt ($9 billion) which is the biggest receiver of FDI in Africa. Iraq's FDI inflows remain negative ($ −3 billion) but saw a $1.8 billion improvement from 2018 (UNCTAD, 2020). One important question to probe is, "Can recent variations in the political and economic systems as well as the existing business regulations illuminate possible future opportunities for foreign firms to enter and operate in the Middle East markets?" For conducting a comparison and understanding the political system of each considered country effectively, the chapter adopts the ABCD framework: advantages, benefits, constraints, and disadvantages (Aithal, 2017). This framework offers an analysis of both the positive and negative aspects of doing business in each of the three considered countries. The main aim of this analysis is to provide information that foreign managers can utilize to make decisions concerning starting business operations within the Middle Eastern countries.

The next section of the chapter discusses the political and economic environment for the UAE, Egypt, and Iraq, respectively. Subsequent to this, the present business regulations for each of these countries are explained.

Political and Economic Environment

The political environment of a country constitutes the basis of the business environment in that country. Issues within the political system can produce varying and sporadic consequences that affect a country's economic and social environment (Zhu et al., 2018). There is a need to give more weight and relevance to the political situation in decision-making and research (De Villa et al., 2015). The political system has the power to facilitate or hinder business operations and impact a firm's capability to sustain profits. Periods of substantial political change and instability have been witnessed across most of the Arab world (Khakhar and Rammal, 2013). There is evidence that in the presence of political stability, businesses get affected positively, whereas political instability within a nation can substantially affect the operations of a company (Hamiza et al., 2020). Therefore, understanding the political environment is crucial to running successful businesses.

The UAE

The UAE is one of the member states of the Gulf Cooperation Council (GCC). It is a federation of seven emirates: Dubai, Abu Dhabi, Sharjah, Fujairah, Ajman, Ras Al-Khaimah, and Umm Al-Quwain, where Abu Dhabi and Dubai are the two most prominent emirates (Akoum, 2008). It is one of the youngest nations in the Middle East and is known for its rapid development and high standard of living. Approximately 90% of its workforce consists of expatriates (Singh et al., 2019). The country is driven by Islamic traditions, but expatriates tend to practice their own cultures.

Although the UAE is one of the highly liberal nations in the Gulf, politically, it is an authoritarian country. UAE's political system is a constitutional monarchy. Each emirate is governed by an emir. These emirates have their own administration where every emir oversees his emirate's resources separately. The Supreme Council which constitutes the seven emirs elects the president among them. Thus, the form of government of the UAE can also be referred to as a federal presidential elected monarchy. The stature and influence of each emirate is manifested in the allocation of positions within the federal government. The current ruler of Abu Dhabi is also the president of the UAE, due to its size and wealth of being the country's chief oil producer. The ruler of Dubai is the vice president and prime minister of the UAE as Dubai is the country's commercial center. Although the political system of the country is inflexible, the distribution of power is almost never contested. However, rivalries among the distinct emirates exist. The Federal National Council which is the federal authority of the UAE consists of forty members; twenty are appointed by the rulers of the seven emirates and twenty are indirectly elected (Freer, 2018).

Advantages and Benefits of the UAE's Political and Economic Environment

The UAE is the most competitive economy in the Arab world followed by Qatar and Saudi Arabia, and the 25th most competitive economy in the world. The nation has been successful in attracting a big number of international businesses to all seven emirates. It is the largest recipient of FDI in the Greater Middle East, attracting half of the total investment that came into the region in 2019 (Schwab, 2019).

The UAE is considered to have one of the most politically stable regimes in the Middle East, displaying a low to moderate political risk. It has demonstrated long-term stability where the federation has been able to retain political stability since the unification in 1971. The nation has good political relationships with many countries which has helped it build healthy trade relations across the globe (Bing and Al-Mutawakel, 2018).

The country has abundant natural resources as it is one of the oil-rich countries in the Middle East (Bing and Al-Mutawakel, 2018). Nevertheless, it focalizes economic diversification that has shown effective endeavors at lowering the GDP portion based on yielding oil and gas. By focusing on different sectors, it has reduced its vulnerability to oil price fluctuations and offered opportunities in a variety of sectors. Its prosperous trade and commerce have been one place where the government has concerted efforts as part of the country's development and economic base diversification. Another sector that has been given a lot of attention in the government's strategic plans is tourism (Akoum, 2008). In the UAE, foreign businesses have opportunities in diverse sectors, such as banking, trade, tourism, manufacturing, construction, education, entertainment, and health services. The greatest FDI, however, lay in financial and insurance activities (Mosteanu, and Alghaddaf, 2019). Additionally, Abu Dhabi has invested in alternate forms of energy production as well as in the nation's first nuclear power station, the Barakah Power Plant. Even though the UAE has been affected by several inauspicious factors, such as the 2009 debt crisis in Dubai and the 2014 oil price decline, the country has been able to maintain growth momentum (Bing and Al-Mutawakel, 2018). Dubai, that has always been the shining commercial hub of the Gulf, is under a lot of debt and there was a worry that Expo 2020, which it was relying on to boost its economy, especially in the sectors of tourism, retail, communication, and transportation, would impact the country's economy negatively when it was postponed due to COVID-19 (Oxford Analytica, 2020). Nevertheless, the postponed big event has taken place at the right time, contributing to the country's economy (Kane, 2021).

Further, the UAE has an extraordinarily high per capita income and one of the lowest unemployment rates in the world. It also has one of the lowest crime rates in the world and a rich infrastructure (Bing and Al-Mutawakel, 2018). Another advantage of the UAE is that its wealth will allow it to acquire the newest devices and equipment that would position it in the forefront of technological advancement.

Constraints and Disadvantages of the UAE's Political and Economic Environment

Even though the UAE and Saudi Arabia have the most diversified economy among the GCC countries, the UAE's economy remains very dependent on oil, except for Dubai. However, when Dubai suffered the economic crisis in 2007, it was bailed out by Abu Dhabi's oil wealth. Nevertheless, the country is working toward a plan to further diminish the economy's reliance on oil exports by the year 2030, and several projects are already taking place to help achieve this. Khalifa Port that opened in Abu Dhabi at the end of 2012 was part of this plan (Bing and Al-Mutawakel, 2018). Additionally, the nation's currency remains pegged to the dollar, minimizing its power to confront inflationary pressure, and therefore is also considered a constraint (Donboli and Kashefi, 2005).

Furthermore, the UAE's location in a relatively unstable region may, to some extent, affect the investor perceptions regarding the risk of conducting business in the country. For example, the country has been involved in diplomatic rows between several Arab states and Qatar that occurred in 2017 when the UAE cut ties with Qatar and accused it of supporting terrorism. However, in 2019, the country eased the ban placed on shipping of goods between the UAE and Qatar, and there has been a slow move toward normalizing the shattered relations (Miller, 2019). The country has also occasionally had minor political conflicts with neighboring countries concerning ownership of oil or land. For example, the country's relations with Iran have been strained due to ongoing territorial disputes regarding Gulf islands. Nevertheless, conflicts within the Middle East have also benefited the UAE. The Arab Spring in 2011, for instance, drove people and businesses to relocate to the UAE and increased tourism and capital inflows (Ali et al., 2012).

The above information revealed that the UAE's advantages lie in its stable political regime, economic diversification, growth momentum, high income, low unemployment, low crime, rich infrastructure, and technology advancement. Its disadvantages lie in remaining largely oil-dependent, having a pegged currency, and being located in a generally unstable region. This information is useful for foreign firms that are keen to operate in a politically stable environment in the Middle East rather than one that is instable and would, hence, result in frequent changes of policies, generating volatility and adversely affecting company performance (Aisen and Veiga, 2013). It is useful for firms seeking operations in a strong economy where unemployment is low and where the danger of crime is small. Operating in such an environment means that foreign businesses do not need to cope with corruption which negatively links to firm growth (Gaviria, 2002).

Egypt

Egypt is a republic situated in the North African part of Greater Middle East. It is best known for its long and popular history. Currently, it is the most populous nation in the whole region (Sweed, 2016).

The country is one of the nations that played a major role in the Arab Spring that began in late 2010. It was successful in ousting its authoritarian leader in a military coup. The revolution helped the Muslim Brotherhood, the oldest and largest religious political organization that has long been active in the Egyptian political arena, to successfully reach the focal point of the administration of the Egyptian regime (Yu and Liu, 2019). Political tensions in Egypt continued to be heightened, and the country failed to achieve any reforms set by the International Monetary Fund (IMF). Nevertheless, the military seized power in 2013, removing the first freely elected president who belonged to the Muslim Brotherhood. This removal put an interim government in place that enjoyed a broad support from the Egyptian public and revised some disputed articles in the constitution. Optimism was developed once President Sisi was appointed in 2014, making reforms and adopting the new version of the constitution (Hecan, 2016). The president of Egypt is elected using the two-round system (i.e., the president is elected by obtaining the plurality of votes. A second round of voting is needed when there are more than two candidates running for the elections). When he was elected, the country was able to pay back more than $6 billion that it owed to foreign oil companies over two months.

In 2015, Egypt chose the banks to handle its successful return to the international bond market after a hiatus of five years, marking the return of economic and political stability in the country for the first time since the 2011 revolution (Ouki, 2018).

Advantages and Benefits of Egypt's Political and Economic Environment

The United Kingdom is currently the biggest investor in Egypt. However, the country has seen augmented investment from the GCC economies that are preparing themselves to make the transition toward a post-oil future and thus have started to grow their presence across the region. The UAE, for example, has investments in various sectors of Egypt, such as real estate, education, tourism, communication, and agriculture. There has been a discovery of more gas reserves across the country and the sector with the greatest FDI is oil and gas. Nevertheless, Egypt has also sought and seen various routes for economic growth in different sectors, such as tourism, construction, manufacturing, real estate, and financial services (Joya, 2017).

Egypt maintains good political relations with other Arab nations, mainly the Gulf countries. When it initially failed to make reforms and negotiate with the IMF, it was successful in finding alternative financial resources offered by several countries within the Middle East, such as Saudi Arabia, the UAE, and Kuwait (Hecan, 2016). Nevertheless, with the current president ruling, Egypt was able to receive a loan from the IMF in 2016 which pushed the nation's external debt to $60 billion. The loan came after an intense foreign exchange shortage that crippled the country's economy and allowed for the Egyptian pound to be devalued. The Egyptian government raised the VAT and reduced subsidies to succeed in financing its deficit (Abdou and Zaazou, 2018). The economic reform program that was launched as part of its $12 billion bailout agreement was designed toward attaining more inclusive, sustainable, and private sector–led growth which would enhance the living standards of the people of Egypt. The country was successful in accomplishing the full-grown economic reform program in 2019 and became one of the fastest growing emerging markets. Egypt now has one of the highest growth rates in the whole region and its unemployment rate has been plummeting after having reached one of its highest points in 2015. The Egyptian government has mainly concentrated on growth initiated through enhancing their economic policies and focusing on increasing tourism, large infrastructure projects, and investments in the private sector as well as aiming to draw in more international investors. Thus, the present Egyptian government is currently on a path toward high economic stability along with political stability (Farzanegan et al., 2020).

Because of Egypt's recent success, in June 2020, the IMF approved a one-year Stand-by Arrangement which aims to assist the country in coping with the challenges proffered by the pandemic. The program would assist the country in maintaining its macroeconomic stability achieved over the past few years by supporting spending related to social and health services and preventing extreme accumulation of public debt. It will also keep inflation low and maintain financial stability, placing Egypt on a strong foundation for a sustainable recovery with more job opportunities and a powerful growth. The program will also boost governance and transparency as well as competition (IMF, 2020).

Constraints and Disadvantages of Egypt's Political and Economic Environment

Egypt has different political parties that can exist and operate (McCants, 2012). With over a hundred registered political parties in Egypt, it is easy to forget that the government's first duty is toward the general interest of the Egyptian people. Such a political environment also makes the long-term political outlook of Egypt uncertain. Although the political risk of the country has improved in recent years, it remains higher than some other Middle Eastern nations such as the UAE.

Furthermore, Egypt has experienced some terrorist attacks in the past few years. For example, in 2017, it suffered terrorist attacks on a mosque and on Coptic churches, by Wilayat Sinai, a terrorist organization based in the Sinai Peninsula that emerged following the overthrow of President Hosni Mubarak in 2011 and declared its allegiance to the Islamic State. The terrorist organization has also conducted attacks on Egyptian military (Gormus and Joya, 2015). Additionally, Egypt faces a terrorist threat in its Western Desert where Al-Qaeda exists. In 2018, nevertheless, the Egyptian military was ordered to defeat Wilayat Sinai by President Sisi who also launched antiterrorism laws to tackle the threats in the Sinai Peninsula and Western Desert of Egypt (CFR, 2020).

The above information revealed that Egypt's advantages consist of the country being a growing emerging market with a relatively stable political and economic situation, witnessing growth in all its diverse sectors, and maintaining good relations with other Arab countries. Nevertheless, the nation suffers from occasional terrorist attacks, and its long-term political outlook remains uncertain. This information is relevant for foreign operators who wish to conduct business in a flourishing emerging market within the Middle East region. It is easier for companies to establish themselves in such markets, in any sector. They will also benefit by being part of a growing infrastructure (Pendleton, 2019).

Iraq

Iraq is an oil-rich federal parliamentary republic that is often associated with thoughts of violence. The president of the country is elected by the Council of Representatives and does not hold significant power in decisions. Iraq has divisive politics in a context of political sectarianism (Kathem, 2020). The political system of the country is epitomized by the continuous exercise of power sharing among the three main ethno-sectarian groups in the country: the Kurds, Shias, and Sunnis. This is known as the Muhasasa system where positions of power are distributed based on quotas and different ethno-sectarian groups which were initially created to secure minority representation (Clausen, 2019). The government has been mainly Shia-led. The Kurdistan region of Iraq, inhabited by the Kurds, is a semi-autonomous region of the country with its own government (Stansfield, 2013).

At the present, the most influential armed non-state actors in Iraq are the Popular Mobilization Forces (PMFs) that consist of a collection of militias. The PMFs are not only security actors but also political actors with significant impact (Mansour and Abd al-Jabbar 2017). Militias have become a regular feature in Iraqi politics, functioning either independently or in coalition with other groups which have contributed to normalizing the presence of armed groups within Iraqi politics.

Advantages and Benefits of Iraq's Political and Economic Environment

The amount of violence in Iraq has tremendously decreased after the 2003 American-Iraqi war. In 2017, Iraq announced a military victory over the Islamic State and began to re-emerge as an appealing destination for international trade and investment (Speckhard et al., 2017). The defeat of the Islamic State along with the formation of a new government in May 2020 after six months of uncertainty (discussed below) may be indicators that the political environment in the country is finally advancing toward a more stable outlook as it is becoming less favorable to explicit sectarianism. Despite the country's hardships, companies have been able to conduct profitable business (Arango and Krauss, 2013). There has also been an increased political and economic interest in Iraq from the GCC countries. In a study conducted by Clausen (2019) in Baghdad, international representatives often described the past few years as a window of opportunity for Iraq. Moreover, there is an ongoing tussle among politicians to place themselves in a position where the public sees them as the defenders of Iraq.

Constraints and Disadvantages of Iraq's Political and Economic Environment

Although Iraq has natural resources, a system of corruption and nepotism under the Muhasasa system exists and is extremely hard to demolish, despite the prevalent agreement that it explains the ineffectiveness of the public sector. Iraq struggles with rebuilding its infrastructure and is unable to satisfy fundamental needs and deliver basic public services such as electricity and clean water. In addition to this, in Iraq, there is a common dependence on connections to secure work and income where the politicians represent specific ethno-sectarian groups rather than the Iraqi state. This system has created problems, such as hiring public sector employees who are not qualified for the position they hold and implementing a process of ghost employees, paying salaries to employees who either do not show up or do not even exist. Thus, government employment deeply burdens the fiscal system and the pressure on the public sector keeps on augmenting as the population in Iraq continues to hastily grow (Clausen, 2019).

Furthermore, Iraq is struggling to adapt to the low oil price environment as it has an almost total dependence on its oil. Although economic diversification remains high on the country's economic agenda, action toward achieving this diversification has been minimal as its non-oil sectors have only grown a little. FDI that is unrelated to the oil sector usually comes from private companies that are based within the Greater Middle East, such as Turkey and the Gulf countries. Its unstable political environment, corruption, and poor infrastructure tend to make private companies from outside the region reluctant to invest in the country's various non-oil sectors. There is also a tremendous dominance of the state economy which leaves very little room for the private sector to grow. Additionally, the uneven distribution of oil resources has increased sectarian disputes across the nation. The fact that identity remains a vital element in politics is incessantly contributing to the political disagreements (Matsunaga, 2019).

The lack of public services and a very high unemployment rate were the key reasons behind the large protests that took place in the South of Iraq in 2018 (Clausen, 2019). Subsequently, uprisings in Baghdad and the South of Iraq in October 2019, which have been referred to as the October revolution, were a way to demand the cease of corruption, unemployment, and the lack of efficient public services. The protestors wanted to end the current sectarian-divided political system that came into effect since the invasion of the United States and the fall of Saddam Hussein as well as end Iran's influence over the Iraqi politics. The demonstrations to change the whole political regime showed the Shia leaders that currently hold a dominant position within the Iraqi political system that changes need to be made. The Iraqi prime minister resigned in December 2019 which left the country without a government for six months. Further to this, the killing of two prominent Shia leaders, Qasem Soleimani, the head of Iran's Islamic Revolutionary Guard Corps' Quds Force, and Abu Mahdi al Muhandis, the deputy chief of PMF in Iraq, at the beginning of 2020 increased the strain and pressure that the leaders with a close relationship to Iran were facing after the protests of October. In addition to this, the COVID-19 pandemic effects along with the reduction in oil prices jeopardized the collapse of the country's economy. This further augmented the hitches felt by Iraq, leaving the country with very few and tough decisions to make, such as requesting foreign aid from nations amid the situation of most nations having taken difficult positions against Iran and its connections in Iraq (Dagher, 2020). Thus, political uprisings seem to be an ongoing phenomenon in Iraq, and the political risk remains high, compared to other Middle Eastern nations.

The above information indicates that although Iraq has started to make the way toward a more stable political outlook, it suffers from high corruption, unemployment, uprisings, and strong dominance of the state economy. It also struggles to satisfy fundamental needs and rebuild its infrastructure. Foreign firms thinking of entering the Iraqi market would have to carefully plan how to navigate these circumstances. Nevertheless, with the state that the country is in, there is plenty of room and, therefore, opportunities that firms can take advantage of (Clausen, 2019).

Regulations

Firms that consider entering a foreign market do not solely take into account the political and economic environment of that market, but also the existent business regulations (Contractor et al., 2020). As regulations are imposed and altered by the government, they are highly connected to the political environment.

The UAE

Formerly, the UAE did not have a value-added tax (VAT) rate. However, in 2018, it implemented a rate of 5% based on a common VAT agreement among the GCC (Zafarullah, 2018). The customs duty tax has been fixed at a rate of 5% (excluding alcoholic and tobacco products that are subject to a rate of 50% and 100%, respectively).

Advantages and Benefits of UAE's Regulations

The UAE's tax regime is very attractive as there currently are no corporate, personal, or withholding taxes. The only entities that pay corporate tax are the oil and gas companies and subsidiaries of foreign banks. The country has one of the most liberal trade regimes in the Gulf area. Moreover, there are no currency exchange or capital repatriation restrictions (Akoum, 2008).

In each emirate, there are at least two free trade zones. There are more than 30 free zones in Dubai. Each zone has its own rules and regulations. If the entity is set up in a free trade zone, it is not required to have any UAE national shareholder as foreigners can possess full ownership of the business. Companies can conduct businesses within the free trade zones and abroad. The regulations for setting up a business are rather simple as an initial approval from the free trade zone authority needs to be obtained, followed by a license. The regulations for starting a business in the zones are less complicated and time-consuming than starting a business onshore/on the mainland UAE. Nevertheless, the benefit of having an onshore entity is fewer restrictions with respect to conducting business activities and no restriction on the location of the entity provided it is onshore (Shayah and Qifeng, 2015; Additional details and the list of the free trade zones can be accessed via UAE's Ministry of Economy's website (linked at the end of the chapter).

Formerly, foreign investors could hold up to only 49% of ownership of a Limited Liability Company (LLC) operating onshore in the UAE. Nevertheless, the country issued Federal Decree-Law number 19 of 2018 on FDI, presenting a framework under which foreign shareholders can own up to 100% of an LLC in some sectors in the UAE. This comes with an aim to develop the nation's investment environment (Al-Gamrh et al., 2020; Mosteanu and Alghaddaf, 2019). Cabinet Resolution number 16 of 2020 specifies the sectors qualified for full ownership and lays out requirements that ought to be met. These requirements pertain to staff headcount, research, and development contribution, and advanced technology investments

(KPMG, 2020). This will undeniably transform the prospect of foreign ownership in the UAE and bolster the country's attraction as an investment focal point.

Constraints and Disadvantages of UAE's Regulations

There are constraints on owning 100% of the shares of a foreign company as it depends on the sector in which the company operates. A company does not qualify for complete ownership in the UAE if it operates within the oil and gas sector or the banking sector. This also applies to other sectors such as telecommunication and medical retail (Townsend, 2019).

Egypt

Companies operating in Egypt must pay a corporate tax of 22.5%, while companies whose activities involve oil and gas must pay a tax rate of 40.55%. The VAT rate decreases from 14% to 5% on imported goods that are needed to set up a business or to be used in production (Benzell et al., 2017).

Furthermore, regarding the free zones, there are two kinds of zones: private and public (private free zones represent one independent project or encompass several projects performing related activities). Egypt has nine public zones (i.e., Alexandria, Damietta, Ismailia, Keft, Media Production City, Nasr City, Port Said, Shebin El Kom, and Suez). Goods exported and imported for the purpose of practicing business for free zone projects are exempt from income tax, custom taxes, and VAT (Al-Youm, 2018); additional information on the free trade zones can be accessed via an Egyptian governmental website linked at the end of the chapter.

Advantages and Benefits of Egypt's Regulations

The customs rate for the imported goods needed to set up a business is 2%. If a foreign corporation operates in Egypt by creating a branch, the established branch can remove a head office charge of a total up to 10% of its taxable income. Apart from that, the branch is exposed to normal Egyptian taxes. Additionally, the Central Bank of Egypt relaxed restrictions on the transfer of foreign currencies after the Egyptian pound floated in 2016. Another advantage is that an LLC can be 100% owned by foreign investors (Schofield, 2019).

Egypt passed the new Investment Law number 72 in 2017, which comes with the aim of bringing more FDI into the country. The new law contains investor incentives, such as ensuring that companies can import and export their products without the need to be registered in the importers and exporters registers, guaranteeing foreign investors' residence in Egypt during the term of a project, granting investors the right to transfer their profits abroad, and assuring that permits issued for the business and lands cannot be eradicated unless the investor has already been notified of the violation and been granted a grace period of 60 days to repair the grounds of the breach (Hashish, 2019).

Constraints and Disadvantages of Egypt's Regulations

Formerly, an LLC was required to have one Egyptian manager. This requirement was abolished in 2018. Nevertheless, exceptions to this still apply to a few activities like importing goods and commercial intermediation, where an LLC is obliged to have one manager of Egyptian nationality (Bayomy, 2019).

Iraq

The corporate income tax rate in Iraq is a flat rate of 15%. This rate increases to 35% for oil and gas companies. The customs duty rates range between 0.5 and 30% (excluding some products such as alcoholic beverages and cigarettes; Deloitte, 2020).

There are currently three free trade zones in Iraq (i.e., Khor al-Zubair, Nineveh's Flaifil, and Al-Qayim) where, akin to the other countries, businesses are exempt from taxes. Further free zones are being developed. Investors apply for a free zone license by submitting an application to the General Commission for Iraqi Free Zones together with a $100 fee. Upon receiving approval, they are obliged to sign a lease within 30 days (Shakespeare, 2014).

Advantages and Benefits of Iraq's Regulations

The key advantage of the Iraqi regulations is that there is no VAT in Iraq (Bird et al., 2005).

Constraints and Disadvantages of Iraq's Regulations

In 2004, the Companies Law stated that a foreign investor can hold 100% of ownership of Iraqi companies, but this law was amended in 2019 to entail that the company be at least 51% Iraqi-owned for new LLCs and joint stock companies, which may well hinder future foreign investment. Also, although foreign investors can transfer funds and profits abroad, it is usually challenging to repatriate funds due to a common foreign currency shortage and the complex documentation process that is essential to be submitted to the bank (Deloitte, 2020).

Conclusion

This chapter provided a general overview of pertinent aspects that relate to evaluating decisions to invest in the Middle East through a comparative analysis of three countries that represent different case studies within the region. There is no doubt that the Middle East offers enormous potential for foreign investors. It is midway between the east and the west and very welcoming to FDI as the different nations make amendments to encourage and promote foreign investment. Also, according to international standards, government debt positions in all Arab nations, apart from Lebanon, are not particularly high (Abdou and Zaazou, 2018).

With political stability, economic openness, security, low unemployment, rich infrastructure, and an attractive tax regime, the UAE remains an appealing country for investors, and still constitutes one of the most important international investment markets in the world (Bing and Al-Mutawakel, 2018). Showing great potential for a booming economy, Egypt's rate of growth, reforms, and new Investment Law have contributed to the development of a strong emerging market with great investment opportunities. Nevertheless, the analysis showed that the constraints and disadvantages of Iraq's different features exceed their advantages and benefits. With political instability, corruption, and poor public services, Iraq has not shown enough change that would land it on the path toward a positive investment environment. However, such a system might be suited for foreign investors with a huge appetite for risk.

Useful Websites

https://www.moec.gov.ae/en/free-zones (free zones UAE)

https://www.gafi.gov.eg/English/eServices/Pages/free-zones.aspx (free zones Egypt)

https://www.meed.com/economic-zones-in-iraq/ (free zones Iraq)

https://www.investmentmonitor.ai/analysis/investors-guide-to-the-middle-east

References

Abdou, D. S. and Zaazou, Z. (2018). Arab Spring future challenges: evidence from Egypt. *Review of Economics and Political Science*, 3(2), pp. 56–69.

Aisen, A. and Veiga, F. J. (2013). How does political instability affect economic growth? *European Journal of Political Economy*, 29, pp. 151–167.

Aithal, P. S. (2017). A critical study on various frameworks used to analyse International Business and its environment. *International Journal of Applied Engineering and Management Letters*, 1(2), pp. 78–97.

Ali, A., Arifin, Z. and Hasi, M. (2012). The challenges of tourism in the countries of the Arab Spring Revolutions. *Advances in Natural and Applied Sciences*, 6(7), pp. 1162–1171.

Al-Youm, A. (2018). *Egypt's free zone exports increased $1 bn in 2018*. Egypt Independent.

Akoum, I. F. (2008). Conducting business in the UAE: a brief for international managers. *Global Business and Organizational Excellence*, 27(4), pp. 51–66.

Arango, T. and Krauss, C. (2013). China is reaping biggest benefits of Iraq oil boom. *The New York Times*, p. 2.

Al-Gamrh, B., Al-Dhamari, R., Jalan, A. and Jahanshahi, A. A. (2020). The impact of board independence and foreign ownership on financial and social performance of firms: evidence from the UAE. *Journal of Applied Accounting Research*, 21(2), pp. 201–229.

Bayomy, M. (2019). *Egyptian companies no longer required to have at least one Egyptian manager*. Middle East Insights.

Benzell, S. G., Kotlikoff, L. J. and LaGarda, G. (2017). *Simulating business cash flow taxation: an illustration based on the "Better Way" corporate tax reform* (No. w23675). National Bureau of Economic Research.

Bing, Z. Y. and Al-Mutawakel, O. (2018). Infrastructure developing and economic growth in United Arab Emirates. *Business and Economic Research*, 8(1), pp. 95–114.

Bird, R., Gendron, P. P. and Rotman, J. L. (2005). *VAT revisited. A new look at the value added tax in developing and transitional countries.* USAID.

CFR-Council on Foreign Relations (2020). Instability in Egypt.

Contractor, F. J., Dangol, R., Nuruzzaman, N. and Raghunath, S. (2020). How do country regulations and business environment impact foreign direct investment (FDI) inflows? *International Business Review*, 29(2), 101640.

Clausen, M. L. (2019). *Breaking the cycle: Iraq following the military defeat of Islamic State* (No. 2019: 02). DIIS Report.

Dagher, M. (2020). *The new three-dimensional political situation in Iraq: an Iraqi point of view.* Center for Strategic and International Studies.

De Villa, M. A., Rajwani, T. and Lawton, T. (2015). Market entry modes in a multipolar world: untangling the moderating effect of the political environment. *International Business Review*, 24(3), pp. 419–429.

Deloitte (2020). *Doing business guide – Understanding Iraq's tax position.* Deloitte & Touche (M.E.)

Donboli, J. H. and Kashefi, F. (2005). Doing business in the Middle East: a primer for US companies. *Cornell International Law Journal*, 38, pp. 413–455.

Farzanegan, M. R., Hassan, M. and Badreldin, A. M. (2020). Economic liberalization in Egypt: a way to reduce the shadow economy? *Journal of Policy Modeling*, 42(2), pp. 307–327.

Freer, C. J. (2018). *Rentier Islamism: the Influence of the Muslim Brotherhood in Gulf Monarchies.* Oxford University Press.

Gaviria, A. (2002). Assessing the effects of corruption and crime on firm performance: evidence from Latin America. *Emerging Markets Review*, 3(3), pp. 245–268.

Gormus, E. and Joya, A. (2015). State power and radicalization in Egypt's Sinai. *The Canadian Journal for Middle East Studies*, 1(1), pp. 399.

Hamiza, O., Francis, T. M., & Rashid, T. (2020). The role of socio-political environment in business success: a case of small businesses in Uganda. *International Journal of Academic Research in Business and Social Sciences*, 10 (10), pp. 783–799.

Hashish, M. (2019). *What you should know about the new investment law of 2017 in Egypt.* Mondaq.

Hecan, M. (2016). Comparative political economy of the IMF arrangements after the Arab uprisings: Egypt and Tunisia. *The Journal of North African Studies*, 21(5), pp. 765–793.

IMF (2020). *Egypt takes proactive approach to limit the pandemic's fallout.* Available at: https://www.imf.org/en/News/Articles/2020/07/09/na070920-egypt-takes-proactive-approach-to-limit-the-pandemics-fallout (Accessed 24 July 2020).

Joya, A. (2017). Neoliberalism, the state and economic policy outcomes in the post-Arab uprisings: the case of Egypt. *Mediterranean Politics*, 22(3), pp. 339–361.

Kane, F. (2021). How investment in Expo 2020 will pay off for UAE economy, burnish Dubai brand. *Arab News*. Available at: <https://www.arabnews.com/node/1938241/middle-east>

Kathem, M. (2020). Cultural (dis)continuity, political trajectories, and the state in post-2003 Iraq. *International Journal of Heritage Studies*, 26(2), pp. 163–177.

Khakhar, P. and Rammal, H. G. (2013). Culture and business networks: International business negotiations with Arab managers. *International Business Review*, 22(3), pp. 578–590.

KPMG (2020). *UAE Cabinet approves 100% foreign ownership rules for all 122 economic sectors –* Tax Flash.

Lythreatis, S., Mostafa, A. M. S. and Wang, X. (2019). Participative leadership and organizational identification in SMEs in the MENA Region: testing the roles of CSR perceptions and pride in membership. *Journal of Business Ethics*, 156(3), pp. 635–650.

Mansour, R. and Abd al-Jabbār, F. (2017). *The popular mobilization forces and Iraq's FUTURE* (Vol. 28). Carnegie Endowment for International Peace.

Matsunaga, H. (2019). *The reconstruction of Iraq after 2003: Learning from its successes and failures.* The World Bank.

McCants, W. F. (2012). *The lesser of two evils: the Salafi turn to party politics in Egypt.* Saban Center at Brookings.

Miller, R. (2019). Managing regional conflict: the Gulf cooperation council and the embargo of Qatar. *Global Policy*, 10(2), pp. 36–45.

Mosteanu, N. R. and Alghaddaf, C. (2019). Smart economic development by using foreign direct investments–UAE case study. *Journal of Information Systems and Operations Management*, 13(1) pp. 9–20.

Ouki, M. (2018). *Egypt–a return to a balanced gas market?* The Oxford Institute for Energy Studies, University of Oxford.

Oxford Analytica (2020). *Dubai Expo 2020 delay will deepen likely recession.* Emerald Expert Briefings.

Pendleton, E. (2019). *The advantages of doing business in an emerging market.* Chron.

Shayah, M. H. and Qifeng, Y. (2015). Development of free zones in United Arab Emirates. *International Review of Research in Emerging Markets and the Global Economy*, 1(2), pp. 286–294.

Schofield, M. (2019). *Doing business in Egypt: a tax and legal guide.* PWC.

Shakespeare, A. (2014). *Economic zones in Iraq.* Middle East Business Intelligence.

Schwab, K. (2019). *The global competitiveness report.* World Economic Forum.

Singh, S. K., Pereira, V. E., Mellahi, K. and Collings, D. G. (2019). Host country nationals characteristics and willingness to help self-initiated expatriates in the UAE. *The International Journal of Human Resource Management*, 32(8), pp. 1707–1730.

Speckhard, A., Shajkovci, A. and Yayla, A. (2017). Following a military defeat of ISIS in Syria and Iraq: what happens next after the military victory and the return of foreign fighters? *Contemporary Voices: St Andrews Journal of International Relations*, 8(1), pp. 81–89.

Stansfield, G. (2013). The unravelling of the post-First World War state system? The Kurdistan Region of Iraq and the transformation of the Middle East. *International Affairs*, 89(2), pp. 259–282.

Sweed, H. S. (2016). Population ageing: Egypt report. *Middle East Journal of Age and Ageing*, 83(4013), pp. 1–8.

TownseNd, S. (2019). *UAE defines industry sectors eligible for up to 100% foreign ownership.* The National. Available at: <https://www.thenationalnews.com/business/economy/uae-defines-industry-sectors-eligible-for-up-to-100-foreign-ownership-1.881898>

UNCTAD (2020). World Investment Report.

Yu, Z. and Liu, Y. (2019). Strategic communications of the Muslim brotherhood in Egypt. *Asian Journal of Middle Eastern and Islamic Studies*, 13(1), pp. 93–109.

Zafarullah, M. (2018). Impact of VAT on UAE Economy. *Asian Development Policy Review*, 6(1), pp. 41–49.

Zhu, Y., Freeman, S. and Cavusgil, S. T., (2018). Service quality delivery in a cross-national context. *International Business Review*, 27(5), pp. 1022–1032.

4

CHANGING LEGAL FRAMEWORK OF THE GCC COUNTRIES

T.P. Ghosh

Introduction

The GCC countries (namely Bahrain, Kuwait, Oman, Saudi Arabia and the United Arab Emirates) initiated reforms in legal and administrative framework to achieve economic diversification and reduction in dependency in hydro-carbon revenue privatizing key economic sectors through FDI participation. Evidently, these reforms could reverse the downfall in net FDI inflows witnessed post-2014 oil price collapse. Critical reforms in the FDI law and the commercial company law, and the introduction of a protective composition scheme through bankruptcy law along with other administrative reforms improved ease of doing business across the GCC and helped to attain wider participation of foreign investors during 2017–2019. However, lacklustre response to GCC reforms in foreign ownership in listed companies requires further studies to identify the reasons thereof and the adoption of renewed strategic stances required to improve the participation of foreign investors in secondary markets. Against, this backdrop, the key aim of this chapter is to review changes in the FDI and company laws targeted to attract a higher level of FDI to attain economic diversification and sustainable growth. The information provided in the chapter should be helpful for the present and prospective foreign investors and lenders interested to do business in the GCC countries.

In the context of economic diversification strategy of GCC countries presented in Section 2, we have examined the efficacy of liberalization in the FDI law allowing 100% foreign ownership in Section 3. In Section 4, we have examined the changes in the commercial company law primarily from the angle of choice of corporate structure in FDI projects, minimum capital requirement and highlighted reform in foreign ownership in public joint stock companies and its effectiveness. We have also highlighted the need for improving corporate governance

DOI: 10.4324/9781003005766-5

mechanisms and argued for allowing 100% foreign ownership in listed companies. A summary of the key regulatory reforms in the GCC countries is presented in Appendix I (Table 4.4) with a list of positive and negative sectors for 100% FDI participation in Appendix II (Table 4.5). Data relating to the dependency of GCC countries to hydro-carbon revenue as presented in Figure 1 are provided in Appendix III (Table 4.6). This chapter does not address the possible impact of COVID-19 on the prospect of economic diversification and FDI flows because of non-availability of relevant data.

Economic Diversification, Ease of Doing Business and FDI Flows to GCC

Non-oil diversification strategy in the GCC countries adopted to wither away oil price–driven economic volatility and build sustainable and resilient economy has gained traction in recent years because of sustained low oil price during 2013–2017. Two consecutive oil price collapses in 2009 and 2014–2016 and resultant severity of sustained low oil price on GCC economies prompted respective governments to envision long-term goals of sustainable development through economic diversification. Economic plans of the GCC countries are targeted to reduce oil dependency and achieve accelerated growth supported by foreign direct investment (FDI) to non-oil sectors. Amidst dwindling FDI flows during 2013–2017 (see Table 4.1) that caused massive roadblocks to the process of fast-track economic diversification and private capital infusion, the GCC countries adopted deep-rooted structural reform in recent years to improve ease of doing business. The state of oil dependency in the GCC countries is depicted in Figure 4.1 using three parameters, i.e., (i) Hydro-carbon sector GDP as % of GDP, (ii) Hydro-carbon revenue as % of GDP and (iii) Hydro-carbon export as % of export, which shows relatively higher degree of oil dependency in Oman, Kuwait, Qatar and Saudi Arabia than Bahrain and the UAE. The highest net FDI flows to the UAE (67% of net FDI flows to the GCC) and recent improvements in FDI flows to Bahrain justify the relatively higher degree of decoupling of oil dependency of these countries.

Saudi Arabia was the major recipient of FDI compared to its GCC peers till 2012, but lack of reform pushed down FDI to just $1419 million in 2017 (4.85% of 2010 net FDI flow), and eventually investor-friendly reforms helped to improve net FDI flows to $4563 million in 2019 (15.61% of the 2010 net FDI flow). Presently, the UAE attracts a major portion of FDI flows to the GCC which have increased over the years from $8,797 million in 2010 to $13,787 million in 2019 – a phenomenal growth of 156.73% over the 2010 level. FDI flows to Oman significantly increased during 2016–2019 in view of the liberalized FDI law, improved corporate law, tax holidays and other administrative reforms. Similarly, dwindling FDI flows to Bahrain and Kuwait have been improved in 2019 while Qatar still faces net FDI outflows possibly because of the blockade within the GCC. There is an indication

TABLE 4.1 Foreign Direct Investment, Net Inflows (in US$ million)

	2010	2011	2012	2013	2014	2015	2016	2017	2018	2019
Bahrain	156	781	1500	3728	1519	65	243	519	111	942
Kuwait	1305	3259	2873	1434	486	285	292	113	−21	675
Oman	1243	1629	135	1612	1286	−2172	2265	2917	5941	3419
Qatar	4570	939	396	−840	1040	1071	774	986	−2186	−2813
Saudi Arabia	29233	16308	12182	8865	8012	8141	7453	1419	4247	4563
UAE	8797	7152	9567	9765	11072	8551	9605	10354	10385	13787
	45303	**30068**	**26653**	**24563**	**23414**	**15940**	**20632**	**16308**	**18477**	**20573**
% Change in FDI, Net Inflows		−33.6%	−11.4%	−7.8%	−4.7%	−31.9%	29.4%	−21.0%	13.3%	11.3%

Source: World Bank, https://data.worldbank.org/indicator/BX.KLT.DINV.CD.WD.

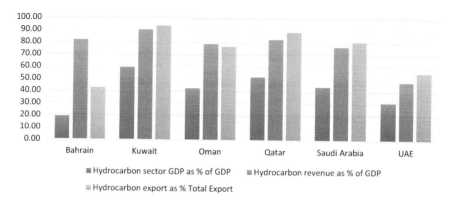

FIGURE 4.1 State of Oil Dependency in GCC Countries: Average of 2012–2018.

Data Source: World Bank Group, Gulf Economic Update, Issue 5/Dec. 2019. See Data Table 4.6 in Appendix III.

from UNCTAD (World Investment Report 2020) that global FDI flows to decrease by up to 40% in 2020 because of COVID-19 crisis.

However, the proportion of non-oil GDP has improved in 2018 over 2000/2010 in all GCC countries except Kuwait, although at varied intensity. Bahrain and the UAE achieved better non-oil diversification than other peers while Oman, Qatar, and Saudi Arabia reached more than 50% level of non-oil GDP (see Table 4.2). Recent studies of the World Bank and OECD (WB, 2019; OECD, 2020) also observed that traditional diversification strategies of GCC which leveraged on hydro-carbon value chain have been recently shifted towards lower-carbon industries.

GCC governments have made substantial progress in implementing structural reforms to improve various indicators of ease of doing business, e.g., starting a business, dealing with construction permits, getting electricity, registering property, protecting minority investors, paying taxes and trading across borders and enforcing contracts while getting credit and resolving insolvency require further attention.

TABLE 4.2 Non-Oil GDP as % of GDP in GCC Countries

	2000 (%)	2010 (%)	2018 (%)
Bahrain	44		82
Kuwait		50	48
Oman	33		59
Qatar	43		53
Saudi Arabia	40		57
UAE		69	70

Source: World Bank Group (WB, 2019).

In particular, increased number of corporate restructuring cases across GCC countries during COVID-19 period is a cause of concern. All six GCC countries adopted long-term vision to achieve economic diversification and sustainable growth, and majority of the economic sectors are opened up for 100% FDI to attract broad based FDI flows. Reforms in the legal framework include, inter alia, amendment to FDI law, corporate law, code of corporate governance and bankruptcy law.

Liberalization of FDI Law in GCC Allowing 100% FDI Participation

GCC countries except Bahrain have introduced foreign investment law which focuses on:

i. establishment of "one window" solution for granting various licenses and registration of FDI-related companies in shortest possible time;
ii. transparency in the "list of FDI restrictions" notifying positive list of economic sectors wherein 100% FDI participation is permitted (see Appendix II – Table 4.5);
iii. allowing repatriation of dividend and closure capital by the FDI company, and salaries and other benefits by employees of such companies and
iv. alternative dispute resolution mechanism.

Bahrain permits 100% FDI derogating the Article 65 of the Commercial Company Law (KOB, 2018) and allowing incorporation of public joint stock companies with foreign capital and expertise, whilst empowering the Minister of Industry and Commerce to impose foreign ownership restrictions within certain business sectors or undertaking certain activities.

The UAE has taken the lead in creating FDI-friendly investment climate allowing 100% foreign ownership in 122 economic activities across 13 sectors (Appendix II – Table 4.5), abolishing requirement of 51% Emirati ownership outside free zone area in the positive list business and granting long-term visas to the foreign investors. Bahrain, Saudi Arabia and the UAE allow foreigners to have freehold ownership of land and properties in investment zones shifting from the previously followed lease agreement. Kuwait and Qatar continue to allow long-term lease agreement. FDI laws and/or policies across the GCC established specialized institutional framework, e.g., Bahrain Economic Development Board (of the Ministry of Industry, Commerce and Tourism), Oman Public Authority for Investment Promotion and Export Promotion, Kuwait Direct Investment Promotion Authority (DIPA), Saudi Arabian General Investment Authority (SAGIA) (now Ministry of Investment in Saudi Arabia (MISA), and UAE Foreign Direct Investment unit to provide "single window" mechanism for granting commercial, employment and all other licenses curtailing possible bureaucratic delays.

Bahrain focuses on Free Trade Agreements (FTA) for attracting FDI and expects to attract FDI in Bahrain International Investment Park (BIIP) allowing special privileges. The Ministerial resolution No. 17 of 2018, as amended, sets out conditions in order to waive the foreign ownership restriction in certain activities that require 51% or more Bahraini ownership:

- The company must be present in at least three international markets.
- That the capital of the parent company must be at least BHD20 million or its equivalent in foreign currency (1 BHD = 2.65 USD - 2020).
- The capital of the Bahraini company must be at least BHD 2 million.

As per Article 10 of the Foreign Investment Law of Oman (SOO, 2019], the Council of Ministers may allow 100% foreign ownership in any Omani company on a recommendation from the Ministry of Commerce and Industry, subject to the following conditions:

- The capital of the company being at least OMR500,000.
- The company's projects contributing toward economic development.

If a foreign company secures a government contract, a foreign company may also be able to register a branch or 100% subsidiary. Oman allows 100% ownership in foreign companies by US natural and corporate persons by virtue of US-Oman free trade agreement. The FDI law offers exemption from custom duty on imported plant and machinery for setting up FDI projects and five-year tax holiday in selected industries specified in Article 8.1 of the Foreign Investment Law.

Decline in net FDI flows in Kuwait is attributable to delay in many anticipated projects designed to boost economic diversification and foreign investment. In accordance with the commercial company law (SOK, 2017) any foreign investor seeking to establish their business in Kuwait could either establish a company with limited ownership of 49% of the company's shareholding and the remaining 51% must be owned by a Kuwaiti partner or operate under an agency scheme through a Kuwaiti agent. The ownership restrictions had been a major hurdle to foreign entities with a limited control over management as major decisions would require the consent of the local partner. The new FDI law (SOK, 2013) allows the foreign investors 100% ownership of a Kuwaiti FDI company, and to manage it completely without needing a Kuwaiti partner. Since the introduction of new FDI law, many companies started business in Kuwait which include Berkeley Research Group (99%), GE Technological Centre Kuwait (97%), Huawei Technologies Kuwait (100 %), IBM Kuwait (100%), Malka Communications Group (60%) and NTG Clarity Networks Inc. (100%).

Qatar's foreign investment law requires that FDI-funded projects should match with development plan of the State and it gives preference to projects that targeted to achieve optimal utilization of domestic raw materials, export industries, or project that proposes a new product or in which modern technology is used, and projects that seek to locate worldwide leading industry or develop and qualify national cadre. Qatar's foreign investment law (SOQ, 2020) in general requires not less than ownership of 51% Qatari partner(s) and up to 100% foreign ownership based on Ministerial decision in selected sectors (Appendix II – Table 4.5). Also FDI projects are allotted land with a 50-year lease in contrast to land ownership offered to foreign investors in Bahrain, Saudi Arabia and UAE.

Foreign investment licenses in Saudi Arabia primarily takes either of the two forms – (i) firms jointly owned by a national and foreign investor, or (ii) firms wholly owned by foreign investor. FDI projects are licensed under the Foreign Investment Law [KOSA, 2015a] FDI projects are granted the following:

- all privileges, incentives and guarantees extended to a national project;
- permitted to acquire necessary real estate for operating the licensed activity and housing of staff;
- investments may not be confiscated without judicial ruling and
- disputes between the Government and the foreign investor should be settled amicably or as per relevant laws.

Saudi Arabia reformed residency law to allow foreigner investors unlimited residency visa and land ownership for the project.

UAE Changes Nominee Shareholder Arrangement

The Nominee Shareholder Arrangement (NSA) is an arrangement by which a UAE national becomes majority shareholder of a limited liability company (LLC) but agrees to waive all rights attached shareholding, e.g., right to (i) receive dividends, (ii) exercise votes in general meetings and (iii) receive any proceeds of the sale of the shares held by the company. The waiver is based on the presumption that the Company law does not distinguish between beneficial and legal interests in shares of a company. However, contradictory signals have been observed in legal decisions wherein the NSA has been both upheld and struck down by UAE courts causing legal uncertainty surrounding the arrangement. Earlier Federal Anti-Concealment Law No. 17 of 2004 (also termed as the "Anti- Fronting Law") intended to prohibit the NSA including both civil and criminal penalties to all parties with possibility of deregistration. In the recent case of NMC debt trouble, it is reported that the shares of the majority shareholders have been pledged without their knowledge and also there remains a confusion regarding the legal stake of the minority shareholders. Because of the inherent legal uncertainty, many foreign investors structured their onshore business through Abu Dhabi Global Market (ADGM) Free Zone that recognizes English law trust structure. Easing of FDI norms and abolishing the Emirati partnership mechanism in the UAE primarily injects booster to small and medium enterprises spread across the country while it is effective even for "on-shore" big projects.

> **ACQUISITION OF 100% OWNERSHIP IN ONSHORE BUSINESS BY MARS**
>
> Global food and confectionery conglomerate Mars owned 49% of the shares in the Dubai-based limited liability company to the extent of maximum percentage of foreign ownership previously permitted for a company incorporated "onshore", i.e., outside of a free zone in the UAE.
>
> Mars is a privately owned food company owning some of the world's best-known confectionery and food brands such as Dolmio and Uncle Ben's, and pet food brands Whiskas, Royal Canin and Pedigree. The company invested about $150 million in its UAE operations setting up an offshore business within Jebel Ali Free Zone in 1993 and thereafter entered into an onshore joint venture in 2013. Mars has acquired all of the shares in its Dubai-based subsidiary taking advantage of the new Foreign Investment Law.
>
> Switching from 49% ownership to 100% ownership taking advantage of the new FDI requires simple steps:
>
> i. The foreign investor has to apply for switch with prior approval of the Emirati Partner(s) in the Emirates concerned (Emirate FDI Authority) and obtain preliminary approval.
> ii. The foreign investor shall then apply for obtaining FDI license to the competent authority which evaluates and grant license with 5 working days.
> iii. In case the FDI request does not fall in the Positive or Negative List, the competent authority may submit the request to the FDI committee for approval which may require submission of additional documents.
> iv. If FDI request is referred to the FDI committee, the approval is granted by UAE Cabinet.

However, despite non-oil diversification target, the oil sector continues to be the recipient of a significant portion of the FDI flow in the UAE. Abu Dhabi National Oil Corporation (ADNOC) got big foreign investors (investment value about $20.7 billion) in infrastructure projects led by US firm Global Infrastructure Partners, Singaporean sovereign wealth fund GIC, Canadian investor Brookfield Asset Management and the Ontario Teachers' Pension Plan Board. The foreign investors will acquire 49% of a new ADNOC subsidiary, which will have leasing rights to 38 gas pipelines spanning 982 km for a period of 20 years, in return for a volume-based tariff subject to upper and lower caps [Arab News, 2020].

Changing Commercial Company Law Structure to Host 100% FDI

Article 2 of the UAE Commercial Company law [GOUAE, 2015] sets objective of the new companies law [GOUAE, 2015] which echoes underlying principles of amending commercial company law in the GCC countries:

> The law has for objective to the development of the working environment and capacities of the State and its economic position in regulating companies according to the various international norms related to governance rules and the protection of shareholders and supporting foreign investment and promoting corporate social responsibility of companies.

The GCC countries offer a wide range of choices in selecting corporate form, amongst which single person company, limited liability company and closed joint stock company are most suitable for 100% FDI. Public joint stock companies across the GCC restricts maximum foreign shareholding to 49% which has been relaxed in case-by-case basis in respect to many listed companies (see Paragraph 4). The UAE allows 100% FDI companies in the mainland (outside free zone) which can take the form of either limited liability company (LLC) or private joint stock company, and exempts application of Article 151 regarding nationality of board members and Article 209 regarding disposal of shares that reduces shares of UAE nationals. So far LLC remained the most favoured corporate structure by foreign investors in GCC countries.

In Saudi Arabia, a favoured structure for 100% FDI is Branch of a foreign parent, with a minimum capital requirement of SAR 5,00,000 which can be established with license from SAGIA. A Branch operates as an extension of its foreign parent company without pursuing detailed documentation and procedures of a company formation. The SAGIA licensed Branches:

- can engage in projects in both the public and private sector; and
- may promote and solicit its SAGIA-licensed business throughout the Kingdom.

However, Branches are not allowed to conduct promotion, marketing and trading activities. As per Invest Saudi [https://investsaudi.sa/en/] more than 1,100 licenses for foreign investors were issued in 2019 which are 54% more than in 2018 and 300% of 2017. Pan-Asia, EDS Renewables, WngFu, McDermott, GlaxoSmithKline and Unibio are some of the major investors licensed by SAGIA in 2019 [General Authority of Statistics https://www.stats.gov.sa/en].

Earlier Bahrain commercial company law restricted majority shareholding of public joint stock company to Bahraini and other GCC nationals, and US investors who are US citizens are treated at par with the GCC citizens in the Kingdom of Bahrain in accordance with the Bahrain-US Free Trade Agreement (FTA). By virtue of Article 65 [as amended by Law No. (50) of 2014] of Bahrain commercial company law (KOB, 2020):

Bahraini public shareholding companies may be established with the participation of foreign capital or expertise. Subject to an order by the Minister concerned with trade affairs, the percentages of participation of foreign capital or expertise in certain sectors or activities may be specified.

The liberalized article keeps the option open for increasing the foreign shareholding in public joint stock company.

FDI investor (100%) can operate in Kuwait through limited liability company or closed shareholding company. Likewise other GCC peers Kuwait offered flexibility of allowing foreign companies to establish and operate through a 100% foreign-owned "branch" or "representative office" in Kuwait.

The GCC sets 100% FDI even with small capital investment with view to attract MSMEs which dominate GCC business. Minimum capital requirement for establishing 100% FDI companies are stated in Table 4.3.

Improving Governance in Public Joint Stock Companies and Protecting Composition Scheme

The amended commercial company law along with code of corporate governance attempted to strengthen governance of public joint stock company and improve protection of minority shareholders with a view to attract foreign shareholding up to 49% in general and even up to 100% in selected companies (see Paragraph 4) incorporating several measures including:

- increased public participation restricting founder's capital to 35%;
- board composition comprising majority non-executive directors;
- compulsory transfer to legal reserve before payment of dividend;
- submission of business plan to shareholders in AGM in case of significant loss of capital;
- right of shareholders to file complaint against directors for wrongdoing and
- right to minority shareholders to initiate complaint against decisions which are considered detrimental to the interest of the company and shareholders.

In addition, global best practices on corporate governance have been adopted in code of corporate governance issued by various capital market authorities of GCC ensuring inclusion of independent directors in the Board of public listed companies, formation of board committees, e.g., nomination committee, remuneration committee and audit committee and introducing risk management mechanism. GCC countries also enacted bankruptcy law incorporating international practices of "protective composition" in the case of debtors experiencing financial hardship and requiring assistance to reach settlement with creditors which is of great significance for ensuring court-monitored business re-organization in distressed economic conditions like the 2008 economic crisis and the recent COVID-19 crisis. Useful remedial measures under this scheme include ability to raise priority funding

48 T.P. Ghosh

TABLE 4.3 Minimum Capital Requirement in LLC and Private Joint Stock Company Structure in the GCC

Country	Minimum Capital Requirement	
	Limited Liability Company	*Private Joint Stock Companies*
Bahrain KOB(2020)	BHD 20,000	BHD 250,000
Kuwait SOK (2017)	Pursuant to Ministerial Decision no. 234 of 2015, minimum capital requirement is KD 1000	Pursuant to Ministerial Decision no. 234 of 2015, minimum capital requirement is KD 25,000
Oman SOO (2019a)	No statutory minimum capital	Article 91: Omani Riyals 500,000
Qatar SOQ. (2015)	No statutory minimum capital requirement. Ministry of Commerce and Industry requires that minimum capital of a limited liability company which is 100% owned by a foreign entity under a Ministerial Exemption be not less than QAR 3,000,000–4,000,000.	QAR 2,000,000
Saudi Arabia KOSA (2015b)	Article 158: Not less than SAR 500,000. SAGIA also prescribes project-specific minimum capital requirement: • Service/property investment project value SAR 30 million • Service/property financing projects SAR 200 million with 40% Saudi shareholding • Service/transport SAR 500,000 • Contracting: SAR 500,000 (but have revenue/asset value requirements) • Commercial (100% foreign): SAR 30 million and commitment to invest at least SAR 200 million over the first five years	Article 49: Not less than SAR 2,000,000
UAE GOUAE (2015)	Adequate capital The de facto minimum capital requirement is AED300,000.	Not less than AED 5 million and must be paid in full

on secured or unsecured basis to continue the business and provision for creditor-led supervisory committee to monitor implementation of the scheme.

Extending Reform to Ownership Structure of Public Joint Stock Companies

Development of a strong secondary market with investment alternatives in equity shares in diversified economic sectors is an essential precondition for economic diversification and growth. Bahrain and Oman have implemented liberalized foreign ownership beyond the critical 49% level, while other GCC countries are still experimenting with the idea of 100% foreign ownership in selected listed companies.

Liberalization of share ownership in public joint stock company is expected to attract investments from foreign institutional investors to domestic as well as FDI companies and enhance the scope for expansion of these companies because of better access to capital. Exploring ADR and GDR routes for accessing foreign capital is also linked to relaxation of share ownership norm and improved corporate governance practices. Current reforms discussed above are based on the essentially presumption of business expansion by a foreign company. Indeed, large FDI projects should be encouraged to adopt the form of a public listed company which becomes integral part of the GCC economy. Traditionally, multinational companies (MNCs) establish foreign subsidiary and list such subsidiary in the host countries to participate in the local market.

Bahrain is the only GCC countries which permits 100% foreign ownership in 40 out of 41 listed companies except Bahrain Family Leisure in which 49% restriction has been retained. Oman allows more than 49% foreign ownership in 74 out of 119 listed equities, although foreign ownership exceeded 50% only three companies, namely, Al Kamil Power Company (65.01%), Oman Cables Industry (51.36%) and Phoenix Power Company (52.49%).

Kuwait in general restricts foreign ownership in listed companies to 49%. It has recently relaxed foreign investment norms for 100% ownership in banks subject to approval of the Central Bank of Kuwait for buying shares exceeding 5%. Foreign shareholding in 7 out of 20 listed companies in Kuwait exceeds 10%, and only in 2 companies the foreign ownership exceeds 50%. In Ahil United Bank of Kuwait and Humansoft Holding foreign ownership have been relaxed to 100%, and actual foreign shareholdings reached 56.37% and 53.64% respectively.

Foreign ownership in Qatari listed companies has been increased to 49% from the earlier upper limit of 25% which had boosted foreign investment of $2.2 billion. Still actual foreign ownership in 39 public listed companies is well below 49%. Only in 17 companies foreign ownership is in the range of 10–31.3%. Despite the relaxation of foreign ownership limit to 100% in Salam International (engaged in contracting and trading, retail and distribution, real estate and investment) and Qatar First Bank actual foreign ownership reached just 11.26% and 9.97% respectively.

In the Dubai financial market cross-listed companies of Bahrain and other countries have relaxed foreign ownership limit up to 100%. Among Emirati companies, 100% foreign ownership has been permitted in Emirates Integrated Telecommunications (DU), but actual foreign ownership is only 0.49%. As regards Abu Dhabi Stock Exchange listed securities, foreign shareholding is permitted up to 49%, and foreign ownership exceeding 10% is found only in financial and insurance companies.

Recent listing of Saudi Aramco with just 10% public offering is a case in point. Out of the state-controlled Saudi Aramco's record $25.6 billion initial public offering (IPO), nearly 80% was subscribed by Saudi nationals. The proceeds of the stake sale were planned to be injected in domestic projects. It has been argued that it helps to mobilize domestic savings of Saudi investors which would have been otherwise invested outside the Kingdom. But the Aramco IPO is considered as a missed opportunity to attract foreign capital with other supportive plan to retain domestic savings within the country. International listing of Aramco has been abandoned on valuation issues. Gross (2019) observed that selling to local owners somewhat defeats the purpose of economic diversification. Saudi shareholders are still dependent on Aramco's performance (remain oil dependent), just through a different mechanism.

Also, foreign investment in all listed companies in Tadawul (Saudi Arabia stock exchange; https://www.tadawul.com.sa) is very low despite the 49% upper limit. Out of 205 listed companies, foreign shareholding is below 10% in 180 companies and in the range of 10–29.6% in 25 companies. However, the current reform allowing strategic investments garnered significant strategic investments in six listed companies belonging to the oil and gas sector and in banking and insurance: Allianz Saudi Insurance (51%), Arab National Bank (40%, Bupa Arabia Insurance (43.25%), Chubb Arabia Insurance (30%), Rabigh Refining (37.5%) and Saudi British Bank (30.99%). Strategic investment in public listed companies could be another alternative strategy for inviting foreign capital.

This analysis shows inadequate response of foreign institutional investors in the GCC secondary market despite relaxed foreign ownership limit in many stock exchanges which could be because of small size of individual stock market, non-availability of good quality equity stocks of varied industrial sectors, cyclicality of real estate stock and in general financial performance and growth prospect of GCC equity. Many of these issues would link back to oil dependency and economic uncertainty arising out of sustained low oil price.

Concluding Remarks

It has been studied that the GCC countries progressed at a varied degree to improve business environment and participation of private sectors including foreign investors in key economic sectors. Revival of FDI flows across the GCC in the recent years should be considered as a success indicator of structural reform initiatives. Reform in the FDI law, the commercial companies law and the code of corporate governance coupled with allowing land ownership for FDI projects and granting long-term residency visa to investors are proved to be game-changing strategies in improving ease of doing business and achieving the objective of economic diversification attracting foreign investment. Also, the Mars case provides an early response to conversion of existing 49% business with local partner into 100% ownership. This would bring necessary operational efficiency and flexibility with resultant improved profitability in functioning of the MSME sector. However, the GCC countries have yet to make progress in establishing major non-oil manufacturing projects that could significantly reduce oil dependency.

Although in many GCC listed companies 100% foreign ownership is permitted, foreign participation is evidently very low. Further research is necessary to analyse reasons thereof including financial performance and growth prospect of public companies in the GCC. Most importantly, FDI companies which meet the listing requirements should be encouraged to operate as public listed company rather than as LLCs or closed joint stock company which would increase investment alternatives in the secondary market.

Although this chapter covers GCC countries, a similar trend of liberalization can be observed in the broader Middle East region. Of course, improvement in investment climate in Egypt requires a special mention. Post–November 2016 currency crisis, Egypt could successfully restore investors' confidence using IMF fund facility of $13 billion and related reform package. Egyptian pound was allowed to float by 48% devaluation and reopening of interbank foreign exchange market. Other important reforms include (i) adoption of new investment law (72 of 2017) aimed at reducing barriers to international companies to invest and operate in Egypt and (ii) bankruptcy law in 2018. The new investment law offers special incentives and reintroduced private-owned free trade zone. The United Nations Commission on Trade and Development (UNCTAD) has ranked Egypt as the top FDI destination in Africa between 2015 and 2019, and FDI inflows to Egypt grew from $8.1 billion in 2018 to $9 billion in 2019. The investment climate in Turkey, on the other hand, has negatively impacted because of political factors, weak Turkish Lira and high level of foreign exchange–denominated debt of Turkish banks and other corporates. The geopolitical risk, concern over rule of law and weakening relationship of Turkey with the United States and the EU led to a historical low level of FDI flow to the country. Similarly, American embargo and economic sanctions have affected the investment climate in Iran. Long-standing bilateral commercial relationship between Israel and the United States makes Israeli investment climate altogether different from other Middle East countries which require separate analysis.

Challenges for Investment in the GCC and Broadly in the Middle East

- Impairment of banks' loan assets because of COVID-19 which may increase to at least 20%;
- Ongoing COVID-19 impacted debt restructuring in large companies under the realm of the newly established bankruptcy law;

52 T.P. Ghosh

- Volatility of economic performance linked to oil price volatility;
- Geo-political tensions and proximity to conflict zones; and
- Domination of expat work force in GCC economies and low degree of acceptance of the collective bargaining principle.

Key Takeaway

- GCC economies have been pursuing planned non-oil economic diversification.
- Supportive foreign investment law facilitates One hundred per cent foreign direct investment in a wide range of economic sectors in the GCC.
- Changes in the company law and bankruptcy law, and other administrative reforms, enhanced ease of doing business in GCC countries.
- GCC countries have initiated wide-ranging capital market reform including adoption of globally benchmarked corporate governance principles.
- Although COVID-19 caused temporary business disruptions and economic turmoil, oil-rich GCC nations have ability to provide stable business environment and therefore remained as preferred FDI destination.

Useful Websites

- Foreign investment in Kuwait Santandertrade.com https://santandertrade.com/en/portal
- Foreign Direct Investment in UAE https://u.ae/en/information-and-services/finance-and-investment/foreign-direct-investment
- Investing in Bahrain https://www.bahrain.bh/wps/portal
- Invest in Egypt, Arab Republic of Egypt, General Authority for Investment and Free Zones https://www.investinegypt.gov.eg/english/Pages/default.aspx
- Invest in Oman, Omanuna. https://www.oman.om/wps/portal
- Invest Saudi https://www.investsaudi.sa
- Invest Qatar https://www.invest.qa
- MEED Middle East Business Intelligence https://www.meed.com
- Secretariat General of the Gulf Cooperation Council
- https://www.gcc-sg.org/en-us/Pages/default.aspx
- Zawya – Middle East's Trusted source of business, financial and economic new
- https://www.zawya.com/uae/en/

Appendix I: Reform in the Legal Framework in GCC – at a Glance

Presented in Table 4.4 is an overview of the long-term vision adopted by the GCC countries and initiatives taken to attract FDI participation to achieve an economic diversification.

Changing Legal Framework of the GCC Countries 53

TABLE 4.4 Key Reforms in the Legal Framework of GCC Countries

Country	Economic Vision	Summary of Changes in Legal and Institutional Framework
Bahrain	Economic Vision 2030,[1] inter alia, focuses on enhancing the role of private sector productivity including attracting FDI and stimulating diversification in high-potential sectors.	i. Carried out key changes in the Commercial Company Law in 2018 and 2020, and updated Corporate Governance Code in 2018; ii. Adopted its new Reorganisation and Bankruptcy Law (Bahrain Law No. 22/2018) on May 30, 2018 iii. Amended trust law to recognize trust governed by law of a foreign jurisdiction; iv. Introduced protected cell companies and investment limited partnership in the banking and financial sector; v. permitted freehold property right foreign investors; vi. Instituted two commercial courts for dispute settlements involving foreign investors; vi. Established Gateway project which is a free trade zone and Bahrain Investors Centre to support incoming investors and facilitating business registration process.
Kuwait	New Kuwait 2035 Plan[2] has been initiated to overcome challenges in maintaining high economic growth arising out of sustained low oil price.	i. Introduced foreign investment law (Law no. 116 of 2013); ii. Amended company law issued in 2012 (Law no. 15 of 2017); iii. Established Kuwait Direct Investment Promotion Authority (KDIPA) in 2013; https://www.kdipa.gov.kw/en/ iv. Allowed foreign banks to open multiple branches; v. Introduced Preventive, Settlement, Restructuring and Bankruptcy law in 2019; and v. Granted of income-tax and custom duty exemptions.
Oman	Oman Vision 2040,[3] inter alia, focused on creating wealth through economic diversification and private sector partnership.	i. Introduced new foreign capital investment law (Royal Decree no. 50/2019); i. Introduced new companies law (Royal Decree no. 18 /2019) and updated code of corporate governance for public listed companies in 2016; iii. Enacted Bankruptcy Law (Decree No. 53/2019); and iv. Exempted custom duties on import of equipment and raw material, and corporate tax for the first five years of activity.

(Continued)

54 T.P. Ghosh

TABLE 4.4 (Continued)

Country	Economic Vision	Summary of Changes in Legal and Institutional Framework
Qatar	**Qatar National Vision 2023**[4] is built on four pillars, i.e., human development, social development, economic development, environmental development. It proposes transition from uncontrolled development relying on low-productivity, low-skilled and low-paid expatriate workers, to a diversified post-carbon economy relying on a high-productivity, highly skilled and highly educated labour force.	i. Adopted Second National Development Strategy in 2018–2022; ii. Introduced new company law (Law no. 11/2015); iii. Introduced executive regulations on foreign capital investment law (Law no. 13/2020) and reformed labour laws; and iv. There is no specific law governing bankruptcy and therefore bankruptcy issues are addressed by Commercial Code.
Saudi Arabia	**Saudi Vision 2030**[5] and supporting action plan National Transformation Programme launched in 2016 set " thriving economy" target through increased private sector contribution of 65% of GDP by privatization of state-owned companies in various industrial sectors	i. Introduction of new companies law (Royal decree no. M3 of 2015) and amended foreign investment law (Royal decree no. M1 of 2015; ii. Permitted 100% participation in retail and wholesale space, real estate, healthcare, education, courier services and publishing; iii. Relaxed 49% limit for foreign strategic investors in shares of listed companies; iv. Enacted new bankruptcy law in 2018; v. Permitted land and property ownership to foreign investors; and vi. Reformed residency law to allow foreign investors unlimited residency visa.

UAE	**National Vision 2021**[6] supported by National Agenda 2021 aims at achieving economic diversification expanding new strategic sectors that is less reliant on oil. It has been followed up by the **2030 Agenda for Sustainable Development**	i. Introduced new commercial companies law in 2015 and further amended the law in 2020 annulling the requirement for commercial companies to have a major Emirati shareholder or agent and allowing full foreign ownership to expats of onshore companies; ii. introduced foreign investment law in 2018; iii. Introduced new bankruptcy law (Decree no. 9/2016); iv. Reformed labour law and introduced anti-commercial fraud law; v. Permitted land and property ownership to foreign investors; and vii. Reformed residency law to allow foreign investors long-term residency visa.

1 Bahrain Economic Vision 2030, Economic Development Board, Bahrain. http://www.bahrainedb.com/en/EDBDocuments/EDB-Vision-2030-May-2013.pdf
2 Kuwait Vision 2035. http://www.newkuwait.gov.kw/en/
3 Oman Vision 2024, https://www.2040.om/wp-content/uploads/2019/02/190207-Preliminary-Vision-Document-English.pdf
4 Qatar National Vision 2023. https://www.gco.gov.qa/en/about-qatar/national-vision2030/
5 Vision 2030: Kingdom of Saudi Arabia, https://vision2030.gov.sa/sites/default/files/report/Saudi_Vision2030_EN_2017.pdf
6 United Arab Emirates, Vision 2010. https://www.vision2021.ae/
United Arab Emirates, UAE and the 2030 Agenda for Sustainable Development, Excellence in Implementation 2017. https://sustainabledevelopment.un.org/content/documents/20161UAE_SDGs_Report_Full_English.pdf

Appendix II

TABLE 4.5 Positive and Negative Lists for 100% FDI Participation in GCC Countries

Country & FDI Law	Positive List	Negative List
Bahrain	Residency, food, administrative services, arts, entertainment and leisure, health and social work, information and communications, manufacturing, mining and quarrying, water supplying and professional, scientific, technical and real estate activities.	The Ministry of Industry, Commerce and Tourism (MoICT) maintains a small list of business activities that are restricted to Bahraini ownership, including press and publications, Islamic pilgrimage, clearance offices, and workforce agencies.
Kuwait		Ministerial Resolution No. 75 of 2015 sets out the Negative List, which includes 10 different sectors that are not eligible for an investment license, including: i. extraction of crude oil; ii. extraction of natural gas; iii. manufacturing of coke ovens and products related thereto; iv. manufacturing of fertilizers and nitrogenous formulas; v. manufacturing of coal gas and distribution of gaseous fuels through main pipelines; vi. real estate activities, except for construction development projects for private operations; vii. activities related to security and investigations; viii. membership organizations; or ix. activities for the sourcing of labour, including household workers.

Changing Legal Framework of the GCC Countries 57

Oman Law No. 50/2019 Foreign Capital Investment Law

The Minister of Commerce and Industry has issued a negative list setting out a list of 37 business activities in which foreign investment is prohibited in Annexure 1 to Law No. 50/2019 Foreign Capital Investment Law. Most of these prohibited sectors cater to the indigenous and small-scale industry like translation, taxi operation and fishing.

Banks and insurance companies, commercial agency rights and trading in real estate.

Qatar Law No. 13 of 2020 on Organization of Foreign Capital Investment in Economic Activity

Article 2(2): Agriculture, industry, health, education, tourism, development and exploitation of natural resources, energy or mining provided that such projects match with Development plan of the State (Qatar)

Saudi Arabia Supreme Council of Economic and Development Affairs

Under the Negative List, certain economic activities are currently closed to foreign interests:

i. In the industrial sector, exploration, prospecting and production of petroleum substances, excluding services related to the mining area;

ii. In the service sector, the following economic activities are, at present, closed to foreign interest:
 a. catering to military sectors;
 b. security and detective services;
 c. real estate investment in Makkah and Medina;
 d. tourist orientation and guidance services related to Hajj and Umrah
 e. recruitment offices;
 f. commission agent;
 g. services provided by midwives, nurses, physical therapy services and quasi-doctoral services; and
 h. fisheries.

(*Continued*)

TABLE 4.5 (Continued)

Country & FDI Law	Positive List	Negative List
United Arab Emirates (UAE) Decree no 19 of 2018 regarding foreign direct investment	Article 7(1): Positive List Resolution covers three broader sectors: Agriculture (19 activities), Manufacturing (51 activities) and Services (52 activities) are eligible for full 100% foreign ownership in mainland UAE. Positive list activities include construction, educational activities, health care, hospitality and food services, renewable energy, etc.	Article 7(2): UAE negative list includes important sectors like exploration and production of petroleum materials, banking, financial services, insurance, land and air transport services, and telecommunications.

Sources: Various FDI Laws in GCC and rules.

Appendix III

TABLE 4.6 Indicators of State of Oil Dependency in the GCC Countries

GCC Countries	2012	2013	2014	2015	2016	2017	2018	Average
Bahrain								
Nominal GDP, US$ billion	31	33	34	31	32	35	38	
Hydrocarbon sector as % of GDP	18.9	20.7	20.4	19.8	19.2	18.3	17.7	19.29
Hydrocarbon revenue as % of GDP	87.2	88.3	86.2	78.1	75.7	75.1	82.4	81.86
Hydrocarbon export as % Total Export	50.5	47.8	45	33.3	33.3	40.3	47.4	42.51
Kuwait								
Nominal GDP, US$ billion	174	174	163	115	109	120	142	
Hydrocarbon sector as % of GDP	64.5	62.7	61	59.7	60.3	54.2	54.1	59.50
Hydrocarbon revenue as % of GDP	93.6	92.1	90.3	88.6	89.2	89.3	89.6	90.39
Hydrocarbon export as % Total Export	95.5	94.7	94.9	92.1	91.9	93	93.8	93.70
Oman								
Nominal GDP, US$ billion	77	79	81	69	66	71	79	
Hydrocarbon sector as % of GDP	44.9	43.8	42.5	42.4	41.8	40.4	40.8	42.37
Hydrocarbon revenue as % of GDP	84.7	85.7	84.3	78.7	68.2	72.9	78.2	78.96
Hydrocarbon export as % Total Export	83.6	81.7	81.7	74.97	70.5	72.1	74.4	77.00
Qatar								
Nominal GDP, US$ billion	187	199	206	162	152	167	191	
Hydrocarbon sector as % of GDP	58.1	55.7	53.2	51.1	49.5	48.4	47.4	51.91
Hydrocarbon revenue as % of GDP	77.1	92.4	82.2	81.9	82.4	81.5	83.3	82.97
Hydrocarbon export as % Total Export	92.5	91.9	90.8	87.5	85.1	85.7	88.2	88.81

(*Continued*)

TABLE 4.6 (Continued)

GCC Countries	2012	2013	2014	2015	2016	2017	2018	Average
Saudi Arabia								
Nominal GDP, US$ billion	736	747	756	654	645	689	787	
Hydrocarbon sector as % of GDP	45.2	45.3	42.7	43.2	44.6	42.9	43.2	43.87
Hydrocarbon revenue as % of GDP	91.8	89.8	87.8	72.9	64.2	63	67.5	76.71
Hydrocarbon export as % Total Export	87.4	86.4	84.9	75.1	75.6	77.3	80.2	80.99
United Arab Emirates								
Nominal GDP, US$ billion	375	390	403	358	357	378	414	
Hydrocarbon sector as % of GDP	32.6	32.0	30.7	30.8	30.6	29.6	30.0	30.90
Hydrocarbon revenue as % of GDP	67.7	63.6	62.9	45.3	22.8	36.1	36.1	47.79
Hydrocarbon export as % Total Export	61.0	59.8	61.2	54.4	44.9	48.0	58.4	55.39

Source: World Bank Group, Gulf Economic Update, Issue 5/Dec. 2019.

References

Arab News (2020), Abu Dhabi wins $10bn FDI in gas pipeline deal, June 23. https://www.arabnews.com/node/1694286/business-economy

Government of United Arab Emirates (GOUAE) (2015). Federal Law No 2 of 2015 on Commercial Company Law issued on 1 April 2015 and further amended on by a decree on November 23, 2020.

Gross, S. (2019), The Saudi Aramco IPO breaks records but fell short of expectations, Brookings, Dec. 11. https://www.brookings.edu/blog/order-from-chaos/2019/12/11/the-saudi-aramco-ipo-breaks-records-but-falls-short-of-expectations/

Kingdom of Bahrain (KOB) (2018). Corporate Governance Code. Ministry of Industry, Commerce and Tourism, Bahrain.

Kingdom of Bahrain (KOB) (2020). Legislative Decree No. 28 of 2020 concerning the amendment to certain provisions of the Commercial Companies law promulgated by Legislative Decree No 21 of 2001.

Kingdom of Saudi Arabia (KOSA) (2015a). Law of Companies, Royal Decree No M3 dated 28/1/1437H (i.e. 10/11/2015G).

Kingdom of Saudi Arabia (KOSA) (2015b). Foreign Investment Law in the Kingdom of Saudi Arabia, Royal Decree No. M/1.

OECD (2020). The impact of coronavirus (COVID-19) and the global oil price shock on the fiscal position of oil-exporting developing countries, OECD Policy Responses to Coronavirus (COVID-19), September. https://www.oecd.org/coronavirus/policy-responses/the-impact-of-coronavirus-covid-19-and-the-global-oil-price-shock-on-the-fiscal-position-of-oil-exporting-developing-countries-8bafbd95/

State of Kuwait (SOK) (2013). Law No. 116 of 2013 Regarding the Promotion of Direct Investment in the State of Kuwait.

State of Kuwait (SOK) (2017). Law No. 15 of 2017, Company Law, Council of Ministers.

State of Qatar (SOQ) (2015). New Commercial Companies Law No. 11 of 2015.

State of Qatar (SOQ) (2020). Law No. 13 of 2020, on Organization of Foreign Capital Investment in Economic Activity, Ministry of Economy and Commerce.

Sultanate of Oman (SOO) (2019). Royal Decree No. 50/2019, Foreign Capital Investment Law.

Sultanate of Oman (SOO) (2019a). Royal Decree No. 18/2019 Promulgating the Commercial Companies Law.

World Bank Group (WB) (2019). Economic diversification for a sustainable and resilient GCC, Gulf Economic Update, Issue 5/December.

5
WASTA IN THE MIDDLE EAST
A Corruption or an Opportunity

Mohammad Ta'amnha, Susan Sayce and Olga Tregaskis

Introduction

Understanding cultural aspects and settings where businesses are conducted is a major concern of international businesses (IBs). This is particularly true when it comes to the Arabic region where less is known about business environments compared with developed countries. The main purpose of this chapter is to develop a practical instrument that can be used to understand and measure a social capital mechanism namely "Wasta". This Arabic relational form of social capital is dominant in Arabic business setting. It plays key roles in facilitating business transactions and other social activities, though it is considered in many cases a corruption. The findings of this study were drawn from data gathered from professionals who work in the IT sector in Jordan.

The findings reveal that the usage of Wasta is increasing because of the harsh economic challenges caused by the global pandemic. In this chapter the authors present a 14-item Wasta legitimacy scale (WLS), which was developed around the dimensions of pragmatic legitimacy, normative legitimacy, and cultural-cognitive legitimacy. These dimensions reflect the perceptions of Jordanian IT managers and employees regarding Wasta. This scale is helpful to understand the cross-cultural issues around Wasta.

Wasta can be seen as "the intervention of a patron in favor of a client to obtain benefits and/or resources from a third party" (Mohammad and Hamdy, 2008, p.1). Wasta is a phenomenon (Marktanner and Wilson, 2016) that is prevalent and integrated deeply into the social fabric of Arabic societies (Barnett et al., 2011). Wasta has a long history that affects how decisions are made in that part of the world (Makhoul and Harrison, 2004, Cunningham and Sarayrah, 1993, Khakhar and Rammal, 2013). It is part of day-to-day Arabic language and activities

(Al Maeena, 2010, Berger et al., 2015). Wasta is an effective mechanism of social capital that leads to difference sort of supports. It leads to obtaining jobs (Ezzedeen and Swiercz, 2001), facilitating procedures (Arab Archives Institute, 2000), and improving business and social interactions (Tlaiss and Kauser, 2011b). However, doing Wasta is also associated with negative practices such as allocating resources according to the principle of "who you know" more than "what you know". Wasta affects the significant managerial decisions such as staffing decision (Hutchings and Weir, 2006), allocating organizations' training and developmental opportunities (Altarawneh, 2009), and promotion and career advancement opportunities (Tlaiss and Kauser, 2011a). Thus, Wasta is accused of causing about a half of deficiency in the development of the Arabic economics (Marktanner and Wilson, 2016).

Therefore, Wasta is perceived as a form of corruption that implies breaching the laws and regulations enacted to ensure justice and equal opportunities among the societies' members (Hutchings and Weir, 2006). Nevertheless, Wasta is widespread in Arabic societies and continues to be used and in times of economic turbulence may be more used.

A poll conducted in August/October 2019 about the corruption in the Middle East by the Global Corruption Barometer Middle East and North Africa (2019) found that the percentages of using Wasta in some of the Middle Eastern countries was rather high in several sectors in comparison with other form of corruption (i.e. bribery) (see Table 5.1).

Table 5.1 shows that Wasta is widely used in several Arabic institutions. Therefore, our main objective in this chapter is to understand why Wasta is widely spread in the Middle East in general and in the Arabic context (i.e. Jordan) in particular. We adopt the institutional viewpoint to pursue our inquiry, mainly by employing the legitimacy perspective. This standpoint explains why Wasta is still widely used in the Arabic context, even though it is perceived as corruption and against Arab states' laws and regulations.

TABLE 5.1 Bribery and Wasta Rates Based on People Who Received These Services from Government Departments

Country	Corruption type	General average (%)	Public schools (%)	Public clinics and health centers (%)	Identification services (%)	Public utility (%)	Police (%)	Judges (%)
Jordan	Wasta	25	15	20	13	21	15	16
	Bribe	4	4	1	2	5	2	0
Palestine	Wasta	39	22	31	24	21	30	29
	Bribe	17	11	9	9	8	11	14
Lebanon	Wasta	54	40	45	45	51	42	65
	Bribe	41	26	27	37	36	36	48

Source: Global Corruption Barometer Middle East and North Africa (2019).

Wasta and Business

Wasta is deeply rooted in the business activities in the Arabic countries. For instance, Khakhar and Rammal (2013) found that Wasta is widely used by Arab negotiators that they described it as a referent power that facilitates the negotiation processes in this regions. Al-Ma'aitah et al. (2021) found that Wasta significantly affects the long-term buyer–supplier relationships. Wasta is also found to play a significant role in relationships with customers and ensuring their loyalty (Zhang et al., 2021). Berger et al. (2021) found that Wasta significantly and positively affects the satisfaction, and relationship and organizational performance among business people. Sefiani et al. (2018) found that Wasta plays significant roles in SMEs. They found that using Wasta enables the SMEs to get access to up-to-date information that is critical for the success of these enterprises. In addition, they found that Wasta enables SMEs to get financial resources in the form of trade credits from their suppliers. Loewe et al. (2008) found that investors use Wasta to speed up governmental procedures and get special access to services and information. This is perhaps due to lack transparency and accountability on all levels of the Jordanian administrations. Loewe et al. found that entrepreneurs rely mainly on their social capital and Wasta more than investing on their productive capital to succeed in the Jordanian market.

The usage of Wasta in the business setting stems from the key components and attributes of wasta that make it an effective mechanism in Arabic markets. Wasta is an informal social institution (Ta'Amnha, 2014) because it is a well-established practice and a key component of Jordanian culture, comprising shared social understandings and meanings; it enables people to increase the levels of coordination and cooperation between them, helping them to achieve their shared objectives; it comprises many roles that are carried out through several parties involved in its activities; it involves expectation and obligation. Each person taking part in Wasta expects to receive something and is also obligated to provide something in return. Wasta is an institution because there is hierarchy in its structure, reflecting the structures in the societies, cultures, and norms that govern and coordinate the behaviors of the societies' members; it has its own boundaries, as it is not accessible easily to everyone. Wasta is a changing institution. It used to be a family practice but is now used among friends, colleagues, and business partners; Wasta guides people's behavior according to certain acceptable manners, leading to the gaining of benefits or the avoidance of undesirable practices and actions. In other words, Wasta is an institution because of the embedded legitimacy associated with its practices and behaviors.

Even though Wasta is widespread in Arabic societies, it is a form of corruption and implies breaching the laws and regulations enacted to ensure justice and equal opportunities among the societies' members. The influences of Wasta in decision-making processes result in available resources and benefits being given to some people at the expense of others who may deserve them more. Certainly, Wasta violates the fundamental notion of equity in the workplace, which supports assigning the right people to the right jobs. Favoritism in distributing available jobs and other resources corrupts the typical procedures of recruitment, selection, and promotion. The priority in organizations is about who has influence with the decision-makers. In other words, with Wasta the qualifications of candidates are not highly valued. Indeed, personal relationships are the cornerstone of the hiring and promotion of decision-making process in Arabic societies and organizations.

Scale Development (with 14 Items) – Phase 1 of Study

In order to develop a scale for Wasta, we employed in-depth semi-structured interviews (Creswell and Creswell, 2017). The topics discussed in the interviews were driven from social capital, Wasta, and institutional literatures. Considering the exploratory perspective, the interviews were conducted to collect new ideas, experiences, and feelings of the participants. At the beginning of the interviews the interviewer explained the purpose of the study, and clarified the concepts of interest, mainly Wasta and legitimacy. Then the interviewees were asked to discourse briefly on their employment history, to create rapport. The Wasta and its legitimacy questions were then asked and probed.

Semi-structured in-depth interviews were conducted with 35 employees of 16 IT companies working in Jordan. Each interview length ranged between 35 and 55 minutes. The first five interviews represented pilot interviews that were found to be very useful for trying the interviews questions, and enhancing the interview protocol and procedures (Harding, 2018, Castillo-Montoya, 2016). Interviews were audio-recorded, with participants' permission.

After conducting interviews, the recordings were transcribed verbatim, which helped achieving data immersion, then data were analyzed using thematic analysis following the six phases described by Braun and Clarke (2006). Initial sub-themes were identified that were grouped into main themes that were given names after careful scrutinizing. Finally, the researchers worked to make theoretical sense from the emerging themes and related data.

To improve the trustworthiness and validity of the study's findings, member-checking technique (Cresswell, 1998) was carried out by asking six participants to review the research data and interpretation (Iivari, 2018), to make sure that the research interpretations are in line with their original inputs and understanding (Moroko and Uncles, 2008).

The interviewees included 19 males and 16 females, their ages ranged from 21 to 56, with an average of 34. Their length of experience in IT sector ranged from less than 1 year to 27 years, with an average of 18 years. 14 participants were single, and 21 were married. In terms of highest level of education, 7 had high school diplomas, 23 had first degrees, and 5 had master's degrees.

Wasta Legitimacy

Legitimacy is achieved when people accept or adopt certain behaviors and practices that can be categorized into three types: (1) pragmatic legitimacy; (2)

moral legitimacy; (3) cultural-cognitive legitimacy. Below, a brief description of the 14 items of the scale is presented.

Pragmatic legitimacy of Wasta

Item 1: Wasta is offered to companies' clients to keep and enhance their relationships with them IT companies rely hugely on their networks to succeed in the Jordanian market. This is because the IT services are offered by large number of competing companies. Therefore, IT companies do their best to attract and gain the loyalty of their customers. The data showed some companies doing Wasta to their clients to keep and enhance their relationships with them.

> it is very important to keep strong relationships with customers. The market so competitive and we need to maintain our current customers. We use many strategies, our prices have dropped hugely in this period and we try to serve customers as much as we can … are you asking me about Wasta? yes … we do Wasta to our customers, … do we used it more currently?… yes we tend to use Wasta sometimes as much as we can as long as we keep our VIP customers … why not … I think we are more tolerant with Wasta more than before given the current harsh conditions in the market.
>
> *(M, 12)*

Item 2: Wasta is used to speed up certain processes especially when dealing with governmental institutions that suffer from ineffective bureaucracy The data also revealed that sometimes Wasta is used to speed up certain processes especially while dealing with governmental institutes that are characterized by slow bureaucratic systems. Wasta is used to reducing waiting times and costs such as in the case of getting importing and exporting license, custom, and clearance of goods from ports and boarders.

> Wasta is also used to avoid endless procedures to get some licenses or permissions or in case of clearance our products from the port … bureaucracy cost us money and time. Wasta sometimes very helpful to reduce all these obstacles.
>
> *(F, 28)*

Item 3: Wasta is used because it leads to recruit and hire well-connected employees in the market who bring business to the employing companies Wasta receives more legitimacy when it enables companies to recruit and hire a well-connected person in the market. Some employees indicated that they hire employees mainly to get access to their contacts that will enable them to expand their operations in the market. Certainly, Wasta generates another form of Wasta and therefore it considers as a mechanism of the social capital that leads to several benefits when it is invested rightly.

> we hired last week a new account manager who was working with [name of competitor], it was our sales manager's recommendation because this person is well connected with corporate customers from his previous jobs … we hope that he will attracted those customers to do business with us.
>
> (M, 9)

Item 4: Wasta is used in doing business and getting best offers and deals such as getting tenders Wasta is also used in doing business and getting best offers and deals (Sefiani et al., 2018). It is a way to get access to the decision-makers in organizations. People accumulate their social capital through doing favors to other parties and therefore expecting to get something in return.

> we use Wasta also to get good conditions when making deals with our suppliers, or to get some projects and tenders.
>
> (F, 28)

Item 5: Wasta is used to hire family's members because their competences and experiences are well known by the recruiters The legitimacy of Wasta is also granted when people do Wasta for their acquaintance, friends, and relatives. This reduces the associated risk of hiring someone whose skills and experiences are not known by the employing company.

> I know the personal and professional history of my friends, I cannot take a huge risk to hire someone strange, I know nothing about him or hire … friends is one of the effective sources of hiring employees… this is specially very important nowadays … let me tell another thing … friends and even relative when we hire them in our company, they are more patient if we cannot pay them the full salaries rather some of them asks to delay the whole salary if the company needs that…. What we need more … yes Wasta produces problems but let's have consider its advantages.
>
> (F, 32)

Item 6: Wasta is used to hire family's members because they are more likely to be committed to their family business and give it a maximum effort Even though most of the times the literature on Wasta tends to highlight its negative impacts on the organizations, the data showed that sometimes the family companies tend to hire their family members for several reasons. Mainly, hiring family business not only shows the supplicants' commitment to their families and their members but also this practice may bring benefits to these companies such as higher performance since it is widely believed that those employees working for their families' companies will identify themselves with family companies and align their successes with these companies' achievements. Therefore, they show high levels of enthusiasm and cooperation, working hard to enable their companies to achieve their objectives. In addition, hiring family members and friends sometimes enhances the effectiveness of hiring decisions. This is because the knowledge and attributes of those family employees are well known by the recruiters.

> during these difficult times we select employees very carefully ... I will tell this ... maybe you will criticize me ... but this is the reality ... yes sometimes relative do not perform what we expect from them, and sometimes it is sensitive to be firm with your relatives, but from my experience hiring relatives in the company beats hiring people from outside the family ... family members are more committed to the business ... they perceive the company as their whole life so they look after the company as they look after their families and kids ... given the current difficult and challenging conditions ... I expected the prevalence of Wasta will increase ... and people will accepted more and more as long as it leads to benefits to them.
>
> *(M, 10)*

Normative Legitimacy

Item 1: Wasta is used to show the commitment and obligation to the families and their members The family is an essential component of the Jordanian social fabric. Family members share the same values and norms of solidarity, loyalty, and cooperation. Dependency and emotional attachment are also high among those members. Therefore, people feel obligated to support their family's members and offer them all possible support and protection. However, the motive for a number of families' members to support their relatives sometimes stems from their desire to avoid unfavorable consequences; for example, if they refuse to assist their relatives by doing Wasta for them, social punishments may ensue. This sort of pressure plays a significant role in keeping family ties very strong, with the threat of punishment for anyone who breaches the terms of this implicit contract. Currently, there is a consensus among the staffing employees that they have been facing increasing pressures from their relatives to find jobs for them inside their companies as a result of the increasingly downsizing activities and layoffs of employees in the Jordanian labor market.

> you can't imagine the pressure that I am under from my relatives, I am obligated to support my relatives during normal times, and this pressure has increased currently ... people are fighting over the few jobs available now in the market.
>
> *(M, 3)*

> I am between two fires … how to meet my obligations towards my relatives and how to meet my jobs responsibilities and ethical practices … to be honest with you … I have no choice but to support my relatives even if it at the expense of the working ethics.
>
> *(F, 25)*

Item 2: Wasta is used to meeting friendship expectations of supports Wasta also plays a significant role in strengthening the ties between friends. People sometimes do Wasta for their friends to demonstrate their backing and support when they need them. This increases the level of cooperation and strengthens the relationships among friends. The data showed that the staffing employees themselves try to do Wasta to their friends and not when they asked directly from them. This increases the acceptance and legitimacy of Wasta during this pandemic.

> as we say a friend in need is a friend indeed, one my friend lost her job, I can't leave her facing this difficult situation when I can do something for her … she is a single mom with two kids … I offered her a job in our company as an assistant admin in the marketing department, she accepted and I am really happy because I was able to help her.
>
> *(F, 34)*

> When my friend asked me for a job who lost his job recently, I imagined myself in his position, it is really difficult time to lose one's job. I really empathized with him and offered him a job in our company … yes it was not at the same level of his previous job but it is better than nothing.
>
> *(M, 18)*

Item 3: Wasta is used to practices Islamic principle "shafa'a" Wasta is inextricably linked with Islam. This is very obvious in respect of Shafa'ah Wasta, which occurs when the intercessor intercedes with the decision-makers to provide a certain benefit to the supplicant, who deserves such support but cannot obtain it by his/her own efforts (Faisal, 1990).

> I do Wasta because I am committed to the Islam principles that encourage us to help with justice for weak people who cannot get his or her rights because they don't have strong support from tribal society.
>
> *(M, 14)*

Item 4: Wasta is used as an act of charity The data showed that the charity deeds is one of the key motives of exercising Wasta for some people who try to offer their supports to other people in the society in finding jobs and other benefits.

When I find some in need I offer him or her my support, this really makes me feel happy. As long as I can help people to get job or governmental subsidies why not to do it.

(F, 23)

This part explained the conditions in which moral legitimacy is granted to Wasta. This type of legitimacy is given when the exercising of Wasta corresponds to society's norms and manners. This section is divided into four categories: family obligation, friendships, Shafa'ah, charity work.

Cultural-Cognitive Legitimacy of Wasta

Item 1: Wasta is exercised because it gives status and feeling of satisfaction to the Wasta person The data showed that sometimes Wasta is done because it satisfies people needs for recognition and social esteem. Arabic societies are traditionally hierarchal structured where those who are at the top receive more respect and status. Doing Wasta reinforces this situation.

People sometimes exercise Wasta because this put them in higher position in the Arab societies that appreciate who are able to offer support and help to other people who are in need.

(M, 16)

Item 2: People who have strong Wasta (supplicant) feel powerful and protected in the society One of the key motives of having Wasta is getting protection and having more power to reach the available organizational and society resources. So, this gives Wasta and asking for Wasta more legitimacy that contributes to spreading Wasta in the society.

There is no doubt that having support is so important in our society, even people boast of the people they know. Having Wastas is necessary in our society, it offers protection and tranquility.

(F, 20)

Item 3: People use Wasta as a result of absence of the social justice One of the major reasons why Wasta prevails in Jordanian society is the absence of social justice. People typically rely on Wasta to secure their rights or obtain what they deserve. Given that people believe that there is absence of fairness and equal rights and chances of finding jobs in the labor market, people use Wasta more and more.

We are not living in the virtuous city, we have problem in every aspect of our lives, politically, economically and socially … the social justice is very low here in our society … nothing goes as it should be … I have to use Wasta whenever I go … in finding jobs Wasta is above everything … it comes first … there are very few job opportunities, and we use powerful Wasta than other to get jobs.

(M, 6)

Item 4: People use Wasta because they believe that nothing can be achieved or reached without Wasta in the labor market The data showed that some of the participants believe that nothing can be performed or attained without Wasta interventions in this time of global turbulence around the pandemic, more than any time before. There is no doubt among the Jordanian people that jobs cannot be reached without a strong support from relatives and friends. People have no trust in the idea that jobs will be given to who deserve them based on their competences or meritocracy. They believe that Wasta will be the powerful mechanism to get job more than any time before.

I can't do anything without asking for Wasta, in any institution … governmental or business I try to find Wasta before I visit them.… Wasta is part of our lives and it play a key role in speeding up the process and overcomes the mood of officers who sometimes try to put stakes in the wheel to just stop the process … so I try find Wasta whenever I go to ensure that I get what I looking for … no you ask me about Wasta … defiantly the demand on Wasta and the usage of Wasta has been increasing since this COVID-19 destroyed our lives.

(M, 8)

The Jordanian people consider Wasta an essential cultural aspect in their lives and therefore rely on its intervention to meet their needs and achieve their objectives. Wasta affects Jordanian people's sense-making processes in their lives and how they deal with their external world. This section explains how Wasta has become a typical practice under certain circumstances. A large proportion of Jordanians believe that nothing can be done without Wasta, particularly when seeking jobs. Wasta also gives status to the Wasta people and they feel powerful because of their supplicants. Finally, people rely on Wasta because of the absence of social justice.

Discussion

Even though Wasta faces different sorts of deinstitutionalizing pressures such as functional, social, and political (Ta'Amnha, 2014), the findings of this study show that Wasta is being more institutionalized and getting more support. Companies that are aiming at conducting business in the Arabic world need to understand the reasons behind the prevailing of Wasta, and how it intervenes in facilitating and establishing business.

The findings showed that Wasta is used extensively in the IT sector and affects their decisions because of the various desirable outcomes and resources it delivers to organizations and individuals. To achieve the target of this chapter the legitimacy perspective was employed; in particular we focused on three key types of legitimacy that are pragmatic, moral, and cultural-cognitive legitimacy.

Wasta receives pragmatic legitimacy. The nature of IT businesses, like any other service business such as insurance and banking, relies strongly on the quality of relationships with clients. This therefore offers fertile ground for Wasta to flourish and be accepted (Khakhar and Rammal, 2013). The Jordanian IT companies find that, by doing Wasta for their customers, they increase the possibility of retaining them for longer period, thus improving their financial results. In doing so, companies maintain their current resource and be able to generate more resources such as financial profits by doing more business with their customers. In addition, this situation is explained by the reciprocity tenet in social exchange theory (Molm et al., 2012). IT companies can enhance their customer satisfaction by offering Wasta support to their customers. IT companies' clients feel dissatisfied and thus think of switching to other competitors when their Wasta requests are declined. These findings support the result of Zhang et al. (2021), who found that Wasta positively relates to customer loyalty. Certainly the desirable outcomes that are derived from exchanging benefits are found to be a significant predictor of the client's loyalty and satisfaction (Berry, 2000).

In addition, Wasta plays a key role in enhancing the relationships with suppliers. This finding provides further support to Al-Ma'aitah et al. (2021) who found that Wasta play a key and significant role in the relationships with suppliers. And it is a powerful bargaining tool for Arab managers during negotiations with foreign parties (Khakhar and Rammal, 2013). This is because Wasta involves Mojamala as an emotional component in Wasta, which is a social tie between business partners that determines its quality and reflects the Arabs' desire to accommodating to enhance harmony and avoid confrontation during business negotiations (Berger et al., 2021). Indeed, in the MENA shame-honor culture, maintaining relationships is the honorable and is the right thing to do over values; this therefore contributes to normalizing corruption such as in the case of Wasta (Biaggi and Barkanian, 2020).

Largely, these companies seem to prefer hiring family members whose loyalty and commitment to their social groups are expected to encourage them to work hard to achieve their organizations' objectives. They will do so because they consider these companies as extensions of their families, and they thus exert their efforts to enable them to achieve their goals. Stewardship theory, for instance, provides useful insights into this process. It assumes that assigning family members to run family-controlled companies will lead to better results such as reducing managerial opportunistic behavior and the cost of agency problems (Davis et al., 1997, Eddleston and Kellermanns, 2007, Fox and Hamilton, 1994). This is because family employees usually work not for their own short-term interests but to achieve their organization's objectives, as they consider their personal success to be part of the company's success. Several studies support this proposition, pointing out how family-run companies outperform other companies (Miller and Breton-Miller, 2006, Dekker et al., 2015, Gomez-Mejia et al., 2001, McConaugby et al., 2001, Fama and Jensen, 1983, Burkart et al., 2003, Zahra et al., 2008, Anderson and Reeb, 2003). Moreover, the findings of this research support a previous research by Sefiani et al. (2018), who found that business owners rely on Wasta in order to hire a qualified staff.

Moral legitimacy is another type of justification for using Wasta in the Jordanian IT sector. Wasta is an effective mechanism that sometimes operates harmoniously with tribal and Islamic manners and norms, as relationships among family members are characterized by high levels of attachment and dependability. People expect to receive support when they need it from their influential relatives, who feel obligated to meet their requests (Ta'Amnha et al., 2016). In addition, the usage of Wasta under the Shafa'a principle also gives it more acceptance, given that the values and attitudes held by individuals in the Middle East are deeply held on the Islamic work ethics (Whiteoak et al., 2006). Shafa'a – an Islamic concept that indicates to the support given to those who are in need or who are qualified but cannot get what they deserve through normal procedures. According to the *Fatwa* from Dar Al-Ifta' in Jordan (the official authorized body of *Fatwa* in Jordan) (*Fatwa number 3322 on 25/9/2017 and number 830 on 14/7/2010*), Wasta is acceptable as long as it is employed to promote justice in the society, solving conflicts, and restoring the rights of others (Megdadi, 2020). In this case, Wasta is acceptable and receives normative legitimacy.

The permeation of Wasta into the Jordanian IT companies also refers to cognitive legitimacy/a "taken-for-granted" quality. Using Wasta to obtain a job or promotion in Jordan in general and in the IT sector in particular is usually inevitable because of the difficult economic conditions, and because Wasta is typically what people rely on for their careers in the Jordanian IT labor market. Jordanian jobseekers find it challenging to use other alternatives that may not lead to the same gains as those provided by Wasta. Wasta is therefore considered as a key mechanism used to gain more resource from the labor market in Jordan. There is thus a tension associated with the use of Wasta arising from the perceived need on the one hand and, on the other, the acknowledgment that it may not be open and fair to all.

Phase 2: Scale Validation

Expert Opinion

The scale comprises 14 items generated from employing inductive and deductive approaches. These items were reviewed by three academics who have practical and academic expertise in international businesses. The aim of this step is to check the content validity of the measure, to check to what extent it reflects Wasta legitimacy, and to assess the scale comprehensibility and the appropriateness of the items. The final version of the scale is shown in Table 5.2. This final draft of the instrument was subject to further quantitative investigation.

TABLE 5.2 Items for Wasta Scale

Pragmatic legitimacy
1. Wasta is used by companies to their clients to keep and enhance their relationships with them.
2. Wasta is used to speed up certain processes especially while dealing with governmental institutes that are characterized by bureaucratic systems.
3. Wasta is used because it leads to recruit and hire a well-connected person in the market who brings business to the employing companies.
4. Wasta is also used in doing business and getting best offers and deals such as getting tenders.
5. Wasta is used to hire family's members and friends because their competences and experiences are well-known by the recruiters.
6. Wasta is used to hire family's members because they are more likely to be committed to their family business and give it a maximum effort

Normative
1. Wasta is used to show the commitment and obligation to the families and their members.
2. Wasta is used to meeting friendship expectations of supports
3. Wasta is used to practices Islamic principle of "shafa'a"
4. Wasta is used as an act of charity

Cultural-Cognitive legitimacy of Wasta
1. Wasta is exercised because it gives status and feeling of satisfaction to the Wasta person
2. People who have strong Wasta (supplicant) feel powerful and protected in the society
3. People use Wasta as a result of absence of the social justice
4. People use Wasta because they believe that nothing can be achieved or reached without Wasta in the labor market.

Scale Testing

After developing the scale, it was subjected to a purification step through actual data. We contacted again the IT companies that agreed to take part previously in the qualitative interviews of this study to fill out a questionnaire using Google Forms. We got 185 useable questionnaires at the end during January 2021. The participants comprises 87 females and 98 males. Their length of experience in IT sector ranged from less than 1 year to 29 years, with an average of 19 years. Eighty-two participants were single, and 103 were married. In terms of the highest level of education, 34 had high school diplomas, 136 had first degrees, and 15 had master's degrees.

Data Analysis

Several steps and validation tools were employed to analyses the data including assessing the construct reliability, conducting exploratory factor analysis (EFA), and lastly confirmation of the finding through the confirmatory factor analysis (CFA).

Exploratory Factor Analysis (EFA)

The EFA was conducted on the 14 items. These items were developed based on empirical data analysis that represents a solid theoretical ground.

Prior to performing the EFA, the fitness of data was checked. This was conducted by the application of Kaiser-Meyer-Olkin value, which reached 0.81 that is greater than the acceptable values which is .6 (Kaiser and Rice, 1974). Accordingly, KMO value is acceptable.

The maximum likelihood with promax rotation was carried out. Factors were extracted as per the MINEIGEN criterion, which means that the eigenvalues of all the factors should be greater than 1. The Bartlett's test of sphericity also found to be significant ($p<0.01$), indicating that the correlation matrix is an identity matrix.

A minimum cutoff criterion for item deletion was that of factor loadings (<0.5) (Hair et al., 2006). All factors loaded ($>.5$), so no items were deleted. The maximum likelihood revealed the presence of three factors that together explained 55.21 per cent of the variance.

The coefficient Cronbach's α for reliability ranged from 0.786 to 0.868, thus supporting the validity and reliability of the instrument.

Confirmatory Factor Analysis (CFA)

The 14-item scale developed was further validated through CFA. AMOS 20 was used to perform CFA. CFA is suitable for scale development that is executed when the measurement has a strong theoretical foundation (Hair et al., 2006).

The model showed a good fit (CMIN/df=1.83, p=0.000, CFI=0.94, RMSEA=0.7, GFI=0.9, NFI=0.90, and IFI=.95).

The measurement model confirms the proposed three structures of the Wasta scale. All the items loaded significantly to their priori dimensions (see Figure 5.1).

The object of this study is to develop and validate a scale to measure Wasta legitimacy. The result of EFA identified three dimensions of the Wasta legitimacy, namely: pragmatic (six items), normative (four items), cultural-cognitive (four items). The results showed that the three dimensions are distinct and interrelated construct. This scale contributes to Wasta and social capital literature and thus enables the international companies to understand the meaning of Wasta more and the reasons behind its spreading in the Arabic societies and their institutions.

Takeaway

International companies that are working or thinking of doing business in the Middle Eastern markets such as Jordan should be aware of the business climates and specific social capital mechanisms such as Wasta, its meaning, sources, and influences. The validate measure offers enriched explanation of Wasta and its dimensions that the international companies should be aware of.

76 Mohammad Ta'amnha et al.

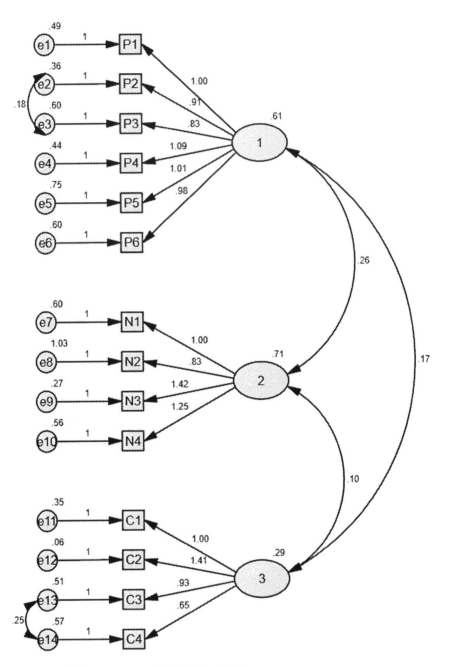

FIGURE 5.1 Measurement model for Wasta Scale.

Here is some advice to international businesses:

1. Doing Wasta to clients ensures their loyalty, especially when it is delivered to the influential clients. So companies have not been reluctant in offering Wasta to their VIP customers. However, offering Wasta should be done with careful calculation. IBs need to invest their time and effort to build strong relationships with local business partners through building trust and support. Certainly, the reciprocity principle facilitates conducting businesses in the Middle East region. IBs need to be aware that the shame-honor culture of Arabs emphasizes keeping relationships over value. Therefore IBs do not have to perceive Wasta totally as a form of corruption (Luo, 2008), but as a form or a mechanism of the social capital that enables them to get access to resources and increase their likelihood of success (Velez-Calle et al., 2015).
2. Wasta is an effective tool that can be used by IBs to speed up the governmental processes and avoiding delay in the bureaucratic procedures that suffer from lack of transparency and accountability (Loewe et al., 2008). Therefore, it is recommended to the IBs to hire local agents to deal with the local governments. However, IBs need to remember that "Wasta comes with prices" (Biaggi and Barkanian, 2020, p.129).
3. Hiring well-connected people is critical sometimes for the success of business, so IBs need to try to hire who are well known and well connected in markets to enhance their chances of success. IBs need not to forget that most of Arab societies are tribal that emphasize the importance of solidarity, trust, loyalty, and mutual support.
4. Wasta is an effective mechanism that can be used in negotiation with suppliers. It is necessary to build trust first and then doing business with the suppliers under competitive conditions (Brandstaetter et al., 2016).
5. Wasta can be used as an effective recruiting and monitoring tool. It helps first to hire people who are known by the company, and Wasta can be used in monitoring and evaluating and behavioral modification of who are not performing as expected. It can also be part of conflict resolution processes.
6. Sometimes Wasta can be used to hire families' members in businesses because they are more committed to the business and its sustainability. Therefore, IBs should be tolerant sometimes in respect of allowing their local managers to hire their relatives.
7. IBs need to be aware of the pressures their local managers may face from their relatives and friends to hire them. Therefore, IBs need to be more tolerant with this to keep their successful mangers, or they may have to rely on international mangers to avoid such pressure in case the connection in the local market is not that important. Certainly, being culturally intelligent is required in this region.
8. Sometimes Wasta is exercised to meet Islamic teaching or as a charity act, especially the principle of Shafa'a. In this case Wasta is conducted to support who are in need and deserve getting support but can't reach them for many reasons such as lack of Wasta or social status.

9. Some people exercise Wasta to show their power and status. In addition, same feeling is experienced by who are connected with strong and influential Wasta (supplicants).

Case Study

Isaac is a businessperson whose business mainly concentrates on used trucks, cars, and parts. He buys these products from the UK and ships them to Jordan. The working conditions of the used vehicles and parts markets according to Isaac are as follows:

1. It is difficult to predict the supply of the used vehicles and parts; it depends mainly on the availability and opportunities.
2. The demand for used vehicles and parts increases in Jordan during the winter period, mainly during January, November, and December, due to the suspension of many projects during this heavy rainy period. Therefore, the construction companies use this period to plan for spring, and to perform maintenance works, and this increases the demands for the used vehicles and their parts.
3. Therefore, during this period, the demand for shipping from the UK to Jordan is high, and it is difficult to obtain cargo holds during this demanding period.

The importer Isaac, whom we interviewed, mentioned that he can always get cargo holds whenever he needs through his relationship with the brothers of a marine agent (Khaled) who has a fright forward company headquartered in Germany – Frankfurt, and one of its shipping lines goes to Jordan every 11 days.

Khaled gives Isaac priority in cargo holds, even if there is no prior reservation, due to the unpredictability in the used vehicles and parts market as explained above. Khaled tends to postpone the shipments of other importers and gives priority to Isaac, due to the intercession of his brothers.

Isaac added that this situation enables him to obtain a competitive advantage in the used vehicles market in Jordan because:

1. He is able to supply used vehicles and parts to the merchants in Jordan during winter.
2. He sells his used vehicles and parts at a cheaper price compared to the competitors due to preferential shipping prices he gets from Khaled.
3. He is perceived as a credible supplier to the merchants in Jordan because he delivers goods on time, unlike some other used vehicles and parts importers.
4. Isaac also explained that he uses his connection with Khaled to sell cargo holds to other importers at preferential prices, which also enables him to maximize his profits.

In conclusion, Wasta plays a major role in the business sector in Jordan or with Jordanians, even if they are working in Western countries. Wasta is a crucial mechanism to get preferences in prices and services. This highlights the importance of

Wasta and its role in reducing the transactional cost, and therefore we can say that Wasta is a "Success Factor" in doing business in the Middle East that cannot be ignored or underestimated.

References

Al Maeena, K. 2010. Vitamin WAW. Arab View. Retrieved on 27 December, 2010 from http://www.arabview.com/articles.asp?article=81
Al-Ma'Aitah, N., Soltani, E. & Liao, Y.-Y. 2021. Wasta effects on supply chain relationships in the middle East Region. In Mehdi Khosrow-Pour (ed.), *Encyclopedia of organizational knowledge, administration, and technology*. IGI Global.
Altarawneh, I. I. 2009. Training and development evaluation in Jordanian banking organizations. *Research and Practice in Human Resource Management* 17, 1–23.
Anderson, R. C. & Reeb, D. M. 2003. Founding family ownership and firm performance: Evidence from the S&P 500. *Journal of Finance*, 58, 1301–1327.
ARAB ARCHIVES INSTITUTE 2000. A survey on Wasta in Jordan. Towards Transparency in Jordan conference in cooperation with Transparency International held in Amman-Jordan on 22, May 2000.
Barnett, A. H., Yandle, B. & Naufal, G. 2011. *Regulation, Trust, and Cronyism in Middle Eastern Societies: The Simple Economics of 'Wasta'* [Online]. Retrieved on 21 October, 2012 from http://www.pearlinitiative.org/tl_files/pearl/data/Wasta-2011.pdf
Berger, R., Barnes, B. R. & Silbiger, A. 2021. Scale development and validation for measuring business-to-business Wasta relationships. *Journal of Business & Industrial Marketing*, 36(12), 2201–2218.
Berger, R., Silbiger, A., Herstein, R. & Barnes, B. R. 2015. Analyzing business-to-business relationships in an Arab context. *Journal of World Business*, 50, 454–464.
Berry, L. L. 2000. Cultivating service brand equity. *Journal of the Academy of Marketing Science*, 28, 128–137.
Biaggi, C. E. & Barkanian, J. A. 2020. Culture and corruption: Plagiarism, wasta and bribery in the MENA region. *The International Journal of Business Management and Technology*, 4.
Brandstaetter, T., Bamber, D. & Weir, D. 2016. 'Wasta': Triadic trust in Jordanian business. In Mohamed A. Ramady (ed.), *The political economy of Wasta: Use and abuse of social capital networking*. Switzerland: Springer.
Braun, V. & Clarke, V. 2006. Using thematic analysis in psychology. *Qualitative Research in Psychology*, 3, 77–101.
Burkart, M., Panunzi, F. & Shleifer, A. 2003. Family firms. *The Journal of Finance*, 58, 2167–2202.
Castillo-Montoya, M. 2016. Preparing for interview research: The interview protocol refinement framework. *Qualitative Report*, 21.
Cresswell, J. W. 1998. *Qualitative inquiry and research design: Choosing among five traditions*. Thousand Oaks, CA, Sage.
Creswell, J. W. & Creswell, J. D. 2017. *Research design: Qualitative, quantitative, and mixed methods approaches*, Sage Publications.
Cunningham, R. B. & Sarayrah, Y. K. 1993. *Wasta: The hidden force in Middle Eastern society*, Westport, Connecticut: Praeger.
Davis, J. H., Schoorman, F. D. & Donaldson, L. 1997. Toward a stewardship theory of management. *Academy of Management Review*, 22, 20–47.

Dekker, J., Lybaert, N., Steijvers, T. & Depaire, B. 2015. The effect of family business professionalization as a multidimensional construct on firm performance. *Journal of Small Business Management*, 53(2), 516–538.

Eddleston, K. A. & Kellermanns, F. W. 2007. Destructive and productive family relationships: A stewardship theory perspective. *Journal of Business Venturing*, 22, 545–565.

Ezzedeen, S. R. & Swiercz, P. M. 2001. HR system effectiveness in the transformative organization: Lessons from Libancell of Lebanon. *Competitiveness Review: An International Business Journal incorporating Journal of Global Competitiveness*, 11, 25–39.

Faisal, A. A. 1990. Favouritism (Wasta): An exploratory study of university students. *Journal of King Saud University*, 2, 693–711.

Fama, E. F. & Jensen, M. C. 1983. Separation of ownership and control. *Journal of Law and Economics*, 26, 301–325.

Fox, M. A. & Hamilton, R. T. 1994. Ownership and diversification: Agency theory or stewardship theory. *Journal of Management Studies*, 31, 69–81.

Gomez-Mejia, L. R., Nunez-Nickel, M. & Gutierrez, I. 2001. The role of family ties in agency contracts. *Academy of Management Journal*, 44, 81–95.

Hair, J. F., Black, W. C., Babin, B. J., Anderson, R. E. & Tatham, R. L. 2006. *Multivariate data analysis*, Upper Saddle River, NJ.: Pearson Prentice Hal.

Harding, J. 2018. *Qualitative data analysis: From start to finish*. London: SAGE Publications Limited.

Hom, P. W., Tsui, A. S., Wu, J. B., Lee, T. W., Zhang, A. Y., Fu, P. P. & Li, L. 2009. Explaining employment relationships with social exchange and job embeddedness. *Journal of Applied Psychology*, 94, 277.

Hutchings, K. & Weir, D. 2006. Guanxi and wasta: A comparison. *Thunderbird International Business Review*, 48, 141–156.

Iivari, N. 2018. Using member checking in interpretive research practice. *Information Technology & People*, 31, 111–133.

Kaiser, H. F. & Rice, J. 1974. Little jiffy, mark IV. *Educational and Psychological Measurement*, 34, 111–117.

Khakhar, P. & Rammal, H. G. 2013. Culture and business networks: International business negotiations with Arab managers. *International Business Review*, 22, 578–590.

Lawler, E. J. 2001. An affect theory of social exchange. *American Journal of Sociology*, 107, 321–352.

Loewe, M., Blume, J. & Speer, J. 2008. How favoritism affects the business climate: Empirical evidence from Jordan. *The Middle East Journal*, 62, 259–276.

Luo, Y. 2008. The changing Chinese culture and business behavior: The perspective of intertwinement between guanxi and corruption. *International Business Review*, 17, 188–193.

Makhoul, J. & Harrison, L. 2004. Intercessory wasta and village development in Lebanon. *Arab Studies Quarterly*, 26, 25–41.

Marktanner, M. & Wilson, M. 2016. The economic cost of wasta in the Arab world: An empirical approach. In Ramady M. (eds.). *The political economy of wasta: Use and abuse of social capital networking*. Cham: Springer. https://doi.org/10.1007/978-3-319-22201-1_6

McConaugby, D. L., Matthews, C. H. & Fialko, A. S. 2001. Founding family controlled firms: Performance, risk, and value. *Journal of Small Business Management*, 39, 31–49.

Megdadi, O. 2020. The effects of the Islamic ruling 'Fatwa' on business relationships in Jordan: The case of 'Wasta'. *Journal of Halal Service Research*, 1, 38.

Miller, D. & Breton-Miller, L. 2006. Family governance and firm performance: Agency, stewardship, and capabilities. *Family Business Review*, 19, 73–87.

Mohammad, A. A. & Hamdy, H. 2008. The stigma of Wasta: The effect of Wasta on perceived competence and morality *German University in Cairo*, Working paper No. 5.

Molm, L. D., Whitham, M. M. & Melamed, D. 2012. Forms of exchange and integrative bonds: Effects of history and embeddedness. *American Sociological Review*, 77, 141–165.

Moroko, L. & Uncles, M. D. 2008. Characteristics of successful employer brands. *Journal of Brand Management*, 16, 160–175.

Sefiani, Y., Davies, B. J., Bown, R. & Kite, N. 2018. Performance of SMEs in Tangier: The interface of networking and wasta. *EuroMed Journal of Business*, 13(1), 20–43.

Ta'Amnha, M. 2014. *An investigation of Wasta and the effects of human and social capital on Jordanian insurance employees' career experiences and success.* PhD thesis, University of East Anglia.

Ta'Amnha, M., Sayce, S. & Tregaskis, O. 2016. Wasta in the Jordanian context. In Pawan S. Budhwar and Kamel Mellahi (Eds.), *Handbook of human resource management in the Middle East*. Edward Elgar Publishing.

Tlaiss, H. & Kauser, S. 2011a. The impact of gender, family, and work on the career advancement of Lebanese women managers. *Gender in Management: An International Journal*, 26, 8–36.

Tlaiss, H. & Kauser, S. 2011b. The importance of wasta in the career success on Middle Eastern managers. *Jouranl of Eurpean Industrial Training*, 35, 467–486.

Velez-Calle, A., Robledo-Ardila, C. & Rodriguez-Rios, J. D. 2015. On the influence of interpersonal relations on business practices in Latin America: A comparison with the Chinese guanxi and the Arab Wasta. *Thunderbird International Business Review*, 57, 281–293.

Whiteoak, J. W., Crawford, N. G. & Mapstone, R. H. 2006. Impact of gender and generational differences in work values and attitudes in an Arab culture. *Thunderbird International Business Review*, 48, 77–91.

Zahra, S. A., Hayton, J. C., Neubaum, D. O., Dibrell, C. & Craig, J. 2008. Culture of family commitment and strategic flexibility: The moderating effect of stewardship. *Entrepreneurship Theory and Practice*, 32, 1035–1054.

Zhang, M., Hartley, J. L., Al-Husan, F. B. & Alhussan, F. B. 2021. Informal interorganizational business relationships and customer loyalty: Comparing Guanxi, Yongo, and Wasta. *International Business Review*, 30, 101805.

PART II
Conducting Business in the Middle East

6
ENTRY MODES TO MIDDLE EAST-GCC MARKETS

The Case of the UAE

Vijay Pereira, Bhaskar Dasgupta, Daicy Vaz and Glenn Muschert

Introduction

Multinational corporations (MNCs) undertaking foreign direct investment (FDI) through the internationalization strategy would incrementally base it on their ability to learn and adapt over time. This also stands true for such investors when planning entry into the Middle East-GCC, especially given the volatile nature of these emerging markets (Luo & Tung, 2007). Thus, these entities investing or entering into the region could minimize substantial risks when deciding to invest in Middle East countries, as weak political, commercial, and institutional environments characterize them. We identify and characterize the context of the Middle East-GCC broadly, but are more specific on the UAE, as a case. Through our case, we envisage, investors would lead to superior elements of deliberate and planned actions as well as emergent strategies, mitigating the levels and types of risk, which will determine their entry mode.

There is a large body of international business literature on the topic of "entry modes", which depicts how MNCs strategize in terms of decision making when they want to enter a new country (Brouthers, 2013; Pereira et al., 2021). Theoretically, two key lenses, i.e., the institutional theory that portrays a country's institutions, and the transaction cost economics theory, an economic theory that calculates the economic sense of entering a country, become key on how MNCs choose their entry mode. This is important for these investing MNCs, as they can then overcome the multiple challenges and risks of undertaking FDI in a particular new country. The understanding of several post-entry changes over time could be incremental or alternatively it could be a linear process of increased commitment. This is mostly dependent on the ability of the said MNE to learn more about the foreign host country and thereby adjust their firm-specific advantages to a particular new market (Johanson & Vahlne, 2009). We envisage that our contribution

DOI: 10.4324/9781003005766-8

would help them to be able to firstly identify, pre-empt, mitigate, and secondly then manage the various risks inherent in Middle East countries by taking on board and developing various capabilities that successfully then become part of their internationalization strategies (Figueira de Lemos et al. 2011, Budhwar et al. 2019). This we envisage would lead to superior elements of deliberate and planned actions as well as emergent strategies (Mintzberg and Waters 1985), mitigating the levels and types of risk, which will determine their entry mode. In what follows, we list out the feasible modes of entry into the GCC together with stating the legal frameworks and possible considerations that an investor will need to consider.

Legal Frameworks Governing Market Entry in the GCC

Based on our analysis and experience, we have identified several key mechanisms for firms desirous of doing business in the GCC. Thus, we list the following broad mechanisms (International Trade Administration, 2020):

- *No presence*: To sell remotely into GCC without opening an office or appointing an agent. These can be for limited products and services such as technology, education, consulting, etc.
- *Appointing commercial agents*: Recruiting a local agent can assist in having a local presence with local networks and relationships to sell the products and services of the firm. There is regulation in place for these agencies, by statutes and a requirement of registration by the Ministry of Commerce. These agencies are usually 100% owned by local GCC Nationals, although in some cases, the foreign company could own up to 49% of the firm. This coverage of these agencies is also usually for the specified territory / country.
- *Branch offices*: Foreign companies may establish branch offices directly, although their roles are usually limited to sales, support, and marketing activities. They usually also need a local sponsorship which may entail a fee.
- *Subsidiaries*: Foreign companies can establish a subsidiary in the GCC, usually with a shareholding cap of 49%, thereby requiring a local partner. There is a need for registering these subsidiaries by the Ministry of Commerce and may require further approvals and licensing from other bodies.
- *Free trade zone companies*: Many of the GCC countries have now established Free Trade Zones where a 100% foreign-owned company can be established (MEED, 2014).
- *Requirement of specific rules*: Certain sectors have special rules such as Defense, Aerospace, and oil and gas. They may involve requiring local presence, local investments, local employees, and local shareholding.

Irrespective of the means and mode of entry, foreign firms operating in the GCC can face and experience up to five distinct legal frameworks, especially when it comes to commercial law cases. That said, given the requirements for local participation in many business activities as enumerated above, the personal law elements (succession planning, dispute resolution, asset recovery, etc.) also play a role in commercial decisions such as if the commercial engagement is with a local agent.

- *Sharia Law.* The word Sharia relates to the body of knowledge, which includes the Quran along with the sayings and teachings, behaviors, and actions (Sunnah) of the Prophet Muhammad. The interpretation of this body of knowledge is different by different schools of law, namely the Hanafi, Maliki, Shafi'i, and Hanbali for Sunni Muslims and, to a lesser extent in the GCC, the Ja'fari School for Shia Muslims. As life developed in the Muslim world (after the Quran was revealed), various jurists in the different schools of law would normally rely on the Quran and Sunnah to opine on legal cases. In addition, they would also use independent reasoning, intellectual judgment or customary practice to extend the legal corpus to handle the ever more complex requirements of personal and commercial laws. This framework still governs much of personal law within the GCC (Azzam, 2021).
- *Civil Law*: The influence of European culture started to increase in Muslim countries within the GCC from the early 19th century onwards. For example, the Napoleonic Code or the French Civil Law system heavily influenced the development of the Egyptian Legal system. In this system, which descends from the framework of Roman law, core principles are codified into a system, which serves as the primary source of law. This is the most widespread system of law and in force in various shapes and forms in more than 150 counties around the world. The law code is a systematic collection of interrelated articles, in an agreed classification and order.
- *International Treaties and Membership*: In the GCC, taking the lead from the Egyptian system, the legal system based on civil law for commercial, civil, and criminal disputes, while as already mentioned, Sharia Law applies to personal cases for Muslims to handle cases relating to divorce, property distribution, succession planning, child custody, etc. It is noteworthy that there is an incorporation of an ever-increasing body of legal influences into local civil law from international treaties and membership of bodies such as the World Trade Organization or from other countries such as the adoption of commercial bankruptcy laws from the UK and/or US legal codes.
- *Mixed Common and Civil Law*: In the Dubai International Financial Centre, Dubai, UAE, there is an establishment of a unique legal system, which has its own laws, regulations, courts, and arbitration center. It is independent of the UAE civil and commercial laws, but subject to the criminal laws of the UAE. The basis of legislation is on best practices of the world's financial centers; principle-based and constitutes a commercial code including common laws as well as civil laws (Grassa & Gazdar, 2014). These laws include Companies Law, Contract Law, Arbitration Law, Insolvency Law, Regulatory Law, Markets Law, Data Protection Law, etc.

- *Common Law*: The Abu Dhabi Global Market, Abu Dhabi's International Financial Centre, UAE is governed under laws which are broadly modeled on the English Judicial Common Law system. Unlike the civil law system, the common law system, also known as case law system, is derived from the judicial decisions of courts. These decisions arise as precedent. A common law court looks at previous decisions and synthesizes the previous cases to opine on the extant case. If the cases were similar, then there is an expectation that the honorable judge will follow previous case law but if not, then the judges will state an opinion with reasoning to establish a precedent. The drawing up of most international commercial contracts and trade is under common law, which is due to the higher level of predictability and responsiveness to new circumstances.

Investment Promotion Policies in GCC Markets

The Middle East largely depends on FDI apart from their major earnings from oil and gas sector. Nevertheless, since GCC had restrictions to the foreign ownership of business within their borders, investing in the Gulf was not favored. The first bank in the UAE, i.e., HSBC Middle East bank, was set up in 1946, there onward funding the investors. UAE initially began exporting pearls and ventured into exporting oil and gas trade from 1962 onward (Mosteanu & Alghaddaf, 2019). With the realization that the Gulf has finite natural resources, the six GCC countries (the UAE, Qatar, Oman, Saudi Arabia, Kuwait, and Bahrain) opened up to investors providing them relaxation in business operations in free trade zones (FTZ).

Free Trade Zones

The main intention behind the concept of free trade zones was to develop sectors such as manufacturing, logistics, infrastructure, and banking, so that the economy of Gulf countries will no more be solely dependent on oil. Jebel Ali was the first port in Dubai, declared as free zone in 1985 in the UAE (MEED, 2014). UAE now owns around 40 free zones (e.g., Jebel Ali free zone and Dubai internet city in Dubai, Masdar city free zone and Abu Dhabi Airport free zone in Abu Dhabi, to name a few). The advantages of FTZs are that there is no local ownership required. Moreover, customs on imports/exports, taxes on profits, and income are waived off, and there is no cap on minimum capital investment (Hossain, 2015a). This is a key advantage for investors who look to start business in the GCC. The FTZs are compelled to have 49% foreign ownership only if they need to sell products in the local UAE market. Nevertheless, if the products are only for regional sales, then the local ownership is not a necessity (International Trade Administration, 2020). It is, thus, not surprising that many business offices are set up in the free trade zones across UAE.

Foreign Direct Investment

The UAE explored real estate, attracting huge FDI and grew fast in this sector from 2000 to 2008 until the financial crisis. In 2007, Emirates Investment Authority was formed to maintain and advise on the economic growth of UAE (Mosteanu & Alghaddaf, 2019). The UAE once again gained momentum through free zone regulations and "Smart City" plans that boosted tourism and created opportunities for investors with quality living standards. In the UAE, Abu Dhabi Investment Authority, Abu Dhabi Investment Council, Dubai International financial center and Dubai investment corporations govern the foreign investments and the Emirates investment Authority regulates all investments in the UAE (Mosteanu, 2019; Mosteanu & Alghaddaf, 2019).

Investors intending to start business in the UAE will need to consider the competition from the local companies as well. For example in the airlines sector, Etihad Airways and Emirates Airlines are leading in global competition, Du and Etisalat are very well established in telecom industry, Aramex and DP World in logistics sector (TWFR, 2013). Taxes on business apart from Oil, telecommunication and banking are nil, and VAT kept at 5%. UAE legislation is also working toward increasing the shares of foreign investors beyond 49%, which would increase foreign investor ownership in the non–free trade zones, something that every investor looks forward to. All these relaxations on the business front would attract higher FDI and make the UAE independent of solely depending on oil and gas for economy (Mosteanu & Alghaddaf, 2019).

Trade Routes

The GCC is actively considering reviving of the trade routes between GCC and Asia, i.e., the new Silk Road (TWFR, 2013), with China being the first trade partner of the GCC, European Union the second largest in 2020 (European Commission, 2021). The bilateral ties between China and GCC are multifold. China, as an emerging economy, is a large importer of oil from the GCC with 16% import from Saudi Arabia and liquefied natural gas from Qatar as per the LNG contract signed in 2018. GCC geographical locations are also a key interest to China. Further, for enhancing trade and movement within the GCC, rail projects are in force with investment of USD 100bn (Frost & Sullivan, 2011).

Human Capital

The UAE benefits from its large oil resources, willingness to diversify and the ability to purchase products and services. With ease in regulations, UAE and Bahrain are known to be liberal toward business investors and operations. Saudi Arabia and Kuwait, on the other hand, are not as liberal yet (Mosteanu & Alghaddaf, 2019). The UAE depends on large human capital, has a huge number of migrants (Beblawi, 2011), and has now begun to issue a ten-year visa to scholars and highly educated professionals. This just exhibits the country's willingness to open doors to innovation and development.

Theoretical Lens

Theoretically, one can explain mode of entries by MNEs or investors into a foreign location through three distinct lenses (Arregle, Hébert & Beamish, 2006). The transaction cost economics (TCE) theory (Williamson, 1993; Coase, 1937) suggests that there are different types of transaction costs that needed to take into consideration when entering into a new market. These three costs are broadly categorized as (1) information costs, i.e., costs that are needed to find out, enquire, consult, etc., about entering into a new market; (2) negotiation costs where firms negotiate in order to pursue a mode of entry into a new market; (3), monitoring costs that include the cost of entry itself, setup, and start operations.

The institutional theory focuses on the varied social, political, and economic institutions or systems within a particular country, in terms of both its operations and its legitimacy. These would include governments, legal systems, educational institutes, and interest groups – to name a few. The key argument here is that MNEs and investors need to understand and appreciate these institutional challenges before they enter a new market (North, 1990; Scott, 2001).

Organizational learning theory (OLT) suggests that organizations learn from previous experiences, both positive and negative. It is expected that previous positives are encouraged whereas previous mistakes are rectified, based on their previous learning. The positioning of these learnings are at three different levels, i.e., individual, groups, and organizational (Schön & Argyris, 1996).

Risk Mitigation in GCC Market Entry

This section will review some of the major, real, and perceived risks of operating in the ME/GCC region and will discuss some modern risk mitigation tools in terms of how to implement them. These risks are broadly categorized under three main risks, i.e., institutional, commercial, cultural, and political risks.

1. *Institutional Risk*:
    a. Foreign firms accustomed to dealing with democratic regimes and institutions may feel uneasy about undertaking business in countries, which place ultimate authority in a ruler and his family. This may lead them to believe that expropriation of intellectual property or assets may happen without legal recourse. That said, these firms should note that such a situation could arise in democratic countries as well, such as with Eminent Domain cases. In the GCC, it should be noted that there is a deep-seated cultural preference for consensus, centuries-old tradition of private businesses and asset protection, availability of arbitration and mediation frameworks, and the availability of a legal system for resources does mitigate this risk (Linklaters, 2019).

b. Another concern which arises is the absence of judicial review of government actions and the difficulty in predicting judicial results in some of the legal frameworks discussed in the previous section. This legal risk can be mitigated by exploring pure common law jurisdictions, where the legal certainty is higher (Linklaters, 2019; Kamrava et al., 2016).
2. *Commercial Risk*:
    a. The foreign exchange risk is minimal due to lack of exchange control mechanisms and very strong currency pegs generally to the ($) USD, which makes operations lower risk. The low levels of taxation further assist in making GCC businesses more profitable and predictable (MEED (2014). The benefit of having large pools of private patient capital to co-invest means that businesses in the GCC can afford to take the longer-term value creation view.
3. *Cultural and Religious Sensitivities*:
    a. GCC strictly follows Islamic norms of praying five times a day and fasting all day long during the holy month of Ramadan. During Ramadan, the business meetings or deals are dealt with at a slower pace (Expat guide, 2010). In addition, it is important to remember that Friday is a day off from work unlike Sunday in western countries.
    b. It is paramount and extremely important that cultural differences need studying and understanding, to assimilate into the values of GCC nations. The nationals strongly believe in developing true bonds and only rely on people they trust. Therefore, "Wasta", i.e., mutual friends and contacts, can work better in this system (Budhwar et al., 2019; Expat guide, 2010).
4. *Political Risk*:
    a. Geopolitical risk is always high on the agenda in the GCC due to the historical incidence of wars, revolutions, counter-revolutions, riots, and the similar events. That said, within the GCC, these incidents have been much lower than the wider GCC, hence is comparatively safer. Whilst all countries around the world have seen country ratings challenged in 2020, it is a mixed bag for GCC, with some countries downgraded, but Saudi Arabia and Abu Dhabi having their ratings reaffirmed (TWFR, 2013).
    b. Risk of corruption and non-compliance risk is a traditional risk in every country, and the GCC is no exception. Based on the Transparency International Corruption Perceptions Index 2019, the GCC countries are notably less corrupt compared to the neighbors in the wider region with steady improvement in rankings. In the case of the UAE it is ranked higher than countries such as France and the United States (Transparency International, 2020; see also https://www.transparency.org/en/cpi#).

Promoting Responsible Conduct in GCC Markets

IMD World Competitiveness ranking ranks the UAE among the top ten democracies for business (IMD, 2020). One of the main reasons is the political stability in this country. Unlike Iraq, Iran, Syria, and other countries, the UAE has not let political tensions affect the economy at large (TWFR, 2013). The UAE is actively paving its way toward achieving the UN SDGs by 2030. The National Climate Change Plan of the United Arab Emirates (2017-2050) sets guidelines for management of greenhouse gas emissions and tackling climate change. The UAE is a part of the revolution for clean energy and pledged to generate 24% of its electricity from such sources by 2021. The efforts against clean energy are evident with the results from CO2 emission per person dropped from 32.6 tonnes in 1990 to 21.9 in 2010 (The UAE's government portal, 2021). For every UN SDG, there are vision plans and projects launched to ensure that the SDGs are achieved (The UAE portal for the Sustainable Development Goals).

Another field that attracts FDI in the GCC are the Brownfield and Greenfield projects. Brownfield projects refer to the mergers and acquisitions across borders and benefit greatly in terms of reducing investment in infrastructure, R&D, and an already existing operational network. Greenfield investments are new projects started in a foreign country and can face challenges of period and legal procedures for the startup (Schneidhofer, 2017). Greenfield FDI in Dubai has been significant with investments accounting for 88.5% of total FDI in 2016. Canada (30%), the United Kingdom (13%), France (11%), Spain (8%), and the United States (7%) were among the top FDI contributors. Dubai also calls for alliances and joint ventures, subcontracting and license agreements, mergers and acquisitions as entry modes for business (Dubai FDI Monitor, 2016). The key areas here being nonresidential building construction, food and accommodation, research and development, real estate, and wholesale trading.

Sector-Related Concerns for Investors

The oldest sector of the GCC that is well known and established is the oil sector. Though GCC has survived its economy through oil extraction and export, there is always a question on political agenda, i.e., how long will GCC depend on oil for economy? The Gulf adopted the "allocation state" model wherein the focus was mainly on sales of extracted oil. This model thereby led to distribution of wealth, increased demand of migrant labor, and undermined the productive assets of Gulf region (Hvidt, 2013). The two outcomes of this scenario that obstruct development of the GCC are that there was no stable income generation and decreased employment opportunities for the new educated generation (Hvidt, 2011).

Renewable Energy Sources

The oil sector that is government owned draws huge income for the country due to which the government need not rely on taxes, thereby making it an "allocation state" rather than a "production state" (Hvidt, 2013). The Omani government had envisioned to decrease the contribution of oil and gas in GDP from 49% in 2005 to 20% by 2020 (Hossain, 2015b). The oil reserves in the ME are known to last for another 50 years at the least (TWFR, 2013). Having known that oil resources are exhaustible, wavering, and the only source of income (Hvidt, 2013), the GCC has begun to diversify into other sectors. One such sector is renewable energy (Ferroukhi et al., 2013), but it is greatly challenged by cheaper prices of conventional energy sources such as petroleum, natural gas, and oil, thus making the renewable energy projects more expensive (El-Husseini et al., 2009).

Development of Smart Cities

Sustainable innovation is a focus of the GCC (see Ferroukhi et al., 2013 for details on projects and collaborations). All six GCC countries have outlined a vision plan, i.e., Economic Vision 2030 in Bahrain, New Kuwait 2035, Vision 2020 & Vision 2040 in Oman, National Vision 2030 in Qatar, Vision 2030 in Saudi Arabia, and Vision 2021 in the UAE, which comprise initiatives and programs for e-governance and smart cities (Asmyatullin, Tyrkba & Ruzina, 2020). These countries are thus looking to diversify and digitalize with use of latest technology to attract tourists and enhance trade (Saxena & Al-Tamimi, 2018). Some indicators of smart cities are GDP growth, innovation and R&D expense, foreign investment, education expenditure, environment, governance, people, and mobility (Giffinger et al., 2007; Nam & Pardo, 2011; Barrionuevo, Berrone & Ricart, 2012; Lombardi et al., 2012). In the UAE, "Masdar City" and "Zayed Smart City" in Abu Dhabi adopt technically advanced solutions of artificial intelligence and solar power. The UAE is one among the eight eco-city initiatives (refer Eccles et al., 2012).

Outward Foreign Direct Investment (OFDI)

The FDI saw a peak in the GCC from 2002 to 2010 as per a report by World Bank (2017). However, the GCC is seeing a downfall in FDI since 2010 (EU, 2018). While the FDI has reduced, OFDI is on an exponential growth mainly in the UAE and Qatar (Durani et al., 2021). We can determine the economic growth of a country by the value of its capital accumulation, boosted by its domestic investment. OFDI improves the rate of goods exported and enhances domestic production, thereby increasing domestic investment (Hejazi, 2005). The UAE has significantly invested in defense, aerospace, and aviation (Davidson, 2011). Through diversification (mainly vertical), a country can benefit from stabilized earnings, expand revenues, and retain or increase value-addition (Hvidt, 2013). Researchers have called for diversification into private sectors for two main reasons. First, because the private sectors create job opportunities for the population excluded from oil sector employment, and second, because FDI can be attracted only by private firms (Hvidt, 2013).

Sovereign Wealth Funds (SWF)

Sovereign wealth funds (El-Kharouf, Al-Qudsi & Obeid, 2010) allow the Gulf countries to have stable earnings in the longer run through investment of oil incomes.

For example Kuwait holds a reserve fund in London (Kuwait investment office established in 1953) which amounted to USD 100 billion by the 1990 Gulf war and in 2020, Kuwait held USD 533 billion and Abu Dhabi held USD 579 billion worth SWF (Investopedia, 2020).

Property Ownership

There are three types of property ownerships in the GCC. First is the "contractual lease" which is short-term contract, second is the long-term lease of 99 years, and third is full ownership. These contractual interests differ depending on the nationality of investor. Local nationals have maximum ownership, followed by GCC nationals and then the foreigners. The ownership rights exercised depends on the investment zones, whether it is restricted or not. In the "Investment zones", full ownership of the land is given to the foreign investor depending on the sector of business, whereas foreign ownership maybe restricted totally in non-investment zones. However, in the UAE, the long-term lease is divided into "Musataha" (up to 50 years) which demands mandatory development of land and "Usufruct" (up to 99 years) where the development of land is not permitted. It is also possible to combine Musataha and Usufruct leases by first opting for Musataha and developing the land and then leasing it out for 99 years without developing it further (CCBJ, 2012).

Conclusions

As a case of entry modes in the GCC, we portrayed the UAE's strategic location, political balance, economic stability, pro-business policies, tax-free income, 100% foreign ownership in free zones, global trade network, and interest in greenfield and brownfield projects making it an attractive hub for business (Mathews, 2006).

As one of the key attractions for investors, we notice that the free zones appear to be most liberal when it comes to doing business in the GCC, but they can have their own challenges and restrictions. The free zones can have restrictions on the sort of business carried out, such as either trading or logistics. Secondly, the company in a free zone is bound to carry out business within the free zone only and not the entire GCC. Though the GCC promotes tax-free business in free zones, one needs to bear in mind about the living and rental costs. Moreover, costs and time-related setup of facilities, infrastructure, legal procedure, and resources need consideration before investing in a business.

We conclude that the GCC mainly looks to promote businesses in the area of education, logistics, aviation, smart city and infrastructure, artificial intelligence, banking, and retail. Through these areas, they intend to achieve the 17 United Nations Sustainable Development Goals (UN SDGs) and already have started achieving a few of them. Though there is a long way to go, the GCC countries seem aligned, showing commitment and focusing on achieving these. Investors looking to enter the GCC can consider entry through these sectors with a concrete business plan. With ten-year visas now available to highly educated professionals in the UAE, and other relaxations in work contracts, the intention of the GCC to absorb the cream of every sector is very evident. Tax-free earnings are very lucrative to foreigners as well.

We envisage that comparatively the easier way of entering the GCC may be through the brownfield projects and franchises. A number of businesses have succeeded through mergers and acquisitions, and franchises have been prominent too. Risks of political warfare and corruption are minimal especially in the UAE, and business investors looking to proceed with legal procedures need not be skeptical about the monarchy. Though the GCC mostly works under a monarchy, the laws are strictly in place and followed diligently by all nationals.

References

Arregle, J. L., Hébert, L., & Beamish, P. W. (2006). Mode of international entry: The advantages of multilevel methods. *Management International Review*, 46(5), 597–618.

Asmyatullin, R. R., Tyrkba, K. V., & Ruzina, E. I. (2020). Smart Cities in GCC: Comparative Study of Economic Dimension. In *IOP conference series: Earth and environmental science* (Vol. 459, No. 6, p. 062045). IOP Publishing.

Azzam, A. A. F. (2021). Whether Sharia law is an obstacle to the development of commercial arbitration in the countries of the gulf cooperation council? (*Masters' Thesis*).

Barrionuevo, J. M., Berrone, P., & Ricart, J. E. (2012). Smart cities, sustainable progress. *Iese Insight*, 14(14), 50–57.

Brouthers, K. D. (2013). Institutional, cultural and transaction cost influences on entry mode choice and performance. *Journal of International Business Studies*, 44(1), 1–13.

Budhwar, P., Pereira, V., Mellahi, K., & Singh, S. K. (2019). The state of HRM in the Middle East: Challenges and future research agenda. *Asia Pacific Journal of Management*, 36(4), 905–933.

Coase, R. H. (1937). The nature of the firm. *Economica*, 4.

Corporate Counsel Business Journal (CCBJ) (2012). Real Estate Investing In The Middle East: Foreign Ownership Restrictions In The GCC https://ccbjournal.com/articles/real-estate-investing-middle-east-foreign-ownership-restrictions-gcc

Davidson, C. (2011). *Power and politics in the Persian Gulf monarchies*. London: Hurst.

Dubai FDI Monitor (2016). https://www.dubaifdimonitor.ae/application/annual_reports/pdf/Dubai_FDI_MONITOR_Highlights_Report_2016.pdf?v=20210423-055953

Durani, F., Ameer, W., Meo, M. S., & Husin, M. M. (2021). Relationship Between Outward Foreign Direct Investment and Domestic Investment: Evidence from GCC Countries. *Asian Economic and Financial Review*, 11(4), 278–291.

Beblawi, H. El, (2011). Gulf industrialization in perspective. In J.-F. Seznec and M. Kirk (Eds.), *Industrialization in the Gulf: A socioeconomic revolution*. London: Center for Contemporary Arab Studies, Georgetown University/Routledge, pp. 185–97.

Eccles, Robert G., Annissa Alusi, Amy C. Edmondson, and Tiona Zuzul. (2012). "Sustainable Cities: Oxymoron or the Shape of the Future?" In Spiro Pollalis, Andreas Georgoulias, Stephen Ramos, and Daniel Schodek (eds.), *Infrastructure Sustainability and Design*, pp. 247–265. New York: Routledge.

El-Husseini, I., Fayad, W., El Sayed, T., & Zywietz, D. (2009). *A new source of power – The potential for renewable energy in the MENA region*, New York, NY: Booz & Co.

El-Kharouf, F., Al-Qudsi, S., & Obeid, S. (2010). The Gulf Corporation Council sovereign wealth funds: Are they instruments for economic diversification or political tools? *Asian Economic Papers*, 9(1), 124–151.

EU. (2018). *GCC investment report*. A Project Implemented by Euro-support Consortium – AESA.

European Commission (2021). *Countries and regions*. https://ec.europa.eu/trade/policy/countries-and-regions/regions/gulf-region/

Expat guide (2010). *Doing Business in the GCC*. A Simple Guide to the Westerner.

Ferroukhi, R., Ghazal-Aswad, N., Androulaki, S., Hawila, D., & Mezher, T. (2013). Renewable energy in the GCC: status and challenges. *International Journal of Energy Sector Management*, 7(1), 84–112.

Figueira de Lemos, F., Johanson, J. & Vahlne, J. E. (2011). Risk management in the internationalization process of the firm: A note on the Uppsala Model. *Journal of World Business*, 46 (2), 143–153.

Frost & Sullivan (2011). "*Strategic Insight on the GCC Rail Sector*" The prominence of railways in GCC's transportation sector set to rise due to major rail projects developed in the region.

Giffinger, R., Fertner, C., Kramar, H., & Meijers, E. (2007). *City-ranking of European medium-sized cities*. Cent. Reg. Sci. Vienna UT, 1-12.

Grassa, R., & Gazdar, K. (2014). Law and Islamic finance: How legal origins affect Islamic finance development? *Borsa Istanbul Review*, 14(3), 158–166.

Hejazi, W. (2005). Are regional concentrations of OECD exports and outward FDI consistent with gravity? *Atlantic Economic Journal*, 33(4), 423–436.

Hossain, M. Z. (2015a). Free trade zones in Oman: A descriptive analysis. *Journal of Applied Management Science*, 9(4), 64–73.

Hossain, M. Z. (2015b). Free trade zones in Oman: A descriptive analysis. *Journal of Applied Management Science*, 9(4), 64–73.

Hvidt, M. (2011). Economic and institutional reforms in the Arab Gulf countries. *The Middle East Journal*, 65(1), 85–102.

Hvidt, M. (2013). *Economic diversification in GCC countries: Past record and future trends*.

IMD (2020). *IMD World Competitiveness Ranking 2020*: showing strength of small economies. https://www.imd.org/news/updates/IMD-2020-World-Competitiveness-Ranking-revealed/

International trade administration (2020). *Market Entry Strategy* https://www.trade.gov/knowledge-product/united-arab-emirates-market-entry-strategy

Investopedia (2020). *Sovereign Wealth Fund* (SWF) https://www.investopedia.com/terms/s/sovereign_wealth_fund.asp

Johanson, J. & Vahlne, J. E. (2009). The Uppsala internationalization process model revisited: From liability of foreignness to liability of outsidership. *Journal of International Business Studies*, 40(9), 1411–1431.

Kamrava, M., Nonneman, G., Nosova, A., & Valeri, M. (2016). *Ruling families and business elites in the Gulf Monarchies: ever closer?*

Linklaters (2019). *GCC Quarterly review* https://www.linklaters.com/en/insights/publications/gcc/gcc-quarterly-review/q3-2019

Lombardi, P., Giordano, S., Farouh, H., & Yousef, W. (2012). Modelling the smart city performance. *Innovation: The European Journal of Social Science Research*, 25(2), 137–149.

Luo, Y. D. & Tung, R. L. (2007). International expansion of emerging market enterprises: A springboard perspective. *Journal of International Business Studies*, 38(4), 481–498.

Mathews, J. A. (2006). Dragon multinationals: New players in 21-st century globalization. *Asia Pacific Journal of Management*, 23(1), 5–27.

MEED (2014). GCC free zones https://www.meed.com/gcc-free-zones/
Mintzberg, H. & Waters, J. A. (1985). Of strategies, deliberate and emergent. *Strategic Management Journal*, 6(3), 257–272.
Mosteanu, N. R. (2019). Intelligent Foreign Direct Investments to boost economic development–UAE case study. *The Business & Management Review*, 10(2), 1–9.
Mosteanu, N. R., & Alghaddaf, C. (2019). Smart economic development by Using Foreign Direct Investments–UAE case study. *Journal of Information Systems & Operations Management*, 13(1), 9–20.
Nam, T., & Pardo, T. A. (2011, June). Conceptualizing smart city with dimensions of technology, people, and institutions. In *Proceedings of the 12th annual international digital government research conference: Digital government innovation in challenging times* (pp. 282–291).
National Climate Change Plan of the United Arab Emirates (2017–2050). https://u.ae/en/about-the-uae/strategies-initiatives-and-awards/strategies-plans-and-visions/environment-and-energy/national-climate-change-plan-of-the-uae#:~:text=National%20Climate%20Change%20Plan%20of%20the%20UAE%202017%E2%80%932050%20is,a%20better%20quality%20of%20life
North, D. C. (1990). *Institutions, institutional change and economic performance*. Cambridge, UK: Cambridge university press.
Pereira, V., Temouri, Y., Shen, K., Xie, X., & Tarba, S. (2021, forthcoming). Exploring multi-level innovative ecosystems and strategies of EMNEs through disruptive global expansions- A case of a Chinese MNE. *Journal of Business Research*, 138(2022), 92–107.
Saxena, S., & Al-Tamimi, T. A. S. M. (2018). Visioning "smart city" across the Gulf Cooperation Council (GCC) countries. *Foresight*, 20(3), pp. 237–251.
Schneidhofer, Z. (2017). *The Opportunities and Challenges of Foreign Direct Investment in the United Arab Emirates* (Doctoral dissertation, Empire State College).
Schön, D., & Argyris, C. (1996). *Organizational learning II: Theory, method and practice* (Vol. 305, No. 2). Reading: Addison Wesley.
Scott, W. R. (2001). Organizations, overview. *International Encyclopedia of the Social and Behavioral Sciences*, 16, 10910–10917.
The UAE portal for the Sustainable Development Goals https://uaesdgs.ae/en/goals
The UAE's government portal (2021) *The UAE's response to climate change* https://u.ae/en/information-and-services/environment-and-energy/climate-change/theuaesresponsetoclimatechange#:~:text=In%20order%20to%20reduce%20its,CO2)%20per%20capita%20have%20decreased
The world financial review (TWFR) (2013). *Entry Strategies for Middle Eastern Markets* https://worldfinancialreview.com/entry-strategies-middle-eastern-markets/
Transparency International (2020). *Corruption perceptions index* https://www.transparency.org/en/cpi/2020/index/usa
Williamson, O. E. (1993). Transaction cost economics and organization theory. *Industrial and Corporate Change*, 2(2), 107–156.
World Bank. (2017). *World investment report*. Washington D.C: World Bank.

7

EMPLOYMENT RELATIONS IN THE MIDDLE EAST AND NORTH AFRICA (MENA)

Mike Leat and Ghada El-Kot

Introduction

The employment relationship involves an exchange of labour quality and quantity for rewards. Inherent to the relationship are both conflicting and mutual interests, the parties both want to obtain the best deal for themselves but they also need the relationship and for it to continue. The terms of the exchange agreement may comprise a legally enforceable contract (Leat, 2007).

Elements of the terms and nature of the individual employment relationship may be determined and influenced through the interactions of collective organizations representing the interests of groups of employees and employers/managers. Commonly, we would expect representative actors to comprise trades unions and employers' organizations, and the processes of interaction to include Joint Consultation, Social Dialogue and Collective Bargaining. This relationship does not occur within a vacuum, labour markets, legislative frameworks and religious and cultural values and norms all provide context to the interactions, expectations and outcomes.

The structure of the chapter therefore comprises an initial identification of the countries comprising the region, followed by sections on: labour markets and regulation, religious and cultural contexts; management in practice and collective employee relations. Finally, we draw some conclusions regarding the current state of collective employee relations in the region.

Countries and Clusters

There are various interpretations and terms used to refer to the countries and region that are the focus of this book. We use the larger MENA region and within that we include the six Gulf Cooperation Council (GCC) countries – Bahrain, Kuwait, Oman, Qatar, Saudi Arabia, and the United Arab Emirates, the non-GCC Arab states of Iraq, Syria, Jordan, Lebanon, Yemen, and the Occupied Palestinian Territory. In North Africa – Algeria, Morocco, Egypt, Tunisia, Libya. However, Iraq, Syria, Libya, Yemen and Palestinian Territory have experienced civil strife and armed conflict in recent years, there is relatively little data available for these countries and it is difficult to discuss legislative and employee relations frameworks, rights and freedoms, processes and institutions when the rule of law cannot be guaranteed.

What this means in practice is that the majority of the material in this chapter will concern the GCC countries, Jordan, Lebanon and four of the countries in North Africa – Egypt, Morocco, Tunisia and Algeria.

In order to explain widespread regional variations in labour standards and labour market flexibility, Cammett and Posusney (2010) used a typology of post-independence political economies based on oil dependence and political regimes and identified three main groupings – the oil-rich monarchies (the six GCC countries), non-oil-rich monarchies of Morocco and Jordan, and a group of low-income single-party republics including Tunisia, Egypt, Algeria, Syria and Yemen. We refer to this typology at relevant points in the ensuing discussion.

Labour Markets and Regulation

The MENA region is polarized in terms of wealth and income per head, with the GCC Oil monarchies leading the way. As noted above, a number of non-GCC Arab states have recently experienced armed conflict and war, and Jordan and Lebanon in particular experienced a large influx of refugees. Together, the Arab states have a high proportion of both foreign workers and refugees. In Saudi Arabia, the UAE and Qatar, native citizens constitute less than half of the population and in the UAE, non-natives constitute almost 90% of the population (International Trade Union Confederation – ITUC, 2020). Visser (2019) noted the proportion of international migrant workers in the Arab states at 35%, the highest in the world. Unskilled migrant workers in the GCC states, Jordan and Lebanon have been exposed to the potential for human rights abuses, vulnerability and exploitation as a consequence of the use of immigration sponsorship schemes such as *Kafala*, which place primary responsibility for regulating the employment relationship with the employer (International Labour Organisation – ILO, 2017). The ITUC (2020) refers to these schemes as enabling modern slavery, acknowledges the actions of Qatar in dismantling the system but asserts that other countries in the region still rely on it.

A number of states in the region, including all GCC states, are pursuing localization programmes aimed at increasing the employability, employment opportunities and active participation of native citizens in states' economic development. Forstenlechner and Baruch (2013) suggest these programmes breach the traditional national psychological contract.

Traditionally, states in the region exhibited a national-level psychological or social contract or ruling bargain between government and its citizens. This included a sense of entitlement on the part of native citizens and large public sectors with ample and guaranteed secure jobs, terms and conditions, salaries and status all higher than in the private sector. Forstenlechner and Baruch (2013), Meijer (2016), Sparrow (2018) and Lies et al. (2012) all refer to this tacit agreement unravelling in recent decades, and Meijer notes the influence of neoliberalism and the contribution the unravelling played in the popular uprisings that constituted the Arab Spring.

CASE

Kuwaitization

The Kuwaiti labour market is strongly segmented, with the majority of the workforce being nonnationals and representing 82% of the total workforce, and the majority of nationals being employed in the public sector, i.e. 74% and in high-paying parts of the private sector (incl. finance, insurance, mining). The private sector, which employs the majority of migrant workers, generally provides wages and benefits that are well below public sector standards or at least those accepted by Kuwaiti nationals. This is an important factor behind Kuwaitis' low enthusiasm in migrating to the private sector and the failure of Kuwaitization efforts of the government.

Nationalisation of the private sector workforce is a key priority for the government. Nationalisation policies in Kuwait are centred on long-term wage subsidies for nationals employed in the private sector along with Kuwaitization measures including bans on the recruitment of foreign workers. While there has been an increase in nationals' share of private sector employment, the private sector continues to be a less attractive option for Kuwaiti jobseekers, and more comprehensive reforms and policies are needed to achieve long-term and sustainable outcomes in terms of productivity and employment.

In fact, the Kuwaiti government has one of the most extensive private sector employment support programs in the region. In order to close the gap between private and public sector wages, the Kuwaiti government provides substantial financial incentives to nationals working in the private sector with the aim at equalizing the wages for Kuwaitis working in the private sector to those of public sector workers.

(DWCP Kuwait 2018–20 ILO)

In many states in the region the legal regulation of the labour market leads to rigidity and inflexibility in those sectors where the law applies, commonly the public sector and large private sector employers. Migrant labour, domestic labour and agriculture are often excluded from the formal frameworks of regulation.

Mellahi and Forstenlechner (2011) and Waxin and Bateman (2016) point out that if employers have more powers and control mechanisms over expatriate workers and native workers are more difficult to dismiss, then this may act as an incentive to employ migrant labour. Cammett and Posusney (2010) incorporated the ease of hiring, firing and adjusting working hours in their measure of labour flexibility and labour protection. They concluded that single-party republics tended to have relatively rigid labour contracts to protect employees but that in practice these were widely ignored or circumvented. The oil monarchies had traditionally preferred relatively flexible labour contracts, but there was evidence of increasing rigidity and protection being introduced for native citizens in order to comply with international pressures on labour standards.

Schurman and Eaton (2012) argue insufficient or absent legislative and regulatory frameworks, and social protection schemes, are what define informal work and informal workers suffer from a range of insecurities including income and representation insecurity. As noted above, large sectors of the labour forces are excluded from legal protection in MENA. Trades unions traditionally played a key role in helping workers address these insecurities, and Visser (2019) identifies the size of the informal economy as a factor of overwhelming importance for trade unions and their future. He suggests the revitalization of the trade union movement necessitates that they successfully address organizing and representing what he refers to as the "new unstable workforce" in the digital economy. The ILO (2020) estimates that 67% of workers in North Africa are in informal work, while Awad (2019) suggests that in Morocco it is close to 80% and in MENA overall 46% of workers are in informal work.

The key takeaway from the above presentation is that many governments in the region are seeking to encourage the employment and economic participation of native citizens in the private sector. The employment of native citizens is much more likely to entail an employment relationship and contract that is regulated, relatively inflexible and which provides employees with employment and social protection. The same degree of regulation, inflexibility and protection is less likely to apply to the employment contracts of the large proportions of foreign and migrant labour, and the terms of the contract are much more likely to be at the discretion of the employer.

CASE

Exclusion of workers from labour protection

While **Qatar** has dismantled the kafala system, other countries in the region still relied heavily on this system of modern slavery and maintained the exclusion of migrants, the vast majority of their workforce, from the rights to freedom of association and collective bargaining.

> In the **United Arab Emirates**, foreign workers represented 89 per cent of the workforce in 2020. Under the kafala system, any attempt at escaping or fleeing an employer in the UAE is punishable by law. Runaway workers are imprisoned, deported, and face significant financial costs, including paying back their employers for the sponsorship fees without receiving salaries earned.
>
> In **Lebanon**, over 250,000 migrant domestic workers, from African and Asian countries, were employed in private households in 2020. Horrendous reports of abuses have been exposed, like the case of a Filipino 28-year-old domestic worker, Halima Ubpah, who came to Lebanon in 2007, leaving behind her husband and three daughters, with a promised monthly salary of US$100. For ten years Halima was beaten and psychologically abused on a daily basis and her employers would lock her up in a room to sleep every night before the start of the next day. Concerns about exploitation and the lack of legal protection for migrant domestic workers in Lebanon led a number of sending countries, including Ethiopia, Nepal and the Philippines, to impose a ban on their nationals from travelling to work as domestic workers in Lebanon.
>
> **(ITUC Global Rights Index 2020)**

Management in Practice

Branine and Pollard (2010) confirm that a gap exists between the theory of Islamic management and the practice of management in Arab countries. They argue management in Arab countries is informed and heavily influenced by non-Islamic tribal, traditional and national cultural values, norms of different countries and by western management thinking. They note two dominant management practices which are inconsistent with core Islamic principles:

- authoritarian management and centralized and bureaucratic organizations, and
- nepotism in recruitment, treatment and promotions (*Wasta* and *Piston*).

Branine and Pollard (2010), Iles et al. (2012) and Budhwar and Mellahi (2018) note authoritarian management and a disinclination to delegate, share decision-making or allow employee participation all inconsistent with the Islamic teachings encouraging consensus and consultation-based decision-making. Iles et al. (2012) conclude that subordinates do not expect to participate and indeed that they view joint decision-making as indicating weakness. Al-Jahwari and Budhwar (2016) cite Kabasakal et al. (2012), who argues that in MENA region, consultation is not used for power sharing but as means of showing that the leader cares about his subordinates and values their opinions. Budhwar and Mellahi (2018) identify the strong impact of high power distance on managers' negative perceptions towards delegation of authority and employee participation in decision making. Branine and Pollard (2010) further conclude that organizations in the region are centrally controlled and bureaucratic and an atmosphere of low trust and political gamesmanship pervades. There is also a lack of management skills and communication tends to be poor.

Wasta is an institutional form of nepotism which may be consistent with certain dominant cultural values, but as Budhwar et al. (2019) note, its use in recruitment and compensation, in GCC and North African countries, is not consistent with core Islamic values of equity and fairness. Aldossari and Robertson (2016), in their study in KSA, argue that Wasta, which is consistent with in-group and family collectivism, loyalty to family and friends and the importance attached to social relationships, permeates employment relationships in the region and also encourages a mindset of dependency. Branine and Pollard (2010) confirm it does not matter how much you know but who you are and who you know.

The dominant authoritarian style of management, centralized and bureaucratic organizations, and the widespread use of nepotism signify an employment relationship reality quite different from that indicated by Islamic values and the IWE (Islamic work ethic), which emphasize and encourage equitable and fair treatment of employees, justice, consultation and consensus in decision-making.

Hence, styles of management are predominantly authoritarian, and the employment relationship is characterized by low trust and poor communication. Employees do not expect delegation of authority or to participate in decision-making; the latter is commonly regarded as a sign of weakness on the part of management. Institutionalized nepotism or Wasta is widespread in recruitment, treatment and promotions.

Collective Employee Relations

As noted in the introduction section, employment relationship is one based on an exchange of labour for reward; the terms of this exchange may be determined and agreed between the individual actors, but it is also common for the terms of the exchange to be the product of a mixture of individual, collective and legislative regulation.

At the collective level, the actors are normally trade unions representing the interests of employees and employers' associations representing the interests of employers. In each case, the parties form and join collective organizations in order to enhance their bargaining power in the determination of the terms of and in the conduct of the employment relationship. The parties may also collaborate with others within national-level confederations, and national-level federations may also associate with other like-minded organizations internationally. Both may also seek to gain advantage and influence by associating themselves with political parties in order to influence the legal and institutional national context within which they operate (for details see Leat 2007).

The primary processes through which the collective organizations seek to regulate the terms and conduct of the employment relationship are collective bargaining (CB) and social dialogue (SD). Evidence of the prevalence and utilization of these processes in the MENA region is provided in a later section.

Legislative Frameworks

Government may influence the terms and conduct of the relationship through legislation, and this may have a number of functions: it may seek to protect the interests and rights of the parties, it may seek to promote or prevent particular behaviours and it may be restrictive in seeking to determine the rules within which the various individual and collective relationships are conducted. Government may also engage with the collective organizations through tripartite discussions and negotiations; they are also involved as major actors as employers of the public sector (Leat 2007).

Collective employee relations are dependent on the formation, participation and effectiveness of trade unions and employers' associations, and there are a number of prerequisites that need to be facilitated by the legislative and institutional frameworks in a country:

- workers and employers must have the freedom to associate, to form and join collective organizations
- once formed they need to be free and willing to engage in joint processes with each other, and arguably free to withdraw their labour or institute a temporary closure or cessation of work.

The ILO conventions and recommendations constitute the international standards, and there are a number of them which address these basic legal and human rights freedoms. ILO member states should ratify these conventions and give effect to the rights and protections contained within them by statute or some other measures appropriate to national conditions.

The two main ILO conventions regarding the right to form unions and employers' associations and engage in collective bargaining are:

Convention No 87 on the Freedom of Association and Protection of the Right to Organize (1948), which provides that "workers and employers, without distinction whatsoever, shall have the right to establish and, subject only to the rules of the organization concerned, to join organizations of their own choosing without previous authorization."

Convention No. 98 on the Right to Organize and Collective Bargaining (1949). This convention seeks to protect workers from anti-union discrimination and employer interference and to encourage and promote "the full development and utilisation of machinery for voluntary negotiation between employers or employers' organisations and workers' organisations, with a view to the regulation of terms and conditions of employment by means of collective agreements."

In the MENA countries, ratification of these conventions is patchy and effective implementation tends to be partial and conditional. Only Kuwait of the GCC countries has ratified both of these Conventions, whereas Convention No. 87 has been ratified by Algeria, Egypt, Kuwait, Libya, Syria, Tunisia and Yemen; and Convention No. 98 by Algeria, Egypt, Iraq, Jordan, Lebanon, Libya, Morocco, Syria, Tunisia and Yemen.

Slaiby (2018) examined ratifications and implementing legislation and concluded that many of the countries that had ratified the Conventions had not fulfilled the requirements in national legislation.

Commonly, where the Conventions have been ratified, the rights created within countries are limited to citizens of the country (thereby excluding migrant workers, a large section of the workforce in some GCC countries) and to particular sectors of the economy and types of work; domestic and agricultural sectors are commonly excluded. There are some examples of migrant workers being able to form and join trade unions, e.g., in Jordan and Lebanon.

Based on the above analysis, the key takeaway is that in the MENA countries, effective national legislation to support and enforce the implementation of rights to form trade unions and employers' associations and engage in collective bargaining is uncommon, and where it does exist, it is often limited in scope and jurisdiction.

Freedom to Associate

There are trade unions in most of the MENA states, even in some where the conventions have not been ratified; however, they are explicitly banned in both Saudi Arabia and the UAE. The ITUC Global Rights Index 2020 reports that of 18 countries in the MENA region (Saudi Arabia was excluded in 2020 because of ongoing legislative changes) all excluded some workers from the right to establish or join a trade union. It is also common to have restrictions on the freedom to associate in terms of a need for a trade union to be registered by the state. Rishmawi (2013) notes two regimes for establishing trade unions: the notification and the registration regimes. The former is preferable in terms of enabling trade union organization and freedom. A requirement for the state to agree to registration provides opportunities as, for example, in Algeria and Egypt for dissolution, delay, and other forms of interference. Tunisia was one of the very few countries in the region utilizing a notification regime. Awad (2019) notes that recent changes to the Labour Law in Jordan have increased restrictions on trade union formation and they now face obstacles in registration. The ITUC regards any such requirement to be a violation of the rights embodied within Conventions 87 and 98 and identified Bahrain, Egypt (where independent trade unions were dissolved in March 2018 and 27 were still awaiting re-registration at the end of 2019) and Algeria as particular culprits, though they claim that all but two of the MENA countries impeded the registration of trade unions.

Rishmawi (2013) notes that the ILO stresses that Freedom of Association requires guaranteeing the possibility of multiple unions and federations within a country and that laws which prohibit or limit this are inconsistent with the Conventions. If workers are unable to organize and join trade unions of their own choice, the union movement is arguably not free and independent. Omeira (2008) noted little freedom of association in countries (such as Jordan, Kuwait, Yemen and Syria) where the state effectively imposed and controlled a single trade union federation. Cammett and Posusney (2010) concluded that single-party republics like Tunisia, Egypt, Algeria,

Syria and Yemen all had single trade union confederations linked to the ruling political party and unions were subject to registration requirements and government monitoring of finances. In terms of union pluralism and competition, they concluded that union competition was virtually non-existent in the region other than in Morocco and Oman and that workers in Morocco had the greatest degree of freedom. They acknowledged the influence of French Unions in both Morocco and Tunisia during colonization. In Morocco, the movement is fragmented with four representative unions each with particular political/religious affiliations. The Union Marocaine du Travail (UMT) is the oldest Union and claims independence but is often associated with the monarchy. The Confédération des Travailleurs Marocains (CDT) is close to the USFP Socialist Union. The Union Générale des Travailleurs Marocains (UGTM) is close to the Istiqial independence party, and Union Nationale des Travailleurs Marocains (UNTM) is close to the Islamic movement.

Slaiby (2018) found that most of the countries in the region had union movements and central federations controlled by governments who utilized a range of mechanisms to achieve domination. The only countries in which independent national centres were still active were Tunisia, Morocco and Bahrain, though in Egypt, Algeria and Jordan there were some independent unions created as a reaction to government domination. But without registration, these unions face great difficulties in being effective. Ramadan and Adly (2015) refer to post–Arab Spring governments in Egypt reimposing authoritarian state corporatism and legal restrictions on independent free unions, delegitimizing them in favour of the state-affiliated Egyptian Trade Union Federation (ETUF) which had been granted a legal monopoly on representing workers. Meijer (2016) also refers to the ETUF as a state organ established to control the workers' movement and concludes more widely that trades unions have been incorporated into the state in Algeria, Egypt and Syria.

Another potential indicator of trade union freedom is affiliation to the ITUC which is open to democratic, independent and representative national trade union centres. At the end of 2019, 11 countries in the region had union organizations affiliated to the ITUC. In eight countries, namely, Bahrain, Iraq, Jordan, Kuwait, Oman, Palestine, Tunisia and Yemen, only one organization was affiliated to the ITUC. Egypt had two affiliated unions which did not include the ETUF (the Egyptian Democratic labour Congress, EDLC, and Egyptian Federation of Independent Trade Unions, EFITU), as did Algeria (Confederation generale asutonome des traveilleurs en Algerie, CGATA and Union Generale des Travailleurs Algerians, UGTA). Morocco had three unions affiliated to the ITUC (UMT, CDT and UGTM). There were no ITUC-affiliated organizations from the UAE, KSA, Libya, Lebanon, Syria and Qatar.

Accordingly, we deduce that the freedom of employees and employers in the MENA region to associate, to form and join collective associations is limited. There are limitations on who are eligible, obstacles and restrictions on formation, registration, recognition, plurality and competition, and many national governments either oppose or seek to co-opt, integrate and control union movements within a form of state corporatism.

> **CASE**
>
> **Dismantling of independent unions and violent attacks on workers**
>
> In **Algeria** and **Egypt**, most independent unions were still unable to function as the authorities refused to grant them recognition, while prominent trade union leaders faced state persecution. In **Egypt**, at least 27 independent unions still sought registration with the authorities, following their arbitrary dissolution in March 2018. In **Algeria**, CGATA offices were administratively closed by the authorities on 3 December 2019, without any cause. Furthermore, **Kaddour Chouicha**, a CGATA executive member, was briefly detained on 24 October 2019 in Oran for his participation in a peaceful sit-in calling for the release of political dissidents. On 9 December 2019, as he returned to the police station to recover his cell phone, which had been confiscated, he was again arrested on spurious charges, summarily prosecuted the next day and sentenced to a one-year prison sentence.
>
> (for details see ITUC Global Rights Index 2020)

Collective Bargaining and Social Dialogue

The ILO (2013) defines SD broadly to include collective bargaining and consultation as:

"Social Dialogue includes all types of negotiation, consultation and exchange of information between, or among, representatives of governments, employers and workers on issues of common interest." It suggests that the main purpose of SD is to promote consensus building and democratic involvement among the main stakeholders at work and can occur at a number of different levels from workplace up to national tripartite dialogue between the representatives of workers, employers and managers and government.

The ILO (2019) argues that collective representation of workers and employers through SD is at the heart of democracy; it helps promote peace and social justice, provides institutional capabilities for navigating the future of work and should be promoted through public policy. SD is a major mechanism for achieving satisfactory working conditions and their (ILO) Decent Work agenda.

Further, the ILO (2013) identified certain preconditions for successful Tripartite SD: a democratic regime, freedom of association, independent and representative social partners, political will and commitment, and institutional support. Slaiby (2018) concluded that while there are variations between countries in the region all of these preconditions can be evaluated as weak in MENA. Omeira (2008) noted that tripartite platforms as envisaged in National Social Dialogue hardly existed. In their review of tripartite SD in Jordan, Tunisia and Morocco, De Koster et al. (2015) conclude that the potential for SD is underutilized, as are the systems and regulatory frameworks in place. Tunisia had the more active SD, but the authors nevertheless felt that none of these industrial relations systems could effectively deal with the socio-economic issues confronting the countries. There was a lack of political will on the part of government, the trades unions were weak, while stronger employers' associations were more focused on trade and economic development.

Convention No. 98 identifies CB as a process whereby employers and trades unions seek to determine and regulate terms and conditions of employment through voluntary negotiation and agreement; implicitly this requires both parties to be prepared to compromise in order to agree and accept that they cannot be autonomous. This tends to be a more difficult issue for employers and managers, and we have noted earlier their apparent reluctance to share decision-making and delegate authority in the MENA region. Processes of consultation without the pre-requisite for reaching an agreed outcome tend to be more popular with employers and managers.

In MENA countries, where there are legislatively supported freedoms to engage in CB, restrictions tend to be applied, scope may be limited, process restrictions may be strict, agreements may need to be ratified by government which gives a power of veto and employers may be unwilling to participate. Yemen, Bahrain, Oman, Kuwait, Qatar, Jordan and Morocco are all examples of countries where collective bargaining is allowed but heavily restricted (Slaiby, 2018; De Koster et al., 2015; Mellahi and Forstenlechner, 2011).

CASE

Social Dialogue

Kuwait has the longest experience in tripartite participation among the Arab States, with long-standing national tripartite consultative bodies. The government publicly supports its social partners, yet issues remain with regard to freedom of association, and particularly the right to strike. Kuwait is one of the few Arab states that have ratified both C87 and C98. However, the law imposes some restrictions on workers' ability to join and form unions, incl. a requirement that new unions must have at least 100 founding members, of which 15 have to be Kuwaiti citizens. Non-citizens may not hold union office and have to obtain official approval to join a union.

(DWCP Kuwait 2018–20 ILO)

Tunisia is an exception within the region, there is legislative support and provision for CB at a range of levels, and for agreements to be extended into employment contracts for all applicable workers subject to government approval. Some agreements are concluded at national level, but very little bargaining occurs at the level of the sector or the enterprise. Nevertheless, according to the ILO data on CB coverage, Tunisia had coverage for 57 % of employees in 2014 and is the only country from the MENA region for which recent ILO CB coverage data is available. De Koster et al. (2015) estimate CB coverage to be 90% at all levels in Tunisia.

The ITUC GRI 2020 reports that 17 of the 18 MENA countries violated the right to CB. Slaiby (2018) concluded that the nepotism and crony capitalism that characterize the authoritarian regimes in MENA create relationships between government and employers that trivialize both CB and tripartite SD.

Based on the above analysis, we can say that the effective use of CB and SD to enhance democracy, constrain the autonomy of employers and determine terms and conditions of employment is rare in the MENA region. Where processes and structures ostensibly exist and operate, the mixture of weak legislative support and willingness to promote and engage on the part of governments and employers leads to trivialization and ineffectiveness.

Right to Strike

As noted earlier, trades unions are banned in the UAE and KSA, strikes are explicitly a criminal activity and workers can be suspended or dismissed without pay or deported for taking strike action. However, in the other oil monarchies like Bahrain, Qatar, Oman and Kuwait, the non-oil monarchies and single-party republics, there are limited rights or freedom to strike but with procedural and other restrictions on taking strike action.

The ITUC GRI 2020 reports that all 18 countries violated the right to strike with 13 either prohibiting or cracking down on strike action and freedom of assembly being restricted. Explicit mention is made of repression and violence, arrests and police detention in Egypt and Morocco.

CASE

Right to strike

Egypt

In October 2017, in a context of increasing state repression, the **Egyptian** prime minister issued an order to refer cases of protest, strike and sit-in to State Security Courts after they have been tried by the general courts.

On 6 June 2019, State security forces arrested seven employees of the **Egyptian Railway Maintenance and Service Company** (Ermas) who had organised a strike to demand a pay rise. The charges brought against them were "inciting strike and public disorder".

> On 14 September, workers at the **Orglo** factory staged a strike to claim the payment of an overdue allowance. Security forces arrested 19 workers and referred them to the Ismailia prosecution. Thirteen of them were released while six others were charged with "gathering, blocking road traffic, rioting, damaging the economy and disrupting vital facilities". They all were sentenced to a 15-day prison sentence.
>
> On 6 October, seven protesting workers at the **Eastern Tobacco Company** met the same fate, as they were arrested for "inciting strike" and condemned to a prison sentence and a fine.
>
> In October 2019, 26 shipyard workers were condemned by the military court to a suspended one-year jail term and a fine of 2,000 Egyptian pounds for their participation in a strike.
>
> (for details see ITUC Global Rights Index 2020)

Labour Protection

Cammett and Posusney (2010) compared the de jure rights and de facto experience of labour protection in countries in the region. They define labour protection to include collective labour rights (freedom of association, CB and the right to strike), and labour market flexibility (the ease with which employers can hire, fire and adjust working hours). Their conclusions were that the Middle East region as a whole had the lowest levels of labour protection in the world. There were wide variations; the non-oil monarchies (Jordan and Morocco) had levels of protection above the world average, but the Gulf Oil Monarchies (Bahrain, Kuwait, Oman, Qatar, Saudi Arabia, and the United Arab Emirates) had low levels of protection, with UAE, Saudi Arabia and Kuwait being particularly poor. They also concluded that in all countries in the region de jure rights surpassed de facto experience and enforcement, noting wider gaps and a widespread lack of compliance in the non-oil monarchies and single-party states (Tunisia, Egypt, Algeria, Syria and Yemen) than in the Gulf oil monarchies. However; this was due to the lower levels of de jure protection in the oil monarchies. Overall, they conclude that authoritarianism associated with widespread restrictions on the ability of workers to organize and mobilize meant that workers had very little ability to defend their rights in practice. Meijer (2016) concludes that the GCC countries rely on imported migratory labour which has few, if any, rights and the rest of the Arab world is characterized by an increasing marginalization of labour and chiselling away of rights and protections. Awad (2019) argues that the IMF has been instrumental in encouraging states in the region to improve labour market flexibility as a condition of loans and the ensuing policies have effectively reduced labour rights. He argues that non-unionized labour has the most to lose in these circumstances and unions are weak in the region.

The ITUC GRI 2020 argues that MENA is the worst region in the world for workers' rights and protection. They note that in Libya, Palestine, Syria and Yemen rights could not be guaranteed because of ongoing armed conflicts and a breakdown of the rule of law. Of the other countries in region, KSA was excluded as explained earlier. Egypt was in the ten worst countries in the world, and Iraq, Kuwait and the UAE were all ranked particularly poorly.

Accordingly, we can conclude that there are wide variations in levels and the extent of social protection throughout the MENA region with de jure rights commonly exceeding de facto experience. Levels of protection have traditionally been low in many states; however, there are instances of recent enhancement of rights, and there are also signs of improvement in de jure experience.

CASE

Labour protection in Qatar, dismantling Kafala

In a historic move, the State of Qatar has introduced major changes to its labour market, ending the requirement for migrant workers to obtain their employer's permission to change jobs, while also becoming the first country in the region to adopt a non-discriminatory minimum wage.

Following the adoption on 30 August 2020 of Law No. 19 of 2020, migrant workers can now change jobs before the end of their contract without first having to obtain a No Objection Certificate (NOC) from their employer. This new law, coupled with the removal of exit permit requirements earlier in the year, effectively dismantles the "kafala" sponsorship system and marks the beginning of a new era for the Qatari labour market.

In addition to removing the need to obtain an NOC, the adoption of Law No. 18 of 2020 provides greater clarity regarding termination of employment. To terminate an employment contract and change jobs, workers must provide at least one month's written notice if they have worked with the employer for two years or less, or two months' notice if they have worked with the employer for over two years.

Additional legislation, Law No. 17 of 2020, adopted today also establishes a minimum wage of 1,000 Qatari riyals (QAR) which will enter into force six months after the law's publication in the Official Gazette. The new minimum wage will apply to all workers, of all nationalities and in all sectors, including domestic workers. In addition to the basic minimum wage, employers must ensure that workers have decent accommodation and food. The legislation also stipulates that employer pay allowances of at least QAR 300 and QAR 500 to cover costs of food and housing respectively, if they do not provide workers with these directly – a move that will help ensure decent living standards for workers.

The adoption of these laws supports the transition towards a more skilled and productive workforce, which is a key goal in Qatar's National Vision 2030.

> It will also help promote economic recovery from the fallout of the COVID-19 pandemic, as well as the growth of the economy over the longer term.
>
> Increased labour mobility is expected to provide numerous benefits to Qatar as it transitions towards a knowledge-based economy. Employers will be able to hire experienced staff locally instead of from overseas, thus greatly reducing recruitment costs. Enhanced mobility will also generate more job opportunities and increase job satisfaction for workers
>
>> By introducing these significant changes, Qatar has delivered on a commitment. One that will give workers more freedom and protection, and employers more choice. We are witnessing what can be achieved when governments, workers and employers work together with the ILO to promote decent work for all.
>>
>> (Guy Ryder, ILO Director-General)
>
> Minister of Administrative Development, Labour & Social Affairs Yousuf Mohamed Al Othman Fakhroo said, "The State of Qatar is committed to creating a modern and dynamic labour market. In line with Qatar Vision 2030, these new laws mark a major milestone in this journey and will benefit workers, employers and the nation alike".
>
> (August 2020, DOHA, ILO News)

TU Membership

Slaiby (2018) comments that information on trade union membership rates in the region is limited and open to manipulation by both governments and trade unions. He concludes that with the exception of Tunisia, trade union membership rates are low and unions are weak.

Visser's (2019) comprehensive review of the state and possible futures for the trade union movement worldwide aggregated trade union membership density data for the Arab and North African regions (Iraq, Syria, Yemen and Libya were excluded due to the civil strife and armed conflict in those countries). He concludes that the rates in 2016 for the Arab region were 5% of employees and 3.3% if you include the self-employed, own-account workers and the informal sector. For North Africa, the rates were substantially higher at 33.9% and 22.7% respectively. The Arab states rates are the lowest of any region in the world. However, he notes that the North African region (Morocco, Tunisia, Egypt and Algeria), against global trends, has shown spectacular growth in absolute numbers of trade union members since the Arab Spring of 2011.

Unfortunately there is no detailed specific analysis of the membership growth in the North African countries, but Visser does identify a number of relationships that might be relevant. Generally there are positive relationships between unionization and ethnic homogeneity and economic development (the Gulf states are an exception to this), and negative relationships between unionization and poverty, the proportion of migrant workers and workers in the informal economy, and labour rights violations (all variously present in the Arab states but less so in North Africa). Further, there are also positive relationships with centralized collective bargaining, not common in MENA, and union recognition, which is subject to restriction. However, another factor which he highlights and which applies to Egypt and North Africa is a very clear positive relationship between the existence of union-related unemployment and social insurance, pension funds or health insurance. Another factor that might be applicable to the growth in Tunisia and Morocco is the cooperation between the union centres (De Koster et al., 2015).

Visser (2019) identified four potential futures for trade union movement globally, and it is difficult not to conclude that in the vast majority of MENA states, trade unions are marginalized and there appear to be few signs of or reasons to envisage revitalization. Accordingly, we can conclude that across the region and with the exception of Tunisia and other North African states trade union membership is low and their influence is weak. They are marginalized, and there are few reasons to believe that this will change in the foreseeable future.

Conclusions

The evidence suggests that the autonomy of management is largely unconstrained in MENA, not by legislative frameworks granting de jure rights and protections nor by de facto compliance or enforcement and not by a strong and effective trade union movement. Large sections of the labour force are in informal work and unprotected, including the large numbers of foreign and migrant labour in the GCC states, Jordan and Lebanon, who are vulnerable and liable to exploitation by employers. Managements' approach tends to be authoritarian with little delegation or sharing of decision-making, and there is widespread practice of nepotism in the workplace and in wider society. Employment relationships would not appear to be consistent with some core principles of Islam or the IWE, and the individual employee can have little power in the relationship, is expected to work hard, obey and not show dissent.

Governments are predominantly authoritarian, institutions are centralized and bureaucratic, democracy exists in only a few states and governments only partially enact the principles of International Labour Rights Conventions and Standards. The traditional social contract or ruling bargain may be unravelling given the demands of neoliberalism and long-term economic sustainability, and native citizens find themselves confronted by additional pressures to be economically active and to work in the less secure and protected private sector. Tripartite SD seems to be largely non-existent and SD and CB both appear to suffer due to a lack of political will by governments, lack of interest on the part of employers and weakness of trades unions and the labour force. Trades unions lack legislative support and protection, they lack membership and strength and are marginalized with little reason to believe in upcoming revitalization.

Websites

ITUC https://www.ituc-csi.org/
ILO https://www.ilo.org/global/lang--en/index.htm

References

Aldossari, M. and Robertson, M. (2016). The role of wasta in repatriates' perceptions of a breach to the psychological contract: A Saudi Arabian case study. *The International Journal of Human Resource Management*, 27(16), pp. 1854–1873.

Al-Jahwari, M., & Budhwar, P. S. (2016). Human resource management in Oman. In P. S. Budhwar, & K. Mellahi (Eds.), *Handbook of Human Resource Management in the Middle East* (pp. 87–122). Edward Elgar.

Awad, M. (2019). The impact of trade and investment on labour standards in the MENA region. *International Journal of Labour Research*, 9(1–2), pp. 215–233.

Branine, M. and Pollard, D. (2010). Human resource management with Islamic management principles: A dialectic for a reverse diffusion in management. *Personnel Review*, 39(6), pp. 712–727.

Budhwar, P., Pereira, V., Mellahi, K. and Singh, S. K. (2019). The state of HRM in the Middle East: Challenges and future research agenda. *Asia Pacific Journal of Management*, 36, pp. 905–933.

Budhwar, P. and Mellahi, K. (2018). *Human Resource Management in the Middle East*. Edward-Elgar.

Cammett, M. and Posusney, M. P. (2010). Labor standards and labor market flexibility in the Middle East: Free trade and freer unions? *Studies in Comparative International Development*, 45, pp. 250–279.

De Koster, A. and Oechslin, E. and Trabelsi, M. and Said, M. (2015). *Social Dialogue in Morocco, Tunisia and Jordan*, Regulations and Realities of Social Dialogue. European Commission and ITC-ILO.

Forstenlechner, I. and Baruch, Y. (2013). Contemporary career concepts and their fit for the Arabian Gulf Context A sector level analysis of psychological contract breach. *Career Development International*, 18(6), pp. 629–648.

International Labour Organization (2013). *National Tripartite Social Dialogue, An ILO Guide for Improved Governance*. Geneva.

International Labour Organization (2020). *World Employment and Social Outlook Trends 2020*. Geneva.

International Labour Organization (2017). *Employer-Migrant Worker Relationships in the Middle East: Exploring Scope for Internal Labour Market Mobility and Fair Migration*.

International Labour Organisation (ILO) (2019). *Women in Business and Management. The Business Case for Change*. Geneva. https://www.ilo.org/global/publications/books/WCMS_700953/lang--en/index.htm

International Trade Union Confederation (2020). *ITUC 2020 Global Rights Index. The World's Worst Countries for Workers*.

Kabaskal, H., Dastmalchian, A, Karacay, G. and Bayraktar, S. (2012). Leadership and culture in the MENA region: An analysis of the GLOBE project. *Journal of World Business*, 47, 519–529.

Lles, P., Almhedie, A. and Baruch, Y. (2012). Managing HR in the Middle East: Challenges in the public sector. *Public Personnel Management*, 41(3), pp. 465–492.

Leat, M. (2007). *Exploring Employee Relations*. 2nd ed. Butterworth-Heinemann.

Meijer, R. (2016). The workers' movement and the Arab uprisings. *Internationaal Instituut voor Sociale Geschiedenis, IRSH* 61, pp. 487–503.

Mellahi, K. and Forstenlechner, I. (2011). Employment relations in oil-rich Gulf countries. In: M. Barry & A. Wilkinson, ed., *Handbook of Comparative Employment Relations*, Edward Elgar.

Omeira, M., Esim, S. and Alissa, S. (2008). Labor governance and economic reform in the Middle East and North Africa: Lessons from Nordic countries, *ILO Working*, Paper no. 436.

Ramadan, F. and Adly, A. (2015). *Low-Cost Authoritarianism: The Egyptian Regime and Labor Movement Since 2013*, Carnegie Middle East Center. https://carnegie-mec.org/2015/09/17/low-cost-authoritarianism-egyptian-regime-and-labor-movement-since-2013-pub-61321

Rishmawi, M. (2013). Freedom of Association in Arab Countries: A Toolkit, *Arab NGO Network for Development (ANND)*.

Schurman, S. J. and Eaton, A. E. (2012). *Trade Union Organizing in the Informal Economy: A Review of the Literature on Organizing in Africa, Asia, Latin America, North America and Western, Central and Eastern Europe*. Rutgers University.

Slaiby, G. (2018). *The Power Resources Approach in the MENA Region*. Tunis, Friedrich-Ebert-Stiftung.

Sparrow, P. (2018). The psychological contract within the comparative HRM literature. In: C. Brewster, W. Mayrhofer, E. Farndale, ed., *Handbook of Research on Comparative Human Resource Management*, 2nd ed. Edward Elgar, Cheltenham.

Visser, J. (2019). *Trade Unions in the Balance*. ILO ACTRAV Working Paper.

Waxin, M. F. and Bateman, R. (2016). Labor localisation and HRM practices in the gulf countries. In: P. Budhwar, K. Mellahi, ed., *Handbook of Human Resource Management in the Middle East*, Cheltenham.

8
BANKING AND FINANCIAL INSTITUTIONS IN THE GULF COOPERATION COUNCIL REGION

Vikash Ramiah, Vijay Pereira, Bhaskar Dasgupta, Alex Frino and Huy Pham

Introduction

According to the behavioural finance literature, investors are prone to several heuristic-driven biases, and when it comes to international investments, home bias tends to be the main issue. In simple terms, home bias is the fear of the unknown combined with a preference for what is usually familiar (Ardalan, 2019; Graham et al., 2009). We believe and posit that investors are susceptible to such bias when making decisions about investing when it comes to the Middle East context. This chapter attempts to provide a plausible remedy for this issue in terms of educating investors about the banking and financial realities in the Gulf Cooperation Council (GCC) region. Accordingly, the main goal of this chapter is to demonstrate how the banking and finance structures of the Middle East are like and what they are currently exposed to in their day-to-day working life. We plan to demonstrate that like developed markets, the GCC banking and finance industry is governed by financial mathematics, robust regulatory framework and market integrity. Just like every developed market possesses its own idiosyncratic factor, the GCC market has its own unique factors. These are important to unbundle and understand from varied stakeholders perspectives, and hence, for this key reason, it is important for us to highlight the similarities and differences.

The chapter is organised as follows. Section 2 identifies the literature as a source of the asymmetric difference in knowledge. Section 3 shows that the banking regulatory framework is universal and not unique to the GCC, and Section 4 reveals that different national legal system is not necessarily a deal breaker. Section 5 illustrates that history favours doing business with the Middle East, Section 6 highlights the similarities and differences in the roles of Central Banks, and Section 7 discusses the types of financial institutions in the GCC. Section 8 discusses how the UAE has

DOI: 10.4324/9781003005766-10

the characteristics of an emerging equity market, Section 9 shows how the GCC is vulnerable to crises, and Section 10 concludes the chapter.

Source of the Asymmetric Difference in Knowledge

The way business is carried out within the financial and banking regulatory framework has been extensively documented within developed markets (for details see Ellert, 1976; Eckbo, 1983, 1985, 1992; Eckbo and Wier, 1985; Aharony et al., 1988; Slovin et al., 1991; Bittlingmayer, 1992; Sundaram et al., 1992; Amoako-Adu and Smith, 1995; Akhigbe and Whyte, 2001; Spiegel and Yamori, 2003; Benczur et al., 2017; Madura, 2020; Musthaq, 2020). This enables the business community to understand how to conduct business in a developed market and thus explaining the existing preference for developed markets. During the late 2000s and 2010s, the attention changed to emerging markets (Fu and Heffernan, 2009; Lin and Zhang, 2009; Goddard et al., 2012; Gan et al., 2014; Pham et al., 2017; Ramiah et al., 2018) as there are major business opportunities. Given the performance of the Middle Eastern markets recently, there is a growing interest in terms of learning about this market. As this is a major gap in the literature, businesses who are figuring out how to embrace the Middle Eastern success cannot find the answer in the literature. Consequently, our chapter contributes to this discussion by explaining the financial aspects of conducting business in the region to educate investors.

Banking Regulatory Framework Is Universal and Not Unique to the GCC

According to the above-cited literature, the banking regulatory framework can be summarised by the following headings: information reporting, central bank management, corporate governance, entry and exit requirements, financial management, financing, lending, mergers and acquisition, monetary policy, operating rules, taxation, ownership structure, reserve requirement, securities trading, risk management, foreign investment, transaction management and many more. How do businesses react to announcements of these policies? The literature does not provide a clear answer as the empirical findings appear to be mixed. First, we observe clear sectoral effects implying that each sector will have a distinct reaction (positive, negative, or no effect). Second, it depends on whether the policy implemented is stringent or lax. Third, the effects are highly dependent on how either the revenue or the cost function of an organisation is affected by the policy. Fourth, these regulations affect the systematic risk of businesses. Fifth, when subsequent adjustments are made to a particular regulation, a diamond risk structure is discerning—suggesting a risk-shifting behaviour. Finally, most sectors appear to be affected. The literature justifies our book chapter in that implicitly suggests that each market is different, and, with unpredictable outcomes, we must study the market we plan to enter. This book chapter offers some insights into the GCC market, namely Saudi Arabia,

Kuwait, the United Arab Emirates (UAE), Qatar, Bahrain and Oman as they have achieved the highest financial development scores in the region.

Different National Legal System Is Not Necessarily a Deal Breaker

The national legal systems that we observe around the world revolve around four basic systems: civil law, common law, statutory law and religious law. Nevertheless, certain countries can opt to have a hybrid between these systems. Except for Saudi Arabia, the remaining GCC countries (Kuwait, the UAE, Qatar, Bahrain and Oman) tend to have a combination of civil law, common law and religious law where the religious law is Islamic law. The civil law tends to follow the Egyptian law, which is a derivative of the French Law (Napoleonic Code) whilst the common law tends to follow the English Law. From this perspective, conducting business in the GCC country is like the rest of the world (except for Saudi Arabia). For instance, the UAE follows the Egyptian civil law and the Islamic Law but certain areas in Abu Dhabi (Abu Dhabi Global Market, also known as ADGM) and Dubai (Dubai International Financial Centre) follow the English Law.

Example of the Usage of English Law in Dubai International Financial Centre (DIFC)

One of the goals of the UAE is to become the leading financial hub in the Middle Eastern region and in the world. The DIFC has already established this goal in Middle East, Africa and South Asia (MEASA) region and is among the top ten global financial centres in the world. In a truly Dubai style, the DIFC district was established to offer all the infrastructure to conduct business namely state-of-art buildings, office space, residential apartments, green parks, entertainments, retail outlets, art galleries and other aspects that are conducive to conduct business. This centre focuses on banking and finance businesses but is opened to a limited number of non-financial businesses as well.

One of the reasons for the success of the Emirates Airlines internationally is the geographic location of Dubai—midpoint between the East and the West—and DIFC is exploiting the same strategic geographic advantage by providing the East and the West a pathway to the emerging markets. For example, the DIFC (1) bridges the time-zone gap between London and New York, and Hong Kong and Tokyo; and (2) enables access to the MEASA region which is expanding thanks to strong economic and demographic growth.

As of 2020, more than 2,400 companies have taken advantage of this onshore financial centre to access the MEASA region. With an independent regulatory and legal system, the DIFC has made the setting up and operations of businesses relatively simple and efficient. It can be regarded as a one-stop shop for businesses as DIFC handles the registration, incorporation, licensing to leasing and employee sponsorship processes, commercial property ownership, query handling, issue resolutions, expansion assistance and client induction.

The financial activities that are offered by the DIFC are as follows:

1. Banking
2. Private Banking
3. Investment Banking
4. Brokerage
5. Capital Markets
6. Innovation Licence
7. Insurance
8. Fund Management
9. Asset Management
10. Wealth Management
11. Private Equity
12. Islamic Finance
13. Fintech

The DIFC is one example of how financial infrastructure has been developed in the region. In terms of launching financial centres, Oman can be seen as the leading country, followed by Bahrain who came on board in the 1980s and then Qatar in the 1990s. The DIFC started in the 2000s, and it was followed by Saudi Arabia. More recently, ADGM emerged (mid-2010) as an international financial centre in the free zone area of Abu Dhabi. The ADGM accommodates for both financial (banking, capital markets, wealth and asset management, virtual assets activities, securities, fintech and special purpose vehicles) and non-financial businesses (corporate, professional services, family business, tech start-ups, associations and special purpose vehicles). It is worth mentioning that ADGM is the leading fintech hub in MENA region with the setting up of the first fintech Regulatory regime and the first FinTech RegLab—which is the world's second most active fintech sandbox. In addition, it is a leading platform that regulates and facilitates the use of virtual asset. According to the FSRA, a "Virtual Asset" is defined as a digital representation of value that can be digitally traded and functions as (1) a medium of exchange; and/or (2) a unit of account; and/or (3) a store of value but does not have legal tender status in any jurisdiction. Furthermore, a "Virtual Asset" is: (a) neither issued nor guaranteed by any jurisdiction, and fulfils the above functions only by agreement within the community of users of the Virtual Asset; and (b) distinguished from Fiat Currency5 and E-money6. In simple terms, ADGM is taking the lead in cryptocurrency in the world.

Implications of the Difference in the Legal Systems

The implications for international investors are fourfold. First, conducting business in this region can be similar if the country of origin uses these types of law (combination of French, English, Egyptian and Islamic Law). Second, Saudi Arabia is different from the rest of the GCC with its unique reliance on Islamic Law. Third, if the country of origin does not have the Islamic Law element, it is not a deal breaker as there are specific areas designated to attract foreigners. Fourth, when studying these markets, it is important to differentiate between onshore and offshore financial centres.

Can History Provide the Strategic Advantage of Doing Business in the Middle East?

According to evidence, humans reached the Middle East a significant period before they reached Europe. Arab merchants were able to take advantage of the Spice and Silk Routes as they were able to reach the East before anyone else (and vice versa). The commodities traded at that time were spices, silk, porcelain, dates, textiles, slaves, gold and many others. Such geographical advantage is still being exploited, for example (1) Emirates Airline linking the entire world, (2) the DIFC acting as link between the East and the West, and (3) not to forget oil and gas.

The history of international trade shows us that capitulatory agreements reduced sovereign risk which then acted as a catalyst for bankers to finance operations. With a lower sovereign risk, the cost of capital is reduced and investments in the region became more attractive. In a similar manner, today the GCC countries have various trade agreements with the rest of the world. For example, the Australia-Gulf Cooperation Council Free Trade Agreement allows Australia and the GCC countries to interact in terms of trade and investment across a variety of goods (livestock, meat, dairy products, vegetables, sugar, wheat and other grains) and services. Australia finds the GCC market attractive as the GCC has a GDP of US$1.5 trillion (2017), GDP per capita of US$26.7 (2017), population of 56 million (2018) and student[1] number of 12.0 million (2015). These indicators translate to a total merchandise trade with Australia of AU$11.02 billion (2019). Similar agreement exists with Europe through the European Free Trade Association (EFTA) and the Agreement covers areas such as trade in goods, rules of origin, sanitary and phytosanitary measures, technical barriers to trade, trade remedies, trade in services, investment/establishment, protection of intellectual property, government procurement, competition, institutional provisions and dispute settlement. The GCC has bilateral agreements with several countries and is constantly in negotiations with new partners. The success of existing business collaborations is anecdotal evidence that the financial system has delivered the services.

The Role of Central Banks in the GCC Are Like Any Other Country Except for Islamic Banking and Possibly Fintech

Like any central bank or reserve bank, in the GCC the central bank is a financial institution that looks after the production and distribution of money and credit for the country, and it has the responsibility to formulate monetary policies and regulate other financial institutions. One unique feature of the central banks in the GCC is that they have a segment on Islamic banking—whereby they ensure that Islamic financial institutions have the environment to follow the Sharia Law (a set of religious principles which form part of the Islamic culture). As the region embraces technological innovations, we also notice a growing interest in Fintech

TABLE 8.1 Central Banks Operating in the GCC

Country	Central Bank	Abbreviation	Founded
Saudi Arabia	Saudi Arabian Monetary Authority	SAMA	1952
Kuwait	Central Bank of Kuwait	CBK	1969
UAE	Central Bank of the United Arab Emirates	CBUAE	1980
Qatar	Qatar Central Bank	QCB	1973
Bahrain	Central Bank of Bahrain	CBB	2006
Oman	Central Bank of Oman	CBO	1974

and cryptocurrencies which central banks in other countries are yet to catch up with. Table 8.1 shows the basic details about the various central banks that operate in the GCC region.

The websites that links the central banks are as follows.

(1) Saudi Arabian Monetary Authority: https://www.sama.gov.sa/en-us/pages/default.aspx
(2) Central Bank of Kuwait: https://www.cbk.gov.kw/en
(3) Central Bank of the United Arab Emirates: https://www.centralbank.ae/en
(4) Qatar Central Bank: http://www.qcb.gov.qa/English/Pages/default.aspx
(5) Central Bank of Bahrain: https://www.cbb.gov.bh/
(6) Central Bank of Oman: https://www.cbo.gov.om/

It important to explain the basic roles central banks play in the GCC region through an example. The UAE central bank promotes both monetary and financial stability whilst maintaining sustainable economic growth, and it is achieved predominantly through effective supervision, prudent reserve management, building robust financial infrastructure and meeting international standards and practices. The three overarching objectives of the central bank are to (1) maintain stability of the national currency, (2) promote and protect the stability of the financial system, and (3) manage foreign reserves. To achieve these objectives, the central bank has various functions including organising licensed financial activities, protecting customers of licensed financial institutions, credit control and maintaining the integrity of the financial infrastructure systems. Unlike most other central banks, the UAE central bank has been proactive in developing the infrastructure for digital currencies. Another distinct feature from countries outside the Middle East is an authority named "Higher Shari`ah Authority" which provides advice on the jurisprudence of Islamic financial transactions. The Higher Shari`ah Authority overlooks the rules, standards, financial instruments and general principles applicable to Sharia-compliant businesses and activities.

The financial activities governed by the central bank includes deposit taking, credit and facilities, currency exchange and money transfer services, monetary intermediating services, stored values services, electronic retail payments, digital money services, virtual banking services and arranging/marketing licensed financial activities. In addition, they oversee the activities of financial institutions in terms of foreign exchange, financial derivatives, bonds and sukuk, equities, commodities and any other financial products.

Although the central bank is responsible for the entire UAE market, there are two instances where other regulatory bodies are involved. The Dubai International Financial Centre (DIFC) is governed by the Dubai Financial Services Authority (DFSA), whilst the Abu Dhabi Global Market (ADGM) is regulated by the Financial Services Regulatory Authority (FSRA). In simple terms, the regulations in these centres are more robust when compared to an offshore centre as offshore centres are predominantly tax havens and are susceptible to money laundering. This uniqueness has been attested recently (see Kapar et al., 2020).

Types of Financial Institutions Supervised by the Central Banks in the GCC

One of the roles of a central bank in the GCC is to supervise financial institutions that market participants can safely use as they are regulated and licensed. For this section, we collected and analysed the data from the websites of central banks of the GCC to understand the financial services that are available in the region. Tables 8.2–8.5 show the various financial institutions for Bahrain, UAE, Saudi Arabia, Kuwait and Oman respectively. The official central bank website for Qatar does not provide us with the data for our analysis.

Table 8.2 shows the various types of financial institutions available in Bahrain, and from this table we can see clearly that there is a distinction between conventional and Islamic finance. Conventional finance relies on the paradigms of finance which boils down to making decisions based on risk and return while considering business ethics and sustainability. Islamic finance follows similar decision-making process with an additional dimension which is governed by the Sharia Law. For example, the Sharia principle advocates profit-sharing and loss-bearing (Mudarabah), safekeeping (Wadiah), joint venture (Musharaka), cost-plus (Murabahah), leasing (Ijara) and other aspects. As the Qur'an prohibits riba (which means increase), it created an ongoing debate around whether "interest" constitutes an "increase" within the Muslim community. Furthermore, investments in businesses that are considered as sinful (haraam) by the Qur'an are prohibited, and examples of these products are alcohol and pork. In simple terms, Islamic finance creates a "clientele effect". From Table 8.2, we can see that Islamic finance has similar characteristics to conventional finance in terms of having retail banks, wholesale banks, Islamic windows of conventional banks (a segment of conventional bank that offers Islamic finance products), Takaful companies (Islamic insurance companies) and re-Takaful companies (re-insurance companies).

In the UAE, we find 11 categories of financial institutions, namely wholesale banks, foreign banks, national/domestic banks, finance companies, exchange businesses, payment service provider, representative offices, monetary intermediaries, investment bank, investment companies and finance companies (see Table 8.3).

TABLE 8.2 Different Types of Financial Institutions in Bahrain as of July 2020

Type of Financial Institutions	Number
Conventional Finance	
Retail Banks	30
Wholesale Banks	68
Foreign Banks	16
Representative Offices	7
Insurance Companies	36
Investment Business Firm	52
Specialised Licensees	53
Islamic Finance	
Retail Banks	6
Wholesale Banks	15
Islamic Windows of Conventional Banks	14
Takaful Companies	6
Re-Takaful Companies	2
Unclassified	
Other	80
Total	**385**

TABLE 8.3 Different Types of Financial Institutions in the UAE as of July 2020

Type of Financial Institutions	Number
Wholesale Banks	11
Foreign Banks	27
National Banks	21
Finance Companies	23
Exchange Businesses	105
Payment Service Provider	1
Representative Offices	75
Monetary Intermediaries	9
Investment Bank	1
Investment Companies	22
Finance Companies	26
Total	**321**

It is important to highlight two types of institutions that flourished based on the flow of funds concept and these two categories are exchange businesses and representative offices. Exchange businesses are permitted to buy and sell foreign currencies and traveller's cheques from/to customers who are physically present in the UAE. This business thrives due to the following: (1) around 80% of the population comes from over 200 different countries, (2) the need to send money back home as remittance, (3) the geographical location of the UAE and (4) tourism industry.

Representative offices are small service facilities that are staffed by a parent bank personnel as they are a cheaper option when compared to setting subsidiaries. These offices assist clients of the parent bank in their dealings with the bank's correspondents or with information about local business practices and credit evaluation of foreign customers. For example, Bank of America, Societe General Bank, HSBC, Bank of Singapore, Credit Suisse and many other major banks from other parts of the world operate in this environment to service their domestic customers who conduct business in the UAE. It is important to highlight that most of the banking business is either retail or transaction banking—which is a consequence of the trade flow between North and South, East, and West, India and the UAE, and Africa and China.

Two aspects worth pointing out in the Saudi Arabia market is the high concentration in the insurance business and the growing fintech business (see Table 4). As part of the Saudi Vision 2030, the Crown Prince of Saudi Arabia Mohammed bin Salman is working towards diversifying the Saudi economy, and this has created several opportunities for the insurance sector. The insurance sector is (1) comprised of a lot of participants and (2) heavily regulated. Licensed insurance companies, insurance brokers, insurance agency, actuaries, loss assessors and loss adjusters, insurance claims settlement specialists and insurance advisors are regulated by SAMA. The Middle Eastern countries have invested significantly in blockchain technology and have the ideal environment to move into the next stage of this technological revolution—fintech. Saudi Arabia is a good example to illustrate how central banks are creating the right platform to host fintech companies, and Table 8.4 shows the 24 permitted fintechs registered thus far.

TABLE 8.4 Different Types of Financial Institutions in Saudi Arabia as of July 2020

Type of Financial Institutions	Number
Saudi Banks	13
Foreign Banks	18
Insurance and Reinsurance Companies	
Licensed Companies	35
Insurance Brokers	78
Insurance Agency	76
Actuaries	2
Loss Assessors and loss Adjusters	14
Insurance Claims Settlement Specialists	10
Insurance Advisors	8
Money Exchangers Group A	4
Money Exchangers Group B	61
Financial Leasing	2
Credit Bureaus	2
Permitted FinTechs	24
Payments Systems and Payment Service Providers	6
Total	**353**

TABLE 8.5 Different Types of Financial Institutions in Kuwait and Oman as of July 2020

Type of Financial Institutions	Number
Kuwaiti Banks	
Conventional	5
Islamic	5
Specialised	1
Foreign Banks	12
Finance Companies	1
Investment Companies	
Conventional	23
Islamic	30
Exchange Companies	39
E-Payment of Funds Companies	8
Total	**124**
Oman	Number
Local Banks	7
Specialised Banks	2
Islamic Banks	2
Foreign Commercial Banks	9
Leasing & Financial Institutions	6
Money Exchange Companies	16
Total	**42**

Table 8.5 shows the financial institutions for Kuwait and Oman respectively. These two countries have relatively lower number of institutions when compared to Bahrain, the UAE and Saudi Arabia. Despite the low number of financial organisations, they offer both conventional and Islamic products. Additionally, we notice the presence of specialised banks in both markets, and they refer to organisations such as housing banks or development banks.

As we can see the types of financial institutions in Kuwait and Oman are similar to those in Bahrain, the UAE and Saudi Arabia. To avoid repetition from the above discussion, we do not elaborate on them.

GCC Has the Characteristics of an Emerging Equity Market

Countries that are working towards becoming a developed market such as the United States is usually referred to as an emerging market. These countries work towards increasing market efficiency, fairness, regulatory framework, developing their stock exchanges and other characteristics. Emerging markets are attractive to investors as they tend to offer higher growth potentials, and the UAE market fits this category. The UAE has two stock exchanges, namely Abu Dhabi Securities Exchange (ADX) and the Dubai Financial Market (DFM).

The DFM is a leading establishment in Dubai, and it provides (1) a platform for various traders to trade, and (2) the entire infrastructure for the transaction to be completed. In simple terms it provides all the facilities provided by a traditional exchange in terms of clearing, settlement and depository of securities, efficiency of the market, transparency and liquidity environment. The DFM is a Sharia-compliant exchange that is regulated by the UAE Securities and Commodities Authority (SCA), and following a consolidation with NASDAQ Dubai in 2010, investors have access to more asset classes. In essence, it is a secondary market for public listed companies, local and federal bonds, mutual funds and other financial instruments.

As of 2020, the DFM covers 10 sectors with 74 stocks. The sectors and their corresponding number of stocks in brackets are follows: Banks (13), Investment and Financial Services (11), Insurance (14), Real Estate (9), Transportation (4), Industrials (2), Consumer Staples and Discretionary (7), Telecommunication (2), Services (3), Private Joint Stock Companies (1) and Nasdaq Dubai (8). Examples of parties offering domestic Sukuk are the Government of Dubai, Emaar and Damac while international markets can be represented by Indonesia, Hong Kong and others. In the government bond market, the typical players are the government of Dubai and Emirates while the players in the commercial market tend to be ENBD, Emirates Development Bank, Industrial and Commercial Bank of China Limited operating in the Dubai (DIFC) Branch and many others.

Other equity markets in the region are Muscat Securities Market (MSM) in Oman, Kuwait Stock Exchange (KSE), Bahrain Stock Exchange (BHB), Saudi Stock Exchange (Tadawul) and Qatar Stock Exchange (QSE). It is important to note that business days are from Sunday to Thursday in the Middle East and the holiday periods are different from the rest of the world. When dealing with the equity markets of the GCC, it is important to learn about the opening hours of these exchanges as they tend to be different from other developed markets.

Like the Developed Countries the GCC Is Vulnerable to Crises

Another vein in the literature provides further justification for our chapter. Several studies show how businesses react to crises periods. For example, some researchers explain that the global financial crisis was a consequence of either the deregulation process or lack of regulation or simply inadequate regulation (Acharya et al., 2011; Kawai and Prasad, 2011). Following crises periods, a new wave of regulations emerges to stimulate both developed and emerging economies as both economies are subject to international banking regulation as mandated by the Basel accord. Given the financial structures are different in these two economies, the efforts on emerging economies differ in that they are dedicated towards strengthening the banking system and widening the scope of the formal financial system. Prasad (2011) highlights the top four priorities of emerging market policymakers as (1) establishment of efficient and flexible regulatory structures, (2) reconciliation of

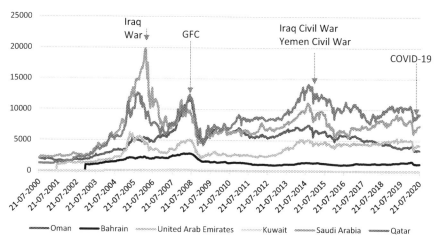

FIGURE 8.1 Financial Crises in the GCC.

the regulatory and financial development agendas, (3) financial inclusions and (4) managing financial institutions.

Figure 8.1 shows how the equity markets in Oman, Bahrain, the UAE, Kuwait, Saudi Arabia and Qatar reacted over the last 20 years. The time series show that most of the markets were affected by Iraq war, global financial crisis (GFC), Iraq civil war, Yemen civil war and more recently by the pandemic (COVID-19). It is worth mentioning that the COVID-19 period covers a brief period where oil prices reached their lowest possible point (negative price of oil). It is clear from this observation that the GCC countries are susceptible to geopolitical risk.

Conclusions

Geopolitical risk in the Middle East region has been dramatised and exploited extensively by the media, and this has created a biased opinion about doing business in the Middle East. This bias has reinforced other biases such as home bias which in turn leads to overreaction—whereby investors perceive the risk to be higher than what it is. For example, if an investor living outside the Middle Eastern region is following the news in their domestic country, they will form a biased opinion due to the overreaction of the media. It is important to understand that the media tend to dramatise events so that they can sell their product. What investors should not forget is that the business community in the Middle East region are constantly working with the leaders to create a safe environment for business. For example, see Din et al.'s (2020) piece where they portray the impact of behavioural biases on herding behaviour of investors in Islamic financial products. The Israel–United Arab Emirates normalisation agreement, officially known as the "Abraham Accords Peace Agreement: Treaty of Peace", is a classical example of how business communities and leaders are working together to create a peaceful business environment.

The fact that investors in the region are continuing to thrive means that overseas entrants have an equal opportunity to a piece of the pie (see Ferziger & Bahgat, 2020 piece discussing Israel's growing ties with the Gulf Arab States).

On another note, the purpose of our chapter is to educate investors about the financial system within the GCC region. We have shown that doing business in the Middle East from a finance point of view is similar to what is offered in the rest of the world. Conventional financing exists and can be used by any market participants. For example in the UAE, it implies that foreign investors will be able to access financial services similar to what is provided in their country and investors will have to understand the idiosyncratic banking and financial regulation of the country (some minor differences exist similar to the rest of the world). The point of difference remains Islamic finance, and we argue in this chapter that this type of finance caters for a particular group of the community and is simply a "clientele effect". Within the Middle East, there is a section of the population that prefers to use sharia-compliant financial institutions, and with this significant portion of demand, we observe a significant supply of Islamic banking.

It is worth pointing out that this part of the world has been quick to explore new opportunities like fintech. For example the UAE has created an unparalleled eco-system for the use of blockchain technology, and we have seen a number of incubators. It is a signal that the UAE is trying to be a leading financial hub in the region, and its success depends heavily on new investors. Expo 2020 Dubai is a platform created for over 190 countries to carry out business, and if we consider the numerous bilateral and multilateral trade agreements, we can see a clear signal that the Middle East is opened to international investors.

Our final conclusion is that investors should not overreact to dramatised news broadcast and must look at the risks in a more rational way.

Note

1 Education is one of Australia's major exports.

References

Acharya, V. V., Cooley, T., Richardson, M. And Walter, I. (2011). Market failures and regulatory failures: Lessons from past and present financial crises, in Kawai, M. and Prasad, E.S. (eds) *Financial Market Regulation and Reforms in Emerging Markets*, Tokyo: Asian Development Bank.

Aharony, J., Saunders, A. and Swary, I. (1988). The effects of DIDMCA on bank stockholders' returns and risk. *Journal of Banking and Finance*, 12(3), 317–331.

Akhigbe, A. and Whyte, A. M. (2001). The impact of FDICIA on bank returns and risk: evidence from the capital markets. *Journal of Banking and Finance*, 25(2), 393–417.

Amoako-Adu, B. and Smith, B. F. (1995). The wealth effects of deregulation of Canadian financial institutions. *Journal of Banking and Finance*, 19(7), 1211–1236.

Ardalan, K. (2019). Equity home bias: a review essay. *Journal of Economic Surveys*, 33(3), 949–967.

Benczur, P., Cannas, G., Cariboni, J., Di Girolamo, F., Maccaferri, S. and Giudici, M. P. (2017). Evaluating the effectiveness of the new EU bank regulatory framework: A farewell to bail-out? *Journal of Financial Stability*, 33, 207–223.

Bittlingmayer, G. (1992). Stock returns, real activity, and the trust question. *The Journal of Finance*, 47(5), 1701–1730.

Din, S. M. U., Mehmood, S. K., Arfan Shahzad, I. A., Davidyants, A., & Abu-Rumman, A. (2020). The impact of behavioral biases on herding behavior of investors in Islamic financial products. *Frontiers in Psychology*, 11, 1–10.

Eckbo, B. (1983). Horizontal mergers, collusion, and stockholder wealth. *Journal of Financial Economics*, 11(1), 241–273.

Eckbo, B. (1985). Mergers and the market concentration doctrine: Evidence from the capital market. *Journal of Business*, 58(3), 325–349.

Eckbo, B. (1992). Mergers and the value of antitrust deterrence. *The Journal of Finance*, 47(3), 1005–1029.

Eckbo, B. and Wier, P. (1985). Antimerger policy under the Hart-Scott-Rodino Act: a reexamination of the market power hypothesis. *Journal of Law and Economics*, 28(1), 119–149.

Ellert, J. (1976). Mergers, antitrust law enforcement and stockholder returns. *The Journal of Finance*, 31(2), 715–732.

Ferziger, J. H., & Bahgat, G. (2020). Israel's Growing Ties with the Gulf Arab States. *Atlantic Council*.

Fu, X. M., and Heffernan, S. (2009). The effects of reform on China's bank structure and performance. *Journal of Banking and Finance*, 33(1), 39–52.

Gan, C., Zhang, Y., Li, Z. and Cohen, D. A. (2014). The evolution of China's banking system: bank loan announcements 1996–2009. *Accounting and Finance*, 54(1), 165–188.

Goddard, J., Molyneux, P. and Zhou, T. (2012). Bank mergers and acquisitions in emerging markets: evidence from Asia and Latin America. *The European Journal of Finance*, 18(5), 419–438.

Graham, J. R., Harvey, C. R. and Huang, H. (2009). Investor competence, trading frequency, and home bias. *Management Science*, 55(7), 1094–1266.

Kapar, B., Olmo, J., & Ghalayini, R. (2020). Financial integration in the United Arab Emirates Stock Markets. *Finance Research Letters*, 33, 101219.

Kawai, M. and Prasad, E.S. (2011) Introduction, in Kawai, M. and Prasad, E.S. (eds) *Financial market regulation and reforms in emerging markets*, Tokyo: Asian Development Bank.

Lin, X. and Zhang, Y. (2009). Bank ownership reform and bank performance in China. *Journal of Banking and Finance*, 33(1), 20–29.

Madura, J. (2020). *Financial markets & institutions*, Boston, USA: Cengage Learning.

Musthaq, F. (2020). Development finance or financial accumulation for asset managers? The perils of the global shadow banking system in developing countries. *New Political Economy*, 26(4), 1–20.

Pham, N. A. H., Ramiah, V., Moosa, I. and Nguyen, H. (2017). The effects of regulatory announcements on risk and return: The Vietnamese experience, *Pacific Accounting Review*, 29 (2), 152–170.

Prasad, E. S. (2011). Financial sector regulation and reforms in emerging markets: An overview, in Kawai, M. and Prasad, E.S. (eds) *Financial Market Regulation and Reforms in Emerging Markets*, Tokyo: Asian Development Bank.

Ramiah, V., Pham, H. N. A., Moosa, I. and Moyan, L. (2018). The wealth effects and diamond risk structure of financial regulation. *Applied Economics*, 50(16), 1852–1865.

Slovin, M., Sushka, M. and Hudson, C. (1991). Deregulation, contestability, and airline acquisitions. *Journal of Financial Economics*, 30(2), 231–251.

Spiegel, M. M. and Yamori, N. (2003). The impact of Japan's financial stabilization laws on bank equity values. *Journal of the Japanese and International Economies*, *17*(3), 263–282.

Sundaram, S., Rangan, N. and Davidson, W. N. (1992). The market valuation effects of the Financial Institutions Reform, Recovery and Enforcement Act of 1989. *Journal of Banking and Finance*, *16*(6), 1097–1122.

9
ACCOUNTING AND TAXATION SYSTEMS IN THE MIDDLE EAST

Peter Rampling and Albert Wijeweera

Introduction

This chapter examines and critiques the differences and similarities in accounting and taxation practices in the Middle East and North Africa (MENA) region when compared to international accounting and taxation standards. An overview of the region's dominant accounting and taxation systems will first be provided followed by an exploration of the challenges foreign investors and multinational companies (MNCs) may experience in adapting to these systems. The religious and cultural contexts of accounting and taxation systems in the MENA region are a pervasive theme throughout this chapter and reflect the vital role these play in determining how modern accounting and taxation standards both derive and manifest in these economies.

The accounting and taxation systems of a country are influenced by unique institutional, historical, economic, and sociocultural factors. Hence, institutions cannot be assumed to be homogenous between countries based solely on the proximity of their geographic locations. If all MENA nations were united by common taxation and accounting systems, business dealings in the region would be far less formidable. Unfortunately for foreign investors, this is not the case. In fact, the differences in the accounting and taxation systems between MENA countries can serve to be as much of a barrier for inexperienced investors as the barriers which exist between local MENA and international accounting standards.

There exists an interdependent relationship between tax accounting as a social practice and the factors that are inherent in its operating environment (Alsharari, 2019). These factors may include general levels of national inflation and the administration of taxation; hence, taxation systems can also influence accounting practices (King, 2008; Henrekson et al., 2010). In addition, taxation is vital as a source of government revenue, and the amount of tax collected will vary between nations, depending on economic, demographic, institutional, and political structures; as a result, differences among taxation systems are time- and jurisdiction-dependent (Daniel et al., 2010). Therefore, the chapter first reviews taxation systems in the Middle East and then expands the analysis to the MENA region.

Taxation

The Middle East and MENA Countries

The definition of the Middle East is geographically arbitrary and does not constitute precise borders. Rather, it is a definition of a cultural area. Several definitions have been used in the past and continue to be used today; however, for this chapter, we will proceed with the group classification of MENA (the Middle East and North Africa) countries by the International Monetary Fund (IMF), which divides the Middle East countries into two main groups of non-resource countries (oil importers) and resource-rich countries (oil exporters) (see Table 9.1). Within these classifications, there are two subgroups under non-resource countries and three subgroups under Resource-rich countries. Out of six Maghreb countries, four belong to non-resource countries and the other two belong to the resource-rich group. The GCC countries refer to the six countries that comprise the Gulf Cooperation Council, while OME (Other Middle Eastern) countries are Iran, Iraq, and Yemen. While countries placed within these classifications still differ in their economic, political, and taxation systems, there are commonalities within these countries that allow for certain generalizations to be made that are useful for our purposes.

We consider the differences in accounting and taxation practices between the MENA nations and internationally and between the five sub-classifications of countries within the MENA region outlined above. According to the IMF report, MENA comprises 21 countries, namely, Algeria, Bahrain, Djibouti, Egypt, Iran, Iraq, Jordan, Kuwait, Lebanon, Libya, Mauritania, Morocco, Oman, Qatar, Saudi Arabia, Somalia, Sudan, Syria, Tunisia, the United Arab Emirates, and Yemen. As shown in Table 9.1, some MENA countries are excluded from this chapter.

TABLE 9.1 The Middle Eastern and North African Countries

Non-resource countries		Resource-rich countries		
Maghreb	Mashreq	Maghreb	GCC	OME
Mauritania	Egypt	Algeria	Bahrain	Iran
Morocco	Lebanon	Libya	Kuwait	Iraq
Tunisia	Jordan		Oman	Yemen
	Syria		Qatar	
			Saudi Arabia	
			UAE	

Source: International Monetary Fund (2015).

It is important to reiterate that our basic premise within this chapter and indeed this book is that the shared Islamic context of the Middle East is sufficient to differentiate these countries from the rest of the world. Consequently, the following sections will outline practices that must be considered within an Islamic context to be fully appreciated.

History of Taxes and Types of Taxation

Taxation has a very long history. For thousands of years, people have been paying various forms of tax to authorities. Interesting facts about the history of taxation are provided in "A Brief History of Taxation" by the D'Amore School of Business. According to the description, the first record of organized taxation comes from Egypt around 3000 BC and is mentioned in numerous historical sources, including the Bible. It also explains the tax collection practices of the Egyptian kingdom, citing an example of the pharaoh sending commissioners to take one-fifth of all grain harvests as a tax. Taxes in Islam are only collected to raise the amount necessary to cover the deficit in the obligatory expenditure of the Bait-ul-Mal, or the financial institution responsible for the administration of taxes in Islamic states. When imposing taxation, no consideration is given to the notion of preventing the increase of wealth or preventing richness or increasing the revenues of the Bait-ul-Mal. If the government's objective is to redistribute income, it should set taxes according to the ability-to-pay principle. The tax policies in Islamic countries are complex due to the concept of Zakat (i.e., a religious duty for Muslims to give away a certain percentage of yearly earnings that are over and above what is required to provide the essential needs for charitable causes). Zakat is one of the five pillars of Islam and is closely connected to the community development tax in the Western economies. As per Ahmed et al. (2014), all taxes imposed by governments in Islamic countries need to reflect the fact of Islamic ruling for it. Whether taxes should be imposed should be answered in the light of Sharia principles.

Taxation is regarded as an essential and multifaceted role of governments. It provides the funding for large-scale developments such as public educational institutions, health care systems, and public transport systems that ultimately benefit the wellbeing of citizens (Henrekson et al., 2010). Without tax collection, governments are unable to finance essential services for their populations. This is particularly important in developing nations where governments need to mobilize and direct a society's savings towards the most critical investment projects, such as social and economic infrastructure investments. Additionally, taxation can serve as an effective and necessary means of income redistribution through the funding of social welfare programs, particularly in countries with a significant disparity in wealth between wealthy and disadvantaged populations. On the other hand, taxes can be used as an incentive to discourage undesirable activities such as gambling, alcohol consumption, and tobacco smoking.

While the underlying aims of taxation systems are similar, the rates and forms of tax imposts vary between countries. Understanding the implications of taxation has become critical to corporate entities in their investment decision-making. Lower taxes help corporations to generate higher revenues or set lower prices (Daniel et al., 2010; Henrekson et al., 2010). Macroeconomic variables such as interest rates, taxes, and inflation are often linked in any economy. For instance, a decrease in interest rates or tax will often encourage more people to borrow more money (King, 2008), resulting in consumers having an increased amount of money to spend, thus causing growth in the economy and a rise in inflation (Bowler et al., 2017). An elevated or rising inflation rate in a country will often force the government, in turn, to increase the level of tax on goods and services because of their greater price to stabilize consumption and aggregate expenditure (Azam et al., 2010; Henrekson et al., 2010). On the other hand, higher inflation could benefit government coffers, particularly in income tax, because some taxpayers will move to higher tax brackets due to inflation and not a rise in the real income. In other words, a rising inflation rate could produce the same consequences that a higher tax rate does to individuals and investors.

The forms of taxation may be classified in several different ways. However, the most intuitive is the distinction that is made between direct and indirect taxation. Direct taxation is imposed upon a person, property, or institution responsible for paying the tax. In contrast, an indirect tax is imposed upon the manufacture or the sale of goods and services. In some instances, such as corporate profits tax, the tax may be shifted forward by increased costs of products or backward by reducing input costs such as the wages paid to workers.

Consequently, it is not always clear whether a tax should be categorized as direct or indirect. Therefore, this chapter adopts a classification first proposed by (Musgrave 1987) classifying direct and indirect taxes. These definitions are important in understanding the current taxation systems in place in the MENA region and being informed and prepared for changes in taxation practices in the future.

An Overview of the Current Taxes in the Middle East

In ideal terms, a good taxation system should be able to allow governments to raise necessary revenue without discouraging or inhibiting economic activity. The Middle East region has arguably the least demanding taxation system globally, consistently ranking well below the world average (PwC and World Bank, 2017, also see Table 9.2). Several countries within the GCC, such as the United Arab Emirates and Qatar, have also been recognized previously as being world leaders in the ease of paying taxes (PwC, 2017).

TABLE 9.2 The Middle East vs Global Comparison for Tax Rates and Compliance

	Total Tax Rate (%)	Compliance Time	Average Number of Payments
Middle East	24.2	157 hours	17.1 payments
Global	40.6	251 hours	25 payments

Source: PwC Paying Taxes 2017 Analysis.

The corporate tax rates vary significantly among Middle Eastern countries. For example, in Saudi Arabia, the standard corporate income tax rate is 20%. However, as Ahmed (2021) states, the tax rate for taxpayers engaged in the production of oil and hydrocarbons in Saudi Arabia is determined based on the company's capital investment. As far as the UAE is concerned, there is no legal concept of corporate income rate in the country (Ahmed, 2021), but oil and gas companies are taxed. The corporate tax rate in both Kuwait and Oman is 15%, and interestingly, in Kuwait, it does not matter whether the company is in Kuwait if the company is doing business there. Compared to the above three countries with corporate tax rates, Qatar has the lowest corporate tax rate of 10%. There are certain recent developments with strong tax implications in the GCC countries. Several countries, including Oman, UAE, and Qatar, have removed restrictions on foreign ownership of local companies. For instance, in 2020, Oman introduced up to 100% foreign ownership, while the UAE relaxed restrictions and allowed foreign investors to own up to 49% of the shares in a UAE mainland-registered company.

Historically, the Middle East region has imposed low taxation rates due to the presence of sufficient government revenue from petrochemical industries. In particular, the GCC countries have lower government revenues from taxation and higher government revenues from hydrocarbon operations than their non-oil-producing counterparts. This has mainly been in response to GCC governments prioritizing policies that favor foreign direct investment and promoting expatriate labor to support rapid growth and broaden economic activity over the past several decades (IMF, 2016). These policies allowed the GCC nations to maintain some of the lowest rates of taxation globally. Oil revenues accounted for between 50 and 90% of total government revenues between 2012 and 2015 across the GCC countries. A comparative group of resource-rich countries not in the GCC had an average of only 24% of government revenue from oil production. During the same 2012–2015 period, only 1.7% of GDP was generated in non-oil taxation revenue. At present, the non-oil sources of government revenue are composed primarily of customs duties, profit tax on foreign companies, withholding tax, Zakat, value-added tax (VAT), and revenue from fines and government fees. There are currently no income taxes on GCC nationals or expatriates in the GCC except for Qatar and Saudi Arabia, which have limited income taxes on expatriates who carry out business or professional activities.

Nonetheless, the volatility in demand for petroleum products has brought about a recent shift in the overall policy direction of the GCC nations. The rapid and sustained decline in oil prices since 2015 has led to a decline in economic activity and led to a fiscal deficit projected to widen above 5% of GDP in 2021 (IMF, 2016). The COVID-19 pandemic further exacerbated the situation. To illustrate, on 20 April 2020, the US oil benchmark West Texas Intermediate (WTI) fell from $17.85 at the start of the trading day to negative $37.63 on close on 20 April 2020, creating history with a negative price for oil. However, oil-exporting countries might ease their cautious approach as they have seen a steady increase in the oil price in recent months. It is interesting to note that oil price has increased by around 50% in 2021.

To further illustrate, Brent crude futures rose to $77.78 a barrel on 5 July 2021, trading around their highest since October 2018, while West Texas Intermediate rose to $76.92 a barrel, its highest since November 2014. Although the oil price recovered to the pre-pandemic level within one year of hitting rock bottom level, oil-producing countries are still following a cautious approach in taxation and fiscal policies.

Considering the expectation that oil prices may remain low and the acceptance of governments' over-reliance on oil revenue, the GCC countries initiated fiscal reforms to diversify budgetary revenues. Most notably, the GCC countries decided to impose a VAT system at a flat rate of 5% on the supply of goods and services. All countries of the GCC have now legislated and imposed the VAT, the most recent being Oman in April 2021. Saudi Arabia has increased the VAT rate to 15% from July 2020. The initiation of a VAT system in the GCC is likely the beginning of a gradual transition into increased taxation reforms and fiscal consolidation that will be made to ensure adequate government revenue to achieve long-term strategic objectives. Several additional reforms to increase non-oil revenue have been proposed, which may impact the decision-making of foreign investors and MNCs who wish to enter the GCC. These include the expansion of business profits tax, taxation on remittances, and expatriate income tax (IMF, 2016). Therefore, it is crucial to consider the possibility of the introduction of these taxes when initiating business dealings in the GCC. While increased tax revenue can increase government earnings if collected efficiently, there is a global trend toward lower corporate taxation to prevent profit shifting and cross-border adjustments for multinational corporations (MNC) (Riskjell, 2014). However, having low tax rates has served the hydrocarbon-focused MENA region well historically, and tax avoidance isn't as significant an issue in the MENA region as in the United States and China. The lower corporation taxes function as incentives for MNCs to pay taxes within the region of operation rather than engaging in illicit financial practices such as tax evasion and profit shifting.

Poudineh et al. (2018) point out that as the world pushes ahead with the deployment of renewable energy, resource-rich MENA economies are lagging. This observation is common to resource-rich MENA countries, including GCC, OME, and the Maghreb. For the region to catch up, new policies are required to remove barriers of entry to the industry and create investment incentives. In addition, sensible tax policy should provide incentives for renewables deployment through a partial renewable subsidy program and partial fossil fuel price reform in a way that balances the fiscal pressure on the government against political acceptability. As the authors state, resource-rich countries are behind advanced economies in alternative energy electricity sector reforms. However, this might give them a last-mover advantage in the sense that they can tap into years of international experience with a properly structured tax system to avoid design mistakes and create a sustainable solution that is compatible with renewables deployment and their own context.

Resource-rich Maghreb countries face several issues in crafting a tax system that could help the growth and concurrently lessen income inequality and income distribution. First, many of these countries do not have an established tax collection system, and the relevant institutions do not exist. For example, tax revenues comprise a very small fraction of government revenues; hence powerful institutions dedicated to collecting taxes do not exist. Second, taxation is a politically sensitive issue because introducing new taxes completely undermines a government's source of legitimacy and public support, which are obtained through the distribution of resource rents. Therefore, under the current conditions, it would be difficult to formulate a tax policy based on hydrocarbon use (Poudineh et al., 2018). Third, as far as the non-resource Maghreb countries are concerned, they have limited natural resources to develop institutions and support the discovery of those natural resources. Therefore, these countries should develop and efficiently extract natural resources, make concerted efforts to transform underground wealth to above-ground assets, and support the development of other sectors instead of displacing them.

Taxation policies in the MENA North African nations have recently begun to focus more on economic development than the resource base. As a result, the tax revenue to GDP ratio significantly varies among MENA countries. For instance, while the ratio is about 12% for Mashreq countries, it is a meager 1% for some MENA countries such as Bahrain. The impact of these differences could be better understood if taxes are analyzed against revenue, equity, and efficiency measures. The study of tax policy in the MENA region often revolves around revenues from natural resources and the need to diversify them. Yet, the region is one of the most diverse in the world, politically, economically, and geographically. Endowments of natural resources vary significantly across countries; political systems include quasi-democracies, monarchies, and kingdoms; many countries are experiencing a difficult period of socio-political transformations mainly due to the Arab Spring. Many attribute the Arab Spring to a strong perception of inequities in how governments have conducted economic policy, particularly in taxation. The number of fragile states has increased in the past decade due to unsuccessful political reforms following revolutions and wars. As IMF (2015) states, there are significant differences across MENA economies in terms of size, the colonial inheritance of legal system, openness, migration, and sensitivity of countries' main tax bases to the forces of globalization.

Based on the above analysis, the existing tax benefits enjoyed by the foreign companies operating in the Middle Eastern countries will not last long. As Ahmed (2021) points out, the governments of the Middle Eastern countries, including the energy-driven Gulf Cooperation Council (GCC) countries, are currently facing a double-whammy in oil price shocks and the COVID-19 pandemic which is adversely impacting economic growth. As a result, these governments are compelled to find ways to increase government revenue with minimum damage to the cozy lifestyle enjoyed by their citizens for many decades. Among those new measures, Ahmed (2021) highlights a series of noteworthy new regulations such as the implementation of the Value Added Taxes (VAT) by GCC countries, the introduction of a new Real Estate Transaction Tax (RETT) in the Kingdom of

Saudi Arabia, Economic Substance rules in the United Arab Emirates and Bahrain, personal income tax announcement in Oman, and new Transfer Pricing regulations in Qatar. As these changes are occurring at an unprecedented speed, it is vital for foreign investors and companies operating in the Middle East to devise strategies to respond quickly to any significant changes in tax policies that affect their business.

Challenges for Foreign Investors and MNCs

Over the last few decades, many countries have witnessed enormous growth in their national income, mainly thanks to foreign direct investment inflows by MNCs. In general, MNCs secure funds from the source country, but those who come to MENA countries realized that they could easily borrow funds for their investment from the host nation. However, MNCs that invested in MENA countries had to learn to deal with Islamic financial institutions (IFIs), which are considerably different from the Western financial system. Aribi and Arun (2015) outline that the IFIs are a fast-growing sector of the global finance industry and posing challenges to the ways that existing financial institutions are perceived and experienced around the world. The IFIs follow a zero-interest approach based on equity and risk-sharing and have become a trillion US dollar industry (Sheng and Singh, 2012). These institutions have a unique ethical identity that gives equal importance to social goals and profit and challenges the conventional bias towards debt instruments in the financial sector. The savings and investments of IFIs are settled by real sector economic activities, which focus on long-term goals rather than short-term risk-taking decisions that are popular in the financial sector. The fundamental question is how an institution built on Islamic values continues in a society where economists focus exclusively on economics' mechanics where most decisions are based on maximizing self-interest (Rice, 1999). However, over the years, changes in the arguments of leading economists have appeared over the incessant distributional concerns of international development, encouraged by market turbulence. For instance, in a recent essay on "markets and morality" Bhagwati (2011) has argued that values will determine the player's behavior in the marketplace but further asserts that good policies have "to walk on both legs, positive and normative, and both have to be sound and strong" (p.163).

Mellahi et al. (2011) assert that despite the excellent market potential for MNEs in the region, foreign direct investment (FDI) barriers still exist in most countries. While there has been an increasing trend of FDI inflows to the region compared to other developing and emerging regions of the world, the Middle East emerges as one of the most underperforming regions (Apaydin, 2009). The cluster of Gulf Cooperation Countries (i.e., the UAE, Kuwait, Bahrain, Oman, Qatar, and Saudi Arabia) has attracted only a modest proportion of total world FDI inflows in the early 2000s (Hussein, 2009), but according to the United Nations World Investment Report, total FDI inflows to GCC countries increased to approximately $27.7 billion in 2020. That is a whopping 12% increase considering that the world business was in turmoil and total world FDI inflows contracted by about 35% in 2020.

Most of the FDI inflows to the region have been invested in countries such as Saudi Arabia, the UAE, and Oman that have removed entry barriers and created a climate conducive to foreign investment. To a certain extent, these countries have been able to liberalize their FDI regulations and remove most of the FDI-related entry barriers. The market size also plays an important role in the pattern of FDI inflows. Countries with a larger market size appear to attract more FDI inflows.

Accounting

Accounting Systems in Middle Eastern Countries

Financial management and accounting are not novel concepts for some Middle Eastern countries. On the contrary, they have been used to these concepts for centuries. Karatas (2016) is a good source for historical facts related to Iran and Persian countries on the topic. For instance, in the 10th century, the Great Seljuk Empire began transitioning from nomadic life to settled life. As a result, they made progressive applications in the fields of politics, economics, and finance with the influence of the Persian culture. According to Karatas (2016), two ancient books remained related to financial and accounting practices at that time. The first is the *Siyasetname*, which was written between the years of 1077–1078 AD and contains information about the state's financial management and accounting culture. The second is the *Kabusname*, which was written in 1082 AD which provides information about the private sector's trade and accounting culture. Karatas (2016) evaluates these two books written in the 11th century: a time of stagnation for accounting science in Europe. It shows how important are these two books to accounting literature by demonstrating that the Great Seljuk Empire had applications of the private sector and state accounting far beyond its era. Furthermore, the two books demonstrate that Middle East countries were aware of the most important features of modern accounting practices such as ethical rules, prudence, calculation of profit and profitability, and the management of receivables and debts in the state financial management.

As stated above, accounting is not new to Islamic nations. Trokic (2015) asserts that with the emergence and subsequent development of Islamic economics, including the Islamic financial system and its institutions, there became a need for Islamic accounting. The concept of an Islamic accounting system and processes is not a new one by any means as there is significant historical evidence to show the use of Islamic accounting practices as early as the time of the second Caliph, Umar, in the Islamic State. Some suggest that the Holy Qur'an provides the basis for accounting, with significant Ayahs (verses) demanding that accounting practices be developed and implemented in society. Some scholars even argue that Islamic accounting influenced the development of double-entry accounting in Italy, home of the father of modern accounting (Trokic, 2015).

The MENA countries, in general, tend to follow international accounting practices when they deal with foreign entities. However, Islamic rules are prevalent in domestic affairs. Interested readers may refer to Alsharari (2020) that explains certain Islamic terms and facts that are extremely useful for understanding domestic accounting practices in the Middle East. Like Western countries, Islamic countries prepare and publish accounting statements on a periodic basis. Islamic accounting is done over hawl, an Islamic calendar year that is 354 days long. When it comes to recording economic activity in accounting: cash basis and accrual basis, Islamic law must determine which basis is *halal*, or lawful. When a business has prepared its financial statements at the end of the hawl, it must declare its Islamic taxable obligations that need to be discharged. These taxes will be the responsibility of the owners of the business. Alsharari (2020) further suggests that the taxable amount is to be declared in the statement and charged to the business owners. One interesting fact is that the Islamic economic calculations allow a certain amount of the total profit to be allocated for sustaining the business. However, if there are further profits above this sustainability level, taxes must be paid. According to Alsharari (2020), if a business has many owners and paying Zakat (yearly payment made under Islamic law for charitable and religious purposes) puts one or more owners in a difficult situation, such a context must be declared, and evidence presented. This could be an issue for small- and medium-scale businesses rather than well-organized multinational companies. Another form of tax is the *Khumus*, which is a religious obligation of any Muslims to pay one-fifth of their acquired wealth from certain sources toward specified causes. The recording of these two kinds of Islamic taxes—Zakat and Khumus—in financial statements is done at the end of hawl when the business's total profit is known. Non-Muslim businesses might have to pay *jizya*, a special payment for the protection or for being exempt from certain duties once profits are declared. It is important to note that, as Aghimien (2016) states, while similarities exist in taxation mainly due to the use of International Financial Reporting Standards (IFRS), there are still distinct differences from religious and other contexts.

Challenges Facing Governments and MNCs

If the accounting systems and practices were identical, there would be no problem for international investors in understanding the published financial statements of MENA countries. However, casual observation suggests a notable difference in the accounting systems among the MENA countries. The differences are less conspicuous for the GCC countries that share somewhat similar economic development than other MENA countries. Nevertheless, foreign investors must follow a cautious approach concerning the accounting standard even among the GCC countries. As Abdallah (2008) states, the development of accounting should match the high rates of economic and social growth and provide them with relevant, timely, and reliable information to help entrepreneurs, investors, and MNCs make the right decisions. Given the lack of accounting comparability and harmonization between accounting systems of Gulf countries, it is not surprising that the investing and financing decisions tend to be risky Abdallah (2008).

The lack of consistency among the accounting systems in MENA countries and its consequences are clearly stipulated in IMF (2015) report. As the report reveals, business registration thresholds are low in some countries relative to international norms (e.g., Algeria, Egypt, Morocco, and Tunisia), and their definition is problematic. An excellent example is how value-added taxes are computed. Although defined in terms of turnover, they vary according to activity and the legal form of the business. The argument frequently justifying the use of multiple thresholds is that some businesses add a higher value than others (e.g., services), and therefore should be subject to the VAT at lower turnover levels. There are major flaws with this argument. First, the use of a registration threshold is constrained by the capacity and resources of the tax administration. Second, the accounting capabilities of taxpayers who must meet minimum filing requirements could be limited by the availability and use of accounting standards and familiarity of enterprises with them.

Further, Mousa and Desoky (2014) show how some MENA countries such as Bahrain have moved with the global acceptance of IFRS. On practical-level implications, the results of this study should be of interest to those who engage in improving accounting standards in GCC as well as for the investors planning business activities in GCC. They should also be of interest to practitioners in accounting standard-setting and regulation, as well as academic researchers and educators and the investment community at large. In a related study, Abushamsieh et al. (2014) compare the public financial information disclosed by a group of Middle East Arab countries. These countries belong to a single geographic area and have Arabic as their official language and Islam as their religion; therefore, they can be assumed to share certain socio-cultural characteristics. They have analyzed MENA countries of two distinct groups in terms of their economic development: on the one hand, the GCC countries, the richest in the zone; and on the other, the less developed countries, such as Egypt, Jordan, and Palestine. According to the IPSAS 1 and 2 requirements, Abushamsieh et al. (2014) conclude that despite the important administrative reforms made regarding financial laws, there is still a low level of development in the financial information presented for all the countries studied.

Middle Eastern governments have found themselves with few alternatives but to open their doors to MNEs, thus increasing the number of MNEs operating in their economies. Given the recent increase in the number of MNEs in the Middle East countries, the region has more challenges than before (see Mellahi et al., 2002; 2011). Other researchers (Godley and Shechter, 2008) highlight many pertinent issues regarding MNEs and accounting practices in the Middle East region. Among the questions raised are: Do MNEs apply home country practices? Do they adapt their practices to host countries? How do MNEs enter the region? What are the most appropriate modes of entering the Middle Eastern markets? Further, they discuss how, why, and under which institutional arrangements contribute to MNEs' strategic capabilities that form a basis for competitive advantage in the host country market.

As discussed earlier in this book chapter, substantial reforms in economic and political fronts have been underway in most Middle Eastern countries that may affect MNEs operating or considering entering the region. In addition, foreign investors should understand that many aspects of doing business in the Middle East, including accounting, fall under the jurisdiction of the law of Islam. As Lewis (2001) points out, accounting is central to Islam since accountability to God is paramount to a Muslim's faith. Therefore, multinational companies that understand these cultural and religious nuances could still generate profitable growth in the MENA countries if they adapt their business practices to the existing country's existing accounting and taxation policies and the source country.

Conclusion

We have reviewed the main differences and similarities in taxation and accounting practices in the MENA region compared with the accounting and taxation systems of the rest of the world. We draw several important conclusions based on the review. Firstly, we noted that while similarities exist in taxation mainly due to the use of International Financial Reporting Standards (IFRS), there are still distinct differences from religious and other contexts. As a result, we identified that foreign investors need to approach accounting and taxation practices in the MENA region with care. In particular, the religious and cultural contexts of accounting and taxation systems in the MENA region need to be evaluated as a part of the due diligence process of any significant investment decision. As we have seen, the MENA countries generally tend to follow international accounting practices when dealing with foreign entities. However, Islamic rules are prevalent in domestic affairs. Therefore, good knowledge of specific Islamic terms and facts is beneficial for understanding domestic accounting practices in the Middle East.

Furthermore, MNCs that invested in MENA countries had to learn to deal with Islamic Financial Institutions (IFIs), which are considerably different from the Western financial system. We have discussed a few of the most important concepts, such as Zakat, Khumus, jizya, and their implications on accounting and taxation to multinational companies operating in the MENA countries. While accounting and taxation systems are relatively similar among MENA countries, noticeable variances exist between the two subgroups of resource-rich and non-resource MENA countries.

Secondly, there has been a noticeable shift in the taxation and accounting policies by the MENA countries to attract foreign investments due to the unprecedented volatility in the oil price in the world market. The severity of the volatility is illustrated by the fact that the US oil benchmark West Texas Intermediate (WTI) reported a negative price on 20 April 2020, creating history with a negative price for oil before rising to $77 a barrel on 5 July 2021, its highest in seven years. Although the oil price recovered to the pre-pandemic level within one year of hitting rock bottom level, oil-producing MENA countries might not return to historical low corporate tax policies that they were well known for many decades.

Thirdly, the study suggests that certain MENA countries, particularly the GCC countries, are still favored by multinational companies due to the ease of doing business resulting from low corporate tax rates and less demanding accounting rules.

It is not surprising that countries within the GCC, such as the United Arab Emirates and Qatar, have been recognized as being world leaders in the ease of paying taxes. Empirical evidence suggests that these countries still have a comparative advantage over other groups of countries. This is manifested by the way foreign investment inflows have performed post-COVID-19 era. As we have noted previously, total FDI inflows to GCC countries had increased by double digits in 2020 when the rest of the world experienced a one-third contraction in FDI inflows to their economies. However, it is unwise to anticipate that the foreign companies operating in the Middle Eastern countries' existing tax benefits will last long. As the governments of the MENA region are compelled to find ways to increase government revenue with minimum damage to welfare benefits enjoyed by their citizens, they might expand their tax base by further incorporating multinational companies and their affiliates. More research is necessary to understand the implications of these changes to the multinational corporate entities operating in the MENA countries.

Useful Websites

https://www2.deloitte.com/xe/en/pages/tax/articles/taxation-in-the-gulf.html
https://www.internationaltaxreview.com/jurisdictions/middle-east
https://www.indexmundi.com/facts/indicators/IC.TAX.TOTL.CP.ZS/map/middle-east
https://www.pwc.com/m1/en/services/assurance/financial-accounting.html
https://middleeast-business.com/international-financial-reporting-standards-ifrss-in-arabic/
https://santandertrade.com/en/portal/establish-overseas/united-arab-emirates/tax-system
https://data.worldbank.org/region/middle-east-and-north-africa
https://hbr.org/2017/04/how-multinationals-can-grow-in-the-middle-east-and-africa
https://middleeast-business.com/international-financial-reporting-standards-ifrss-in-arabic/
https://onlinebusiness.northeastern.edu/blog/a-brief-history-of-taxation/
https://santandertrade.com/en/portal/establish-overseas/united-arab-emirates/tax-system
https://www.cia.gov/library/publications/the-world-factbook/geos/print_ku.html
https://www.ey.com/Publication/vwLUAssets/ey-resilience-in-a-time-of-volatility/$FILE/ey-resilience-in-a-time-of-volatility.pdf
https://www.imf.org/external/pubs/ft/wp/2015/wp1598.pdf
https://www.indexmundi.com/facts/indicators/IC.TAX.TOTL.CP.ZS/map/middle-east
https://www.internationaltaxreview.com/jurisdictions/middle-east
https://www.pwc.com/m1/en/services/assurance/financial-accounting.html
https://www2.deloitte.com/xe/en/pages/tax/articles/taxation-in-the-gulf.html

References

Abdallah, W. M. (2008). Accounting standards and practices of the gulf countries. In *Accounting, finance, and taxation in the gulf countries* (pp. 75–93). Palgrave Macmillan.

Abushamsieh, K., López-Hernández, A. M., & Ortiz-Rodríguez, D. (2014). The development of public accounting transparency in selected Arab countries. *International Review of Administrative Sciences*, 80(2) (pp. 421–442).

Aghimien, P. A. (2016). Development of accounting standards in selected Middle Eastern countries in comparison to the United States of America. *Review of International Business and Strategy*.

Ahmed, E. R., Islam, A., & Yahya, S. (2014). Comparative study of Zakat and taxation system for Muslims and Non-Muslims in Malaysia. *Advances in Environmental Biology*, 8(9) (pp. 549–554).

Ahmed, N. (2021). Middle East tax handbook embrace change. Lead with confidence. www2.deloitte.com/content/dam/Deloitte/xe/Documents/tax/me_tax-handbook-2021.pdf

Alsharari, Muhammad. (2020). Towards Islamic Accounting: A Revolutionizing Independence.

Alsharari, N. M. (2019). A comparative analysis of taxation and revenue trends in the Middle East and North Africa (MENA) Region. *Pacific Accounting Review*, 31(4) pp. 646–671.

Apaydin, M. (2009). Analyzing FDI trends in emerging markets: Turkey vs CSEE and the Middle East. *International Journal of Emerging Markets*, 4(1) pp. 72–97.

Azam, M., Khan, H., Hunjra, A. I., Ahmad, H. M., Chani, D., & Irfan, M. (2010). Institutional, macro economic policy factors and foreign direct investment: South Asian countries case. *African Journal of Business Management*, 5, (pp. 4306–4313).

Bhagwati, J. (2011). Markets and morality. *American Economic Review*, 101(3), (pp. 162–65).

Bowler, N. E., Clayton, A. M., Jardak, M., Lee, E., Lorenc, A. C., Piccolo, C., ... & Swinbank, R. (2017). Inflation and localization tests in the development of an ensemble of 4D-ensemble variational assimilations. *Quarterly Journal of the Royal Meteorological Society*, 143(704), (pp. 1280–1302).

Daniel, P., Keen, M., & McPherson, C. (Eds.). (2010). *The taxation of petroleum and minerals: Principles, problems and practice*. London: Routledge.

Demirbag, M., Mellahi, K., & Riddle, L. (2011). Multinationals in the Middle East: Institutional environment and strategies. *Journal of World Business*, 46(4), (pp. 406–410).

Godley, A., & Shechter, R. (2008). Editors' introduction: Business history and the Middle East: Local contexts, multinational responses—A special section of enterprise & society. *Enterprise & Society*, 9(4), (pp. 631–636).

Henrekson, M., Johansson, D., & Stenkula, M. (2010). Taxation, labor market policy and high-impact entrepreneurship. *Journal of Industry, Competition and Trade*, 10(3–4), (pp. 275–296).

Hove, S., & Gamariel, G. (2017). Maximizing the gains from natural resources for sustainable development in Africa. *Quantum Global Research Lab (QGRL) WORKINGPAPER No, 4*.

Hussein, M. A. (2009). Impacts of foreign direct investment on economic growth in the Gulf Cooperation Council (GCC) Countries. *International Review of Business Research Papers*, 5(3), (pp. 362–376).

Karatas, Nilufer & Bekci, Ismail & Apalı, Ali. (2016). Accounting Culture of the State and Private Sector in the Middle East at XI. Century.

King, E. (2008). *Transfer pricing and corporate taxation: Problems, practical implications and proposed solutions*. New York: Springer Science & Business Media.

Lewis, M. K. (2001). "Islam and accounting", *Accounting Forum*, Vol. 25, No. 2, pp. 103–127.

Mellahi, K., Demirbag, M., & Riddle, L. (2011). Multinationals in the Middle East: Challenges and opportunities. *Journal of World Business*, 46(4), (pp. 406–410).

Mellahi, K., Guermat, C., Frynas, G., & Bortmani, H. (2002). Motives for FDI in Gulf cooperation council state: The case of Oman. *Thunderbird International Business Review*, 45(4), (pp. 431–446).

Mousa, G. A., & Desoky, A. M. (2014). The value relevance of international financial reporting standards (IFRS): The case of the GCC countries. *Journal of Accounting, Finance and Economics*, 4(2), (pp. 16–28).

Musgrave, R. A. (1987). Short of euphoria. *Journal of Economic Perspectives*, 1(1), (pp. 59–71).

Poudineh, R., Sen, A., & Fattouh, B. (2018). Advancing renewable energy in resource-rich economies of the MENA. *Renewable Energy*, 123, (pp. 135–149).

Rice, G. (1999). Islamic ethics and the implications for business. *Journal of Business Ethics*, 18(4), (pp. 345–358).

Riskjell, O. K. (2014). *A fundamental tax reform in Norway: A comparison of the allowance for corporate equity system and the comprehensive business income tax system in a Norwegian setting* (Master's thesis).

Sheng, A., and Singh, A., (2012). https://mpra.ub.unimuenchen.de/53044/1/MPRA_paper_53044.pdf

Taxes, P. (2017). The global picture, World Bank Group and PwC. http://www.pwc.com/gx/en/services/tax/payingtaxes-2017.html

Trokic, A. (2015). Islamic accounting; history, development and prospects. *European Journal of Islamic Finance*, 25(2) 103–127.

10
MANAGING HUMAN RESOURCES IN THE MIDDLE EAST

Pawan Budhwar, Vijay Pereira and Mohammed Aboramadan

Introduction

This chapter provides an overview regarding the management of human resources in the Middle East. Considering HRM policies and practices are strongly influenced by contextual factors such as institutions, national culture, competitive environment, amongst others (for details see Budhwar and Sparrow, 2002), it would be sensible to look at the HRM phenomena as part and parcel of the distinctive political, socio-economic, cultural, and institutional system of a given country in the region (Budhwar & Debrah, 2009).

Given the developments in HRM in most countries in the region (see Budhwar & Mellahi, 2006, 2007, 2016), it is important to define HRM in the broadest sense. This is sensible as several HRM approaches can exist within firms in different countries, each of which depends on a number of distinct 'internal labour markets' and approaches to human capital management (Budhwar & Sparrow, 2002). Within the labour market of the Middle East, HRM incorporates a range of sub-functions and practices, which include systems for workforce governance, work organization, staffing, and development and reward systems (Budhwar & Mellahi, 2016). Further, given the dominance of Islam in the region, HRM systems are strongly governed by its principles (Branine & Pollard, 2010). For this chapter, HRM is concerned with the management of all employment relationships in the firm, incorporating the management of managers as well as non-management labour.

An analysis of the existing literature reveals a spike in HR-related research and how best to manage HRs in the Middle East. Also, it presents a jumbled picture of the situation and the distinct lack of a thorough evaluation that may not only help report major progress in the area, but also help advance future research and practice. The chapter's goals are to highlight the current state of HRM development in the Middle East, to present a case study from a GCC country on the utilization

DOI: 10.4324/9781003005766-12

of HRM, and to highlight a set of HR challenges/key takeaway for practitioners. The later should assist HR practitioners in the region to generate context-relevant HRM policies and practices. HR practitioners in the region are called upon to invest in HRM due to its favourable effects on wide work-related outcomes such as productivity, employee engagement, innovation, and corporate and individual performance.

Developments in HRM in the Middle East

Most countries in the Middle East are now emphasizing the development of their human resources, talent management, and organizational development (e.g., Budhwar and Mellahi, 2016, 2018). The countries with rich oil resources in the region have been making serious efforts to reduce their dependence on them and to develop other sectors, which need skilled human resources (Manafi & Subramaniam, 2015; Obeidat et al., 2014). Similarly, the non-oil-producing countries tend to rely on an efficient human resources bank for sustained economic growth. Most countries in the region still tend to rely on a foreign workforce, and, given the rapidly increasing indigenous population and unemployment in the region, there is an increased emphasis on the development of 'locals' and reducing the number of 'foreigners' from the workforce, for example by Saudi Arabia, the UAE, and Oman (Budhwar & Mellahi, 2018; Forstenlechner, 2010; Goby et al., 2015). Indeed, issues related to the creation of the right kind of employable skills in the region and to changing the mindset of locals to work in private sector and lower-level positions are proving to be a major challenge. Such developments have serious implications for the HRM function in the region, in particular related to its role towards improving organizational performance (Budhwar & Mellahi, 2016; Mohamed et al., 2015).

Various scholars have attempted to provide a country-specific HRM overview for the region such as on Iran; see works of Namazie and Tayeb (2006), Namazie and Frame (2007), Soltani and Liao (2010), and Manafi and Subramaniam (2015); on Oman, Al-Hamadi and Budhwar (2006), Al-Hamadi et al. (2007), Katou et al. (2010), Khan et al. (2015); on the UAE, Singh and Sharma (2015), Haak-Saheem and Festing (2020); on Kuwait, Ali and Al-Kazemi (2006) and Zaitouni et al. (2011); on Saudi Arabia, Mellahi (2006), Adham and Hammer (2021), Alqahtani and Ayentimi (2021); on Qatar, Abdalla (2006); on Jordan, Branine and Analoui (2006) and Syed et al. (2014); and on Kuwait, Zaitouni et al. (2011). These scholars present the nature and emerging patterns of HRM and related systems along with their key determinants in the respective countries.

Also, depending on the economic development of a given country in the region, studies covering specific aspects of HRM have been conducted. These include the effects of regulations on HRM in the Saudi Arabia private sector by Mellahi (2007), the impact of HRM on organizational commitment in the banking sector in Saudi Arabia (Cherif, 2020), training assessment challenges in Saudi Arabian higher education (Bin Othayman et al., 2022), on employment policy in Kuwait by Al-Enezi (2002), the impact of HRM on organizational commitment in the banking sector in Kuwait (Zaitouni et al., 2011), the impact of HRM on work engagement and commitment in the higher education sector in Palestine (Aboramadan et al., 2020), the role of a bundle of HRM practices in enhancing employee work-related outcomes such as job performance and extra-role behaviours in the higher education sector in Palestine (Aboramadan, 2022a), human resource development (HRD) in Oman by Budhwar et al. (2002), on Emritazation in the UAE (Forstenlechner, 2008; Rees et al., 2007), the effect of HRM on service innovation in UAE government agencies (Alosani et al., 2021), the link between HRM and organizational performance in the UAE (Farouk et al., 2016), talent management strategies in the UAE (Al Jawali et al., 2022; Singh & Sharma, 2015), management and international business issues in Jordan by El-Said and Becker (2003), electronic HRM in Jordan (Al-Hawary et al., 2020; Obeidat, 2016), high-performance work systems in Jordan (Al-Ajlouni, 2021; Alqudah et al., 2022), on talent management and organizational performance in Bahrain (Kravaritia et al., 2022), on high-performance work systems in Qatari banking system (Obeidat, 2021), and the localization of the workforce in Qatar (Williams et al., 2011). There have also been studies of the impact of cultural value orientations on preferences for HRM by Aycan et al. (2007), the challenges for employment in the Arab region by Shaban et al. (1995); on HRM and innovation in the Iranian electronic industry (Manafi & Subramaniam, 2015), on career development in Oman (Khan et al., 2015), and on general management in the Arab Middle East by Weir (2000).

There are a number of emerging studies that examine women in management-related issues in the Middle East countries (Metcalfe, 2006, for Bahrain, Jordan, and Oman; Metle, 2002, for Kuwait; Tlaiss, 2015 and Abdalla, 2015 for career success/facilitator and barriers for women in the Arab context; Metcalfe, 2008 for women in management in the Middle East; Sidani et al., 2015 for female leadership advantage and leadership deficit; and Marmenout & Lirio, 2014 for female talent retention in the Gulf). There are also publications that debate the transfer of HRM from overseas to the region (Al-Husan & James, 2009, for Jordan). Although not an exhaustive list of all the different studies in the region, this is certainly a good indicator of the kind of HRM-related analysis being carried out.

Emerging studies are investigating a wide range of topics in the area of pro-environmental HRM, which is considered to be the green version of HRM. For instance, in Palestine we notice a number of empirical studies focusing on green HRM in manufacturing (Zaid et al., 2018), green HRM in higher education (Aboramadan 2022b), in hospitality (Aboramadan & Karatepe, 2021), and in non-profit organizations (Aboramadan et al., 2022). The aforementioned studies examine the effect on green HRM on several work-related outcomes such business performance, job performance, green innovative work behaviour, green voice behaviour and others. In Jordan, Ababneh (2021) suggests that green HRM enhances green behaviours via green work engagement. Green HRM was found to influence organizational performance in the Qatari gas and oil industry (Obeidat et al., 2020a, 2020b). Al-Swidi et al. (2021) found, using a sample of private and public employees in Qatar, that green HRM influences green culture and green behaviours. In the UAE, studies were focused on the concept of green HRM from a policymaker perspective (Mehrajunnisa et al., 2022) and the role of green HRM in enhancing link between green values and green creativity in the hospitality sector in the UAE (Al-hawari et al., 2021). In Oman, green HRM demonstrated to affect sustainable performance in a sample of SMEs (Alraja et al., 2022).

Apart from the above, our analysis also highlights the influence of Arab culture and values on its management systems (e.g., Ali, 2010; Branine & Pollard, 2010). Some scholars (Ali, 2010) highlight the immense impact of Islamic values, Islamic work ethics, and Islamic principles on the management of human resources in the Islamic countries of the region (Branine & Pollard, 2010; Budhwar & Fadzil, 2000; Mellahi & Budhwar, 2006). As expected, due to sociocultural similarities, a number of countries (such as Kuwait and Qatar) tend to be similar in various aspects of cultural value orientations, being high on group orientation, strong on hierarchical structures, high on masculinity, strongly following the Arab traditions, and low on future orientation (Kabasakal & Bodur, 2002). In the Turkish context, Yucelt (1984) found that managers in traditional public sector organizations tend to lean towards a benevolent-authoritarian system and less toward a participative style.

Mellahi and Budhwar (2006) report a strong impact of high power distance on managers' perceptions about the delegation of authority to lower levels of employees and interaction with them, in countries such as Kuwait and Saudi Arabia. As a result of this, managers in such countries practise centralized decision-making processes, are less willing to delegate responsibility, and discourage active employee participation. In such circumstances with sociocultural and traditional set-ups, loyalty to one's family and friends is expected to override loyalty to organizational procedures, and this often results in the use of inequitable criteria in recruitment, promotion, and compensation. Ali (2010), Ali and Al-Kazemi (2006), and Mellahi (2006) further highlight the influence of Islamic values: the principle of *shura* – that is, consultation, social harmony, and respect – is manifest in consensus decision-making styles, with respect for authority and age, and concern for the well-being of employees and society at large, in countries such as Kuwait and Saudi Arabia. Ali and Al-Kazemi (2006) reveal that several ideal Islamic values such as equity and fairness are often not adhered to in practice. This explains the widespread adoption of some HRM practices in the Middle East that are not compatible with Islamic values, such as the use of nepotism in recruitment and compensation, known as *wasta*, in the Gulf Cooperation Council (GCC) countries.

Due to significant differences (sociological, economic, legal, political, and so on) between the Middle East and other parts of the world (the 'West', in particular), foreign elements of management tend, at best, not to be conducive to the development of sound management practices in the region (e.g., Ali, 1995; Khan, 2011). An analysis by Saleh and Kleiner (2005) indicates that if U.S. companies want to be successful in the Middle East, they should develop an understanding of the local culture, politics, and people of the region. Research by Goby et al. (2015)

highlights the usefulness of the creation of a positive diversity climate based on Arab cultural traditions in managing the diverse workforce (comprising both locals and expatriates) in the region.

A related theme clearly evident in the literature is that of human resource development where issues are related to the impact of Arab management styles on the effectiveness of cross-cultural negotiations and organizational development activities in the region (Ali, 1995; Kolachi & Akan, 2014), and the need for and mechanisms of management development in the Arab world (Budhwar et al., 2002).

Atiyyah (1991, 1996) emphasizes the usefulness of cultural training and acculturation in the adjustment of expatriates to the region. Matherly and Al Nahyan (2015) propose the need for effective governance of national–expatriate knowledge transfer to build competitiveness; and Goby et al. (2015) highlight the need for the development and practice of interpersonal communication and a diversity climate framework in order to facilitate workforce localization in countries that have an expatriate majority workforce, such as the UAE. Al-Rajhi et al. (2006) reveal the challenges for HRM in the region regarding the adjustment of impatriates. Contributions from Elmuti and Kathawala (1991) and Rodriguez and Scurry (2014a, 2014b) further confirm the need for foreign firms and employees to be strongly responsive and adaptive to local requirements in order to be successful in the Middle East context. Syed et al. (2014) examine the views of local Jordanians towards expatriate managers. This is important given the significant cultural diversity of the foreign workforce in the Middle East, where it is crucial for managers to recognize, understand, and acknowledge the cultural differences of subordinates and accordingly adopt a relevant leadership style. Given the high power distance nature of most Middle East nations, an employee-orientated, paternalistic approach tends to be more successful than others (Zaitouni et al., 2011).

In the absence of awareness, an outsider might believe that there are strong similarities between nations of the Middle East. However, there remains considerable variation across countries in the Middle East that these cultural factors cannot explain. It is now well established in the literature that the management of human resources in a given context is influenced by a combination of national factors (such as the above-mentioned cultural and institutional factors), different contingent variables (such as the size, age, and nature of an organization), and the kinds of policies and strategies an organization pursues (Budhwar & Sparrow, 2002; Budhwar & Debrah, 2009). Many such factors and variables are shaping the HRM function in the Middle East region as well. The rest of this section further highlights the main determinants of the HRM policies and practices of the Middle East.

Over the past couple of decades, a number of countries in the region have also been actively pursuing localization programmes (with an emphasis on offering jobs to locals and reducing the dependence on foreign nationals). This has implications for talent management (Singh & Sharma, 2015), interpersonal communication and diversity management (Goby et al., 2015), management of workplace quotas (Matherly & Al Nahyan, 2015), leadership behaviour of national and expatriate managers (Bealer & Bhanugopan, 2014), and barriers to such localization programmes (Al-Waqfi & Forstenlechner, 2014). The variation in HRM practices based on the size, nature and ownership of the firm (private, public, or multinational) is also evident from an analysis of HRM in countries such as Iran, Kuwait, and Saudi Arabia. Large private sector organizations tend to pay higher salaries than public sector organizations, but job security is low in private sector firms as compared to public sector organizations. In GCC countries (that is, Oman, the UAE, Kuwait, Saudi Arabia, and Qatar), however, public sector organizations pay higher salaries than most private sector organizations, and job security is still relatively high in the public sector (Mellahi & Budhwar, 2006). Iles et al. (2012) highlight the challenges for effective human resource management in the public sector in the Middle East where the impact of *wasta* is strong.

There is also evidence that in many Middle Eastern countries (such as Oman, the UAE, Saudi Arabia, and Iran) the respective national governments are emphasizing the development of human resources and accordingly giving organizations freedom in HRM matters, although within the legal framework. In this regard, the role of HRD in organizational development is being highlighted (Kolachi & Akan, 2014). The names and nature of traditional personnel departments are also changing to emphasize the development of effective HRM systems to help firms compete at home and abroad. However, in the absence of skilled HRM professionals in most Middle Eastern countries, HRM managers have been muddling through, often relying on trial and error, to cope with the impact of market liberalization and severe international competition. In order to cover such skill gaps many countries such as the UAE, Oman, Jordan, Kuwait, Saudi Arabia, and Iran are investing heavily in the development of their human resources. A number of inherent problems with these countries, including a lack of a vocation-based education system, the supply and demand imbalance, negative perception of locals working in the private sector or in lower positions, and the lack of participation of women in the main workforce, are proving to be the main bottlenecks (Mellahi, 2006; Abdalla, 2015; Sidani et al., 2015). Further, the strong emphasis of the above-mentioned localization programmes pursued by many countries in the region is not helping either the private sector or multinational firms to achieve rationalization of their HRM systems (Al-Waqfi & Forstenlechner, 2014).

Based on the above analysis, it can be concluded that there is now an emerging literature on different aspects of HRM systems in the Middle East, although our knowledge remains both limited and patchy, as a result of which it is difficult to draw a conclusive and comprehensive picture of the scene. We cannot confidently say whether there is such a thing as a 'Middle Eastern HRM model', that is, a single HRM model with distinct Middle Eastern characteristics. Perhaps due to a number of reasons related to diversity within the region (including historical contexts, institutional, geographical, cultural, political, legal, social, development stage of nations, support of relevant agencies, national wealth, poverty, national priorities, issues related to terrorism, the role of unions, reliance on foreign labour, increasing security related issues, and global recessionary conditions), it seems that organizations in the Middle East use a whole range of different HRM policies and practices, and that the professionalization of HRM functions is at different stages in different countries.

Case Study: UAE and Technology in HRM

Our case is based on the report produced by KPMG 2019 on UAE human resources management. According to KPMG (2019), UAE is seen as a pioneer in implementing advanced technological solutions at every workplace. Sixty seven per cent of HR executives have outlined that their HRM practices have experienced technological transformation. More than 90% of the surveyed firms by KPMG suggested the inclusion of one or more digital solutions in the last two decades. For instance, innovation-based HRM is led by automation of payroll systems, followed by the adoption of human capital management software, and the use of HR mobile application. According to HR executives of UAE firms, three areas must be addressed in order to ensure a successful implementation of HR digitalization. These are: the capability of the staff to adapt to new solutions, the organization's ability to embrace change, and the institutional capacity to adopt technological initiatives. Despite the current focus of HRM practices in the UAE on performance management, learning, and reskilling, future investment by HR departments needs to be dedicated to digitalized performance management, the use of HR mobile apps, and digitalized talent management systems. This is expected to raise technology budget between 2019 and 2021. With this realization, almost 67% of HR executives in the UAE are seeking change by enforcing digital solutions to transform their departmental functions. To transform the future, two mechanisms were adopted: design thinking and people data analytics. Such analytics are mainly used in hiring decisions and learning and development. Finally, HR executives have suggested that such a process of transformation was faced by several challenges. These include building a new mindset, being ready for disruption, and reshaping the overall HR functions and practices.

Challenges for HRM in the Middle East – Key Takeaway

Based on the above we can say that HRM policies and practices throughout the Middle East are changing, both in terms of the contexts within which they operate, and in terms of the HRM function. There is emerging evidence about major HRM-related changes in the region. A number of forces contribute to this regard, such as changes in the business environment, globalization, increased interest in the region due to ongoing conflicts, and economic developments. For example, de Waal and Sultan (2012) highlight a move towards individualization in HRM policies such as rewards and promotion and high-performance-based HRM systems in the Middle East. These scholars also indicate the efforts being made in most Middle Eastern countries for firms to move away from relationship-based practices and to use more performance-based criteria in recruitment, selection, rewards, and promotion (Mellahi & Budhwar, 2006; Zaitouni et al., 2011). In order to make such changes widespread and to reap their real benefits, there are massive challenges for the HRM function in the region. The first is to convince all concerned about the need to bring such changes. The second is to ensure that these changes take place both quickly and effectively. One of the major hurdles in this regard is changing the mindset of top managers whose beliefs are embedded in old routines and old ways of doing things (Mellahi, 2003). Emerging research evidence (Khan et al., 2015) suggests that, for example, involving employees in career development decision-making process, and increasing transparency and fairness, can create a win–win situation.

Related to changing the mindset of top managers, the creation of a more strategic image and status of the HRM function in the region is another major challenge. Budhwar and Mellahi (2018) conclude that the HRM function in most Middle Eastern countries suffers from low status and is often relegated to a 'common sense' function that, according to top management, does not require professional skills. To a great extent this is an outcome of the poor development of HRM managers, who are not fully capable and ready to manage change and meet current and future challenges. Given some of the inherent problems within the Middle East, such as increasing unemployment, deficiency of employable skills in the available job candidates, pressure to survive, the right size of firms during the difficulties, and reducing over-reliance on the oil economy, it is high time that the HRM function in the region was given the freedom to make the required changes and accordingly make useful contributions towards organization performance, as has happened in many other parts of the world. In this regard, there is a need not only to overhaul the educational and vocational courses and training provided by different institutions in the region, but also to be open and receptive to adopting more of the successful systems of other parts of the world (with the required modifications), as is happening in many emerging markets, resulting in 'crossvergence' of HRM systems (Budhwar & Debrah, 2009). Reinforcing this, an analysis by Deloitte (2015), based on the views of 3000 HRM and business leaders related to human capital trends and challenges, also adds the need to focus on: (1) learning and development to meet the talent-related challenge; (2) reinventing HRM to make it a true partner to the business; (3) development of leaders suitable to be efficient in the present-day context; and (4) development of an organizational culture to encourage employee engagement.

In order to achieve some of these changes, it is important to move away from the inequitable relationship-based HRM policies such as *wasta*, towards a competence- or merit-based approach (Iles et al., 2012). This is now becoming a serious issue, given the aggressive localization programmes pursued by many countries of the region. Simultaneously, firms in the region are being pushed into global economic integration in order to survive and flourish (Afiouni et al., 2014). The absence of skilled local human resources, and open discrimination against overseas skilled employees, might result in serious skill gaps in the region, which will have massive economic implications when many nations in the region are making serious attempts to move into new sectors and reduce their over-reliance on oil-related products. The HRM function in the region has serious tasks at hand to determine how such a transition (towards localization) can take place, and also to ensure that talent is not pushed out of the region, haphazardly creating skills gaps and increasing the cost of attracting, acquiring, and retaining talent. In such conditions the emphasis on talent management (Singh & Sharma, 2015), diversity management (Goby et al., 2015), and on HRD, career, and organizational development (Khan et al., 2015), becomes critical.

This is further aggravated by the problems created by both high unemployment levels and rapidly increasing populations in most Middle Eastern countries. In future times this may be a major destabilizing factor for economic development in the region. Indeed many governments of different countries in the Middle East, along with the private sector, are trying to develop schemes whereby the government contributes towards the cost of training locals, to encourage private sector firms to recruit more local workers (this is happening, for example, in Saudi Arabia, Oman, and the UAE). Dealing with such major issues not only poses major challenges to national governments but also has serious implications for HRM functions (Afiouni et al., 2014).

Given the under-researched scenario of HRM in the region, there is a need for more research to develop a clear view of the key factors that shape the HRM function and determine its performance. This raises another set of challenges, including: in the absence of an established research culture, how can researchers conduct meaningful research? Also, given the sociocultural context of the Middle East and the emerging evidence about the need to adopt and modify Western HRM practices in the region, one needs to be careful of adopting Western HRM constructs, items, measures, and methodologies to conduct investigations in the region. As reported above, some work has been conducted in the past on Arab and Islamic work values and management styles and systems. This can be further developed specifically for the HRM function. In particular, future research should seek to identify and classify the unique region-specific aspects of national culture and other variables, political institutions, and other possible external factors that influence HRM in the Middle East.

In addition, there is a need for both HRM practitioners and researchers to work on issues related to diversity management, female leadership advantage, psychological contracts, HRM and performance, trust and employee engagement, emerging dominant HRM approaches and systems of the Middle East, the kind of internal labour markets suitable for firms operating in the region, tackling nepotism and corruption, ensuring a robust legal framework that works properly to safeguard both local and overseas employees, the creation of relevant employment relations, and how to encourage sharing of evidence-led best practices available with certain case companies in the Middle East. The emphasis should be on further highlighting successful indigenous HRM practices as well as practices developed elsewhere that can be adopted in the region (for example, high-performance work systems, innovative work practices, and specific participatory work practices that are successful in high-power-distance societies).

Dealing with these challenges will never be easy, as they require macro-level changes at the country level and also a change of mindset at the individual level. These are deeply rooted in the sociocultural milieu of the region. This is even more difficult given the existence of the uncertain business environment in the region. It is important to acknowledge that conducting HRM research in most parts of the Middle East is, and will continue to be, a challenging task in an environment where access to reliable data and organizations is very demanding. However, analyses like this one, and indeed others, help us to identify the factors that shape and reshape HRM in the Middle East, and perhaps to understand better the mechanisms by which they do so, and guide us in what we need to do in future.

References

Ababneh, O. M. A. 2021. How do green HRM practices affect employees' green behaviors? The role of employee engagement and personality attributes. *Journal of Environmental Planning and Management*, 64(7): 1204–1226.

Abdalla, I. A. 2006. Human resource management in Qatar. In *Managing Human Resources in the Middle-East* (pp. 139–162). Routledge.

Abdalla, I. A. 2015. Career facilitators and barriers of Arab women senior executives. *International Journal of Business and Management*, 10(8): 218–232.

Aboramadan, M. 2022a. High-performance work systems in an Arab Middle Eastern context: Analysis from multisource data. *Evidence-based HRM*, 10(4), 403–422.

Aboramadan, M. 2022b. The effect of green HRM on employee green behaviors in higher education: The mediating mechanism of green work engagement, *International Journal of Organizational Analysis*, 30(1): 7–23.

Aboramadan, M., Albashiti, B., Alharazin, H. & Dahleez, K.A. 2020. Human resources management practices and organizational commitment in higher education: The mediating role of work engagement. *International Journal of Educational Management*, 34(1): 154–174.

Aboramadan, M. & Karatepe, O. M. 2021. Green human resource management perceived green organizational support and their effects on hotel employees' behavioral outcomes. *International Journal of Contemporary Hospitality Management*, 33(10): 3199–3222.

Aboramadan, M., Kundi, Y. M. & Becker, A. 2021. Green human resource management in nonprofit organizations: Effects on employee green behavior and the role of perceived green organizational support. *Personnel Review*, 51(7), 1788–1806.

Adham, A., & Hammer, A. 2021. Understanding Arab capitalisms: Patrimonialism, HRM and work in Saudi Arabia. *The International Journal of Human Resource Management*, 32(21): 4578–4602.

Afiouni, F., Ruël, H., & Schuler, R. S. 2014. HRM in the Middle East: Toward a greater understanding. *International Journal of Human Resource Management*, 25(2): 133–143.

Al-Ajlouni, M. I. 2021. Can high-performance work systems (HPWS) promote organisational innovation? Employee perspective-taking, engagement and creativity in a moderated mediation model. *Employee Relations*, 43(2): 373–397.

Al-Enezi, A. 2002. Kuwait's employment policy: Its formulation, implications, and challenges. *International Journal of Public Administration*, 25(7): 885–900.

Al-Hamadi, A. B., & Budhwar, P. 2006. HRM in Oman. In P.S. Budhwar and K. Mellahi (eds), *Managing Human Resources in the Middle East*: 40–58. London: Routledge.

Al-Hamadi, A. B., Budhwar, P. S., & Shipton, H. 2007. Managing human resources in the Sultanate of Oman. *International Journal of Human Resource Management*, 18(1): 100–113.

Al-Hawari, M. A., Quratulain, S., & Melhem, S. B. 2021. How and when frontline employees' environmental values influence their green creativity? Examining the role of perceived work meaningfulness and green HRM practices. *Journal of Cleaner Production*, 310: 127598.

Al-Hawary, S. I., Mohammad, A. S., Al-Syasneh, M. S., Qandah, M. S., & Alhajri, T. M. 2020. Organisational learning capabilities of the commercial banks in Jordan: Do electronic human resources management practices matter?. *International Journal of Learning and Intellectual Capital*, 17(3): 242–266.

Al-Husan, F. B., & James, P. 2009. Multinationals and the process of post-entry HRM reform: Evidence from three Jordanian case studies. *European Management Journal*, 27(2): 142–154.

Ali, A. 2010. Islamic challenges to HR in modern organizations. *Personnel Review*, 39(6): 692–711.

Ali, A., & Al-Kazemi, A. 2006. Human resource management in Kuwait. In P.S. Budhwar and K. Mellahi (eds), *Managing Human Resources in the Middle East*: 79–96. London: Routledge.

Ali, A.J. 1995 Cultural Discontinuity and Arab Management Thought. *International Studies of Management and Organization*, 25(3), 1–15.

Alosani, M. S., Al-Dhaafri, H. S. & Awadh Abdulla, A. 2021. Investigating the role of HRM practices on service innovation: Empirical evidence from UAE government agencies. *Management Research Review*, 44(1): 1–24.

Alqahtani, M., & Ayentimi, D. T. 2021. The devolvement of HR practices in Saudi Arabian public universities: Exploring tensions and challenges. *Asia Pacific Management Review*, 26(2): 86–94.

Alqudah, I. H., Carballo-Penela, A., & Ruzo-Sanmartín, E. 2022. High-performance human resource management practices and readiness for change: An integrative model including affective commitment, employees' performance, and the moderating role of hierarchy culture. *European Research on Management and Business Economics*, 28(1): 100177.

Alraja, M. N., Imran, R., Khashab, B. M., & Shah, M. 2022. Technological Innovation, Sustainable Green Practices and SMEs Sustainable Performance in Times of Crisis (COVID-19 pandemic). *Information Systems Frontiers*, 24, 1081–1105. DOI: 10.1007/s10796-022-10250-z

Al-Rajhi, I., Altman, Y., Metcalfe, B., & Roussel, J. 2006. Managing impatriate adjustment as a core human resource management challenge. *Human Resource Planning*, 29(4): 15–24.

Al-Swidi, A. K., Gelaidan, H. M., & Saleh, R. M. 2021. The joint impact of green human resource management, leadership and organizational culture on employees' green behaviour and organisational environmental performance. *Journal of Cleaner Production*, 316: 128112.

Altarawneh, I., & Aldehayyat, J.S. 2011. Strategic human resources management (SHRM) in Jordanian hotels. *International Journal of Business and Management*, 6(10): 242–255.

Al-Waqfi, M. A., & Forstenlechner, I. 2014. Barriers to Emiratization: The role of policy design and institutional environment in determining the effectiveness of Emiratization. *International Journal of Human Resource Management*, 25(2): 167–189.

Atiyyah, H. S. 1991. "Effectiveness of Management Training in Arab Countries", *Journal of Management Development*, 10(7), pp. 22–29. https://doi.org/10.1108/EUM0000000001381

Atiyyah, H. S. 1996 Expatriate acculturation in Arab Gulf countries. *Journal of Management Development*, 15(5), pp. 37–47.

Aycan, Z., Al-Hamadi, A. B., Davis, A., & Budhwar, P. 2007. Cultural orientations and preferences for HRM policies and practices: The case of Oman. *International Journal of Human Resource Management*, 18(1): 11–32.

Bealer, D., & Bhanugopan, R. 2014. Transactional and transformational leadership behaviour of expatriate and national managers in the UAE: A cross-cultural comparative analysis. *International Journal of Human Resource Management*, 25(2): 293–316.

Bin Othayman, M., Mulyata, J., Meshari, A. and Debrah, Y., 2022. The challenges confronting the training needs assessment in Saudi Arabian higher education. *International Journal of Engineering Business Management*, 14: 18479790211049706.

Branine, M., & Analoui, F. 2006. Human resource management in Jordan. In P.S. Budhwar and K. Mellahi (eds), *Managing Human Resources in the Middle East*: 145–159. London: Routledge.

Branine, M., & Pollard, D. 2010. Human resource management with Islamic management principles: A dialectic for a reverse diffusion in management. *Personnel Review*, 39(6): 712–727.

Budhwar, P., & Mellahi, K.. (Eds.). 2016 *Handbook of human resource management in the Middle East*. Cheltenham: Edward Elgar.

Budhwar, P. and Mellahi, K. 2018. Human resource management in the Middle East. In C. Brewster, W. Mayrhofer and E. Farndale (eds) *Handbook of Research on Comparative Human Resource Management*. Cheltenham: Edward Elgar, 487–499.

Budhwar, P. S., Al-Yahmadi, S., & Debrah, Y. 2002. Human resource development in the Sultanate of Oman. *International Journal of Training and Development*, 6(3): 198–215.

Budhwar, P. S., & Debrah, Y. 2009. Future research on human resource management systems in Asia. *Asia Pacific Journal of Management*, 26(2): 197–218.

Budhwar, P. S., & Fadzil, K. 2000. Globalization, economic crisis and employment practices: Lessons from a large Malaysian Islamic institution. *Asia Pacific Business Review*, 7(1): 171–198.

Budhwar, P. S., & Mellahi, K. 2006. Introduction: HRM in the Middle-East context. In P. S. Budhwar and K. Mellahi (eds), *Managing Human Resources in the Middle East*: 1–19. London: Routledge.

Budhwar, P. S., & Mellahi, K. 2007. Introduction: human resource management in the Middle East. *The International Journal of Human Resource Management*, 18(1), 2–10. DOI: 10.1080/09585190601068227.

Budhwar, P. S., & Mellahi, K. 2016. *Handbook of Human Resource Management in the Middle East*. Cheltenham, UK and Northampton, MA, USA: Edward Elgar Publishing.

Budhwar, P. S., & Sparrow, P. 2002. An integrative framework for understanding cross-national human resource management practices. *Human Resource Management Review*, 12(3): 377–403.

Budhwar, P. S., & Varma, A. 2012. Human resource management in the Indian subcontinent. In C. Brewster and W. Mayrhofer (eds), *Handbook of Research on Comparative Human Resource Management*: 576–597. Cheltenham, UK and Northampton, MA, USA: Edward Elgar Publishing.

Cherif, F. 2020 The role of human resource management practices and employee job satisfaction in predicting organizational commitment in Saudi Arabian banking sector. *International Journal of Sociology and Social Policy*, 40(7/8): 529–541.

Deloitte. 2015. Deloitte: Middle East organizations facing human capital trends and challenges. http://www.bq-magazine.com/economy/employment-economy/2015/06/hr-challenges-in-the-middle-east (accessed 10 October 2015).

Elmuti, D., & Kathawala, Y. 1991. An investigation of the human resources management practices of Japanese subsidiaries in the Arabian Gulf region. *Journal of Applied Business Research*, 7(2): 82–88.

El-Said, H., & Becker, K. 2003. *Management and International Business Issues in Jordan*. London: International Business Press.

Farouk, S., Abu Elanain, H. M., Obeidat, S. M. & Al-Nahyan, M. 2016. HRM practices and organizational performance in the UAE banking sector: The mediating role of organizational innovation. *International Journal of Productivity and Performance Management*, 65(6):773–791.

Forstenlechner, I. 2008. Workforce nationalization in the UAE: Image versus integration. *Education, Business and Society: Contemporary Middle Eastern Issues*, 1(2): 82–91.

Forstenlechner, I. 2010. Expats and citizens: Managing diverse teams in the Middle East. *Team Performance Management: An International Journal*, 16(5/6): 237–241.

Goby, V. P., Nickerson, C., & David, E. 2015. Interpersonal communication and diversity climate: Promoting workforce localization in the UAE. *International Journal of Organizational Analysis*, 23(3): 364–377.

Haak-Saheem, W., & Festing, M. 2020. Human resource management – A national business system perspective. *The International Journal of Human Resource Management*, 31(14):1863–1890.

Iles, P., Almhedie, A., & Baruch, Y. 2012. Managing HR in the Middle East: Challenges in the public sector. *Public Personnel Management*, 41(3): 465–492.

Jawali, Hessa Al, Darwish, Tamer K., Scullion, Hugh & Haak-Saheem, Washika 2022. Talent management in the public sector: empirical evidence from the Emerging Economy of Dubai. *The International Journal of Human Resource Management*, 33(11), 2256–2284. DOI: 10.1080/09585192.2021.2001764

Kabasakal, H., & Bodur, M. 2002. Arabic cluster: A bridge between East and West. *Journal of World Business*, 37(1): 40–54.

Katou, A., Budhwar, P. S., Woldu, H., & Al-Hamadi, A. B. 2010. Influence of ethical beliefs, national culture and institutions on preferences for HRM in Oman. *Personnel Review*, 39(6): 728–745.

Khan, S. A. 2011. Convergence, divergence or middle of the path: HRM model for Oman. *Journal of Management Policy and Practice*, 12(1): 76–87.

Khan, S. A., Rajasekar, J., & Al-Asfour, A. 2015. Organizational career development practices: Learning from an Oman company. *International Journal of Business and Management*, 10(9): 88–98.

Kolachi, N., & Akan, O. 2014. HRD role in organizational development (A case of corporate thinking at ETISALAT, UAE). *International Business Research*, 7(8): 160–167.

KPMG. 2019. The future of HR: UAE human resources report. Access on 20. April. 2022. https://assets.kpmg/content/dam/kpmg/ae/pdf/Future-of-hr-2019.pdf

Kravariti, F., Tasoulis, K., Scullion, H., & Alali, M. K. 2022. Talent management and performance in the public sector: The role of organisational and line managerial support for development. *The International Journal of Human Resource Management*, 1–26.

Manafi, M., & Subramaniam, I. D. 2015. Relationship between human resources management practices, transformational leadership and knowledge sharing on innovation in Iranian electronic industry. *Asian Social Science*, 11(10): 358–385.

Marmenout, K., & Lirio, P. 2014. Local female talent retention in the Gulf: Emirati women bending with the wind. *International Journal of Human Resource Management*, 25(2): 144–166.

Matherly, L., & Al Nahyan, S. S. 2015. Workplace quotas: Building competitiveness through effective governance of national-expatriate knowledge transfer and development of sustainable human capital. *International Journal of Organizational Analysis*, 23(3): 456–471.

Mehrajunnisa, M., Jabeen, F., Faisal, M. N. & Mehmood, K. 2022. Prioritizing Green HRM practices from policymaker's perspective. *International Journal of Organizational Analysis*, 30(3): 652–678.

Mellahi, K. 2003. National culture and management practices: The case of GCCs. In M. Tayeb (ed), *International Management: Theory and Practices*: 87–105. London: Prentice-Hall.

Mellahi, K. 2006. Human resource management in Saudi Arabia. In P.S. Budhwar and K. Mellahi (eds), *Managing Human Resources in the Middle East*: 97–120. London: Routledge.

Mellahi, K. 2007. The effect of regulations on HRM: Private sector firms in Saudi Arabia. *International Journal of Human Resource Management*, 18(1): 85–99.

Mellahi, K., & Budhwar, P. 2006. HRM challenges in the Middle East: Agenda for future research and policy. In P. Budhwar, & K. Mellahi (Eds.). *Managing human resources in the Middle East* (pp. 291–301). London: Routledge.

Metcalfe, B. 2006. Exploring cultural dimensions of gender and management in the Middle East. *Thunderbird International Business Review*, 48(1): 93–107.

Metle, M. K. 2002. The influence of traditional culture on attitudes towards work among Kuwaiti women employees in the public sector. *Women in Management Review*, 17(6): 245–261.

Mohamed, M. I., Mutalib, M. A., Abdulaziz, A. M., Ibrahim, M., & Habtoor, N. A. S. 2015. A review of HRM practices and labor productivity: Evidence from Libyan oil companies. *Asian Social Science*, 11(9): 215–225.

Namazie, P., & Frame, P. 2007. Developments in human resource management in Iran. *International Journal of Human Resource Management*, 18(1): 159–171.

Namazie, P., & Tayeb, M. 2006. Human resource management in Iran. In P. S. Budhwar and K. Mellahi (eds), *Managing Human Resources in the Middle East*: 20–39. London: Routledge.

Obeidat, B. Y., Masa'deh, R., Moh'd, T., & Abdallah, A. B. 2014. The relationships among human resource management practices, organizational commitment, and knowledge management processes: A structural equation modeling approach. *International Journal of Business and Management*, 9(3): 9–26.

Obeidat, S. M. 2016. The link between e-HRM use and HRM effectiveness: An empirical study. *Personnel Review*, 45(6): 1281–1301.

Obeidat, S. M. 2021. Do high-performance work practices induce innovative work behaviour? The case of the Qatari banking sector. *International Journal of Innovation Management*, 25(01): 2150003.

Obeidat, S. M., Al Bakri, A. A., & Elbanna, S. 2020a. Leveraging "green" human resource practices to enable environmental and organizational performance: Evidence from the Qatari oil and gas industry. *Journal of Business Ethics*, 164(2): 371–388.

Obeidat, S. M., Al Bakri, A. A., & Elbanna, S. 2020b. Leveraging "Green" Human Resource Practices to Enable Environmental and Organizational Performance: Evidence from the Qatari Oil and Gas Industry. *Journal of business ethics Bus Ethics* **164**, 371–388. DOI:10.1007/s10551-018-4075-z

Rees, Christopher J., Mamman, Aminu & Braik, Aysha Bin 2007. Emiratization as a strategic HRM change initiative: case study evidence from a UAE petroleum company, The International Journal of Human Resource Management, 18:1, 33–53, DOI: 10.1080/09585190601068268

Rodriguez, J. K., & Scurry, T. 2014a. Career capital development of self-initiated expatriates in Qatar: Cosmopolitan globetrotters, experts and outsiders. *International Journal of Human Resource Management*, 25(2): 190–211.

Rodriguez, Jenny K. & Scurry, Tracy. 2014b Career capital development of self-initiated expatriates in Qatar: cosmopolitan globetrotters, experts and outsiders, *The International Journal of Human Resource Management*, 25:7, 1046–1067, DOI: 10.1080/09585192.2013.815254

Saleh, S., & Kleiner, B. H. 2005. Issues and concerns facing American companies in the Middle East. *Management Research News*, 28(2/3): 56–62.

Shaban, R. A., Assaad, R., & Al-Qudsi, S. 1995. The challenge of unemployment in the Arab region. *International Labour Review*, 134: 65–82.

Sidani, Y. M., Konrad, A., & Karam, C. M. 2015. From female leadership advantage to female leadership deficit: A developing country perspective. *Career Development International*, 20(3): 273–292.

Singh, A., & Sharma, J. 2015. Strategies for talent management: A study of select organizations in the UAE. *International Journal of Organizational Analysis*, 23(3): 337–347.

Soltani, E., & Liao, Y.-Y. 2010. Training interventions: Fulfilling managerial ends or proliferating invaluable means for employees? Some evidence from Iran. *European Business Review*, 22(2): 128–152.

Syed, J., Hazboun, N. G., & Murray, P. A. 2014. What locals want: Jordanian employees' views on expatriate managers. *International Journal of Human Resource Management*, 25(2): 212–233.

Tlaiss, H. A. 2015. Neither-nor: Career success of women in an Arab Middle Eastern context. *Employee Relations*, 37(5): 525–546.

de Waal, A., & Sultan, S. 2012. Applicability of the high performance organization framework in the Middle East. *Education, Business and Society: Contemporary Middle Eastern Issues*, 5(3): 213–223.

Weir, D. T. H. 2000. Management in the Arab Middle East. In M. Tayeb (ed), *International Business, Theories, Policies and Practices*: 501–510. Upper Saddle River, NJ: Pearson Education.

Williams, J., Bhanugopan, R. & Fish, A. 2011. Localization of human resources in the State of Qatar: Emerging issues and research agenda. *Education, Business and Society: Contemporary Middle Eastern Issues*, 4(3): 193–206.

Yucelt, U. 1984. Management styles in the Middle East: A case example. *Management Decision*, 22(5): 24–35.

Zaitouni, M., Sawalha, N. N., & El Sharif, A. 2011. The impact of human resource management practices on organizational commitment in the banking sector in Kuwait. *International Journal of Business and Management*, 6(6): 108–123.

11
CONFLICT MANAGEMENT AND NEGOTIATION IN THE MIDDLE EASTERN WORKPLACE

Gita Bajaj and Ahmad Said Al-Shuabi

Introduction

When one or more individuals or parties perceive a divergence of interest or believe that their current aspirations are obstructed by the other party (Pruitt and Rubin, 1986, p. 4; Lewicki, Saunders, and Barry, 2022), there is conflict. However, if they realize that the two parties have differing needs or aspirations that can be achieved through give and take, they negotiate to resolve the conflict. This realization is at the heart of integrative negotiations. Poor negotiation occurs when people cannot see the other party's contribution or wish to amass all value for themselves by use of force or power. But integrative negotiations help create value for all parties. The Middle East (ME) is an exemplary example of such give

Interests and Aspirations

A few decades ago, when the ME countries discovered hydrocarbon resources, their need for skilled human capital far exceeded what was available locally. To develop the sector and the economy, governments adopted attractive tax laws to bring in requisite knowledge and skilled workforce from South Asia, Africa, South East Asia, Europe, the UK, and the United States. The overarching objective was to develop a resilient economy that can leverage fossil fuels without completely depending on them. At the same time, government vision statements and long-term plans also suggest a focus on developing internal capabilities by educating and skilling citizens to reduce dependence on expatriates.

On the other hand, expatriates relocate to ME primarily for better economic opportunities from better salaries and lower or no taxes. In addition, however, they pursue a desire for stability as they lead their lives far away from their home country. In this context, the employees, employers, and organizations function to achieve individual, organizational, and national interests and aspirations.

DOI: 10.4324/9781003005766-13

Sources of Power and Influence

In a broad sense, people have power when they have the "ability to bring about outcomes they desire" or "the ability to get things done the way they want them to be done" (Salancik & Pfeffer, 1977). Presumably, a party with power can induce another to do what the latter otherwise would not do (Dahl, 1957; Kotter, 1979; Lewicki, Saunders and Barry, 2022). When parties are interdependent, both have something that the other needs, which is both the reason for conflict and the power of the other party. How the conflicting parties resolve their conflict depends on how much leverage they have and are aware of, how much they decide to use and how they use it. But what is the source of their power or leverage? According to Lewicki, Saunders, and Barry (2022), power, as it relates to negotiation, can be grouped as follows:

1. Informational sources of power
2. Personal sources of power
3. Power based on position in an organization
4. Relationship-based sources of power
5. Contextual sources of power

We now explore ways that conflicting parties garner these powers in the Middle East.

Informational Sources of Power

Informational power is derived from a negotiator's ability to gather and organize facts and data to support their position. Negotiators may use information as a tool to challenge the other party's position or to undermine the opposing party's arguments. Through this information exchange, a common definition of the situation emerges and serves as a rationale for both sides to modify their positions and arrive at a mutually agreeable resolution.

Like in any other country, immigrants in GCC have to learn the law of the host country to be able to intelligently frame the situations during any negotiation. For this, they must know what rules govern their civil behaviour, organizational participation, business transactions, employer and employee rights and duties, and legal repercussions of any default. In addition, they could face the language barrier, as the legal language is Arabic, though English translations are now available. In case of serious altercations, one would need an Arabic-speaking intermediator. However, the language and cultural barriers can still be daunting for even the educated, let alone the economically and educationally less empowered.

An example of how lack of information could put people in a disadvantaged position is when some employers retain the passport of their employees, alleging that this is governmental regulation, and the employees gullibly agree. However, this is far from the truth, for instance, in the UAE, where the law does not permit an employer to withhold employee passports.

At the organizational level, employees with deep technical knowledge of the market products and regulatory compliance are able to strengthen and forcefully present their arguments to the employers. However, those in a crowded space, like the unskilled or semi-skilled labour or junior level employees, find it hard to express their concerns or negotiate, as the law does not permit unions and associations.

However, there is a shift in this power dynamic with governmental initiatives and greater awareness. For instance, in Dubai, every Industrial Free Zone (IFZ) has a rule book that guides the employer–employee relationship. In some Free Zones, the employer has to deposit one month's salary and the cost of travel back to the home country as a safety net for all hires. On the other hand, an employee cannot switch jobs without clearance from their previous employer. Every Free Zone has also established employer–employee Mediation Centres (MC) to minimize legal proceedings. These MCs have proved to be faster and fairer (According to Geethalakshmi Ramachandran, General Counsel Lakshmi & Co. Legal Consultant, Dubai UAE).

> The Dispute Reconciliation Committee (DRC) within the Ministry of Labor, UAE commendably settles minor labour issues, which therefore do not reach the court for redressal. I would recommend that employers set up a non-partisan redressal committee to address such conflicts before letting authorities come into the picture. Counselling sessions also help greatly.

Power Based on Position in an Organization

Legitimate Power: Legitimate power is derived from occupying a particular position in an organizational hierarchy. The power resides in the title, duties, and responsibilities of the job. In a national context, Heads of State and members of the Parliaments hold positions that vest them with powers to affect the lives of the citizens and residents of that country. How these members assume their positions and how the power is distributed varies from one country to another. See Table 11.1 for a glimpse of the legislative systems in the GCC countries.

At the national level: A state's head holds the supreme and most powerful position in all the countries. While the Kingdom of Kuwait has the most elected members, the Kingdom of Saudi Arabia has none, with the other countries in between (see Table 11.1). In all the countries, there is a change towards a more democratic system, and the most significant shift has happened in Qatar, where all members were appointed until the last election, but in 2021 the maximum percentage (30 of 45) were elected. The powers vested in the elected Councils and the process of election and thereby citizen participation also vary – as in Bahrain, where all citizens vote, to Saudi, where all members are appointed.

Gender participation in governance is also improving, with the UAE leading the pack by ensuring 50% women representation in the government. However, these numbers are much smaller in most other countries, with merely one woman parliamentarian in Kuwait. However, women in elected positions are much less than those appointed, indicating the efforts of the governments to build acceptance.

Foreign nationals who wish to work and live in the Middle East can get a Residence Visa for a limited number of years (for instance, three years in the UAE),

164 Gita Bajaj and Ahmad Said Al-Shuabi

TABLE 11.1 Legislative Systems in the GCC Countries

Country	Year of parliament set up	No of members (appointed/elected/both)	Affiliations	Powers	Gender representation year	Gender representation percentage
Kingdom of Saudi Arabia	1927	150 (All Appointed by the King)	Political parties not allowed to exist	Discuss reports. Cannot pass laws. No oversight of the budget. Can propose laws and amendments	2013	20% women in the Shura Council. Thirty women appointed.
State of Kuwait	1962	50 (elected) + 15 (appointed by the King)	Political parties are outlawed but members can form informal societies.	Most democratic. Passes legislations and can dismiss Ministers	2005	Only one women parliamentarian elected
Kingdom of Bahrain	1973	40 (elected)+40 (appointed by the King)	Political parties not allowed but candidate can align with political associations or run as independent candidates	Can propose laws, may amend the constitution, can call for a no-confidence of ministers and dismiss them. Oversees the state budget and can accept, amend or reject draft laws.	2006	Women secured six seats in the COR and nine seats in the Shura Council, including Fawzia Zainal, who became Bahrain's first female Speaker
State of Qatar	1972	From 2021, 45 (30 elected + 15 appointed). Earlier 35 (all appointed by the Emir)	Political parties are outlawed	Approves general policies and the budget. Can propose legislative bills, proposals on public matters, address interpellation to ministers within jurisdiction	2017	Four members in Parliament

United Arab Emirates	1973	20 (indirectly elected) + 20 (appointed by ruler of each Emirate – 8(Abu Dhabi) 8(Dubai)+other 5 emirates)	Political parties are outlawed	Does not propose laws. Can pass, amend or reject laws and review the general budget. Debates international treaties and agreements. Can question but not dismiss minister.	2006	Since 2019, 50% women in the Council. Seven women elected and 13 appointed. Equal women representation. In 2015, first female Speaker appointed.
Sultanate of Oman	1981	86(elected) + 86 (appointed by the Sultan)	Political parties are outlawed	Can interpellated but not dismiss ministers. Least active in amendments of laws.	1997	2 elected and 15 appointed to state council

Conflict Management and Negotiation **165**

on the basis of an employment offer. For some professions and against investments, some GCC countries also offer longer-duration visas. However, in general, GCC countries do not grant citizenship status to foreign nationals. The government provides a window of a few months for unemployed residents to find a new job and thereby a local sponsor to continue living in the country. If an individual is unable to fetch a job, the alternatives are to initiate a business or return to the home country.

To curb over-reliance on the migrant workforce and build self-reliance, the governments in the GCC countries have adopted labour nationalization policies, such as Kuwaitization in Kuwait, which provide reservations for nationals in key industries, among other measures. By 2008, 60% Kuwaitization was required for banks, 15% for the real estate sector, and 2% for manufacturing industries. So, organizations replaced expatriate workers with Kuwaitis whenever possible, and more capital-intensive technology was imported to reduce dependence on foreign employees. Similarly, Saudi Arabia's Ministry of Labor and Social Development (MLSD) launched a program called "Nitaqat" to encourage Saudi private companies to hire more Saudis under the legal requirements of Saudization (Randeree, 2009). Companies are rated platinum, green, yellow, and red based on compliance. The rating determines their access to government services, especially immigration services. The program also confers employees of yellow- and red-rated companies the right to leave their employer without a letter.

Neal (2010, p. 248) narrates an example of the Omanization of supermarket shop-floor personnel in the early 2000s, where the Filipina females, operating the supermarket checkouts were replaced by Omani women.

A large proportion of the immigrant population is labour from Asia and Africa. The difference in home and host country's salaries makes the ME a lucrative destination for expatriate labour. In return, they willingly work long hours and do more physically demanding jobs.

It is important to note on the other hand that families of many expats have been settled in the ME for many generations now. They have even built big business houses, whose owners have received exceptional visa statuses. With more and more liberal and welcome policies in the ME, the trend of expats wanting to live and work in the ME, especially in progressive countries like the UAE, is only increasing.

Personality and Individual Differences

People differ from each other in psychological, cognitive, motivational, dispositional, and moral orientations. The ideological orientations define one's framing and expectation of any conflict. These vary considerably from one culture to another. In the multicultural environment of GCC countries, these differences, often subtle, get revealed.

For instance, the individual vs collectivist orientation of the people from different countries surfaces in their business conduct. Research indicates that individualistic cultures orient people to make independent decisions for personal gains. In contrast with collectivist cultures prioritize consultative decision-making and group gains.

CASE STUDY 1   WASTA: NEPOTISM, NETWORKING OR DEEP-ROOTED CULTURAL CONNECTION?

Raghav Agarwal was biting his nails. The critical meeting between his company's and client company's sponsors would decide the fate of his previous years of efforts. He had done everything to propose a lucrative deal to their client, but nothing seemed to be moving.

Agarwal was the Chief Marketing Manager at Cargo Global Ltd (CGL). CGL was a leading logistics provider in Oman that moved cargo (90 per cent) and courier (10 per cent) through road, sea, and air routes worldwide. They moved goods from various companies in Japan and Europe and consolidated the consignments at their regional headquarters in Muscat. Agarwal led the negotiations of CGL's long-term contracts in the region, although most of the tariff decisions were made at the headquarters in Denmark.

The previous month, CGL headquarters in Denmark had revised its tariff framework to attract big volume business at reduced costs. The new structure offered an opportunity to get a share of the multimillion-dollar business of the Gulf Oil & Gas Suppliers & Equipment (GOGSE). Agarwal had been eyeing this company, but GOGSE had contractual agreements with ATL, an American logistics company, and it had been next to impossible to get a breakthrough in GOGSE. With the new tariff structure in place, Agarwal, along with Peter Locker, the CGL CEO (a Swedish professional with 20 years of shipping industry experience), had made a strong pitch to George Packard, the CEO of GOGSE (an American professional with about 25 years of oil and gas experience). They showcased how the new tariff structure could save GOGSE USD 2 million annually if they could give CGL the requisite volumes.

This saving could be huge, but it required GOGSE to renegotiate its contract with ATL, which was a time-consuming and challenging job. Its arrangement with ATL was working seamlessly. A single vendor was managing its worldwide movements. So, coordination and paperwork were all organized accordingly. The workflow was smooth, and trust had been built over the long term. Besides, "it is not right to change a contract midway", Packard had asserted. All logic and persuasion were falling on deaf ears. Packard felt the change could jeopardize the business operations of GOGSE and its relations with ATL. CGL team reminded them against putting all eggs in the same basket, but that too did not convince Packard.

When nothing seemed to make a dent with Packard, Locker decided to exploit their sponsor's network. He approached Mohammad Al Balooshi, their sponsor in Oman, to escalate the negotiation to Ahmad Al Zawabi, the GOGSE sponsor in Oman. Few meetings at higher levels were held. A final meeting between the two sponsors and their teams was organized.

The Final Meeting: The meeting started with a polite exchange of greetings and positive assurances. The two sides presented all the logic: CGL presented the possible gains to GOGSE, and GOGSE presented the challenges in fulfilling the requirements. However, no reason or benefit sounded enough to the GOGSE team. Agarwal and Locker had little hope from the meeting now, but they crossed their fingers and hoped for the best.

When all arguments were exhausted, Mohammad Al Balooshi turned to Ahmad Al Zawabi, looked straight in his eyes, and said,

> Do you realize that these efforts will, for the next ten years, bring USD 2 million annually to our country! It would amount to USD 20 million for Oman! Is that a loss we want our country to have, or will you stretch yourself for its sake?

Agarwal and Locker were almost shocked to see what happened after that. They had, for the first time, witnessed in person the Arabic practice of "Wasta"! Ahmad Al Zawabi remained quiet for a few moments and then looked at Mohammad Al Balooshi and nodded his head. Al Balooshi stood up, turned to Peter and Agarwal, and said, "So, it's all done. Please work out things with GOGSE" and walked out.

For the next month, CGL and GOGSE teams worked together to revise the contracts. While ATL served GOGSE for the American business, CGL got the European, Malaysian, Japanese, and Korean regions. These were regions where they could offer better monetary and time gains. The deal amounted to an approximate USD 50 million business over the next five years for CGL.

GOGSE benefitted from the savings and the more favourable image of the company within the country. ATL managed all the business from America and routed its cargo in the region through Dubai, UAE. However, CGL was aggregating from multiple vendors in the region to import directly to Oman. This arrangement of CGL generated employment for many nationals, and GOGSE was projected as a forerunner for the nationalization efforts.

In 2020, almost 25 years hence, Agarwal, having worked in Oman, Qatar, and now the UAE, feels nothing has changed at the more profound level. The cultural values are deep-rooted, and they still surface during negotiations. Interestingly, Agarwal witnessed this sense of responsibility for the collective in all the three countries he worked in – Oman, Qatar, and the UAE – and insists these are held sacred in most of the other Gulf countries as well.

Note: In the above case narration, names of individuals and organizations have been disguised to maintain confidentiality.

This case presents a typical conflict and negotiation situation in the ME, where locals and expatriates from different countries interact and work together daily. In this case, the Swedish CEO and an Indian marketing manager of a European company with a local partner in Oman are involved in a negotiation with an American CEO of an American company with a local partner in Oman. Such multicultural negotiation is more a norm than an exception in the Middle East. To the Swedish and American CEOs and the Indian marketing manager, the logic of commercial gain for the company was evident. However, they were surprised when a patriotic call amidst cut-throat business dealing provided the much-needed breakthrough. This argument was not something any of them could have fathomed in their own countries. This kind of urge to take responsibility for the community is what many researchers have pointed to as collectivism. It takes those from highly individualistic orientation (the Americans and the Swedes) by complete surprise.

Networks and Referent Power

The relational power comes from whatever business flows through that position or person, irrespective of the level in the hierarchy. On the other hand, referent power comes from the respect or admiration one commands because of the attributes like personality, integrity, interpersonal style, etc.

In the Arabic world, this is referred to as "Wasta". Wasta is a person's influence through personal and family networks (Hutchings & Weir, 2006). For instance, Jordan is known for its tribal affiliations: social status, political life, and business life are strongly affected by a system of "soft influences" in which tribal and religious affinity are intertwined. Consequently, it is accepted that "everything, no matter how simple it is, requires a wasta in Jordan" (Al-Said & McDonald, 2001). The same mechanisms can be found across other Arab countries, where wasta is referred to as ma'arifa ("who you know") or a piston ("pulling strings") (Yahiaoui and Zoubir, 2006). This practice in a society that believes in vertical hierarchy implies that the more networked you are in the higher echelons of the local society, the more power you may yield. Although there are systems instituted to restrict the influence of wasta, it remains a pervasive reality.

Some people grumble and humour Wasta, seeing it as nepotism or clout to get favours (Neal, 2010). However, Khakkhar and Hussain (2013) have challenged previous findings of Wasta that frame wasta in a negative light as nepotism. Instead, they point to it as a management tool used by Arabs to leverage referent power during negotiations. Furthermore, they draw its similarities with the Chinese practice of "guanxi", which serves to build trust, commitment, and relationships among the negotiating parties, considered essential by the Arab negotiators for long-term business success.

Caputo (2013) found that attitude towards nepotism tends to influence people's Conflict Management Style (CMS). People use their power passively to get what they want (dominating style), but if it does not work, they accept the situation quietly (submissive style). However, Caputo has recommended more research for a better understanding of nepotism in conflict management.

Contextual Sources of Power

The Middle Eastern context discussed earlier indicates the desires, needs, and fallback options of various parties. The difference in the parties' needs brings them together in the negotiation situation. The fall-back option of each gives them their risk-taking power.

Culture often shapes what kinds of power are seen as legitimate and illegitimate or how people use and react to influence. National cultures also differ in the degree to which people accept inherent inequality in their social structure (Hofstede, 1980a, 1980b, 1989). According to Hofstede (1980a), the Arab world scores high on power distance (PD) dimensions. So, Arabs respect and follow the orders of people in authority. They follow traditional values. In this definition of the Arab world, Hofstede had included Lebanon, Libya, Kuwait, Iraq, Saudi Arabia, and the United Arab Emirates. People from the Indian subcontinent also score high on power distance, though not as high as most of the Middle East's host countries. However, power distance scores are much lower for most Western countries from where the Arab world hosts expatriates.

Hill and Atkins (2013) have furnished in-depth and interesting insights into cultural confluence in the UAE. Contrary to common literature on acculturation, they point to the far more complex phenomena of cultural aspiration. Their study suggests the cultural adaptation exhibited by people from the Indian subcontinent and Arabia converges towards western culture. However, they point to the westerners, mostly retaining their cultural identity and not adjusting to the local or the majority culture.

The westerners consider their management style better than the rest and maintain it both at home and in the office. However, non-westerners display an additional capacity to pragmatically assume multiple identities depending on their need to belong to a group – at home or in the workplace (Suh, 2002). Canadian South Asians, for example, shifted to hybrid identities, whereas the Indians in Dubai adapted to cultural ambiguity (Vora, 2008).

CASE STUDY 2   THE PARADOX OF APPRAISAL IN THE MIDDLE EAST

Rahul, VP Marketing HZE Bank Qatar, was in two minds – should he write an honest appraisal for Sultan Al-Janeibi to be fair to all his team members or be more mindful of Sultan's nationality and wasta? He knew his action could, on the one hand, set a wrong tone for his team culture, and on the other hand, put him in trouble with his seniors. He decided to confront and signed the "Not satisfactory" remark on the appraisal, giving brief reasoning.

While he was expecting some ruffle, the scuffle turned out to be much more intense. Sultan was not just any other employee. He was a local Qatari national with good connections who had helped them get access to some important clients and senior officials over the previous year. However, he never followed up to complete any transaction. Delayed responses, absenteeism, and sheer lack of responsibility made it difficult for the team to work with him.

As expected, Sultan raised much noise on the issue and filed a complaint with the HR Manager. The HR manager called for Rahul to defend his appraisal remarks. Fortunately for Rahul, he had been writing warning emails to Sultan through the year, sometimes guiding him and at other times complaining or warning. However, all his messages had been falling on deaf ears. Rahul printed about 30–40 emails and submitted them to HR. To his surprise, Sultan denied having received any of those emails. Rahul then requested the IT team to verify the emails on the server and provided additional evidence for his assertion. In the meantime, Sultan had reached out to the local sheikh, who was also the bank's local sponsor and a powerful minister. Sultan had escalated the complaint to the bank's highest level, leaving Rahul in a tumultuous state.

Asked again to justify his actions, Rahul thoroughly documented evidence to submit to the Minister. To his relief, the minister could see the team manager's genuine performance concerns and the case was closed immediately. The local Qatari employee was asked to be careful in the future, and a message of merit above wasta was established.[1]

Note: In the above case narration, names of individuals and organizations have been disguised to maintain confidentiality.

Conflict Resolution Styles

Culture influences the way negotiators perceive a situation, put forward their propositions, express and assess needs, desires and powers of self and others, and respond to it. Arabs prefer to resolve conflicts implicitly or indirectly. They conceal their desired wants, needs, or goals during interactions which reflect "musayara" – the desire to be accommodating for the sake of harmony and avoidance of confrontation during negotiations (Gudykunst et al., 1988). So, they avoid direct methods of resolution. Many would rather speak phrases as "we shall see" instead of saying a direct "No".

Due to the high-context behaviour, Arabs also rely considerably on complex nonverbal communication. While most people from the Indian subcontinent are also high context, many from the western countries such as the UK and the United States are from a low-context culture. People from the high-context culture (Arabs and Indians) expect others to understand much of the message through body language and indirect messaging. People from the low context (British and Americans) have no clue of any such expectations or capability to understand the unsaid unless the individual has a high cultural quotient (CQ). They prefer direct and explicit communication; anything short could be confusing and frustrating. To the ones from high context, such direct expression can be rude and offensive. Such differences have the potential for causing miscommunication, creating misunderstandings, and causing conflict.

For instance, in Saudi Arabia, it is considered usual for a person to be aggressive and loud, indicating that they are concerned about the business and the dispute. But this is meant to imply they are passionate and not disrespectful towards the other party. So, it is vital to hear them out patiently and not interject as they speak, which is considered being disrespectful. However, they would be okay with hearing a genuine objection. This style is very different from the Indian negotiation style, where the Indian might consider loud and aggressive as disrespectful but would conveniently interject someone still speaking. This interjection is meant to say, 'I have understood and am responding to it and not offering disrespect as could be perceived by the Saudi national'. The British, on the other hand, might find the loud and aggressive expression as disrespectful. However, people with higher mindfulness and cultural awareness are able to steer their way to a reasoned debate.

Orientation towards time is more relaxed in Arabia, though this is not true for high-profile meetings with senior officials who would expect the most efficient use of their time. It is important to recall here the norms of vertical collectivism where the conduct expectations change with hierarchy. Therefore, the time of the senior official would be more precious, and juniors would be expected to respect their time schedules.

Trust and Relationship in Negotiations

Trust and relationships play a critical role in conflict resolution. The Arabs are highly relationship-oriented, and they prefer to do business with individuals than corporations. Anyone who has worked in the Middle East would know that they need to build relationships and trust before proceeding into a business transaction. Every meeting would invariably begin with some niceties and expressions of care and regard. This is very different from the straight to the business approach of an American or a Dutch. For many in the western world, it is professional to keep the work and relationships separate, much in contrast with the Arabs and the Asians living in this region. Arabs also commonly appeal to the emotions and family relationships and challenges to get concessions, and the other party is expected to appreciate their concerns while assessing the deal. To many, the appeal to personal compulsions might sound unprofessional but not here. Besides personal relations and cultural similarity, religious beliefs also breed trust because people have the same assumptions, beliefs, and values.

Religion plays a vital role in Islamic countries. It guides how people should conduct themselves in the workplace, and its mention can be tangibly noted in workplace conversations. Religious conduct and solidarity are values that the Arabs hold high. As can be seen in Case 1, the cut-throat deal was cracked for a national cause.

Conclusion

Conflict and negotiation are part and parcel of everyone's life all over the world. It usually begins with the parties building trust and relationship followed by information exchange. However, how one would build trust or exchange information would vary considerably for various parties. If the parties are from different countries and cultures, they may not accurately perceive and interpret the other party's approach. This misunderstanding may not only spoil the deal but also sour the relationship forever. On the other hand, dealing with people through stereotypes can also be dangerous. This danger becomes more pronounced if the other side has been influenced by many different cultures besides the category one would cast the party into.

Many companies in the UAE understand the critical importance of managing cultural differences for effective business relations. For example, a senior banker of an Arab bank anonymously shared that they classified their clients in four categories, namely, Asians, Arabs, UAE nationals, and Europeans. To resolve any conflict that could arise with a client from any background, they ensured that the person facing the client was from the same background. This cultural matching helped bridge many communication gaps and softened the clients. Although the language to transact remained English, people from the same cultural background could more accurately understand the non-verbal communication and the meta-messages.

However, all the above are examples of transactional exchanges. Long-term relationships are usually driven by how well someone has learned to deal with these differences to connect personally and individually. If the other side can appreciate the good intentions and the two parties have understood the communication style, they can build trust and work together. A large expatriate community living for two or more generations now in the ME is an indicator of a healthy cultural confluence.

Recommendations: Way Forward

- The governments announce their vision and long-term plans that highlight sectors and competencies they seek to develop. It is prudent to match your competencies to spot an opportunity. For instance, in the UAE, the government has announced a golden visa (ten-visa) for select categories. It is prudent to check the policy documents of the country of interest.
- Make some Arabic-speaking friends. Learn basic Arabic phrases to build initial connect.
- Carefully study the laws of conduct and labour laws of the country. Remember, laws are strictly enforced.

- Stay connected with the embassy of your home country. Participate in the cultural events organized by your embassy. These provide a chance to build relations with people who may have faced similar problems and authorities who can help deal with the issues.
- Read about services offered by the Mediation Centres.
- As an employer, set up a non-partisan grievance or redressal committee to address minor conflicts
- Avoid judging culturally different people and learn to accept and adapt. Behave mindfully.
- Strengthen your documentation, especially when you are challenging a more powerful person or entity.
- Become a member of informal groups of like-minded people. For instance, Inter-nations Expats.
- Do not restrict your interactions with people from your own country for the sake of convenience and comfort. Instead, make friends with people from the host and other cultures.

Useful Links

- Middle East Policy Brief: Vision 2030 https://mepc.org/policy-brief-gcc-vision-2030
- Overview of The Economic Development Strategies In The Middle East's GCC Region https://thefintechtimes.com/overview-of-the-economic-development-strategies-in-the-middle-easts-gcc-region/
- Golden Visa in the UAE: https://u.ae/en/information-and-services/visa-and-emirates-id/residence-visa/long-term-residence-visas-in-the-uae
- UAE labour law https://www.gulftalent.com/repository/ext/UAE_Labour_Law.pdf
- Making Arabic Speaking Friends https://www.arabicpod101.com/lesson/absolute-beginner-3-making-friends-in-arabic/
- Learn Arabic for Free: https://www.conversationexchange.com/s_map/learn.php?language=arabic
- Best Language Learning Apps https://www.rosettastone.com/languages/best-language-learning-app?prid=livemocha_com
- Middle East: Immigration and employment law changes across the GCC https://www.pwc.com/gx/en/services/people-organisation/publications/assets/pwc-middle-east-immigration-and-employment-law-changes-across-the-gcc.pdf
- The Mediation Centre: https://mediationcentre.biz/sample-mediations/
- DMCC Disputes Centre for Dubai Free Zone https://www.dmcc.ae/free-zone/already-a-member/value-added-services/disputes-centre

Note

1 This case is a documentation of a real negotiation. The names of the companies and executives have been changed to maintain confidentiality. The companies and executives are not liable for any breach of sensitive and confidential information.

References

Abaker, M.-O. S. M., Al Titi, O. A. K. & Al-Nasr, N. S., 2019. Organizational policies and diversity management in Saudi Arabia. *Employee Relations*, 41(3), pp. 454–474.

Al-Said, H. & McDonald, F., 2001. Institutions and joint ventures in the Middle East and North Africa: the case of Jordan. *Journal of Transnational Management Development*, 6, pp. 1–2.

Caputo, A., 2013. A literature review of cognitive biases in negotiation processes. *International Journal of Conflict Management*, 24(4), pp. 374–398.

Dahl, R.A. 1957. The concept of power. *Behavioural Science* 2(3), 201–215. DOI:10.1002/bs.3830020303

Gudykunst, W. B., Ting-Toomey, S. & Chu, 1988. Sage series in interpersonal communication, Vol. 8. *Culture and Interpersonal Communication*.

Hill, R. C. & Atkins, P. W., 2013. Cultural identity and convergence on western attitudes and beliefs in the United Arab Emirates. *International Journal of Cross Cultural Management*, 13(2), 193–213.

Hofstede, G., 1980a. Culture and organizations. *International Studies of Management and Organization*, 10(4), 15–41.

Hofstede, G., 1980b. Motivation, leadership and organiztion: do Americans theories apply abroad? *Organizational Dynamics*, 9(1), 42–63. https://scihub.se/https://www.sciencedirect.com/science/article/abs/pii/0090261680900133;https://scihub.se/https://www.tandfonline.com/doi/abs/10.1080/00208825.1980.11656300?journalCode=mimo20

Hofstede, G., 1989. Organising for cultural diversity. *European Management Journal*, 7(4), 390–397. https://www.sciencedirect.com/science/article/abs/pii/0263237389900753

Hutchings, K. & Weir, D., 2006. Guanxi and wasta: a comparison. *Thunderbird International Business Review*, 48(1), pp. 141–56.

Internations (202 Expat Insider Survey), 2021. *The Best and Worst Places for Expats*. https://www.internations.org/expat-insider/2021/best-and-worst-places-for-expats-40108

Khakkhar & Hussain, 2013. Culture and business networks: international business negotiations with Arab managers. *International Business Review*, 22(3), 578–590.

Kotter, J. & Schlesinger, L. 2008. Choosing strategies for change. *Harvard Business Review*, 57, 106–114. DOI:10.1007/978-1-349-20317-8_21.

Kotter, J., 1979. Managing external dependence *Academy of Management Review*, 4(1).

Lewicki, R.J., Saunders, D. & Barry, B. 2022. *Essentials of Negotiation*. McGraw-Hill/Irwin.

Neal, M., 2010. When Arab-expatriate relations work well: diversity and discourse in the gulf Arab workplace. *Team Performance Management*, 16(5/6), pp. 242–266.

Pruitt, D., & Rubin, J. 1986. *Social Conflict: Escalation, Stalemate, and Settlement*. New York: Random House, p. 4.

Randeree, K., 2009. Strategy, policy and practice in the nationalisation of human capital: 'Project emiratisation. *Research and Practice in Human Resource Management*, 17(1), pp. 71–91.

Salancik, G. R., & Pfeffer, J. 1977. Who gets power--and how they hold on to it: a strategic-contingency model of power. *Organizational Dynamics*, 5(3), pp. 2–21. DOI: 10.1016/0090-2616(77)90028-6

Suh, E. M., 2002. Culture, identity consistency, and subjective well-being. *Journal of Personality and Social Psychology*, 83(6), pp. 1378–1391.

Vora, N., 2008. Participatory exclusion: the Emirati state, forms of belonging, and Dubai's Indian middle class. *Anthropological Quarterly*, pp. 377–406.

Yahiaoui, D., & Zoubir, Y. 2006. Human Resource Management in Tunisia. In P. Budhwar, & K. Mellahi (Eds.), *Managing Human Resource in the Middle East*, Middle East. London: Routledge, pp. 233–249.

12
PERFORMANCE MANAGEMENT IN THE MIDDLE EAST

Shahina Javad

Introduction

Performance appraisal (PA) is one of the most common performance evaluation tools used by organizations around the world. It is generally understood as an organizationally sanctioned event that is both formal and discrete, and occurring usually on an annual basis. When human capital was plentiful, the traditional performance appraisal worked well to assign people into two categories: those to be rewarded and those to be fired (Kirkpatrick, 2006). However, when organizations have to constantly compete with each other for human talent, as it is now, the development of the employees becomes a greater concern for them. Further, annual performance appraisals are ill-received because of the potential biases in the evaluation. To counter the flaws/compensate the inadequacies of PA, and to augment the organizational performance, some of the European and American MNCs operating in sectors ranging from technology to manufacturing to professional services have developed broader performance management systems (PMS) that integrate employee performance appraisal with two-way feedback, development, and goal setting. These organizations redesigned their traditional performance management systems by replacing backward looking and time-consuming annual performance ratings/appraisal with frequent performance check-ins between managers and employees (Cappelli and Tavis, 2016; Javad and Sumod, 2015). When PMS works well, it results in significant benefits to both the overall organization and the individual employees. When it does not work well, or worse is ignored, it causes frustration and missed opportunities that are detrimental to the organization.

Due to the significant foreign investments into the Middle East, increased presence of MNEs, domination of foreign workers/expatriates in labors, and introduction of western higher education and training programs, organizations operating in the region are expected to adopt and follow western HR practices. However, scholarly research focused on HRM in the Middle East reports that HRM policies and practices in the region are heavily influenced by a number of cultural and religious factors, and the adoption of western practices vary among different countries in the region (Budhwar and Mellahi, 2016; Budhwar and Mellahi, 2018). For example, while Israel bases much of its HRM policies on western philosophy, HR policies of Morocco are heavily influenced by the national culture (Giangreco et al. 2010).

This chapter has three major goals. First, to highlight the contextual and organizational factors influencing HRM in the Middle Eastern organizations. Second, to review the PA practices in the Middle East, specifically, the influence of western performance management (PM) practices. Third, to discuss key challenges facing effective implementation of PMS in the Middle East. The chapter provides secondary research-based inputs to foreign investors, line managers, and human resource professionals for designing and administering effective performance management systems. It is organized as follows. The first section provides an overview of the major factors that influence performance management practices, the second section presents uses of performance appraisals, and the third section summarizes important features of performance management systems in Middle East–based organizations.

Factors and Sub-factors Affecting PM in the Middle East

Several factors influence HRM practices in the Middle East and, by extension, performance management. These factors can be categorized into external, institutional, and internal factors (Aycan, 2005). Table 12.1 shows the important factors and sub-factors that directly or indirectly affect performance management practices in Middle Eastern organizations.

TABLE 12.1 Factors and Sub-factors Influencing Performance Management in the Middle East

Factors	Sub-factors
External	National/Regional Culture
	• Collectivism
	• Wasta
	• Power Distance
Institutional	Ownership Type
	• State Owned Enterprises (SOEs)
	• Foreign Invested Firms (FIEs)
	• Family-Owned Enterprises (FOEs)
Internal	Technology
	Leadership

Impact of External Factors on PM in the Middle East

In the predominantly Arab-speaking and Islamic countries of the Middle East, cultural practices exert a great influence on all aspects of public and private life of citizens (Behery and Paton, 2008; Haak-Saheem et al. 2017; Suliman, 2006). They also guide the policies and practices of organizations, including HRM practices. Collectivism, wasta/ nepotism, high power distance, etc. are some of the national cultural factors that impact performance management in Middle Eastern organizations.

Collectivism

Arab society is generally characterized by strong collectivism. Collectivism refers to cooperation at the individual, group, organizational, and societal levels and also the extent to which an organization provides benefits to employees (Kirkman, Lowe, & Gibson, 2006). Several authors have suggested that individualistic and collectivistic cultures encourage and endorse different kinds of performance appraisals and have implications for the conduct on individual appraisals (Fletcher, 2001; Ramamoorthy and Carroll, 1998). In a collectivist entity, employees are not hired on the basis of merit but on the basis of personal connections and similarities. Further, within this collectivist framework there are distinctions between the "in-groups" and the "out-groups" of managers. The "in-group" consists of extended family and tribe whilst the "out-group" is non-kin or people from a different religious sect. While the relationship between a manager and his in-group members are characterized by protection and cohesiveness, the relationship of the manager with the out-group members emphasize task achievement and performance targets (Mellahi, 2006). High-performing employees within a group may be disliked by other members of the group and may be perceived as an impediment to the group harmony. Sometimes this may cause conflicts among employees.

In collectivist cultures, loyalty to the superior and in-group is often considered to be more important than productivity. For example, Hebron Public Hospital (HPH), a major public medical treatment facility in Palestine, devised a new framework of performance appraisal system (PAS) based on Western logics in order to professionalize the organization. In the initial phase, the implementation was taken positively by the employees and managers. However, the effectiveness of PAS reduced in the later stages as managers placed lower emphasis on performance but on personal relations and allocated privileges and special treatments to in-group employees regardless of their performance. People were rewarded for their presence and societal status. Consequently, evaluation scores became a representation of status or personal connection instead of performance.

Wasta/Nepotism

Wasta refers to social networks of interpersonal connections rooted in family and kinship ties that are central to the transmission of knowledge and creation of opportunities in the Middle East (Hutchings and Weir, 2006; Khalaf and Khalaf, 2009; Weir and Hutchings, 2005). It is a salient and acceptable practice in Arab culture (Huffpost, 2014). Wasta, characterized by family and personal relations, impacts hiring decisions, performance appraisal practices, and career advancement of employees in Middle Eastern organizations. Although many managers possess some knowledge of Western management practices and may have been educated in the West, Arab culture governing the organizational practices gives precedence to tribe, family, and kin over the objectives of the organization. Working relations in the Arab world are facilitated by an understanding of how to move within relevant power networks. For instance, the performance appraisal policy of SACO, a Saudi Arabian company, shows that is rooted in Western notions of clearly defined goals and objectives. As per the policy document, managers and their staff are required to jointly develop a performance agreement and the resulting performance rating is linked to rewards. However, a study among employees of SACO revealed that the company's performance appraisal outcomes were constrained by wasta (Harbi et al. 2017). Subordinates' personal relationship with the manager was a determining factor in the ensuing appraisal grade. Managers placing personal and political relationships above objective measurement of individual performance contradict the performance evaluation policy. In collectivistic cultures, performance appraisal is more subjective and focuses on soft issues such as loyalty and relationships.

Power Distance

Another factor that influences performance appraisal in Middle East is power distance. Power distance is defined as the degree to which members of an organization or society accept unequal distribution of power (Javidan and House, 2001). In high power distance cultures like Arab countries, power and authority are major determinants of manager–employee relations. In such countries, superiors and subordinates do not consider themselves as equals, and it is considered inappropriate for people in lower positions to express opinions counter to those in superior positions. Hence, subordinates display obedience toward managers, and they rarely oppose managers' decisions. Tolerance for hierarchical solutions, respect for authority, and loyalty mean that subordinates are more likely to accept performance evaluations and subsequent decisions made by their supervisors. It is rare to complain against performance evaluations in high power distance and collectivist cultures.

Impact of Institutional Factors on PM in the Middle East

Ownership type is an important institutional factor that influences HRM practices in the Middle East. For example, there are significant differences between state-owned enterprises, family-owned enterprises, and foreign invested enterprises in terms of their strategic orientation and business performance. These differences result in different HR orientations as well.

State-Owned Enterprises (SOEs)

SOEs or public sector enterprises are the fundamental elements of economic architecture in the Middle East and North Africa (MENA) region. MENA SOEs operate across a wide range of sectors, including manufacturing, electricity and gas, telecoms, postal services, other utilities, real estate, finance, and transportation. The region is home to many competitive and profit-driven public sector companies. Due to higher pay and job security, public sector is the preferred employer of locals in the Middle East, especially in the GCC countries. Many public sector organizations in the Middle East employ large number of experienced, skilled expatriate managers, and professionals in key positions. In order to remain competitive, public organizations adopt best management practices, particularly in human resource management, from the private sector worldwide. They tend to use written procedures, clear rules, job analyses, performance appraisal policies, and structured training programs. For example, performance of all part-time and full-time employees of federal entities in the UAE, except members of judiciary, diplomatic groups, and lower-grade employees, is evaluated based on written standards and established guidelines. On the contrary, though performance appraisals are common in Qatar, they are conducted in a centralized, top-down, subjective, and confidential manner.

A large number of GCC-based SOEs foray into foreign markets as part of their internationalization endeavors. These multinational enterprises (MNEs), owned by the government, try to align their HR practices with the developmental agenda of their home countries. As part of the nationalization policy, Arab MNEs prefer to employ local citizens in international assignments. Local employees are less interested in relocating to foreign countries as a result of their collectivistic attitudes and values. To motivate the local workforce to accept international assignments, HR managers offer them with generous compensation package and career advancement options. Nationals take up international assignments to gain some exposure to foreign cultures and facilitate inward transfer of HRM practices to the home country. Hence, formal performance assessment of local employees during their international stint is not emphasized in state-owned Arab MNEs. Alternatively, to engage national talents, the companies offer non-financial incentives like career development opportunities, and employee recognition programs. For example, Etisalat group, a state-owned MNE headquartered in the UAE, launched a number of recognition programs such as spot recognition award and appreciation certificate in host countries to acknowledge the contributions of employees beyond their official duties. Spot awards are a flexible tool that empowers employees to recognize their managers and peers exhibiting positive behavior in accordance with the Etisalat core value. Under this program, any member of staff can give reward points to colleagues, including their bosses, which can be converted into credit for their mobile bill payments (Etisalat, 2018).

Family-Owned Enterprises (FOEs)

The private sector organizations in the Middle East consist of several small and a few medium-sized family-owned commercial businesses (Basly, 2017). There are roughly 5,000 family firms in the Middle East. These FOEs account for 70% of the region's employment and control over 90% of commercial activities (Alderson, 2011). Majority of these family businesses are agents or dealers for international/foreign brands. In the Arab Middle East, resource boundaries between the family and the business systems are almost absent (Samara, 2020), which often leads to informal human resources practices. Moreover, the practice of wasta influences HR practices of family-owned firms. Due to the centralized structure, outside talents are reluctant to join family businesses as they fear being impeded in their career track by the glass ceiling imposed by familial management succession and probable nepotism. The role of HR varies in family-owned enterprises in the region. For example, in Turkish family-owned firms, the HR departments fulfill traditional personnel-management functions whereas, large family-owned business groups in the UAE follow somewhat formalized human resources practices (Majid Al Futtaim, 2018).

Foreign Invested Enterprises (FIEs)

Regulatory factors inhibit companies from having full foreign ownership in many Arab countries. Hence, foreign firms operating in this market offer the full array of entry choices ranging from simple export to fully owned affiliates such as 100% ownership in free trade zones (Mellahi et al. 2011). Many world-famous multinational banks, consulting firms, IT companies and retail firms have established business in the region, including HSBC, McKinsey, Microsoft, Ikea, etc. Both parent company HR practices and local culture influence international human resource (IHR) practices of multinational companies at subsidiary level (Demirbag et al. 2016; Hannon and Jaw 1995; Nakhle, n.d.). According to Beechler and Yang (1994), the internal environment of the firm, in terms of corporate culture, administrative heritage, organizational structure, and employee characteristics, and the external environment in terms of labor market conditions, alternative job opportunities for employees, host-country regulatory conditions, etc., determines the transferability of parent HR practices to its international subsidiaries. A study examining transferability of HRM practices in international joint ventures in Iran found that private sector as compared to public sector was more flexible to adapt HRM practices from the western partner due to less bureaucracy and stronger drive for performance-based procedures (Namazie 2003). Further, since performance appraisals are not common in Iran, such systems are also often introduced by foreign partners (Iles et al. 2012). Performance assessment is a key factor in successful IHR activities of multinational corporations, especially to retain and motivate existing employees (Varma et al. 2008). For example, H&M, a Swedish multinational clothing-retail company, follows a strong feedback culture in all its international subsidiaries present in 19 markets across the Middle East & North Africa, Russia, Turkey, and Europe. Employee performance assessment process stresses on regular performance reviews followed by individualized development plans aimed at developing and retaining talents (H&M 2021).

Impact of Internal Factors on PM in Middle East

A review of the recent literature suggests that two organizational factors, i.e., technology and leadership, influence the adoption of PM practices in the ME.

Technology

In recent years, due to the rapid development of internet and information technology (IT), public sector and large-sized private organizations in the Middle East have started to increasingly adopt electronic HRM practices. A recent survey by the KPMG (2019) Lower Gulf reveals that HR functions of UAE organizations are undergoing digital transformation (KPMG Lower Gulf, 2019). Digitally driven HR innovations range from automated pay roll to digital human capital to Artificial Intelligence (AI) systems. A case in point is Sharaf DG, Dubai's mega electronics and IT products retailer, that recently introduced an AI-enabled engagement bot to identify employees who are unhappy, disengaged, and are about to leave (Zawya 2019). It is also noteworthy that a number of Middle Eastern organizations adopted digital performance management system. For example, Al-Mansour Group in Egypt, and Ittihad International Investment LLC in Abu Dhabi use cloud-based performance evaluation solutions of SAP for efficient management of employee appraisals (SAP n.d.]. Jumeirah group, a Dubai-based international luxury hotel chain, uses automated performance management system to identify talented people internally, plan for future vacancies and organize talent reviews (CIPD, 2017).

Many federal entities are also at the forefront of digital HR transformation. For example, to automate and integrate different HR processes in federal government entities, the Federal Authority for Government Human Resources (FAHR) in the UAE introduced a HRM information system, called Bayanati in 2014. The application covers employees from all ministries and federal entities. Bayanati manages all stages of performance management electronically and integrates it with other HR processes such as rewards, promotion, and training and development. The automated performance management system allows the user departments to link individual employee's objectives to the strategies and visions of the federal government and monitor and evaluate their performance. The line manager's dashboard displays percentage of completion of the annual evaluation stages and the number of low performing employees who completed the individual development plan. At the end of the appraisal period, appraisal rating is also communicated to employees through Bayanati.

Leadership

CEOs and top management teams play a central role in making strategic changes (Wiersema and Bantel 1992). Young CEOs with international education and/or international experience in foreign countries with greater cultural distance from Middle East are more inclined to adopt performance-oriented and positive work culture in organizations. For example, Tim Murray, an American national with international education and international experience, is credited with transforming Aluminum Bahrain's (Alba) safety culture. Due to the ongoing number of fatalities within the plants, Alba, the second largest single-site aluminum smelter in the world, was not considered as an attractive employer. Tim Murray, who was appointed as the CEO of Alba in 2012, focused on developing a new culture based on safety of people and systems by linking successful safety culture to the financial performance of the company. Everyone at Alba was inducted and trained in health and safety practices. At the start of 2013, the CEO instituted a monthly safety review on the first Wednesday of each month to enforce a strict personal accountability on the performance of safety. As part of this, Alba included safety metrics such as incident categories, inspections, safety training, and corrective actions in plant managers' key performance indicators (KPIs). The monthly CEO safety performance review enabled the management to monitor changes in system condition and performance against established visions, goals, and objectives. The new performance management system introduced by the CEO along with various safety campaigns and training programs improved workplace safety and health in Alba (Alba, 2013; Esty and Sesia, 2005).

Similarly, Pinar Abay, a Turkish national with western education and international experience, is credited with transforming Oyak bank's organizational culture. Oyak bank, one of the largest banks in Turkey, was acquired by the Dutch ING Group in 2007. The company appointed Pinar as the CEO in 2011. Oyak's employees were used to a low-performance culture as the performance appraisal and the reward systems did not differentiate between good and bad performers. Pinar redesigned the old performance management system by replacing branch-level performance target with individual-level performance target. The automated performance management system called Basari Vitrini (meaning the showcasing of success) allowed individual employees to access their performance targets and achievements of theirs and any other employee on a daily basis. Good performance was recognized both monetarily and non-monetarily. The transparency in the performance management system and linking performance to rewards led to dramatic improvements in sales.

Uses of Performance Appraisal

The results of performance reviews are generally used for administrative decisions such as pay and promotions in Middle Eastern organizations. For instance, some public and private sector companies in the UAE like Emirates NBD, ADCB, and

Majid Al-Futtiam link individual and group performance to salary increments (Srinivasan and Çekin, 2020).

Annual appraisal outcome is considered as an important criterion for identifying employee training needs and succession planning. Family-owned private firms such as Zamil Group in Saudi Arabia, Mansour Group in Egypt, and Alghanim Industries in Kuwait link employee performance management with employee training systems. Employees in these organizations are expected to identify the areas in which they wish to grow. At the end of the appraisal period, employees along with their managers prepare employee training and development plans.

Some large family businesses and public organizations use appraisal system for achieving strategic changes. As an illustration, consider how Alghanim Industries used a new performance management system to facilitate a cultural shift from wastacracy to meritocracy. Alghanim is one of the leading family-owned companies in Kuwait, with 30 different businesses in 40 countries (Alghanim 2020). In the initial years, hiring and promotion policies of the group were based on personal relationships and influence (wastacracy) and the company employed a large number of family members in management positions. Omar Kutayba Alghanim, a western-educated fifth-generation CEO of the conglomerate, introduced a culture of meritocracy, and, based recruitment and career advancement decisions exclusively on employees' qualifications, performance, and merit. He revamped the company's performance management and compensation systems to foster meritocracy. Under the new system, employees are evaluated based on clearly defined performance standards and rewarded based on performance evaluation ratings. The company also conducts talent review meetings twice a year in order to review performance gaps and identify potential future leaders of the company and their personal growth needs. New performance management system helped the company to attract and retain best people and align individual goals with corporate goals. In 2020, Alghanim employed more than 14,000 employees from 64 different nationalities. Moreover, the group is now regarded one of the most professionally run companies in the region (Healy and Gallani 2019). Likewise, the Ministry of Saudi Civil Services (SCS) introduced a new performance assessment scheme in 2017 to increase the performance level of 1.5 million Saudis working in the government and develop a work culture based on performance. The new system classifies employees into five categories from excellent to unsatisfactory. All except "unsatisfactory" category receives annual increment based on an annual circular issued by the Civil Services Ministry before the performance assessment period (Harbi 2018).

Legal Uses of Performance Management in the Middle East

A variety of important HR decisions such as confirmation of probation, increment, promotion, and training are linked to the results of performance appraisals in state-owned organizations in the ME, particularly in the UAE. For instance, according to the UAE Federal Decree Law, all government entities are legally required to conduct annual performance appraisals and the result of the performance appraisals form basis for monetary and nonmonetary rewards and promotion decisions. Further, Federal entities are required to analyze employee training and development needs using employee annual appraisals. The decree permits the hiring authority to terminate an employee's service if he/she fails to attain the job performance level prescribed in the Employee Performance Management System, after providing a notice period comparable to the job grade. As per the UAE Labour Law, an employer has to pay up to three months' salary if an employee is terminated for a reason other than the employee's performance.

Features of Performance Appraisal in the Middle East

The following are some of the important features of performance management and performance appraisals in organizations based in the Middle East.

- Regular annual performance appraisal is more common in public sector and mid- to large-sized private organizations. Recently, performance appraisals are being used more extensively for administrative and developmental purposes in the Middle East. Performance appraisals are conducted to meet legal requirements as well (Harbi 2018; Namazie 2003).
- Middle Eastern organizations use broad rating scales and absolute ranking system that measures employee performance against predetermined standards. In order to avoid offending their employees and upset the sense of collectivism and teamwork, many managers provide average or uniform ratings and rarely extend excellent or poor ratings (Hall and Nido, 2017). However, a few organizations use relative performance evaluation system. For example, King Fahd University of Petroleum & Minerals, one of the leading universities in Saudi Arabia, focuses on the achievement of predetermined goals and development of required behavioral competencies when grading employee performance. The grades thus generated are distributed along a bell-shaped curve, and the employees are classified into three major performance categories: top 20% as "top performers", next 70% as "average performers", and the bottom 10% as "non-performers" (KFUPM, 2017).
- Performance appraisals in medium and large private sector organizations are being facilitated by technology.
- Cultural factors such as power-distance and wasta, and favoritism in recruitment, selection, and promotion practices reduce the link between performance and reward. To cope with the influence of the cultural norms, organizations in the Middle East offer long-term training to new employees and customized training to existing employees. Large organizations like ADNOC, Cevital, and Chalhoub group have opened internal training academies across the region to offer upskill training programs (Harbi et al. 2017; Weir and Hutchings 2005).
- Lifetime job security and higher pay and benefits packages reduce the effectiveness of performance appraisals in public sector organizations.

- In the private sector, appraisals are punitive in nature, as private companies are more inclined to use the results to fire poor performers rather than to train them.
- Most organizations in the Middle East use appraisal results only for administration purposes. However, some companies use it for both administration and development purposes. These companies also decouple performance review and talent review sessions as these sessions require managers to possess different kind of skills. While the former session requires managers to have the qualities of judges, the latter requires them to possess the qualities of counselors.
- In recent years, performance appraisal is being used increasingly for administrative and developmental purposes in the Middle East. Performance appraisals in medium and large private sector organizations are facilitated by technology.

Conclusion

Arab culture is classified as high context and uses implicit messages. High-context cultures and firms value flexibility, social harmony, and cooperativeness. Moreover, in Arab countries, loyalty takes precedence over productivity and education, or position takes precedence over people and performance. Consistent with this, many scholars such as Abdalla (2006), Aycan (2006), Harbi et al. (2017), and Mellahi et al. (2011) reported that most of the organizations in Arab countries follow traditional, reactive, and short-term-focused performance appraisals. In fact, performance appraisal is identified as the most culture-bound HR practice in the Middle East.

While performance appraisal is used for control and motivation purposes in western organizations (Cappelli and Tavis, 2016), it serves as a tool for maintaining status quo and hierarchy in the Middle Eastern organizations. Poor implementation of performance appraisal systems does not help organizations to achieve their goals (Dorsey and Mueller-Hanson, 2017; Williams, 1997). This may be the reason why individual performance appraisal designed on western logics fails at the implementation level in Middle Eastern organizations. Past empirical studies found that employee perception of performance appraisal-organizational culture fit is an important determinant of organizational commitment. Therefore, PMS rooted in western logics and meritocracy principles may be more successful in organizations with diverse workforce and performance-oriented culture. In order to get improved performance from appraisals, a continuous process is necessary. It starts with defining and clarifying performance expectations, followed by performance evaluations and ends with development of performance improvement plans. To more effectively manage employee performance, managers should work with employees to identify both skill gaps and new skills that the company may require of its employees in the years ahead and help them to prepare a self-development plan to master the required skills and behaviors.

Case Study

FAHR

The Federal Authority for the Government Human Resources (FAHR) is an independent legal authority established by the federal government of the UAE in 2009. It aims to develop human resources in the UAE Federal Government according to modern concepts and globally applied standards in this field. FAHR is vested with powers and responsibilities to review, manage, and develop HR policies and HR-related legislations for the Federal Ministries and Government entities in the UAE. FAHR, in cooperation with the Ministry of Finance, launched a Human Resources Information Management system called Bayanati to manage human resources tasks electronically.

The Federal Government employee performance management system (EPMS) follows a three-phase cycle: performance planning, interim review, and performance evaluation. The performance planning phase starts during the month of January or February in each year. In order to prepare the annual performance appraisal, the line manager and employee meet at the beginning of the year and agree on the objectives that the employee is expected to achieve by the end of the year. During the meeting, the line manager assigns weight for each objective agreed. After completing the objective setting and weighting processes, the line manager determines the behavioral and technical competencies required by the employee to achieve the desired performance. The interim review phase is conducted during the month of June–July of each year. During this phase, the employee's developments and achievements are reviewed against the planned objectives, in order to reinforce and enhance the performance strengths and identify its weaknesses and provide corrective measures when needed. Annual performance evaluation is the last phase of the EPMS Cycle. It starts during the last two months of the year (November–December). In this phase, line managers review and assess achievement of performance objectives and competencies of their direct reports and rate the overall performance on a five-point rating scale. Distinguished employees, those who received appraisal rating of 3 and above, are eligible for job promotion or financial incentive. Whereas employees whose performance fall under the "need improvement" category are required to follow a six-month performance improvement plan to improve performance.

Relevant Websites

The readers can refer to the following websites to get more information about FAHR performance management system in general:
https://www.fahr.gov.ae/Portal/Userfiles/Assets/Documents/c996dcec.pdf
https://www.fahr.gov.ae/Portal/Userfiles/Assets/Documents/834df64b.pdf
https://www.fahr.gov.ae/Portal/Userfiles/Assets/Documents/8db959c9.pdf

References

Abdalla, I.A., 2006. Human resource management in Qatar. In *Managing Human Resources in the Middle East*, pp. 121–144.

Alba, 2013. *HSE Review*. Available at: https://www.albasmelter.com/mc/newsletters/pdf/booklets/2013/hse%20booklet%20for%202013.pdf (Accessed: 25 May 2021).

Alderson, K.J., 2011. *Understanding the family business*. Business Expert Press.

Alghanim, 2020. *Who we are*. Available at: https://www.alghanim.com/About-us/Who-we-are (Accessed: 25 November 2020).

Aycan, Z., 2005. The interplay between cultural and institutional/structural contingencies in human resource management practices. *International Journal of Human Resource Management*, 16, 1083–1119.

Aycan, Z., 2006. Human resource management in Turkey. In *Managing human resources in the middle-east* (pp. 178–197). Routledge.

Basly, S., 2017. Introduction to "Family Businesses in the Arab world". In *Family businesses in the Arab world* (pp. 1–6). Springer, Cham.

Beechler, S. and Yang, J.Z., 1994. The transfer of Japanese-style management to American subsidiaries: constraints, and competencies. *Journal of International Business Studies*, 25(3), pp. 467–491.

Behery, M.H. and Paton, R.A., 2008. Performance appraisal-cultural fit: Organizational outcomes within the UAE. *Education, Business and Society: Contemporary Middle Eastern Issues*.

Budhwar, P.S. and Mellahi, K. eds., 2016. *Handbook of human resource management in the Middle East*. Edward Elgar Publishing.

Budhwar, P. and Mellahi, K., 2018. HRM in the Middle East. In *Handbook of research on comparative human resource management*. Edward Elgar Publishing.

Cappelli, P. and Tavis, A., 2016. The performance management revolution. *Harvard Business Review*, 94(10), pp. 58–67.

CIPD 2017. *We're not used to Emiratis waiting tables – but everyone has to start somewhere*. Available at: https://www.cipd.ae/news/case-study-jumeirah-group (Accessed: 2 November 2020).

Demirbag, M., Tatoglu, E., and Wilkinson, A., 2016. Adoption of high-performance work systems by local subsidiaries of developed country and Turkish MNEs and indigenous firms in Turkey. *Human Resource Management*, 55(6), 1001–1024.

Dorsey, D. and Mueller-Hanson, R., 2017. Performance management that makes a difference: an evidence based approach. *SHRM Science to Practice Series*.

Etisalat 2018. *Sustainability Report*. Available at: https://www.etisalat.com/en/system/com/assets/docs/general/etisalat-group-sustainability-report-2018.pdf (Accessed: 7 December 2020).

Esty, C.B., and Sesia, A., 2005. Aluminium Bahrain (Alba): The Pot Line 5 Expansion Project. HBSP.

Fletcher, C., 2001. Performance appraisal and management: the developing research agenda. *Journal of Occupational and Organizational Psychology*, 74(4), pp. 473–487.

Giangreco, Antonio, Andrea Carugati, Massimo Pilati, and Antonio Sebastiano., 2010. Performance appraisal systems in the Middle East: moving beyond Western logics. *European Management Review* 7(3), pp. 155–168.

Haak-Saheem, W., Festing, M. and Darwish, T.K., 2017. International human resource management in the Arab Gulf States–an institutional perspective. *The International Journal of Human Resource Management*, 28(18), pp. 2684–2712.

Hall, B., and Nido, S.D., 2017. *YAAS's service center*. HBSP.

Hannon, J.M. and Jaw, B.S., 1995. International human resource strategy and its determinants: the case of subsidiaries in Taiwan. *Journal of International Business Studies*, 26(3), pp. 531–554.

Harbi, S.A., 2018. Criteria for performance appraisal in Saudi Arabia, and employees interpretation of these criteria. *International Journal of Business and Management*, 13(9), pp. 106–117.

Harbi, S.A., Thursfield, D. and Bright, D., 2017. Culture, wasta and perceptions of performance appraisal in Saudi Arabia. *The International Journal of Human Resource Management*, 28(19), pp. 2792–2810.

Healy, P.M., and Gallani, S., 2019. *Building a meritocracy at Alghanim Industries*. HBSP.

Huffpost (2014). *Meritocracy in the Modern World*. Available at: https://www.huffpost.com/entry/meritocracy-in-the-modern_b_6212390 (Accessed: 8 December 2020).

H&M 2021, *Reviews and open dialogues*, Available at: https://career.hm.com/content/hmcareer/en_bh/workingathm/get-to-know-us/grow-with-us.html (Accessed: 0 June 2021).

Hutchings, K. and Weir, D., 2006. Guanxi and wasta: a comparison. *Thunderbird International Business Review*, 48(1), pp. 141–156.

Iles, P., Almhedie, A. and Baruch, Y., 2012. Managing HR in the Middle East: challenges in the public sector. *Public Personnel Management*, 41(3), pp. 465–492.

Javad, S. and Sumod, S.D., 2015. It's time to bring performance appraisal into the twenty-first century. *Human Resource Management International Digest*, 23(7), pp. 23–26.

Javidan, M., and House, R.J., 2001. Lessons from project GLOBE. *Organizational Dynamics*, 29(4), pp. 289–305.

KFUPM 2017. New performance management system for KFUPM staff. Available at: https://www.kfupm.edu.sa/deanships/fpa/docs/Performance%20Management%20-%20Workshop%20English.pdf (Accessed: 16 June 2020).

Khalaf, R.S. and Khalaf, S. eds., 2009. *Arab society and culture: An essential reader*. Saqi.

Kirkman, B.L., Lowe, K.B. and Gibson, C.B., 2006. A quarter century of culture's consequences: a review of empirical research incorporating Hofstede's cultural values framework. *Journal of International Business Studies*, 37(3), pp. 285–320.

Kirkpatrick, D.L., 2006. *Improving employee performance through appraisal and coaching*. Amacom Books.

KPMG 2019. *The future of HR*. Available at: https://assets.kpmg/content/dam/kpmg/ae/pdf/Future-of-hr-2019.pdf (Accessed: 10 December, 2020).

KPMG Lower Gulf 2019. *The Future of HR: UAE human resources report*. Available at: https://www.cmvm.pt/pt/Comunicados/ConferenciasdaCMVM/Documents/STATE%20OWNERSHIP%20IN%20THE%20MIDDLE%20EAST%20AND%20NORTH%20AFRICA.pdf (Accessed: 24 December 2020).

Majid Al Futtaim 2018. *Talent as important as balance sheets*. Available at: https://www.majidalfuttaim.com/en/media-centre/blog-posts/2018/1/talent-as-important-as-balance-sheets (Accessed: 27 November 2020).

Mellahi, K., 2006. Human resource management in Saudi Arabia. In *Managing Human Resources in the Middle-East* (pp. 115–138). Routledge.

Mellahi, K., Demirbag, M. and Riddle, L., 2011. Multinationals in the Middle East: challenges and opportunities. *Journal of World Business*, 46(4), pp. 406–410.

Nakhle, S.F. n.d. *Performance appraisal in multinational companies: The most culturally sensitive HR practice?* Available at: http://sietar.ch/performance-appraisal-in-multinational-companies-the-most-culturally-sensitive-hr-practice-by-dr-samer-francois-nakhle/ (Accessed: 18 December 2020).

Namazie, P., 2003. Factors affecting the transferability of HRM practices in joint ventures based in Iran. *Career Development International*, 8(7), pp. 357–366.

Ramamoorthy, N. and Carroll, S.J., 1998. Individualism/collectivism orientations and reactions toward alternative human resource management practices. *Human relations*, 51(5), pp. 571–588.

Samara, G., 2020. Family businesses in the Arab Middle East: what do we know and where should we go? *Journal of Family Business Strategy*, 12(3), p. 100359.

SAP n.d. *Al Mansour automotive soars employee performance*. Available at: http://ecs-co.com/SuccessStory-assets/StoryPDF/Al%20Mansour-Auto-Success-Story.pdf (Accessed: 28 November, 2020).

Srinivasan, S. and Çekin, E., 2020. *Driving transformation at the Majid Al Futtaim group*. HBSP.

Suliman, A.M.T., 2006. Human resource management in the United Arab Emirates. In *Managing human resources in the middle-east* (pp. 77–96). Routledge.

Varma, A., Budhwar, P.S. and DeNisi, A.S. eds., 2008. *Performance management systems: A global perspective*. Taylor & Francis.

Weir, D. and Hutchings, K., 2005. Cultural embeddedness and contextual constraints: Knowledge sharing in Chinese and Arab cultures. *Knowledge and Process Management*, 12(2), pp. 89–98.

Wiersema, M.F. and Bantel, K.A., 1992. Top management team demography and corporate strategic change. *Academy of Management Journal*, 35(1), pp. 91–121.

Williams, M.J., 1997. Performance appraisal is dead. Long live performance management. *Harvard Management Update*, 2, pp. 1–6.

Zawya, 2019. *Sharaf DG adopts a futuristic strategy to retain 88% at-risk employees with in Feedo's AI-enabled engagement bot: Amber*. Available at: https://www.zawya.com/mena/en/press-releases/story/Sharaf_DG_adopts_a_futuristic_strategy_to_retain_88_atrisk_employees_with_inFeedos_AIenabled_engagement_bot_Amber-ZAWYA20190916075040/ (Accessed: 10 December 2020).

13
EXPATRIATE MANAGEMENT IN THE MIDDLE EAST

Prerna Kumari

Introduction

Middle Eastern (ME) countries are home to expatriates (expats) from around the globe, and this makes them a surreal melting pot of diverse socio-economic and cultural segments. Their geographical location on the world map plays a strategically complimentary role, as Europe-Africa-Asia intersect here. Over the years, expats have become an integral part of the 'whole' populace in the region – blended and co-existent with the natives in harmony, respecting mutual cultures and traditions as well as contributing towards mutual economic goals. As per 2021 demographics, the ME population is approximately 456 million (World Population Review, 2021). The expat population in GCC (Gulf Cooperation Council) countries is over 51% as per the 2016 demographics (www.go-gulf.ae). The highest ratio of expat to local working population exists in this region as per the International Labour Organisation (ILO) (www.ilo.org). Due to COVID-19 pandemic and significant exodus of expat population from the region, there is no recent census that provides the latest population numbers for the ME; the available demographics on population composition are even older. Therefore, 2019 World Bank population estimate and 2021 World Population review have both been considered. Dubai, for example, experienced the sharpest drop in population (8.4%), owing to such exodus (Omar and Mathew, 2019) and the trend is expected to continue across ME in the near future.

Historically, the ME region has been characterised by binding factors of shared language (Arabic, Persian, Turkish), religion (Islam), culture, political structures (monarchy), socio-economic fabric (paternalism) and geographical proximity. These, combined with rising demand for petroleum/energy, which is a natural resource many ME nations are abundantly endowed with, provided an impetus to the prominence of this region on the world economic and political map.

DOI: 10.4324/9781003005766-15

A significant milestone in this development was the establishment of the GCC in 1981, which is an economic and political federation comprising six ME nations: Kingdom of Saudi Arabia (KSA), Kuwait, the United Arab Emirates (UAE), Qatar, Bahrain and Oman. The large-scale immigration of expats into the region was a parallel phenomenon taking shape. This was to play a significant role in combining local and expat knowledge, skills and expertise towards achieving economic growth and development goals of the region. The ME offered lucrative and competitive terms and conditions of employment to incoming expats, thereby making the region a popular destination.

Given this background, expatriate management in the ME becomes unmistakably significant and deserves careful planning and attention on part of organisations and businesses – whether already established in the region or planning to venture therein; as well as for expats themselves. There are multiple social, cultural, economic and political considerations that deserve to be taken into account. This chapter looks at some of these key considerations such as how they facilitate expat management, what challenges they pose and how some of those may be tackled. Furthermore, it provides specific advice and recommendations, based on evidence and experience, to managers and expats aiming to achieve success in the ME region. Additional resources for further referencing have been provided in the appendix (Table 13.1–13.3), for readers interested to find out more about any specific aspect.

Key Contextual Considerations for People Managers and Expats

The expat population in ME may be classified into two predominant categories – 'working' and 'dependent'. The former being employed in any form and generating income (entrepreneurs included); and the latter being dependent on them in terms of visa sponsorship, accommodation, education and other liabilities. In some countries (e.g., UAE), dependents are permitted to undertake certain employment opportunities, subject to terms and conditions such as no-objection-certificate from their 'working' sponsor, without having to change their visa status though their employer needs to obtain a 'Labour Card' before employing them officially. Expats on dependent visa also receive government support in changing visa status, as is the case in Qatar. Whilst there are others (such as KSA) which do not grant permission for expats on dependent visas to undertake employment. Kuwait eased visa transfer regulations in 2021, whereby dependent expats may transfer their visas to undertake private jobs. Likewise, there are travel restrictions to mobility of dependents within the region; for example, to enter KSA, Qatar or the UAE, they must be accompanied by their 'working' sponsor. Many countries such as Bahrain, Egypt and the UAE permit expats to enter the country on long-term visit visas which may be converted to work permit should they find employment.

The 'working' expats may be broadly categorised into skilled, semi-skilled, unskilled and entrepreneurs, each having their respective income brackets, terms of employment and working conditions that deserve consideration while designing expat management policies. The semi-skilled and unskilled working class (blue-collar) usually do not have accompanying dependent expats with them, as they fall within the lower income bracket with fixed-term employment contracts; examples include construction workers, labourers in factories, frontline staff in retail stores, hotel/restaurant support staff, domestic workers and security guards. They usually reside single, in company-provided shared accommodations, and are a large source of regular remittance transfers to their dependents back in the home country.

The following sections look at the overall sociocultural, economic and political context of host countries, factors which ought to be evaluated by potential entrants into the region; and reference to resources where additional information may be found.

Sociocultural Context of Host Country

The sociocultural milieu in ME is a fusion of traditional heritage and modern capability – which has evolved over the decades as change has been embraced by an increasingly amenable society. Cultural diversity and multi-ethnic societies are increasingly becoming commonplace in many ME countries whilst others are still trying to adapt and keep pace; sometimes owing to internal conflict and strife. There is a mix of indigenous as well as foreign residents in these countries. As indicated by the ILO data, the ratio of expats to nationals in GCC countries may average at as high as 89% in some countries such as Qatar and UAE. In fact, KSA and UAE are home to the world's third and fifth largest emigrant community, respectively (Shayah and Sun, 2019).

Family values and tribe-based bonds are very strong and adjure dependence and loyalty among members unanimously. Having long family names is a way of showing respect to one's lineage through titles such as 'Ibn' or 'bin' (son of), 'bint' (daughter of) and 'Abu' (father of).

Another feature of current ME is a fast-expanding indigenous youth base, under 25 years of age. This is the population base that would be or already is, to be absorbed in the working community. Hence, there are intensive efforts by governments and educational institutions to educate them to be employment-ready. The other emergent characteristic in the new millennium has been an increasing number of women not only entering the workforce, but also delivering high performance. It is commonplace to find organisations with a high percentage of female employees, including expats. The improved level of education among women and broad-mindedness of society are accountable for this wave of transition. Women are actively involved in social causes, corporate roles and now even in the Board Room (Forbes ME https://www.forbesmiddleeast.com/). The traditional 'hijab' (head-covering scarf) is mandatory to wear in public places in some countries such as Iran and KSA; whilst not so in others such as Bahrain, Kuwait, Oman and the UAE; and women are receiving more freedom of expression and choice. An example is the right to drive, granted to women in KSA in 2018.

Tangible strand of Westernisation is evident in many ME societies, emulating the best from the West – from language, fashion, food, books, entertainment, housing to other tastes and preferences. Vacation travels to different parts of the world have facilitated this blend of cultures. The other common practice among locals as well as expats is to send their children for higher education abroad – preferably to Western countries. Locals are expected to bring back the learning to contribute to the enhancement of their national interests and achievement of national development goals.

Such considerations must be factored in when any business proposes to venture into the region. Shaykhian et al. (2016) reinforce the importance of cultural adaptation by business leaders of multinational firms when they enter a host country in the ME region. They researched the diminished performance of American firms in the ME context caused by lack of 'culturally competent' business leaders driving such structural, behavioural and organisational adjustment according to local norms and sensitivities.

Hospitality and warmth have been the bedrock of traditional ME culture and culminate in treatment enriched with 'Karam' (generosity) and 'Ihsan' (kindness/graciousness) towards guests. The spirit of nationalism is strong and prevalent – there are magnificent celebrations of flag days, national days and even international days to celebrate the conglomeration of multiple cultures. Loyalty to the nation and a strong spirit of patriotism earmark the common ME culture ('Pan Arabism' as per Britannica) and are a great binding factor among proud members of the society.

The tropical, arid climate in ME makes it a preferred destination for expats from cold countries. There is mostly bright, sunny weather for most parts of the year (very high temperatures for one-fourth of a year); followed by not-so-cold breezy winters; and sparse rainfall. Football (soccer) is the favourite sport in most countries in the region; other popular sports include horse riding, camel racing, motor sports and water sports.

Table 13.1 in appendix contains links to some additional web-based resources that may be accessed for further information with regard to the sociocultural context in the ME region, as the scope of this chapter does not entail such wide array of data. There are comprehensive reports available for download, and those contain insightful information.

Economic Context of Host Country

The economic environment in the ME has been driven by fundamentals of high oil and gas reserves; hence, the worldwide demand and oil prices have been a governing factor for most economies. In addition, sectors such as real estate, construction, telecommunications, automotive, energy, mining, agriculture, retail, eCommerce, healthcare, banking and financial services and travel and tourism are the other predominant quarters of economic activity and attract expat workers in large numbers. Detailed review of the GCC website (gcc-sg.org) is a good starting point and indicator of ongoing activities in the region.

It is recommended to identify information with respect to the target host country – its current economic condition, value of currency, position within the Gulf states, perceived levels of financial security, maturity of markets, international outlook (on forums such as International Monetary Fund and World Bank), industry reports (generated by reputed international analytics firms such as KPMG, E&Y or PwC) and economic policies. These may be further augmented with recent news published in local as well as international newspapers about the host country. The information must be validated from multiple sources before one may base decisions on its veracity. Web links of multiple reliable resources of this kind are listed in Table 13.2 in the appendix.

The other economic consideration is the financial and economic policies of the respective state – the taxable and tax-free elements, cost of living, savings potential, prevailing salary levels and how these may have changed during recent years. For instance, ME was perceived to be a destination for tax-free income by expats for many years, and hence the potential to save was very high. This was augmented by high salary and bonus figures. However, these dynamics have evolved in recent years with the introduction of Value Added Tax (VAT) in the range of 5–15% in various ME countries such as Bahrain, Egypt, KSA and the UAE (PwC ME). This tax is applicable to most goods and services; and has had a direct impact on the cost of living. Soon, countries such as Oman would be implementing VAT as well.

On the other hand, there are ongoing efforts to attract expats into the region. The UAE, for instance, has developed an ecosystem to encourage and welcome entrepreneurs from across the world. There are around 45 free zones within the UAE that encourage the expats to start their fully owned ventures (edarabia.com). These provide import/export and corporate tax exemptions, permit funds/profits repatriation to home country in full and also provide additional support with recruitment, visa formalities and sponsorship. Additionally, the UAE government has recently issued a royal decree to allow foreign nationals to have up to 100% ownership in businesses in the mainland of the UAE. Prior to that, expats could own up to 49% only; remaining stake was to be with a local Emirati sponsor. As per a report published by Global Entrepreneurship Monitor, around 62.3% new businesses were started by non-Emiratis in the UAE in 2017.

Islamic banking and finance (*Sharia*-compliance) are a cornerstone of financial activities and decision-making in the ME and are premised on adherence to *Sharia* (Islamic Laws). Principally, it prohibits charging interest for money lent/invested and propagates profit (or loss) sharing instead. Expanding ME economies have contributed to wider capital base of Islamic banking and financial institutions. Khan and Bhatti (2008, p.709) affirm that these thrive on powerful funding from high net-worth individuals, governments and state-aided institutions in Islamic ME states. These finance bodies can provide additional banking avenues besides conventional banking institutions for the expats moving to ME countries – this information is relevant especially for expat entrepreneurs.

The other prevalent business model in ME is that of the 'family owned businesses' – these are firms created for managing private wealth, investments and finances of large family offices; they have proliferated in ME over the recent decades. Their investments are not limited to any geography and are rather diversified globally in multiple profitable sectors. Some of the top groups are Mansour Group (Egypt),

Al-Futtaim Group (UAE), Olayan Group (KSA) and Alghanim Industries (Kuwait) (Forbes ME).

Further, there are free trade and economic zones such as Abu Dhabi Global Markets, Dubai Silicon Oasis Authority and Jebel Ali in the UAE; and Qatar Science & Technology Park in Qatar; with attractive options for expats (and nationals) to set up their own small and medium enterprises. These facilitate the investment environment within the country. The largest number of such zones is in Jordan and UAE (PwC ME).

Concepts of corporate social responsibility and sustainability are being increasingly embraced by organisations in the region. This serves a two-pronged purpose of alignment with long-term interests of society (diversity, ethics, philanthropy, human rights) at large; and integrating with some of the international best practices. Some of the ME companies with highest ranking on sustainable development parameters include Bee'ah (UAE), NOMADD (KSA) and Masdar (UAE) (WE Forum; Forbes ME). .

Table 13.2 in the appendix contains links to resources containing further information on many of the aspects that have been introduced in this section – further reference is recommended for deeper insights.

Political Context of Host Country

The past political and international strife has had an impact on the ME region, and it has attempted well to brave it and redirect efforts towards growth and development. Government rules and regulations in most countries are well laid out with in-built strict penalties for violations of any kind such as unauthorised photography, use of unlicensed drones, posting inappropriate content on social media, driving under the influence of alcohol, harassment of women and public display of affection, among others. This makes it friendly for expats as there is a sense of citizen care and resident welfare within the policies. There is mutual accountability in terms of compliance on part of residents and presence of redressal mechanisms on part of the government. This also leads to low crime rates as there are strong laws and punishments. The fear of law and enforcement agencies is high and results in good governance overall.

Many ME countries now have young generations of influential rulers and princes (such as Saudi Crown Prince Mohammed bin Salmand and Dubai Crown Prince Sheikh Hamdan bin Mohammed bin Rashid Al Maktoum) who have undertaken roles in the decision-making echelons, adopting a holistic and progressive approach. There is increased emphasis on development of the society, economy, polity and their people rather than letting political conflict undermine them. Expats are usually not employed in politically sensitive government services like police/military; however, some specialised niche expat jobs exist in government companies such as advisory/consulting roles with the government.

Governments in many ME countries such as Bahrain, KSA, Oman, Qatar and the UAE have been driving the 'workforce nationalisation' programme in accordance with their respective state strategies. This implies introduction of regulations to employ a higher number of local citizens in the public as well as private sectors, the objective being to promote employment and development of citizens. However, employment terms, wages, amenities and work conditions usually have a wide gap between private and public sectors. Recently, a November 2022 move by the UAE government, aimed to attract more UAE nationals to work in the private sector, has offered a significantly higher extra compensation per month for joining the private sector (Reynolds and Al Nowais, 2022). A 2017 white paper by ILO contains detailed assessment of the employment sponsorship systems in ME states and the expat worker–employer relationships (ilo.org).

The international relations of the host country also warrant examination in order to understand their relations with countries within the ME region, as well as with other nations (and powers) of the world. In fact, diplomatic relations with source countries of expats have a role to play in the treatment of immigrant labour from the respective countries. For instance, the treatment of white-collar professionals from the United States or Europe may be different from those hailing from Asia or Far East; sometimes also dependent on mutual treaties/agreements. The other reason is the higher income and living standards in their native country – leading to their demand/expectations being higher compared to their Asian counterparts.

The footprints of United Nations, International Labour Organisation and other international forums in the target host country must be evaluated as it would ascertain their overall international status and hence the possible safety and security of potential businesses/employees. Furthermore, the quality of international collaborative development initiatives in the fields of education, healthcare, humanitarianism, innovation and community development can be considered indicators of the political environment prevalent in the said country. A state that is anti-development is less likely to have many such progressive collaborations/initiatives; the reverse holds true as well.

Table 13.3 in appendix contains links to resources containing further information on many of the aspects that have been discussed in this section – further reference is recommended for deeper insights.

The remaining sections of this chapter contain recommendations to people management professionals in charge of expat employees in the ME region and to expats who are considering a move to the ME. These suggestions are also useful for potential entrepreneurs planning to undertake business in the ME.

Recommendations for Excellence in the ME

In order to maximise the capitalisation of diverse opportunities offered by the ME region, people managers and expats need to be planned, prepared and familiarised with the 'way things work' in the region. Having assessed the context of a target host country, as in the preceding sections, it is recommended to consider the suggestions in the following sections, which are suited for the needs of human resource professionals and expats. These pointers can be enablers towards high success and achievement levels in the chosen country and better expat management.

Recommendations for Human Resource Professionals

Dabic et al. (2015) researched the value addition that can be made by expats towards organisational performance; and how human resource management (HRM) policies and practices can facilitate the business performance by recruitment and retention of competent expats. Therefore, the onus of hiring expats with the requisite combination of skills, abilities, aptitude and attitude lies to a great extent on the shoulders of HRM experts within the organisation.

Recruitment and selection practices need to be aligned with the specific country's nationalisation policy, relevant regulations and permissions with respect to expat hiring (for example the *kafala* system of migrant labour sponsorship, as practiced in GCC countries, Jordan and Lebanon, offers protection to migrant workers' rights but also has room for manipulation by employers, thereby leading to an imbalanced employment relationship – country-wise details of these may be found in the ILO 2017 White paper cited in Table 13.3). Local as well as international consulting firms are engaged for expat hiring and provided clear mandates based on the parameters discussed above. In some cases (such as in the UAE and Bahrain), private firms are mandated to screen and interview nationals before they look for expat alternatives, and proceed only if the former were not found adequate for the respective role. This phenomenon has also been identified in Budhwar et al. (2019) as a cause of serious practical challenges to all aspects of HRM in the ME as there is mounting pressure from authorities, and this may lead to dilution of the quality of new recruits. Systematic employee induction practices are therefore highly recommended as there is a gap in this direction, and it can have an impact on expat performance in the new environment.

There is a lot of emphasis on the 'administrative' aspect of people management policies. If a firm is new, it is recommended to put a performance management system in place with key performance indicators, deliverables and possible linkage to performance bonuses. This domain is still nascent in ME, and there is immense potential to streamline and professionalise this. Most performance management systems, where instituted, follow the 180-degree feedback system where manager and employee rate the employee's performance over a one-year cycle, against parameters agreed towards the beginning of the year. Objective, performance-based assessments, evaluation and these being linked to rewards and recognitions can be worked upon to make the ME more attractive to expats from around the world.

Likewise, training and development interventions are picking pace as there is increased emphasis on the importance of ongoing learning and continuous improvement among employees. Expats become direct beneficiaries of these by virtue of being a major part of the overall employee base. Organisations offer in-house training (on-the-job and structured programs); as well as specialised professional training programmes delivered by expert consultants. Technical training is well developed, whilst managerial and soft-skills training is gaining momentum. HRM professionals need to systematically highlight the value-addition that training can do, towards expat performance, and convince top management to invest in this field for the long-term benefit of the organisation. This also indicates the presence of scope for entrepreneurs offering comprehensive, expert-driven learning and development interventions to organisations.

Technology is being increasingly utilised by organisations in order to facilitate establishment of robust people practices. The importance and contribution of the better people management is being progressively recognised, and the tech-spend towards HRM software purchases has been on the rise. In many cases, though, it is still limited to salary/leave management, recruitment and administrative facilitation platforms. There is ample scope to widen this and link with learning, performance management, employee development and so on. Kapoor and Kabra (2014) recommend the increased use of HR Analytics by companies to use HR data and statistics for effective decision-making and evidence-based management as it has a direct impact on firm performance and competitive advantage. It may be noted here that the HRM department structures and practices in ME may differ between family-owned indigenous business groups and multinational enterprises.

It is advisable to carefully plan the cost of hiring an expat employee. Some of the common costs are costs of employment visa, labour contract, residence permit, family visas and residence permits (where applicable), insurance costs (it is mandatory to provide medical and life insurance for all expats blue-collar or white-collar) and relocation allowance where applicable. Additionally, the compensation, housing or child education allowance, annual leave, leave travel (expats are entitled to to-and-fro tickets to their home country once a year) costs need to be calculated in estimating the overall cost of expat recruitment and matching it with the firm's budget. This also helps to identify the preferred nationality of expats that may be hired given these requirements and budget allocations.

The government regulations and requirements with respect to hiring expats may be different across countries. For example, the KSA Ministry of Labor in 2020 changed the rules within its 2011 *Nitaqat* program to encourage companies to enhance their Saudisation levels and restrict their application for foreign national work visas; while Qatar made positive reforms in its foreign national employment regulations by reducing processing fees, easing restrictions on male dependents by enabling them to work without changing sponsorship and introducing 'Temporary Work Visa' (pwc.com). The nationality of expats plays a role in the perception and value attached to them by organisations; hence, the prevailing compensation packages vis-à-vis work levels must be aligned with the company's specific requirements, affordability and budgets. Family status may not be available for all expats, though there are considerations specific to work level, wage level, cost of living and local laws in the country; therefore, company policies vary on this front. Staying away from families is a factor in employment as not all eligible expats may be willing to compromise on this front. HR teams must conduct some benchmarking among firms in similar industries in the host country, and then determine pay grades and terms of employment for expats.

Recommendations for Expats

Expats intending to take up employment opportunities or initiate business ventures in the ME must educate themselves with ample information from all possible resources – first-hand accounts of those who are/have been in the ME, secondary information and data available in public domain, academic research statistics, news and media. All this information must be assimilated and critically analysed before arriving at a decision for or against the proposition.

Expat.com is a highly popular webpage for expats interested in ME and is organised on the basis of separate countries, providing specific information about each county. Also, the Global Power City Index (GPCI) is a credible reference point for expats and businesses as it evaluates and classifies prime cities of the world on the basis of their 'magnetism' to draw capital, labour and business from across the globe. They evaluate cities along six parameters of economy, research and development, cultural interaction, liveability, environment and accessibility. Some of the cities in the ME have been making it to the GPCI reports (Dubai is in the GPCI 2020 list Top-20 for instance).

Overall, cultural adaptability and flexibility may be instrumental enablers for effective expat performance and management. Few additional factors such as prices of real estate, rentals, wage levels, power, water and consumer goods can facilitate rational calculation of cost of living in a host country, by expats. The working days of the week in ME are different from the rest of the world; hence, meetings and discussions must be proposed with this in mind (business week in most countries is Sunday to Thursday except in the UAE) – Friday is the Holy Day and non-working. Similar consideration must be provided to the Holy month of Ramadan and two biggest festivals of Eid al-Adha and Eid Al-Fitr. Work is relatively slow with shorter working hours during Ramadan. Even non-Muslim expats are included in this and all residents observe respect for fasting members and avoid eating/drinking in public places to avoid hurting sentiments. Professional meeting dress code must be kept simple, conservative and non-offensive.

Expats must evaluate compensation packages in great detail and for each component such as fixed/variable components, housing allowance, child education allowance, annual leaves, leave travel tickets for self and dependents, life insurance cover, medical insurance (bear in mind that healthcare is exorbitantly charged in ME, i.e., tough to survive without insurance; medical services are far too expensive), working days, working hours and so on. Further, the prevailing average cost of living, taxation levels and any other financial aspect must be analysed. For instance, even the cost of fuel is not so low anymore in the ME; neither is gold cheap; contrary to popular perceptions of cheaper fuel and gold. Cost of certain items may be different for locals vs expats such as house rent tax slabs or cost of sponsoring domestic service staff. In addition, holistic comparisons must be drawn between home country and the one they plan to migrate to draw up a financial plan, compare to own position in host country; align with career plans/aspirations, family constraints and then decide.

Nolan and Morley (2014) argue that person–environment (PE) fit plays an instrumental part in the expat adjustment in any assignment they undertake. This implies the requirement of synergy between the individual traits (values, beliefs, skills, competencies, aspirations) and work environment features (job description, demands and organisational expectations). Absence of this is likely to impact cross cultural adjustment issues as well as performance issues among expats. This is the rationale behind the recommendations here to ensure such synergy and alignment, hence better adjustment and performance by expats.

Other characteristics of common ME environment include very high safety and security levels especially so in expat residential areas as expat wellbeing is fully taken care of. In fact, there are some residential locales designated for expats and suited to their requirements (for example Abu Dhabi City in the UAE, Saar-Juffair in Bahrain, Maadi-Zamalek in Cairo and Al Sadd-Al Waab in Doha). The living conditions are generally good and there is good quality spacious accommodation; variety of options depending on affordability, easy to access supermarkets, department stores and schools/nurseries and a hospitable environment overall. Purchase of property may not be permitted for expats (in most cases); however, leasing is an option as is the case in the UAE. Most ME countries do not offer citizenship to common expats in return for prolonged stay. Quality of school education is adequate in most ME countries, and there are indigenous as well as international curriculums available – the blend of teachers includes a large proportion of expats; and many international universities also have their establishments in several ME countries.

There are stringent regulations for maintaining law and order in the ME states, enforced with high compliance rates. There are penalties/fines/punishment for violations depending on their severity. For example, bounced cheques/default in bills or bank payments may lead to high penalties or occasional imprisonment; illegal consumption of alcohol by expats without an alcohol permit is liable to fines, imprisonment or even deportation – in KSA, Qatar and the UAE. There are fast-track labour courts and expats get fair trials without discrimination. Cheating, fraud and other crimes are unacceptable and may even lead to deportation.

Expats need to be mindful of a few cultural factors, and it is advisable to demonstrate behaviour which is respectful of local values and traditions, public display of affection is considered offensive even if it involves spouses. Responsible behaviour in the digital space is highly recommended (refrain from making personal, offensive remarks on social media platforms). It is a good idea to pick few basic Arabic language words and terms as it helps establish pleasant communication with locals and improves acceptance and exchange – including workplace bonds.

Professionally, expats must maintain workplace etiquette, dress code, work ethics, integrity and respect cultural boundaries. Understanding the organisational hierarchy, rules, unsaid practices and norms during the first few months is effective as it enables smooth transition and better workplace performance of expats. Work–life balance is reasonably good in the ME as Arabs are very family-oriented and believe in prioritising family alongside professional commitments. In fact, once an expat has moved to the region, mobility between jobs gets better by virtue of the fact that experience within the region is given a clear priority by employers within ME when they advertise their open positions. However, there are specific rules and regulations around this in GCC, Jordan and Lebanon (2017 ILO White Paper – Table 13.3).

In terms of social life, expats (and families) can expect to find friends and build their network of friends-like-family as this is 'home away from home' for all expats. There are multiple social networking opportunities and clubs for expats. Driving license is easy to obtain and for some nationalities (such as Australia, New Zealand, the UK, the United States and within GCC countries) it is even directly transferable. Owning a car is affordable, expat ladies driving is very common and several families have more than one car. Children can stay with parents on dependent visas until the age of 18. There are beautiful weekend getaway destinations for leisure trips both within the country and in nearby countries.

Retails stores in ME are quite modernised and up-to-date, including traditional, local commodities as well as the best of international product and service brands. Speciality cuisines, clothing, fashion and accessories from around the world are easily available. The term 'souq' refers to 'malls' in Arabic.

Prolonged stay in ME can sometimes end up overindulging expats with some of its characteristics, and one may begin to take those for granted. The lifestyles and its comforts can be a deterrent to future relocation. Examples include spacious housing, affordable service staff, luxurious hotels, convenient at-home services and high levels of safety and security. However, the lack of social safety net for expats may also be a factor worth consideration as COVID-19 brought to the surface, and so did the financial crisis of 2008–09. During COVID-19, there has been a mass exodus of blue-collar workers from ME countries due to the low-income brackets they fall into. The situation has been similar for white-collar skilled workers, even though some of them may have sustained for slightly longer period of time 'waiting' to find a job while they try to survive on their savings. Such mass repatriation in times of large-scale crisis is not favourable to anyone but unavoidable at the same time as it is a matter of survival and protection of national interests.

Having said the above, the inextricable link between expats and ME states cannot be undermined and is here to stay as globalisation is shrinking the world. The ME was, and still is, a preferred destination for business/employment, from expats around the world and in fact there are few expats who have been in the region for two or more generations. Therefore, the tips and recommendations cited in this section are likely to aid smooth transition of expats who choose to migrate to ME, after due diligence and careful consideration.

Conclusion

Brewster et al. (2014) acknowledge the complexity of expat performance and discuss the multiple dimensions which play a role in the success of expats in their assignments. The consequences of expat hiring process, their training and development, compensation levels and acclimatisation in the new roles (in a new environment) are evident in the actual outcomes of international roles taken up by expats. This is complicated by many viewpoints, such as that of the organisation, the expat, their non-expat colleagues and family members – regarding the achievement level of the expat in the said role/assignment.

Given the above, this chapter has delved into pertinent, high-impact, but simple, dynamics of expat management in the ME states. The sociocultural, economic and political context of the country an expat considers before entering the ME, must be carefully analysed for ground reality in terms of business environment, facilities, restrictions, legal framework and so on. Such due diligence may then be complimented by the recommendations made for HRM professionals and expats themselves.

Appendix

TABLE 13.1 Resources for Evaluating Sociocultural Context

Academic and International resources	
https://www.un.org/esa/socdev/family/Publications/mtelhaddad.pdf	*Major Trends Affecting Families in the Gulf Countries* (Prof Hadda, Bahrain University, 2003)
http://large.stanford.edu/publications/power/references/baker/studies/tme/docs/TrendsinMiddleEast_MainStudy.pdf	*The Political, Economic, Social, Cultural and Religious Trends in the Middle East and the Gulf and Their Impact on Energy Supply, Security and Pricing* – a study by Institute for Public Policy of Rice University
https://www.csis.org/analysis/ties-bind-family-tribe-nation-and-rise-arab-individualism	Centre for Strategic and International Studies Report on Arab societies (Jon B. Alterman, 2019)
http://graphics.eiu.com/upload/eb/gulf2020part2.pdf	'The GCC in 2020: The Gulf and its People' – a 2019 report from the Economist Intelligence Unit
https://www.un.org/en/development/desa/population/migration/data/estimates2/estimates19.asp	United Nations Department of Economic and Social Affairs Population Division – International Migrant Stock, 2019
Other resources	
http://www.pbs.org/wgbh/globalconnections/mideast/themes/culture/	An article about Middle East themes and culture
https://www.mei.edu/sites/default/files/publications/Sports%20in%20ME.pdf	Sports and the Middle East – Viewpoints special edition by the Middle East Institute, Washington, DC
https://www.weather.org/middle-east/	Website for Middle East weather country wise
https://www.csis.org/regions	Centre for Strategic and International Studies website for overall understanding of region outlook of ME

TABLE 13.2 Resources for Evaluating Economic Context

International resources	
https://www.gcc-sg.org/	Webpage of Secretariat General of the GCC
https://www.worldbank.org/en/region/mena/publication/mena-economic-monitor	The World Bank MENA Economic Update
https://www.imf.org/en/Publications/REO/MECA	The IMF Regional Economic Outlook – Middle East and Central Asia
https://www.unglobalcompact.org/sdgs/action-platforms	The United Nations Global Compact – Sustainable Development Goals

Industry resources

https://home.kpmg/xx/en/home/insights/2016/07/middle-east-and-south-asia.html	KPMG Middle East and South Asia page – contains resources specific to each ME country
https://www.ey.com/en_ae	Ernst & Young UAE – contains relevant industry trends and reports
https://www.pwc.com/m1/en.html	PWC ME page – contains relevant industry trends and reports
https://www2.deloitte.com/xe/en/pages/about-deloitte/articles/back-to-work.html; https://deloittemiddleeastmatters.com/	Deloitte ME PoV Spring 2021 issue and ME matters
https://www.fitchsolutions.com/topic/middle-east ; http://csrmiddleeast.org/page/about-us	Middle East CSR and Sustainability related information

News resources

https://www.arabianbusiness.com/world/middle-east https://gulfbusiness.com/	ME General news sources
https://www.ft.com/world/mideast https://www.cnbc.com/middle-east/ https://www.investopedia.com/terms/i/islamicbanking.asp; http://www.fao.org/3/y1860e/y1860e05.htm	ME financial and investment news and characteristics

TABLE 13.3 Resources for Evaluating Political Context

Political and News resources	
https://www.arabnews.com/middleeast http://www.mideast-times.com/ https://edition.cnn.com/middle-east	ME political news and updates
https://www.bbc.com/news/world/middle_east; https://globalinitiative.net/region/middle-east/	International news reporting on ME
Academic and other resources	
https://www.ilo.org/wcmsp5/groups/public/---arabstates/---ro-beirut/documents/publication/wcms_552697.pdf	'Employer-Migrant Worker Relationships in the Middle East: Exploring Scope for Internal Labour Market Mobility and Fair Migration' – an ILO White Paper 2017
https://merip.org/who-we-are/	Middle East Research and Information Project – a periodical covering the ME since 1971
https://www.jstor.org/journal/middleeastreport	JSTOR ME Report
https://fas.org/sgp/crs/mideast/	Congressional Research Service Reports on the Middle East and the Arab World
https://library.oapen.org/bitstream/handle/20.500.12657/35008/341386.pdf;	*The International Politics of the Middle East* – a book by Raymond Hinnebusch, Manchester University Press
https://ecfr.eu/publication/china_great_game_middle_east/	*China's Great Game in the Middle East*, 2019 policy brief

References

Angrist, M.P. ed., 2010. *Politics & society in the contemporary Middle East*. Lynne Rienner Publishers.

Brewster, C., Bonache, J., Cerdin, J.L. and Suutari, V., 2014. Exploring expatriate outcomes. *International Journal of Human Resource Management*, 25(14), pp.1921–1937.

Budhwar, P. and Mellahi, K. 2006. Introduction: Managing human resources in the Middle East. In P. Budhwar, and K. Mellahi (Eds.). *Managing human resources in the Middle East*: 1–19. London: Routledge.

Budhwar, P. et al., 2019. The state of HRM in the Middle East: Challenges and future research agenda. *Asia Pacific Journal of Management*, 36(4), pp.905–933.

Dabic, M., González-Loureiro, M. and Harvey, M., 2015. Evolving research on expatriates: What is 'known' after four decades (1970–2012). *International Journal of Human Resource Management*, 26(3), pp.316–337.

Kapoor, B. and Kabra, Y., 2014. Current and future trends in human resources analytics adoption. *Journal of Cases on Information Technology (JCIT)*, 16(1), pp.50–59.

Khan, M.M. and Bhatti, M.I., 2008. Islamic banking and finance: On its way to globalization. *Managerial Finance*, 34(10), pp.708–725.

Nolan, E.M. and Morley, M.J., 2014. A test of the relationship between person–environment fit and cross-cultural adjustment among self-initiated expatriates. *The International Journal of Human Resource Management*, 25(11), pp.1631–1649.

Omar, A.A. and Mathew, S. 2019. 'Dubai suffered steepest population drop in Gulf Region, S&P says', *Bloomberg News*, 01 March, 2019. Available at: https://www.bloomberg.com/news/articles/2021-03-01/dubai-suffered-steepest-population-drop-in-gulf-region-s-p-says (accessed 26 December, 2022).

Reynolds, R. and Al Nowais, S. 2022. 'Emiratisation explained: UAE citizens in private sector to get extra Dh7,000 a month', *The National News*, 24 November, 2022. Available at: https://www.thenationalnews.com/uae/2022/11/24/emiratisation-explained-uae-citizens-in-private-sector-to-get-extra-dh7000-a-month/ (accessed 26 December, 2022).

Shayah, M.H. and Sun, Z., 2019, January. Employment in the Gulf Cooperation Council (GCC) Countries–Current Issues and Future Trends. In *2nd International Conference on Social Science, Public Health and Education (SSPHE 2018)* (pp. 412–415). Atlantis Press.

Shaykhian, G.A., Ziade, J. and Khairi, M.A., 2016. How cultural understanding influences business success in Middle East and North Africa (MENA).

PART III
Emerging Themes

14
GENDER ISSUES AT THE WORKFORCE IN THE MIDDLE EAST

Maryam Aldossari and Sara Chaudhry

Introduction

There is growing attention on the manifestation and experience of gender equality in the workplace amongst both research and practitioner communities across the world. However, this debate remains under-explored in the Middle Eastern context; not only because gender equality is a complex and often divisive topic in the region, but also because research in this region is limited due to the methodological and practical limitations of gaining access (Lages et al., 2015). This chapter begins by highlighting the overarching trends in terms of women's employment in the Middle East. This is followed by a discussion of the social-institutional norms and cultural restrictions that impact women's employment in the Middle East. Next, the manifestation of institutionalized gender inequalities, and the dynamic creation and interaction of visible and invisible inequalities, vis-à-vis organizational policies and practices will be discussed. Furthermore, given the fast-changing gender landscape in Saudi Arabia, a section will offer a review of the current structural and institutional changes that are influencing women's employment in this country specifically. Finally, the chapter concludes with some recommendations that address these existing inequalities at the meso/organizational level of analysis.

Women's Employment in the Middle East

Reports on the female participation rate in higher education indicate that there have been significant improvements relating to women's educational development across the Middle East (World bank, 2021). Despite these improvements, the female participation rate in the workforce continues to be significantly low (see Table 14.1). The unemployment rates of young women in the Middle East are considered to be one of the highest in the world – 51.9% of young women

DOI: 10.4324/9781003005766-17

TABLE 14.1 Female Education and Labour Market Participation Rates

Country	Female participation rate in higher education (2016)	Labour-force participation rate, female (2019)	The Global Gender Gap Index rankings (2021)
Egypt	34.8	18	129
Iraq	…	12	154
Saudi Arabia	66.7	22	147
Yemen	6.1	6	155
Syria	42.7	15	152
Jordan	37.5	15	131
United Arab Emirates	53.2	52	72
Lebanon	45.8	23	132
Oman	59.7	36	145
Kuwait	42.7	50	143
Qatar	47.1	57	142
Bahrain	63	45	137

are unemployed compared with 17.8 of young men (ILO, 2020). While the Gulf Cooperation Council (GCC) in the Middle East has a high average GDP per capita, other countries (i.e., the non-GCC group) have high poverty levels, and are either currently entangled in, or are recently emerging from conflict and war (ILO, 2020). Against this uncertain and precarious sociopolitical backdrop, women in particular struggle to secure employment because of systemic labour market inflexibilities and skills mismatch whereby their skills set does not match market demands (O'Sullivan, Rey, and Mendez, 2011). For example, Karam and Afiouni (2014) indicate that the combination of inadequate economic resources and political instability in Lebanon has created significant difficulties for women in terms of their access to formal employment; forcing women into informal employment that is often under-protected and precarious.

One of the main obstacles for women seeking employment in the region is the skills mismatch between their education versus job requirements (Tlaiss and Dirani, 2015). Women continue to remain clustered in traditional fields of education (specifically within the humanities), learning and training, and health care, with fewer women seeking, or achieving, employment opportunities in the burgeoning technical and vocational sectors (Tlaiss and Dirani, 2015). For example, Calvert and Al-Shetaiwi (2002) suggest that women in Saudi Arabia continue to be underrepresented in the educational fields of computing, electronics and accountancy and lack of educational qualifications in these disciplines limit women's ability to secure well-paid, lucrative jobs in the private sector. This story plays out in other countries across the region – for example, women in Qatar were allowed to study certain subjects such as engineering as recently as 2008 (Rutledge et al., 2011). Subsequently, the educational sector in the region contributes to gender inequalities in the labour market by not preparing local women sufficiently in order to compete successfully against local males or expatriates for jobs in the labour market (Romani, 2008).

With the explicit intention of addressing the problem of unemployment/under-employment of nationals (specifically women) and reducing the historical over reliance on expatriates, several countries in the Gulf region (such as Oman, Saudi Arabia and the United Arab Emirates) have introduced 'nationalization' programs to encourage private organizations to employed nationals instead of expatriates (Budhwar and Mellahi, 2016). For example, in Saudi Arabia the government introduced the Saudization (or job localization) programme which reinforced employment quotas for nationals in the private sector (Mellahi, 2007). More importantly, recent Saudization drives have had a progressive gendered focus, whereby feminization of the Saudi workforce is intended to enable Saudi women to become active economic participants; encouraging the recruitment of Saudi women in previously male-dominant sectors such as retail (Varshney, 2019). Similarly, the Emiratization programme aims to encourage national women into employment in the private sector (Rees et al., 2007). Regardless of these top-down government interventions, both Emirati and Saudi women nationals continue to consider the private sector career path unappealing in terms of salary and working hours, as well as being 'culturally inappropriate' (Harry, 2007: 144). Therefore, while labour nationalization programmes have led to minor growth in women's participation rates across the region, (Rutledge et al., 2011), there is clearly a need for more systemic labour market restructuring with an explicit gender focus in order to attract women to the booming private sector. Only through gendered structural mechanisms such as enhanced maternity leave and equal opportunities for training and education will the broader strategic vision of the Saudization and Emiratization drives be realized.

Social-institutional Challenges

In the Middle East, various traditions, customs and religious norms intersect with organizational policies and practices and shape women's experience in workplaces (Hennekam et al., 2017). First, enduring patriarchal structures reinforce a traditional division of labour and responsibilities in line with a dominant male breadwinner model (Metcalfe, 2008). While women are entering the workforce in increasing numbers, the classic patriarchy that characterizes the region imposes certain expectations in terms of what is considered as suitable work/working conditions for women (Haghighat, 2014). For example, in Qatar, recent research found that young Qatari women preferred working in gender-segregated workplaces mainly to accommodate societal and family disapproval of women interacting with men in the workplace (Salem and Yount 2019). Similarly, Kawar's (2000) research on unmarried young women in Jordan showed a distinct preference amongst the participants to work in women-only workplaces in order to uphold traditional values regarding family honour. Overall, patriarchy as a legitimating ideology positions women as representatives of societal/tribal/family honour, conferring men with the right to control them and restrict their educational and occupational choices (Ali, 2015).

Second, patriarchal interpretations of the Islamic faith in the Middle East create additional restrictions for women in terms of their careers (Syed, 2010). Syed et al.

(2005) argue that Muslim women continue to face restrictions in terms of participation in the public sphere due to the maintenance of gender segregation in line with the Islamic concept of modesty. The current conceptualization of modesty in turn creates boundaries for women's mobility, involvement in formal employment and restraints in the interaction of the genders (Sidani, 2005). For example, in Saudi Arabia under Wahhabi Islamic ideology, there are restrictions on women's employment or right to travel without a mahram's (that is, a male guardian like a father/brother/husband) permission (Syed et al. 2018). Given these restrictions, gender segregation is a norm that continues to govern social, educational and work spheres, thereby excluding women from employment and career development opportunities (Al-Rasheed, 2013).

Third, the continuance of tribal and Bedouin traditions in some parts of the Middle East place additional limitations on women's employment and progression opportunities (Syed, 2010). In Jordan, a recent study revealed that tribalism and Bedouin customs were a key barrier that hindered females progressing to leadership positions (Koburtay et al., 2020). Other studies have also found that the maintenance of tribal identities adds another contextually unique layer of patriarchal influence vis-à-vis the societal position of Saudi women (Al Alhareth et al., 2015; Hakiem, 2021). For instance, Alkhaled and Berglund (2018) argue that tribal traditions regard women working in gender-mixed environments as taboo which severely restricts women's entry to specific fields of study (such as STEM subjects) or professions (such as accountancy or architecture). Therefore, these enduring tribal customs enforce restraints on women and significantly impact their decision-making in terms of where to work and what segments of the labour market to be involved in (Sidani, 2005). However, it is also important to note that tribal women experience greater privileges in workplaces relative to non-tribal women in the form of greater access to a range of financial and relational resources (Samin, 2019). For example, Tlaiss and Kauser (2011) found that *wasta*, that is relational influence which relies heavily on tribal affiliations, plays a major role in offering women access to jobs, promotions and lucrative educational/training opportunities within Lebanese organizations. Similarly, research has highlighted how Saudi women's pervasive reliance on wasta (specifically tribal and family networks) facilitates their access to a range of labour market opportunities (Al-Ahmadi, 2011). Overall, the distinctive social-institutional particularities of the Middle Eastern context create institutionalized gender inequalities at the macro level which in turn trickle down to the meso level, impacting organizational values, policies and norms.

Visible and Invisible Inequalities within the Workplaces

Extant research has highlighted several distinctive organizational structures and practices that are informed by the societal-level influences, impacting the career experiences of women in the Middle East (Aldossari et al., 2021; Hutchings et al., 2012; Karam and Afiouni, 2014). In this section we will discuss the manifestation of these institutionalized gender inequalities that can be both visible (such as gendered patterns of vertical and horizontal segregation) and invisible (such as the implications of male-dominated network) within organizations.

In terms of visible inequalities, there is considerable evidence in existing literature that women in the region are employed in what are considered to be 'feminine' fields, principally: health care, education and social care – with a greater concentration of women in lower-level (and, therefore, lower-paid, lower-power) roles (Hutchings et al., 2012). Rutledge et al. (2011) argue that the stigma attached to women working in mixed environments, and freely interacting with men, severely limits women's employment options to a limited number of fields that are considered acceptable by society. However, recent governmental interventions specifically aimed at fostering gender equality have encouraged females into hitherto unexplored occupations such as accountancy services, banking and even the retail sector (Sidani et al., 2015). Nevertheless, several studies focusing on women's own narratives highlight those female employees (and their male counterparts) regarded themselves as tokens hired by their employing organizations as a checkbox exercise to meet nationalization quotas enforced by the government which translated into a lack of genuine career opportunities. For example, Emirati women working in private banking referenced their struggles in progressing beyond entry-level positions, their exclusion from decision-making, lack of training opportunities and limited occupational progression, and their disappointment at being perceived and treated by their male colleagues as 'window dressing' (Farrell, 2008). Similarly, Saudi women working in global Saudi Arabian MNC were perceived by male colleagues and managers as tokens, hired because of their gender and subsequently delegated to subordinate and support roles that they were often considerably overqualified for (Aldossari et al., 2021).

Another component of visible inequality is the underrepresentation of women in senior leadership roles across the Middle Eastern context. In the region there is a clear prevalence of vertical segregation. Recent statistics published by the World Economic Forum (2021) on the representation of women highlight that only 18% of women held management roles in the Middle East, and female representation in senior positions was less than 10% in some countries, such as Syria (8.9%), Egypt (7.4%) and Saudi Arabia (6.8%). According to Metcalfe (2011) women continue to be clustered in lower positions even if they have worked in the same organizations for a long period of time. Research on women's leadership in Lebanon has highlighted that one of the main barriers to women being promoted to leadership roles is the manifestation of patriarchal values within the workplace that tends to prefer men over women with respect to leadership positions (Sidani et al., 2015). This gender bias is also evident in the continued existence and application of stereotypical beliefs that consider men naturally more suited to managerial roles because of their gender and associated personality traits while women are perceived as less capable of performing these leadership roles, and subsequently relegated to lower hierarchical positions, simply because they are women (Abalkhail, 2019). In addition to patriarchal ideology that hinders women's career advancement, several studies have underlined those organizational policies and practices are strongly gendered in the Middle East. For example, there is evidence that women are excluded from access to key organizational information and involvement in strategic planning and decision-making processes (Abalkhail and Allan, 2016); there is lack of mentoring programmes that would enable the progression of women's careers (Tlaiss and Kauser, 2011); and an absence of talent development programmes for female employees (Sidani and Al Ariss, 2014). Consequently, not only are women subjected to socio-institutional norms that restrain their careers both implicitly and explicitly, but organizations also contribute to this narrative of inequality (Karam and Afiouni, 2014).

With respect to invisible inequality in the workplace, its manifestation involves the subtle exclusion of women from professional and social networks that are often male-dominated. This in turn limits their access to key organizational information and their prospects of participating in organizational decision-making processes. As discussed in the previous section, in some countries in the Middle East, professional relationships in the workplace between men and women are actively discouraged. Therefore, women have to creatively resort to relying on their male family members' networks in order to bolster their careers, and to gain access to organizational resources, information and career progress opportunities (Abalkhail and Allan, 2016; Metcalfe 2008). For instance, Singh's (2008) research on female directors in Jordan and Tunisia underscored the importance of family connections for women achieving promotion to higher positions within their organizations. Similarly, in Qatar, participants emphasized that it was vital for women to gain and maintain male family members' support in order to access resources in their workplaces (Salem and Yount 2019). This creates an additional layer of dependency whereby without the support of influential and well-connected male family members, Arab women may find it challenging to access the information and resources needed to thrive in their workplaces.

Country Context: Saudi Arabia's Structural and Institutional Changes

Saudi Arabia has often been positioned relatively low in terms of gender equality compared to other Middle Eastern countries (Syed and Metcalfe, 2017). Nevertheless, in recent years, rapid changes and reforms have been introduced to increase Saudi women participation in the labour market from 22% to 30% in line with Saudi Vision 2030's development plan introduced by the Crown Prince Mohammed bin Salman (Vision 2030, 2016). Several schemes have subsequently been announced by the government to kick-start this increase of female participation in the labour market, principally the feminization of certain jobs and sectors that were formerly the singular purview of men (Khan, 2018); ending the ban on women driving and thereby increasing their mobility/flexibility (Al-Otaibi, 2018); and the amendment of guardianship laws which now allows women over 21 greater freedoms all aimed at removing possible obstacles to their pursuit of careers and access to workplaces (Arab News, 2019). Notably, one year after the introduction of these initiatives, approximately 500,000 Saudi women had entered the labour market (General Authority for Statistics, 2020).

Despite the Saudi government's attempts to promote women's opportunities in workforce and in leadership positions, such as a first appointment of a woman as the Deputy Minister of Labour (Arab News, 2018) and the first female ambassador to United States (The Guardian, 2019), these appointments and transformations can be perceived as artificial, designed to enhance Saudi Arabia's international reputation in the West (Al-Rasheed, 2019). Furthermore, recent research has stressed that conservative tribal factions within Saudi society actively reject reforms introduced by the government to address gender inequalities (Sian et al., 2020). In line with the Wahabi interpretation of Islam, women continue to be perceived within the Saudi society as representatives of family honour and therefore gender segregation is a much-valued and deeply entrenched cultural norm (Syed et al. 2018). Several scholars have argued that limited improvements in social attitudes within Saudi society have influenced how women experience their daily work and which job options are seen as socially acceptable (Alkhaled and Berglund, 2018; Hakiem, 2021; Mazawi, 2005, Syed et al. 2018). For example, Hakiem's (2021) research on Saudi women academics highlights how the higher education sector is seen as a socially acceptable work environment for women as it continues to be gender segregated. Therefore, the current growth in the ratio of Saudi female faculty members may be less related to improvements in gender equity or the feminization drive and more linked to the absence of work prospects outside of the education sector that are considered 'suitable' for women.

At the organizational level, researchers have highlighted the transference of these slow-to-change societal norms, cultural values, traditions and social codes to organizations' formal and informal practices. Sian et al.'s (2020) research in a large global auditing organization in Saudi Arabia showed how management created a female segregated section within the firm to accommodate Saudi Arabia's social expectations of an acceptable work environment for women; with very limited progression opportunities in this all-female section of the organization. Abalkhail's (2017) research findings reveal that men were preferred over women even when they are more qualified in terms of promotion and leadership positions and men continue to be considered the primary breadwinners and heads of their households. Similarly, Aldossari et al.'s (2021) research underlines how Saudi women experience unequal access to career opportunities and gender-based discrimination, such as exclusion from training, development or promotional opportunities, despite working in a large multinational that emphasized gender equality.

Recommendations to Promote Gender Equality in Middle Eastern Workplaces

This chapter has highlighted a range of distinctive socio-institutional features which impact Middle Eastern women's employment opportunities. First, organizations need to redress the issue of gender imbalance in top leadership positions specifically.

Females' lower access to organizational initiatives for career advancement and upskilling as compared to their male counterparts means that organizations fail to develop and subsequently benefit from the knowledge and skills of high-potential female talent. This can be achieved by offering targeted mentorship as a key strategy for strengthening women's career advancement through a range of organizational initiatives such as career counselling, coaching, offering challenging assignments (both across functional and if possible cross-country boundaries), providing psychological support and engaging in proactive monitoring and evaluation of all these initiatives in order to assess whether women are actually benefiting from them (Ibarra, Carter, and Silva 2010; Morley 2013; O'Neil and Bilimoria 2005). Ibarra et al. (2010) argue that without active championing and sponsorship, women not only are less likely than men to be appointed to top roles, but they may also be more reluctant to go for them even if they are qualified. Therefore, there needs to be an explicit recognition that in a context of gender inequality, and low representation of women in senior leadership roles, sponsorship programmes and mentoring will play a critical role for women's career development, specifically in advancing them up the career ladder. A key complication with this recommendation is that in the Arab world women find it difficult to locate a mentor themselves. There are also cultural barriers to women relying on male mentors in the workplaces, which may be unavoidable given the paucity of women in senior leadership positions. Furthermore, there are not many mentoring programmes offered in public organizations specifically, and the few available tend to benefit men more than women (Abalkhail and Allan 2016; Tlaiss and Kauser 2011). In order to address these context-specific dynamics, organizations may need to partner with other organizations and create an inter-organizational mentoring program which can take advantage of the limited females in senior positions across the wider external labour market.

Networking is another key recommendation for encouraging women's entry into diverse segments of the labour market and advancing their careers, thereby reducing their dependence on their own male family members. Extant research in other contexts has highlighted the efficacy of networking in providing support for career development (Mavin and Bryans, 2002). Individuals can gain a range of benefits through networking, including increased visibility, targeted and idiosyncratic support, information exchange, collaboration, career planning and strategizing, and upward mobility both within and outside their employing organization by gaining a better understanding of political and cultural aspects of a workplace (e.g. Bierema 2005; Ibarra 1993; Mavin and Bryans 2002). However, questions have been raised as to whether women benefit from networking in masculine cultures and their likely exclusion from male-dominated networks or 'old boys' networks', given that many of these networks end up reproducing societal (and predominantly patriarchal) structures of power (Ibarra, 1993; Bierema 2005). This has a significant impact on women not only in terms of their career advancement but also with respect to their self-confidence and professional efficacy (Vasil 1996). This situation has led to women sometimes seeking to join women-only networks (Bierema 2005). It has been acknowledged by a number of scholars that women's networks support women in terms of everyday management skills such as exchanging information, giving feedback on work and career plans, problem-solving, advice and simply sharing experiences (Mavin and Bryans 2002; O'Neil, Hopkins, and Sullivan 2011).

Case Study – Saudi Aramco and the Gender Gap

The gender gap is especially wide in the traditionally male-dominated oil and gas sector – with women comprising only 10% of the total workforce (Global Energy Talent Index Report, 2018). Saudi Aramco, as a key player in the sector, has introduced many highly publicized policies aimed at reducing this gender gap and setting itself up as a champion for female employment. Two initiatives were introduced in 2010 – the 'Women in Business' program enabled young females to kick-start their careers while the 'Women in Leadership' initiative was aimed at building senior female employees' key soft skills such as self-confidence, resilience, tolerance, flexibility, assertiveness and awareness. Saudi Aramco's continued focus on reducing the gender gap signals a conscious move away from a not-too-distant past when the company struggled to attract or retain talented females and the small percentage of its female employees predominantly occupied support personnel positions.

Saudi Aramco CEO Amin Nasser highlighted some recent achievements at the Gulf Region Organisation for Women (GROW) forum:

> We have been investing in a wide range of programs for many years to enable women to compete, overcome challenges, and achieve their career aspirations… At Saudi Aramco, we have increased female recruitment to more than 20% of all new hires and doubled the number of women working in our organization over the past 10 years. Meanwhile, in April (2018), we appointed our first female board member.

More innovative practices include partnering with British training institutes to provide targeted professional and vocational training for its female employees. There is also an appreciation that any attempts to close the gender and skills gap can only be efficacious if the overall work culture is supportive of the family responsibilities shouldered by women. Despite a range of public policy initiatives designed to increase female employees' educational and career prospects, Saudi women's home lives embody a male-breadwinner model which make childcare and household responsibilities their sole preserve.

Given the socio-institutional backdrop of the region as well as Saudi Arabia specifically, and the organizational context of proactively tackling the gender gap, critically consider the following issues:

1. Identify the range of socio-institutional characteristics that can inhibit and/or encourage employment opportunities for women in Saudi Arabia.
2. To what extent are the career developmental needs of Saudi Aramco's female employees likely to differ from their expatriate counterparts?

3. What initiatives can the multinational implement to improve women's representation in technical departments (engineering, exploration, drilling, etc.) specifically?

Adapted from:

https://www.oilandgasmiddleeast.com/people/32944-saudi-aramco-has-doubled-number-of-female-employees-in-the-past-10-years

https://www.mckinsey.com/featured-insights/leadership/women-leaders-in-the-gulf-the-view-from-saudi-aramco

References

Abalkhail, J. M. (2017). 'Women and leadership: Challenges and opportunities in Saudi higher education', *Career Development International*, 22 (2), pp. 165–183.

Abalkhail, J. M. (2019). 'Women's career development in an Arab Middle Eastern context', *Human Resource Development International*, 22(2), pp. 177–199.

Abalkhail, J. M. and Allan, B. (2016). 'Wasta and women's careers in the Arab Gulf States', *Gender in Management: An International Journal*, 31(3), pp. 1754–2413.

Al Alhareth, Y., Al Alhareth, Y., and Al Dighrir, I. (2015). 'Review of women and society in Saudi Arabia', *American Journal of Educational Research*, 3(2), pp. 121–125.

Al-Otaibi, N. (2018). 'Saudi Arabia has lifted the ban on women driving – this is what it means for women's rights', *The Independent*, 24 Jane. Available at: https://www.independent.co.uk/voices/saudi-arabia-women-driving-ban-lifted-female-rights-riyadh-middle-east-a8414281.html

Al-Ahmadi, H. (2011). 'Challenges Facing Women Leaders in Saudi Arabia', *Human Resource Development International*, 14 (2), pp. 149–166.

Aldossari, M., Chaudhry, S., Tatli, A. and Seierstad, C. (2021). 'Catch-22: Token women trying to reconcile an impossible contradiction between organizational and societal expectations', *Work, Employment and Society*, pp. 1–14.

Ali, A. H. (2015). *Heretic: Why Islam needs a reformation now.* Knopf Canada.

Alkhaled, S. and Berglund, K. (2018). 'And now I'm free: Women's empowerment and emancipation through entrepreneurship in Saudi Arabia and Sweden', *Entrepreneurship and Regional Development*, 30(8), pp. 877–900.

Al-Rasheed, M. (2013). *A Most Masculine State: Gender, Politics and Religion in Saudi Arabia.* Cambridge University Press, Cambridge.

Al-Rasheed, M. (2019). 'The long drive to prison- The struggle of Saudi women activists', *Journal of Middle East Women's Studies*, 15(2), pp. 247–250.

Arab News (2018). 'First Saudi woman appointed as deputy minister of labor and social development', *Arab News*, 27 February. Available at: https://www.arabnews.com/node/1255331/saudi-arabia

Arab News (2019). 'Saudi Arabia ends restrictions on women traveling: Royal Decree', *Arab News*, 1 August. Available at: https://www.arabnews.com/node/1534241/saudi-arabia

Bierema, L. L. (2005). 'Women's networks: A career development intervention or impediment?', *Human Resource Development International*, 8(2), pp. 207–224.

Budhwar, P. S. and Mellahi, K. (2016). 'The Middle East context: An introduction'. In Budhwar, P. S. and Mellahi, K (eds.) *Handbook of human resource management in the Middle East.* Edward Elgar Publishing, pp. 3–14.

Calvert, J. R. and Al-Shetaiwi, A. S. (2002). ' Exploring the mismatch between skills and jobs for women in Saudi Arabia in technical and vocational areas: The views of the Saudi Arabian private sector business managers', *International Journal of Training and Development*, 6(2), pp. 112–124.

Farrell, F. (2008). 'Voices on Emiratization: The impact of Emirati culture on the workforce participation of national women in the UAE private banking', *Journal of Islamic Law and Culture*, 10(2), pp. 107–68.

General Authority for statistics Kingdom of Saudi Arabia (2020). *Labour Market, Fourth Quarter 2018*. Available at: https://www.stats.gov.sa/sites/default/files/lm_2018_q4_en.pdf [Accessed 8 September 2021].

Haghighat, E. (2014). 'Establishing the connection between demographic and economic factors, and gender status in the Middle East: Debunking the perception of Islam's undue influence', *International Journal of Sociology and Social Policy*, 34 (7/8), pp. 455–484.

Hakiem, R. A. D. (2021). 'Advancement and subordination of women academics in Saudi Arabia's higher education', *Higher Education Research & Development*, 41(5), pp. 1528–1541.

Harry, W. (2007). 'Employment creation and localization: The crucial human resource issues for the GCC', *The International Journal of Human Resource Management*, 18 (1), pp. 132–146.

Hennekam, S., Tahssain-Gay, L. and Syed, J. (2017). 'Contextualising diversity management in the Middle East and North Africa: A relational perspective', *Human Resource Management Journal*, 27(3), pp. 459–476.

Hutchings, K., Lirio, P. and Metcalfe, B.D. (2012). 'Gender, globalisation and development: A re-evaluation of the nature of women's global work', *The International Journal of Human Resource Management*, 23(9), pp. 1763–1787.

Ibarra, H. (1993). 'Personal networks of women and minorities in management: A conceptual framework', *Academy of management Review*, 18(1), pp. 56–87.

Ibarra, H., N. M. Carter, and Silva, C. (2010). 'Why Men Still Get More Promotions Than Women', *Harvard Business Review*, 88 (9), pp. 80–86.

International Labour Organisation (ILO) (2020). World employment and social outlook trend 2020, Available at: https://www.ilo.org/wcmsp5/groups/public/---dgreports/---dcomm/---publ/documents/publication/wcms_734455.pdf [Accessed 12 September 2021].

Karam, C. M. and Afiouni, F. (2014). 'Localizing women's experiences in academia: Multilevel factors at play in the Arab Middle East and North Africa', *The International Journal of Human Resource Management*, 25(4), pp. 500–538.

Kawar, M. (2000). 'Transitions and boundaries: Research into the impact of paid work on young women's lives in Jordan', *Gender & Development*, 8(2), pp. 56–65.

Khan, M. (2018). 'Working Towards Vision 2030: Key Employment Considerations in KSA', *Lexology*, 30 March. Available at: https://www.lexology.com/library/detail.aspx?g=7f0d76f3-afb8-43e2-8f9f-3073bfe156c5 [Accessed 13 September 2021].

Koburtay, T., Syed, J. and Haloub, R. (2020). 'Implications of religion, culture, and legislation for gender equality at work: Qualitative insights from jordan', *Journal of Business Ethics*, 164, pp. 421–436.

Lages, C. R., Pfajfar, G. and Shoham, A. (2015). 'Challenges in conducting and publishing research on the Middle East and Africa in leading journals', *International Marketing Review*, 32(1), pp. 52–77.

Mavin, S. and Bryans, P. (2002). 'Academic women in the UK: Mainstreaming our experiences and networking for action', *Gender and Education*, 14(3), pp. 235–250.

Mazawi, A. E. (2005). 'The academic profession in a rentier state: The professoriate in Saudi Arabia', *Minerva*, 43(3), pp. 221–244.

Mellahi, K. (2007). 'The effect of regulations on HRM: Private sector firms in Saudi Arabia', *The International Journal of Human Resource Management*, 18(1), pp. 85–99.

Metcalfe, B. D. (2008). 'Women, management and globalization in the Middle East', *Journal of Business ethics*, 83(1), pp. 85–100.

Metcalfe, B. D. (2011). 'Women, Work Organization, and Social Change: Human Resource Development in Arab Gulf States', *Human Resource Development International*, 14 (2), pp. 123–129.

Morley, L. (2013). 'The rules of the game: Women and the leaderist turn in higher education', *Gender and Education*, 25(1), pp. 116–131.

O'Sullivan, A., Rey, M. E. and Mendez, J. G. (2011). 'Opportunities and Challenges in the MENA Region', *Arab world competitiveness report 2011*, 2012, pp. 42–67.

O'Neil, D. A., and Bilimoria, D. (2005). 'Women's career development phases: Idealism, endurance, and reinvention', *Career development international*, 10(3), pp. 68–189.

O'Neil, D. A., Hopkins, M. M., and Sullivan, S. E. (2011). 'Do women's networks help advance women's careers? Differences in perceptions of female workers and top leadership', *Career Development International*, 16(7), pp. 733–754.

Rees, C. J., Mamman, A. and Braik, A. B. (2007). 'Emiratization as a strategic HRM change initiative: Case study evidence from a UAE petroleum company', *The International Journal of Human Resource Management*, 18(1), pp. 33–53.

Romani, V. (2008). 'The politics of higher education in the Middle East: Problems and prospects', *Middle East Brief*, 36: 1–6.

Rutledge, E., Al Shamsi, F., Bassioni, Y. and Al Sheikh, H. (2011). 'Women, labour market nationalization policies and human resource development in the Arab Gulf states', *Human Resource Development International*, 14(2), pp. 183–198.

Salem, R. and Yount, K. M. (2019). 'Structural accommodations of patriarchy: Women and workplace gender segregation in Qatar', *Gender, Work & Organization*, 26(4), pp. 501–519.

Samin, N. (2019). *Of sand or soil: Genealogy and tribal belonging in Saudi Arabia*. Princeton University Press.

Sian, S., Agrizzi, D., Wright, T., and Alsalloom, A. (2020). 'Negotiating constraints in international audit firms in Saudi Arabia: Exploring the interaction of gender, politics and religion', *Accounting, Organizations and Society*, in press.

Sidani, Y., (2005). 'Women, work, and Islam in Arab societies', *Women in management review*, 20 (7), pp. 498–512.

Sidani, Y. and Al Ariss, A. (2014). 'Institutional and corporate drivers of global talent management: Evidence from the Arab Gulf region', *Journal of World Business*, 49(2), pp. 215–224.

Sidani, Y. M., Konrad, A. and Karam, C. M. (2015). 'From female leadership advantage to female leadership deficit: A developing country perspective', *Career Development International*, 20(2), pp. 273–292.

Singh, V. (2008)., "Contrasting positions of women directors in Jordan and Tunisia", in Vinnicombe, S., Singh, V., Burk, R. and Bilimoria, D. (Eds)", Women on Corporate Boards of Directors: International Research and Practice, Cheltenham: Edward Elgar, pp. 108–120.

Syed, J. (2010). 'An historical perspective on Islamic modesty and its implications for female employment', *Equality, Diversity and Inclusion: An International Journal*, 29(2), pp. 150–166.

Syed, J., Ali, F., and Hennekam, S. (2018). 'Gender equality in employment in Saudi Arabia: A relational perspective', *Career Development International*, 23(2), pp. 163–177.

Syed, J., Ali, F. and Winstanley, D. (2005). 'In pursuit of modesty: Contextual emotional labour and the dilemma for working women in Islamic societies', *International Journal of Work Organisation and Emotion*, 1(2), pp. 150–167.

Syed, J., and Metcalfe, B. D. (2017). 'Under western eyes: A transnational and postcolonial perspective of gender and HRD', *Human Resource Development International*, 20(5), pp. 403–414.

The Guardian (2019). 'Saudi Arabia appoints its first female ambassador to the US', *The Guardian*, 24 February. Available at: https://www.theguardian.com/world/2019/feb/24/saudi-arabia-appoints-its-first-female-ambassador-to-us [Accessed 12 September 2021].

Tlaiss, H. and Kauser, S. (2011). 'The importance of wasta in the career success of middle eastern managers', *Journal of European Industrial Training*, 5 (35), pp. 467–486.

Tlaiss, H. A., and K. M. Dirani. (2015). 'Women and training: An empirical investigation in the Arab Middle East', *Human Resource Development International*, 18 (4), pp. 366–386.

Varshney, D. (2019). 'The strides of the Saudi female workforce: Overcoming constraints and contradictions in transition', *Journal of International Women's Studies*, 20(2), pp. 359–372.

Vision 2030 National Transformation Program (2016). Vision2030govsa. Available at: https://vision2030.gov.sa/en [Accessed 11 September 2021].

Vasil, L. (1996). 'Social process skills and career achievement among male and female academics', *The Journal of Higher Education*, 67(1), pp. 103–114.

World Bank (2021). *Labor force participation rate, female (% of female population ages 15+) (modeled ILO estimate) - Middle East & North Africa*. Available at: https://data.worldbank.org/indicator/SL.TLF.CACT.FE.ZS?locations=ZQ [Accessed: 3 September 2021].

World Economic Forum (2021). *Global Gender Gap Report 2021*. Available at: http://www3.weforum.org/docs/WEF_GGGR_2021.pdf [Accessed: 1st September 2021].

15
INNOVATION
The Unconventional Gateway to the Middle East

Yassir Nasief and Abdulrahman Basahal

Introduction

The broader region of the Middle East is variously defined but usually encompasses a geographical region, including the Black Sea to the north and the Arabian Sea to the south, along with Iran and Egypt. Analysis of publications and patents illustrates that the regional member countries have shown commitment and progress towards innovation compared to other developed and emerging regions (Global Innovation Index 2021; Ringel et al., 2020). In the past decade, the creation of new knowledge in the form of patents and published research articles from the Middle East has shown progress, and it has the potential to progress further, given the significant resources it can leverage (Ringel et al., 2020).

Technology Transfer

Technology Transfer Reality

Technology has been defined as the specific application of scientific and technical knowledge to the production of goods or services (Office of Technology Assessment, 1984), and in any modern economy, technological innovation is a critical factor in creating social wealth (Davison, 2004). As such, technology can be represented by tangible items such as tools, equipment, documents, machinery, and industrial complexes and also in intangible forms such as patents, licenses, staff knowledge, and skills (Easterby-Smith, Snell, & Gheradi, 1998).

From this perspective, technology transfer is the process of transferring from one nation to another the know-how required to successfully utilise a particular technology (Sarfaraz & Emamizadeh, 1993) in a two-stage process. The first is product transfer, such as machines, equipment, and tools, with this linked to know-how transfer, such as human experience, technical information, and training programmes. Usually, the two are closely related in that an external firm will seek to sell both physical assets and the staff development, training, or software needed to make the best use of those assets. These technology transfers can come into a nation through a variety of means, including foreign direct investment, joint ventures, contracting, franchising, licensing, management contracts, turnkey operations, and exporting.

One problem is that this tends to place the focus on technology transfer as such, but there is evidence this is not sufficient to create the basis for sustaining innovation system (Asheim, Boschma, & Cooke, 2011; Tödtling & Trippl, 2005). Indeed, there is some evidence that too much reliance on FDI can embed existing distortions in the economy with few gains in terms of overall productivity or domestic innovation (Demena & van Bergeijk, 2017). Evidence from Africa suggests that a focus just on technology transfer fails to generate further collaboration between economic and non-economic actors (Daka & Toivanen, 2014; Oyelaran-Oyeyinka, 2014). This creates a problem as it ignores the extent that IK (innovation knowledge) originates from local traditions, and they may utilise it to meet current and future challenges. IK, as a traditional, invariably local, and geographically specific knowledge is developed through generations of continuous adaptation to changing circumstances (Bohensky & Maru, 2011). For innovation to be a sustained process, it needs to access both external resources and adapt to internal expectations and traditions (Ndabeni, Rogerson, & Booyens, 2016).

The GCC countries have historically depended on imported technologies to promote and stimulate their economies. This transfer has been previously funded using the abundant financial resources raised from oil revenues, and the new technologies tended to be concentrated in six major fields: communications, medical services and equipment, petrochemical and chemical industries, military equipment, civil aviation industry, and water and power stations (Alfahhad, 2004).

However, the transfer of both physical technology and related knowledge and training is only part of the process by which the recipient state can make the best use of the new technology. This also requires the ability to absorb the technology into other domestic systems and the indigenous technological capabilities of the recipient to operate, maintain, and modify the foreign Technology (Office of Technology Assessment, 1984).

Indigenous Technological Capability

As noted above, one key factor in the ability to absorb technology is the degree of domestic capacity (Cohen, 2004; Zanello, Fu, Mohnen, & Ventresca, 2016). This capacity is built up from crucial components. First is the complex mix of human skills that embody technical knowledge (mostly a product of the local education systems) (Sillitoe & Marzano, 2009). The second component is the 'institution' through which all the technical knowledge incorporated in individuals is coordinated and developed. At the macro level, the institution that facilitates such collaboration is the government, whereas, at the micro level, this role is played by the enterprise. This also relies on some degree of common purpose as new knowledge is developed and transmitted within an economy, often transmitted orally or through demonstration and imitation, and it is learned by repetition (Rao, 2006; Tödtling & Trippl, 2005), thus having characteristics of the doing–using–interaction (DUI) mode of development (Lundvall, Joseph, Chaminade, & Vang, 2011).

Innovation

This section explores these themes using three countries' examples – Saudi Arabia, the UAE, and Egypt.

Background

Saudi and the UAE are part of the wider GCC and share similar economic, technological, and industrial aspects (Alfahhad, 2004, 2013), such as the following:

1. Their economies attempt to diversify to reduce their reliance on oil and gas. As the energy industry adapts to the shifting dynamics of the global economy, innovation has emerged as a top priority.
2. They have comprehensive national and industrial development plans (Saudi Arabia Vision 2030 and the UAE Vision 2021) aimed at a variety of industries.
3. They have some of the most successful and dedicated inventors regionally and internationally (e.g., Saudi Aramco, SABIC, and Emirates) (Ringel et al., 2020).

By contrast, Egypt is the Arab world's most populous state and possesses a large and highly skilled labour force (Jankowski, 2001). Its economy is relatively underdeveloped, characterised by low wages and below-average productivity (Morsy & Levy, 2020).

The Global Innovation Index (GII)

The GII is an annual survey that mostly uses publicly available statistics to measure innovation at a country level (Global Innovation Index, 2019). To do this, it captures innovation using five input pillars to measure those items of the national economy that enable innovative activities: (1) Institutions, (2) Human capital and research, (3) Infrastructure, (4) Market sophistication, and (5) Business sophistication. Two output pillars are also used to capture evidence of innovation outputs: (1) Knowledge and technology outputs; and (2) Creative outputs.

Each pillar is divided into sub-pillars, and each sub-pillar is composed of individual indicators (80 in total in 2019). Sub-pillar scores are calculated as the weighted average of individual indicators; pillar scores are calculated as the weighted average of sub-pillar scores.

Four measures are then calculated:

- Innovation Input Sub-Index is the average of the first five (input) pillar scores
- Innovation Output Sub-Index is the average of the last two (output) pillar scores

The overall GII score is the average of the Input and Output Sub-Indices. As such, this gives a useful measure of both the level of technology transfer to a country and the level of IK in that country.

Egypt

Egypt regained full sovereignty from Britain in 1952 (it had never formally been a colony) with an economy that relied mainly on agriculture, energy, manufacturing, and textile (International Trade Administration, 2022). Control of the Suez Canal gives some external income, and the Nile has been dammed to generate electricity. However, the economy has never been able to grow fast enough to meet the demands of a rapidly expanding population, whether under Nasser's state management approach (Jankowski, 2001) or the more liberal development model adopted since the mid-1970s. On the other hand, as the most populous nation in the Middle East (and the Arabic-speaking regions of North Africa), Egypt has tended to dominate cultural outputs and has a long-standing, well-regarded tertiary education sector.

The recently adopted National Sustainable Development Strategy (Ministry of Development, 2019) seeks to address some of these problems by encouraging knowledge creation and transfer and the development of SMEs. These goals are supported by the intent to improve the regulatory environment and to improve the partnership between the state and the private sector.

The Egyptian economy historically showed modest progress (Jankowski, 2001). In recent years, the country's economy has been impacted negatively by covid 19 and the war in Ukraine (Abd El Ghany, 2022). Several structural reforms and initiatives related to public finances, business and investment climate, and job creation were introduced by the government to elevate the economic challenges (Hosny, 2021).

In terms of the Global Innovation Index (GII), Egypt is ranked 94th for 2021 (see Figure 15.1). The country is relatively strong in knowledge output, particularly in scientific papers and labour productivity (Global Innovation Index, 2019).

Table 15.1 presents the main actors at the moment in terms of innovation and knowledge creation and transfer.

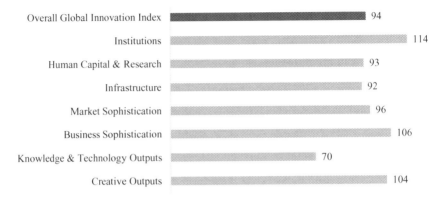

FIGURE 15.1 GII 2021 Rankings Overall and by Pillar, Egypt.

Source: (Global Innovation Index, 2021).

Saudi Arabia

The first Saudi State was established in 1727 (Ministry of Foreign Affairs, 2022). In the early 1990s, the country gained substantial wealth with the discovery of considerable oil reserves. This allowed the development of its economic and social system. Today, Saudi Arabia is one of the world's largest producers and exporters of oil, with an economy considered the largest in the Arab States and the top 20 in the world (The World Bank, 2021). In 2016, Saudi Arabia transparently published its Vision 2030 as a strategic framework for the country, aiming to diversify the economy and improve competitiveness, offering new prospects to reach long-term economic, social, and environmental sustainability (Vision 2030, 2022). In particular, investment and resources were channelled into building industrial zones, economic and smart cities (e.g., NEOM city), as well as enhancing potential economic sectors such as energy, recreation, and tourism (Alyusuf, 2020).

Since 2016, Saudi Arabia has invested heavily in national infrastructure and developed attractive policies to reinforce economic and investment activities, increasing non-oil international trade. Many initiatives have been created to boost economic performance and attract foreign investments. As a result, mega investment deals with global companies were signed (Alyusuf, 2020).

Educational and labour market initiatives were also created to create a competent generation to fulfil the workforce demand of Vision 2030. These changes have resulted in an 18% improvement in the skill set of graduates from 2016 to 2020 (Schwab & Zahidi, 2020) and a significant number of women entering the workplace in a broader range of roles. Female participation in the labour market increased from 19% in 2016 to 33% in 2020 (OKAZ, 2022).

As for the innovation sector, Saudi Arabia ranked 66th in the Global Innovation Index for 2021 (see Figure 15.2). Overall, the country progressed and moved up in the Global Innovation Index ranking in the last two years (Global Innovation

Innovation 227

TABLE 15.1 Egypt's Innovation Ecosystem

Institutions	Human Capital and Research	Infrastructure	Market Sophistication	Business Sophistication	Knowledge and Technology Output	Creative Output
Political environment **Regulatory Environment** **Business Environment**	**Education** **Tertiary Education** **Research and Development**	**ICTs** **General Infrastructure** **Ecological Sustainability**	**Credit** **Investment** **Trade, competition, market scale**	**Knowledge workers** **Innovation Linkages** **Knowledge Absorption**	**Knowledge creation** **Knowledge Impact** **Knowledge diffusion**	**Intangible Assets** **Creative goods and Services** **Online creativity**
Egypt Vision 2030 Minister of Finance Minister of Legal and Parliamentary Affairs Minister of Planning and Administrative Reform Minister of Industry, Trade, and Small Industries General Authority of Investment and Free zones	Minister of Education Minister of Higher Education and Scientific Research Minister of Manpower Minister of Technical Training and Education Cairo University The American University in Cairo Mansoura University Alexandria University Ain Shams University National Research Center (NRC) the Academy of Scientific Research and technology the Egyptian Science, Technology and Innovation Observatory	Minister of Electricity and Energy Minister of Environment Minister of Communications and Information Technology Minister of Climate Change and Environmental Science Egypt e Gov General Authority of Investment and Free zones Telecom Egypt	Minister of Tourism Ministry of Agriculture and Land Reclamation Commercial Banks: HSBC Bank Egypt Commercial International Bank National Bank of Egypt Banque Misr Venture Capital: Algebra Ventures A15 Endure Capital Sawari Ventures	Minister of Investment Sewedy Electric Orascom Construction Limited Global Telecom Holding Company Ezz Steel	General Authority of Investment and Free zones Egyptian Patent Office	Minister of Culture EUNIC Egypt

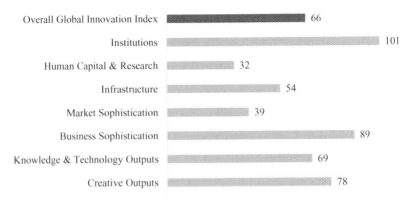

FIGURE 15.2 GII 2021 Rankings Overall and by Pillar, Saudi Arabia.
Source: (Global Innovation Index, 2021).

Index, 2021, Global Innovation Index, 2019). The state unveiled priorities for research, development, and innovation for the coming two decades. As a result, dedicated annual spending on the sector to reach 2.5% of GDP in 2040, and expected the sector to contribute SR60 billion to the National GDP in 2040 (Saudi Gazette, 2022).

In recent years, specialist institutions have been created to encourage innovation, including the King Abdulaziz City for Science and Technology, Saudi Arabia (KACST). In addition, in 2021, the state has established an official Authority named The Research, Development and Innovation Authority (RDIA), linked institutionally to the Prime Minister and is independent financially and administratively (RDIA, 2022), to ensure the innovation sector's growth and prosperity via the following:

1- Acting as a sector enabler, legislator, and regulator;
2- Developing programs and projects;
3- Distributing budget and monitoring performance;
4- Attracting talents locally and globally;
5- Intensifying collaboration with significant research institutions, global businesses, nonprofit organisations, and the private sector (Saudi Gazette, 2022).

Table 15.2 uses the main categories from the GIL report (Global Innovation Index, 2021) to identify the most crucial form they take in Saudi Arabia. So, in terms of 'institutions', an important part of the political environment is the recently adopted Vision 2030 (Vision 2030, 2022, Mitchell & Alfuraih, 2018) and the establishment of The Research, Development and Innovation Authority (RDIA). Table 15.2 provides information regarding the institutions that are very important to the expansion of the innovation sector.

TABLE 15.2 Saudi Arabia's Innovation Ecosystem

Institutions	Human Capital and Research	Infrastructure	Market Sophistication	Business Sophistication	Knowledge and Technology Output	Creative Output
Political environment Regulatory Environment Business Environment	Education Tertiary Education Research and Development	ICTs General Infrastructure Ecological Sustainability	Credit Investment Trade, competition, market scale	Knowledge workers Innovation Linkages Knowledge Absorption	Knowledge creation Knowledge Impact Knowledge diffusion	Intangible Assets Creative goods and Services Online creativity
Vision 2030 CEDA (Council of Economic and Development Affairs) RDIA (Research, Development and Innovation Authority) MISA (Mistry of Investment Saudi Arabia) KACST (King Abdul-Aziz City for Science and Technology) MCIT (Ministry of Communications & Information Technology) Monshaat (Small and Medium Enterprises Authority) SAIP (Saudi Authority for Intellectual Property)	Ministry of Education Tatwer Co. for Educational Services Technical & Vocational Training Corporation KAUST (King Abdullah University of Science and Technology) KFUPM (King Fahd University of Petroleum & Minerals) KAU (King Abdulaziz University) KSU (King Saud University) Science Parks: DTVC (Dhahran Techno Valley Company) Research centers KAPSARC KACARE KAUST Core Labs Home of innovation (SABIC)	Communications and Information Technology Commission (CITC) Electricity Company Saudi E-Gov Portal Elm Digital Solution Company	Commercial Banks: Alrajhi Bank SNB Bank SABB State Funds: SIDF (Saudi Industrial Development Fund) ADF (The Saudi Agricultural Development Fund) SDB (The Social Development Bank) Monshaat (Small and Medium Enterprises Authority) Saudi Venture Capital Company (SVC) 500 Falcons RTF STV Misk Innovation	State Owned: PIF Aramco Sabic Sadara Maaden STC Private Enterprises Almaraie Savola Alolyan Alzamil	Taqnia RPD Innovations IKTVA (In Kingdom Total Value Add) Monshaat (Small and Medium Enterprises Authority) SAIP (Saudi Authority for Intellectual Property)	Ministry of Culture (MOC) and its commissions (Music, theater and performance art, film, and others Misk Art Institute Tilfaz11 Saudi Art Council SAIP (Saudi Authority for Intellectual Property)

UAE

The UAE became independent in 1971 and established its first university, the United Arab Emirates University (UAEU), in 1976. While the UAEU seeks to cover a wide range of academic disciplines, it focuses more on knowledge dissemination to the national community rather than actual knowledge creation. This left a gap in terms of support for innovation and knowledge-intensive activities as means to further economic development (Palacios-Marqués et al., 2016). In recent years, a focus on indigenous research intensity has led to a strategic redirection of UAE federal higher education institutions towards greater efforts in knowledge creation and innovation. A key factor in the production of knowledge is the existence of research-intensive, knowledge-producing institutions (Aljawareen, 2018). This shift of focus improves the capacity to create knowledge and disseminate it.

As with Saudi Arabia, the UAE has created specialist institutions that seek to ease knowledge transfer and creation. This led to the establishment of the Dubai International Academic City (DIAC) in 2007. In October 2014, the UAE government launched the National Strategy for Innovation, which aims to make the UAE among the most innovative countries in the world with a seven-year strategy focussing on seven key sectors: renewable energy, transport, health, education, technology, water, and space (Aljawareen, 2018).

According to the 2021 Global Innovation Index (Global Innovation Index, 2021), the UAE ranks 33rd (see Figure 15.3).

The critical actors in the UAE's innovation Ecosystem using the GII categories are summarised in Table 15.3.

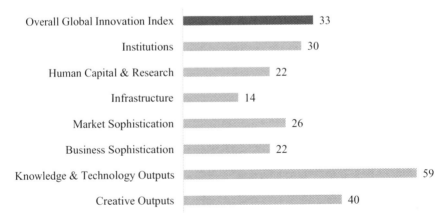

FIGURE 15.3 GII 2021 Rankings Overall and by Pillar, UAE.

Source: (Global Innovation Index, 2021).

Innovation 231

TABLE 15.3 UAE's Innovation Ecosystem

Institutions	Human Capital and Research	Infrastructure	Market Sophistication	Business Sophistication	Knowledge and Technology Output	Creative Output
Political environment **Regulatory Environment** **Business Environment**	**Education** **Tertiary Education** **Research and Development**	**ICTs** **General Infrastructure** **Ecological Sustainability**	**Credit Investment Trade, competition, market scale**	**Knowledge workers Innovation Linkages Knowledge Absorption**	**Knowledge creation Knowledge Impact Knowledge diffusion**	**Intangible Assets** **Creative goods and Services** **Online creativity**
Vision 2021 Federal Supreme Council (FSC) Emirates Investment Authority (EIA) Minister of Cabinet Affairs and The Future Minister of Economy Minister of Culture and Knowledge Development	Ministry of Education Minister of Human Resources and Emiratisation United Arab Emirates University Khalifa University American University of Sharjah UAEU Science and Innovation Park UAEU Research Centers ADNOC Research and Innovation Center	Minister of Infrastructure Development Telecommunications Regulatory Authority (TRA) Minister of Climate Change and Environment UAE EGovernment Portal Etisalat Du Jebel Ali Free Zone	Commercial Banks: Emirates NBD. First Abu Dhabi Bank. Abu Dhabi Commercial Bank. State Funds: Mohammed Bin Rashid Innovation Fund Venture Capital: Wamda Capital Oasis500 MEVP	Abu Dhabi Investment Authority Abu Dhabi National Oil Company (ADNOC) Dubai Ports World Dubai World Emaar Properties PJSC Al-Futtaim Group Al Ghurair Group Lulu Group International Landmark Group Al Naboodah Group	Minister of Culture and Knowledge Development IP Office within the Ministry of Economy	Minister of Culture and Knowledge Development Dubai Design District Dubai Media City Abu Dhabi Film Commission

Conclusion

Considering the innovation ecosystem of the three countries above, we can summarise the main practical guidelines for practitioners and investors planning to work in the region or enter it through the innovation gateway.

Historically, each country has its own strong industries that attract the most national and international interest. For instance, agriculture, tourism, textiles, and logistics are Egypt's key industries (EEDC, 2015). On the other hand, Saudi Arabia has strong industries in energy and chemicals, logistics, mining, and ICT (NCC, 2022). The UAE also has important sectors in energy, commerce, finance and insurance, technology, and advanced manufacturing (UAE Ministry of Economy, 2022).

Potentially, all three countries have evident endeavours in taking steps towards innovation in the advantaged industries and others. First, through their national innovation strategies and established research centres that foster research and development in the country. Practitioners interested in innovation generation in these countries need to explore the country's institutions, human capital, research, and infrastructure actors in Tables 1, 2, and 3. However, if the interest of practitioners is in the technology and innovation application side, they need to explore the country's information on business sophistication, knowledge and technology, and creative output (see the tables in this chapter).

References

Aljawareen, A. (2018). Innovation in the GCC countries.
Alfahhad, J. (2004). Assessing the capability to acquire and absorb technology within the public sector in developing countries: the case of Kuwait. Ph.D., Aston University.
Alfahhad, J. (2013). Technology transfer process to the Gulf Cooperation Council (GCC) countries: An analytical perspective.
Alyusuf, A. (2020). Land of the Future. Saudi Gazette. Retrieved 20 January, 2021, from https://saudigazette.com.sa/article/598327
Asheim, B. T., Boschma, R., & Cooke, P. (2011). Constructing regional advantage: Platform policies based on related variety and differentiated knowledge bases. *Regional Studies*, 45(7), 893–904.
Bohensky, E. L., & Maru, Y. (2011). Indigenous knowledge, science, and resilience: What have we learned from a decade of international literature on "integration"? *Ecology and Society*, 16(4), 6.
Bussola Institute (2022). Saudi Arabia's path to economic diversification through research, development, and innovation. Retrieved 20 September, 2022, from, shorturl.at/abfj5
Cohen, G. (2004). *Technology Transfer: Strategic Management in Developing Countries*. New Delhi, India: Sage Publications India.
Daka, E., & Toivanen, H. (2014). Innovation, the informal economy and development: The case of Zambia. *African Journal of Science, Technology, Innovation and Development*, 6(4), 243–251.
Davison, R. M. (2004). Technology transfer: Strategic management in developing countries. *The Electronic Journal of Information Systems in Developing Countries*, 17(1), 1–2. https://doi.org/10.1002/j.1681-4835.2004.tb00115.x

Demena, B. A., & van Bergeijk, P. A. G. (2017). A meta-analysis of FDI and productivity spillovers in developing countries. *Journal of Economic Surveys*, 31(2), 546–571. https://doi.org/10.1111/joes.12146

Easterby-Smith, M., Snell, R., & Gheradi. S. (1998). Organizational learning: Diverging communities of practice. *Management Learning*, 29(3), 259–272.

EEDC (2015). Why invest in Egypt. Egypt economic development conference. Retrieved 20 January, 2021, from shorturl.at/fnQ01

Global Innovation Index. (2019). *Creating Healthy Lives—The Future of Medical Innovation* (pp. 451). New York, NY: Cornell University.

Global Innovation Index. (2021). *Tracking Innovation Through the COVID-19 Crisis*. Geneva, Switzerland: WIPO.

Hosny, K. (2021). The IMF lists the 5 most important economic reforms in Egypt. Alarabiya. Retrieved 20 September, 2022, from, shorturl.at/gpu 12

International Trade Administration (2022) Egypt - Country commercial guide. Retrieved 20 September, 2022, from, https://www.trade.gov/country-commercial-guides/egypt-market-overview

Lundvall, B.-Å., Joseph, K., Chaminade, C., & Vang, J. (2011). *Handbook of Innovation Systems and Developing Countries: Building Domestic Capabilities in a Global Setting*. Edward Elgar Publishing.

Ministry of Development. (2019). *Sustainable Development Strategy (SDS): Egypt Vision 2030* (pp. 37). Cairo, Egypt: Cairo.

Ministry of Foreign Affairs. (2022). KSA history. Retrieved 20 September, 2022, from, https://www.mofa.gov.sa/en/ksa/Pages/history.aspx

UAE Ministry of Economy (2022). Promising sectors. Retrieved 20 September, 2022, from, https://www.moec.gov.ae/en/promising-sectors

Mitchell, B., & Alfuraih, A. (2018). The Kingdom of Saudi Arabia: Achieving the aspirations of the national transformation program 2020 and Saudi Vision 2030 through education. *Journal of Education and Development*, 2(3), 36–46. https://doi.org/10.20849/jed.v2i3.526

NCC (2022). *Investment Sectors in Saudi Arabia*. National Competitiveness Center. Retrieved 25 September, 2022, from, https://www.ncc.gov.sa/en/Business/Pages/Investors.aspx

Abd El Ghany, M. (2022) Egypt increases social support as economic crisis hurts. Reuters. Retrieved 20 September, 2022, from, shorturl.at/EHQU2

Morsy, H., Levy, A. (2020). Growing without changing: A tale of Egypt's weak productivity growth. *African Development Review*, 32(3), 271–287.

Ndabeni, L. L., Rogerson, C. M., & Booyens, I. (2016). Innovation and local economic development policy in the global South: New South African perspectives. *Local Economy*, 31(1–2), 299–311.

Office of Technology Assessment. (1984). *Technology Transfer to the Middle East* (pp. 610). Washington D.C.: U.S. Congress.

OKAZ. (2022). *Empowering Saudi Women in the Workplace: An Essential Pillar Towards Achieving Sustainable Success*. Retrieved December 26, 2022, from shorturl.at/akrJ6

Oyelaran-Oyeyinka, B. (2014). The state and innovation policy in Africa. *African Journal of Science, Technology, Innovation and Development*, 6(5), 481–496.

RDIA. (2022). About RDIA. Retrieved 20 September, 2022, from, https://www.rdia.gov.sa/index.en.html#about

Palacios-Marqués, D., Welsh, D. H., Méndez-Picazo, M.-T., Palacios-Marqúes, D., Welsh, D., & Méndez-Picazo, M. (2016). The importance of the activities of innovation and knowledge in the economy: Welcome to the Journal of Innovation and Knowledge. *Journal of Innovation and Knowledge*, 1(1), 1–2.

Rao, S. S. (2006). Indigenous knowledge organisation: An Indian scenario. *International Journal of Information Management*, 26(3), 224–233.

Ryan, J. C., & Daly, T. M. (2019). Barriers to innovation and knowledge generation: The challenges of conducting business and social research in an emerging country context. *Journal of Innovation & Knowledge*, 4(1), 47–54. https://doi.org/10.1016/j.jik.2017.10.004

Ringel, M., Trench, S., Khalil, I, Krühler, M., El Hitti, G., & Harnoss, J (2020). *The Middle East Capitalises on Its Commitment to Innovation*. Boston Consulting Group. Retrieved 20 September 2022, from, https://www.bcg.com/publications/2020/the-middle-east-and-a-commitment-to-innovation

Sarfaraz, A. R., & Emamizadeh, B. (1993). Cost estimating for transfer of technology in developing countries. *AACE International Transactions*, L. 5.1.

Saudi Gazette. (2022). Crown Prince unveils priorities for research, development and innovation for coming two decades. Retrieved 20 September, 2022, from, https://saudigazette.com.sa/article/622445

Schwab, K. & Zahidi, S., (2020). How countries are performing on the road to recovery. The global competitiveness report.

Sillitoe, P., & Marzano, M. (2009). Future of indigenous knowledge research in development. *Futures*, 41(1), 13–23.

Sultan, N. (2012). Working for a sustainable GCC future: Reflections on policies and practices. In M. A. Ramady (Ed.), *The GCC Economies: Stepping Up To Future Challenges* (pp. 3–10). New York: Springer.

Tödtling, F., & Trippl, M. (2005). One size fits all?: Towards a differentiated regional innovation policy approach. *Research Policy*, 34(8), 1203–1219.

The Global Competitiveness Report (2011–2012). World Economic Forum.

The World Bank (2021). GDP (current US$). Retrieved 20 September, 2022, from, https://data.worldbank.org/indicator/NY.GDP.MKTP.CD?most_recent_value_desc=true&year_high_desc=true

Vision 2030 (2022). Key projects. Retrieved 20 September, 2022, from, https://www.vision2030.gov.sa/v2030/v2030-projects/

Zanello, G., Fu, X., Mohnen, P., & Ventresca, M. (2016). The creation and diffusion of innovation in developing countries: A systematic literature review. *Journal of Economic Surveys*, 30(5), 884–912.

16
GOVERNMENT E-SERVICES AND REPUTATION
Case of UAE

Fatima Al Ali, Melodena Stephens and Vijay Pereira

Introduction

Governments are the largest service providers in the world (da Silva & Batista, 2007). Adopting e-government leads to cost-saving, improved ease of use and usefulness of services, increased levels of customer service, and more efficient collection and distribution of information for decision making (Evans & Yen, 2006; Sharma et al., 2014). In addition, e-government benefits governments by reducing corruption and improving their financial systems to make them more effective (Kachwamba & Sæbø, 2011). More importantly, e-government encourages democracy and reduces the gap between the government and the citizens (Macintosh, Robson, Smith & Whyte, 2003).

The OECD (2020: 9) highlights the importance of this digital transformation:

> It has, in its own right, forced governments into rethinking organizations, responsibilities, business processes, and collaborative and co-operative arrangements within and across levels of government – and also forced governments to take a whole-of-public-sector view of their service provision to citizens and businesses.

Moreover, many government services are crossing borders making the implication of such e-government services more critical. Some examples are electronic health records, smart contracts, cryptocurrencies, or electronic identities.

E-government or the digitalization of governments is often referred to as Government 2.0 or smart government. It began with World War II and the early space race. Figure 16.1 shows the acceleration of digital technology adoption and government response. The global market size of the smart government is USD

DOI: 10.4324/9781003005766-19

236 Fatima Al Ali et al.

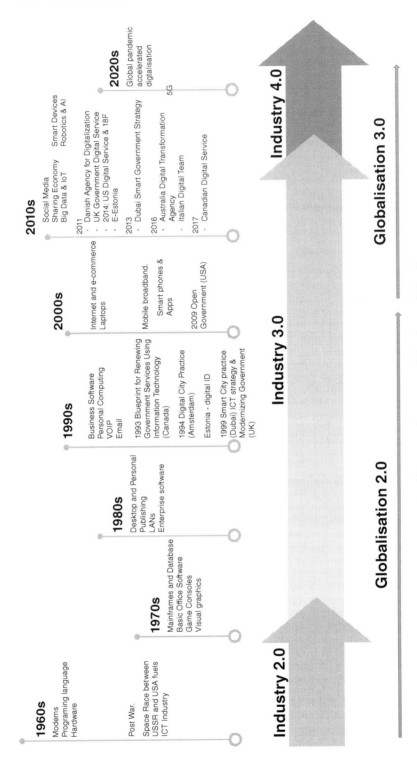

FIGURE 16.1 Innovation in Digital Economy and Public Sector Response – Timeline and Key Events.

Source: Authors (Compiled from McKinsey; Anthopolous, 2017).

28.24 billion for 2022, growing at a Compound Annual Growth Rate (CAGR) of 19.2% (MarketandMarkets, 2021). This growth has been fueled by the digitalization of services, greater outsourcing, big data, AI, and the Internet of All Things (IoT). The COVID pandemic was a tipping point, pushing governments to digitalize faster, whether it was the adoption of health care, education, remote working, or virtual courts. A Deloitte Insights survey of 800 government officials across eight countries found that three-fourths of respondents indicated that COVID-19 accelerated their government's digital transformation (Kishnani et al., 2021).

E-government utilizes ICT and other web-based technologies to improve efficiency in delivering and accessing government services for all kinds of stakeholders in government-to-citizen (G2C), government-to-government (G2G), and government-to-business (G2B) relations (Carter & Bélanger, 2005; Sharma et al., 2014). E-governance is an important topic as it provides *"freedom of expression and freedom of access"* to all citizens (Majeed, Niazi & Sabahat, 2019, p. 112). While traditionally, e-government services have been aimed at the national population, they are also a significant part of international business. In the Middle East, services as a category observed by cross-border bandwidth have increased more than 150 times in the last decade (McKinsey, 2016). Figure 16.2 shows the growth of cross-border services which has grown by 150 times from 2005 to 2015. While the UAE leads in the Middle East, the potential of the region is enormous! Especially as it has 16% of world population.

Government 2.0 is different from Government 1.0, where the flow of information was unidimensional from the government to the public with limited feedback loops from the citizens (Chun et al., 2010). Government 2.0 is a more open, social, communicative, interactive, and user-centered version of e-government (Meijer, Koops, Pieterson, Overman, & Tije, 2012, p. 59). The government becomes a digitally enabled network of public, private, and/or civil society participants, ideally resulting in greater value and lower costs (Tapscott, Williams, & Herman, 2008). But as governments are also embedded in an international network and require greater collaboration and coordination at the global level, questions do arise on the role of the government and its benefits in an international context.

One area where international businesses benefit is through government outsourcing. A study in the UK found that more than 50% of budgets for procurement were for external suppliers (Institute for Government, 2018). This amount is an average of 10% of GDP for OECD countries (OECD, 2011). In some cases, the relationship is simple: Siemens (Germany) was contracted to develop the South African Department of Labour e-Government Portal, or AMD and Intel (USA) worked with the State of Sao Paolo in Brazil to develop citizen service centers. Or in some cases, the relationship is complex: Estonia's National ID Card scheme is managed by a PPP between the Citizens Migration Board (CMB) and two private partners: SK, a joint-venture company, and TRUB Baltic AS. The CMB issues the identity cards to citizens, SK manages the associated electronic services, and TRUB Baltic AS manufactures the card. Estonia's Digital Signatures Act governs the public private partnership (PPP).

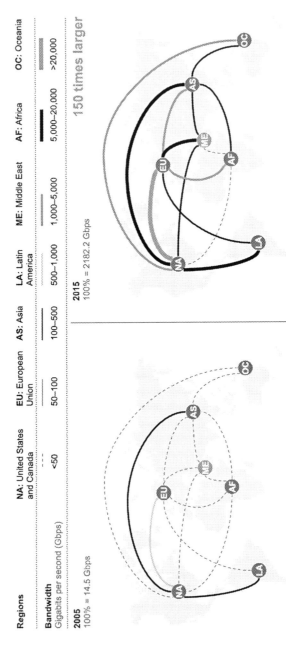

FIGURE 16.2 Global Cross-border Flows 2005–2015 (bandwidth).

Source: Digital McKinsey (2016).

But there have been failures also. In 2018, UK's Carillion, a British MNC listed on the stock market, collapsed. It held 400 public sector contracts, had 43,000 employees, and was operating in the UK, Canada, Qatar, KSA, Egypt, and the UAE, among other countries. This problem is a critical issue for governments as debates emerge around privatization (for efficiency and savings) or outsourcing versus nationalization (for public value control), or insourcing. From an MNC point of view, there is a risk in outsourcing. A major part of Carillion's problems was linked to the inability to recover dues. Carillion attributed £314m of that to its Middle East operations, of which at that time £200m was for a contract for the 2022 FIFA World Cup (GCR, 2018). But for governments, there is the public value component, service delivery, and, more importantly, citizen loyalty and government reputation to consider.

Citizens' behaviors are strongly impacted by their degree of satisfaction with the goods or services provided and trust in the government (Bouckaert & Van de Walle, 2003; Beeri, Uster & Vigoda-Gadot, 2019; Zeng, Hu, Chen & Yang, 2009). Therefore, to ensure satisfaction and loyalty, to avoid civil unrest as experienced in some of the Arab countries during the Arab Spring, governments in the Middle East North Africa region began to proactively shift their mindsets to focus on engaging citizens as an accelerator in improving the quality of their services (Al-Khouri, 2012).

This chapter will focus on the United Arab Emirates (UAE). The first section will look at the complex relationship between the reputation of the country and e-services. The case of the UAE will be used to show how the country put the Government 2.0 agenda at the fore. This section is followed by the unique perspective of who can be considered as the government's customer. This is then followed by the concept of service loyalty in the government context and a discussion section.

Reputation: A Case of UAE e-Government

Anholt (2005) argued that a strong country reputation is recognized when the country's government, actions, initiatives, and investments are aligned with a clear vision. Moreover, country reputation depends on the country images created by the behavior of the leadership and people of that country in different fields and levels (Wang, 2006; Fullerton & Holtzhausen, 2012). Previous research finds that usage of e-government services is a function of trust (Carter, Schaupp, Hobbs, & Campbell, 2012), and reputation is affected by the service quality provided by e-government and the reputation of those entities providing the service (López-López et al., 2018; Alzahrani, Al-Karaghouli, & Weerakkody, 2017). In the 2021 Edelman Trust Barometer, the UAE is one of the few governments for which the government ranks higher than business and NGOs.

One of the key drivers for Government 2.0 was the UAE leadership's ambitious vision, which was to have digitalized government services (TRA, 2018). In 2013, His Highness Sheikh Mohammed, launched a new initiative by directing all government (federal and local) entities to step forward by providing innovative government services through mobile or smartphones within 24 months using the resources in effective and efficient ways and to enable 24 hours a day, 7 days a week (Khaleej Times, 2013). As His Highness said, *"A successful government reaches out to the citizens rather than wait for them to come to it"* (Khaleej Times, 2013).

The UAE leadership adopted the competitiveness approach to help the government sector improve the necessary policies and strategic plans and collaborate with all stakeholders in implementing plans and policies to improve the country's ranking globally in competitiveness reports (FCSA, 2019). The Federal Competitiveness and Statics Centre (previously the Emirates Competitiveness Council) is tasked with monitoring competitive rankings at the national level. In terms of national rankings, the UAE is ranked 24 in the 2020 UN E-Government Development Index. In 2005 it was ranked 42 out of 193 countries. In the 2020 Online Services Index, UAE was ranked 8th globally and 1st in the Arab and the GCC regions, 4th in the Asia region, and in the 2020 eParticipation Index, the UAE ranks 16th globally. For the pandemic response, according to the Pandemic Resilience Index 2021, the UAE ranked 2nd. In addition, each government department is rated on a scale of 2–7 stars for service centers since 2012 (UAE, 2021), and the objective is to be a country that provides Seven Stars Services.

These rankings suggest that the UAE, a pioneer in e-government and smart government, has been executing digital transformation with some degree of success. The earliest initiative was in 2001 and was the introduction of the e-Dirham for collecting revenues between federal entities. In 2004, there followed an infrastructure upgrade for e-government with the Emirates Telecommunications Corporation (Etisalat). The e-government portal was launched in 2005 in the Emirate of Dubai, the objective of which was to conduct 70% of all government services efficiently and effectively (Al Bastaki, 2006). The focus then shifted to the quality of service and delivery method where first it was electronic platforms and then smart platforms in 2013. The focus on artificial intelligence (AI) was reinforced with the appointment of the first Minister of State for AI in the world in 2017. The objective is to become World Leaders in AI by 2031 *"fast adopter of emerging AI technologies across Government, as well as attract top AI talent to experiment with new technologies and work in a sophisticated, secure ecosystem to solve complex problems"* (ai.UAE., 2021). This was spearheaded by the creation of Smart Dubai in Dubai in 2016 and Abu Dhabi Smart Solutions and Services Authority (ADSSSA) or Abu Dhabi Digital Authority (ADDA) in 2019.

Another focus area for the government has been wellbeing and happiness. The government of UAE established the Ministry of Happiness in 2016 (Aljneibi, 2018). One of the vision priorities is to make the UAE the happiest country in the world by focusing on factors and national elements that matter to the citizens, contribute to their happiness, and make them proud to be UAE's citizens (Vision2021, 2020). The UAE government then launched the National Strategy for Wellbeing 2031. Its objective is to support the 2021 vision to be a world-leading country in quality of life by working toward several strategic objectives and initiatives that assure the wellbeing of the society (UAE National Strategy for Wellbeing 2030, 2022). Over ninety strategic initiatives have been adopted to be implemented by the government entities over ten years that aim to enhance the various government sectors that are directly associated with the life of citizens by focusing on areas of physical and mental health, education, lifestyle, social relationships, and government services efficiency (MOCAF, 2020).

The UAE leadership and government is considered unique in the Arab world for its clear vision and strategic objectives (Al Dari, Jabeen & Papastathopoulos, 2018) and, most importantly, its e-government or smart government infrastructure (Khan, 2014; FCSA, 2019). The planning cycle is forward-looking. In 2010, His Highness Sheikh Mohammed bin Rashid Al Maktoum, Vice-President and Prime Minister of the UAE and Ruler of Dubai, launched a vision for the United Arab Emirates for 2021 (Vision 2021, 2020). The vision consists of four main pillars: United in Prosperity, United in Knowledge, United in Destiny, and United in Responsibility.

The main objective in the UAE national agenda is to build a country that has a diversified its oil-dependent economy (FCSA, 2019), where there are substantial opportunities for international business. The UAE government acknowledges the importance of the private sector since 2015 (UAE PPP, 2021) based on the Public–Private Partnership (PPP) model in governing via (1) service contracts; (2) management contracts; (3) leasing contracts; (4) concession contracts; (5) build, operate, transfer (BOT); (6) build, own, operate, transfer (BOOT); and (7) build, own, operate (BOO). The government has responded in an agile and proactive manner to ensure e-services (Awamleh, Stephens, & Salem, 2021). For example, during the pandemic, teleconsultations were used as a digital platform for wellbeing (MoHAP, 2020). As a result, the UAE is ranked 1st in wellbeing and happiness in the Arab region and ranked 21st globally (World Happiness Report, 2020).

Citizen-Centric or Customer-Centric Approach

Whether that the citizen can be viewed as a customer is a topic that is still currently being debated. Some authors reject the notion of calling citizens as customers (Aberbach, 2005; Jung, 2010). However, the fact remains that many countries adopt a citizen-customer approach by treating the citizens as customers (Alford & Hughes 2008; Thomas, 2013). For instance, the United States uses the National Performance Review (NPM) approach under the Clinton administrations to encourage federal organizations to implement customer service standards (Pegnato, 1997; Thomas, 2013). In addition, the United Kingdom uses the Customer Relationship Management (CRM) approach where they treat citizens as customers to maintain a positive relationship with customers, which they believe will lead to an increase in customer loyalty and their long-term value. Such approaches use a deep analysis of customer behavior (King, 2007).

"Citizens expect to be treated as customers, with responsiveness and consideration. That is as truer at the social security office as it is at the supermarket" (Dilulio, Garvey, & Kettl, 1993, p.48). As business values became part of the public administration core business (Denhardt & Denhardt, 2003; deLeon & Denhardt, 2000), these values influence governments to use private sector strategies and transform their interaction and the way of serving their public. The governments are also embracing privatization strategies with respect to how they view the public and overcome the current bureaucracy in providing modern services to solve current problems (Lucio, 2009). Thus, governments use the word "customer" as a reference to their public sector clients (Lucio, 2009).

Many authors support the arguments of calling citizens customers. For instance, according to Barzelay (1992), the customer of government organizations are citizens. He claims that government organizations should be "customer driven and service oriented" (Barzelay, 1992, p.20; Pegnato, 1997, p.398). Osborne and Gaebler (1992, pp. 180–185) also state that government organizations can be customer-driven organizations and become democratic governments to serve their citizen-customers. They claim that there are many advantages to be customer-driven, such as greater responsiveness, more innovation, and less waste.

New Public Management (NPM) is combining the government services with private sector practices to help regain the trust that has been affected by existing public systems, budget deficit, and poor civic perception of government (Lucio, 2009). NPM shows that to enhance government services, increase its effectiveness, and ensure the accomplishment of its tasks, the government should respond to its customers' preferences. Very simply, this means imitating market practices according to customer responsiveness. Thus, this will help governments to achieve their goals in a democratic context (Pierre, 1998). Accordingly, the citizen-customer model considers a good public strategy for the government (Pegnato, 1997).

In some ways, a government can be considered a monopoly, where governments may be unaware of their citizens' dissatisfaction. Citizens cannot switch to another service provider, making the service exit impossible (Hirschman, 1970; Ferrari & Manzi, 2014). Citizens do not have other alternatives for government services (Evans & Yen, 2006). But they can change the government, and hence it is prudent to rethink the way citizens are viewed. It is essential to measure, evaluate, and monitor citizens' satisfaction by using surveys and other methods to listen to their needs (Ferrari & Manzi, 2014; Morgeson, 2014). The main objective of measuring citizens' satisfaction is to enhance their perceptions about government performance, similar to measuring customer satisfaction in the private sector, which will lead to improving the services and products provided by the government (Morgeson, 2014; Evans & Yen, 2006).

The UAE government is also adopting the citizen-customer approach in its 2021 vision. According to the Strategic Planning Manual (SPM), the customer is defined from government sector perspective as *"those individuals and/or enterprises that are beneficiaries of the services provided by government sector entities, e.g., for the Ministry of Education this would be universities, the labor market or students"* (Moca.gov.ae, 2013). SPM states that there two types of customers. The first is the internal customer such as departments, and the second is the external customers such as citizens.

The notion of the citizen in the UAE is important as around 80% of the population are expatriates. In 2019, His Highness Sheikh Mohammed issued an eight-point plan for governance for the Emirate of Dubai. He stated,

> The law does not discriminate between citizens and residents, rich and poor, male and female, Muslims and non-Muslims (Point 2).... We extend a hand of friendship to all those who hold good intentions towards Dubai and the UAE. Dubai is a politically neutral, business-friendly global hub that focuses on creating economic opportunities (Point 3).... Dubai's growth is driven by three factors: a credible, resilient, and excellent government; an active, fair, and open private sector; and public and government-owned flagship companies that compete globally and generate an income for the government, jobs for its citizens, and assets for future generations (point 4).
>
> (The National, 2019)

Moreover, the UAE 2021 vision that has been launched by His Highness Sheikh Mohammed bin Rashid Al Maktoum, Vice-President and Prime Minister of the UAE and Ruler of Dubai, states that under the fourth vision "UNITED IN PROSPERITY" (p.20) *"The UAE will nurture high quality of life built on world-class public infrastructure, government services, and a rich recreational environment"* (UAE Vision2021, p.24).

E-service Satisfaction

Many countries have adopted customer satisfaction in different industries as an important economic indicator for the wellbeing and development of any nation (Sharbat & Amir, 2008). Extensive studies have been conducted to understand customer satisfaction in the online environment (Bansal et al., 2004; Evanschitzky et al., 2004; Ribbink et al., 2004; Yang & Peterson, 2004). Often these studies define customer satisfaction as the positive or negative feelings toward services that have been received from the service provider (Schmit & Allscheid, 1995; Woodruff, 1997; Barnes et al., 2004). Zeithaml (2002) defines e-satisfaction in a similar way and as the evaluation of whether an online service or product meets online customer needs and expectations.

Customer satisfaction can be conceptualized using two approaches. The first approach is by viewing customer satisfaction as an emotional reaction toward the performance of a particular service; it is conceptualized as transaction satisfaction. On the other hand, when satisfaction depends on the elements that occur over repeated transactions, it will be conceptualized as cumulative satisfaction (Shankar et al., 2003; Chang et al., 2009). Thus, overall satisfaction or cumulative satisfaction is an overall experience affected by customers' expectations of the e-service provider and their perceptions about e-service performance over the current and previous period (Johnson et al., 1995; Johnson et al., 2001; Krepapa et al., 2003; Ha & Janda, 2008).

A significant number of studies have investigated customer satisfaction in the online context and e-government context in specific. Lu, Fang, and Feng (2012) investigated the factors that affect users' satisfaction with e-government services. The results show that perceived security is the most important factor of perceived value and perceived fit. The authors claim that the customers are looking for protection of their privacy while using e-government services and their awareness about security affects the value of e-government awareness. Moreover, the study also reveals that both customer satisfaction and perceived value are influenced by perceived fit. This means that customers are willing to use new technology that supports and positively affects their work and that the security system is guaranteed.

Danila and Abdullah (2014) investigated the main factors that affect citizens' intentions and usage of e-government services in Malaysia. This was done by introducing a framework that combines three models: The Technology Acceptance Model (TAM), Theory of Planned Behavior (TPB), and Information System Success (ISS). The results show that the factors in the proposed framework, which are personal innovativeness, perceived usefulness, perceived ease of use, attitude, subjective norm, perceived behavior control, and system quality, have a great influence on users' intentions and usage of e-government services.

Ma and Zheng (2019) investigated the influence of e-government performance on citizens' satisfaction in thirty-two countries in Europe. They argue that this study is unique by investigating the performance of e-government at the country level and citizen satisfaction at the individual level. The data were obtained from 32 countries in Europe. The results show that the performance of e-government is positively associated with citizen satisfaction; however, this association varies depending on the aim of e-government services use. The authors conclude that e-government service features should be added and developed by not only considering the supply as the only party but also citizens as the end party who are affected by the service features.

It can be noticed that most of the e-satisfaction studies concentrate on the main determinants of customer satisfaction in the online context, including e-service quality. Besides highlighting the most important factors of e-service quality that positively or negatively affect customer satisfaction.

This has been reflected in the one of UAE government practices that concerned about customer satisfaction in using e-services, especially mGovernment initiatives. One of the main objectives of mGovernment initiatives is to increase the level of customer satisfaction or – as the UAE government states – customer happiness with the government digital services (UAE, 2022). Accordingly, the UAE government started to invest extensively in innovation and technology including smart devices and big data as government enablers to ensure service excellence (UAE, 2022).

Due to the increased focus on public awareness about the digital services besides their quality, this led to increase the usage level of these services among them. This positively impacted the level of satisfaction or happiness among the customers who use digital services from 70% in 2017 to 87% in 2020 (UAE, 2022).

One approach that helped UAE government to measure the level of customer happiness and helped develop and improve the quality of digital services provided is using the happiness meter (UAE, 2019). Happiness meter is a government tool that is used by the federal government organizations to collect customers' instant or real-time feedback about the service delivered. This approach helps overcome several challenges in obtaining the real data about the customer satisfaction and happiness that will help improve the quality of the services (UAE, 2019).

The main objectives of using this tool are to instantly measure the level of customer satisfaction, provide the necessary analytical data which positively support the improvement process, and provide the decision-makers with accurate statistics for quality improvement process. Accordingly, this system has been installed online in government organizations by April 2019 through different channels including 9 smart applications, 550 online services, and 39 organizations' websites (UAE, 2019).

Implementing this initiative resulted in a significant impact on customer happiness and economic level (see Figure 16.3). It can be said that this project positively affected several areas. First, it has an impact on the number of customer engagement and usage of online services. The statistics showed that the level of engagement and level of customer satisfaction obtained from the evaluation have been increased especially through online channels and platforms. Second, it helped in addressing the unhappy customers which provided an opportunity for taking corrective actions to improve services provided. Third, the happiness meter has been deployed across all the government entities in the federal sector in all seven emirates. This national connectivity provided a holistic view of the happiness and satisfaction level across UAE in online services in 38 government organizations. From economic point of view, happiness meter implementation succeeded in positively influencing the UAE economy due to the continuous improvement on e-service. It has been noticed that the cash flow into UAE economy has been increased by approximately 200 million in one year (UAE, 2019).

E-service Loyalty

The development and penetration of the Internet in the marketing and e-commerce contexts, along with customers' increasing willingness to purchase online, has encouraged several outcomes. First, it has increased the number of organizations doing online business. This will help them to find and maintain new and existing customers for long-lasting profitability (Ulbrich, Christensen, & Stankus, 2010; Valvi & Fragkos, 2012). Second, it has facilitated the development of different e-loyalty models in research (Valvi & Fragkos, 2012).

The concept of loyalty falls into three categories: behavioral, attitudinal, and integrated approaches (Oh, 1998; Chang et al., 2009). The behavior approach looks at the number of repeated purchases and measures customer loyalty by the rate of purchasing, regularity of purchasing, and potential to purchase. The attitudinal approach examines customer loyalty in terms of "psychological involvement" and good feelings toward a certain service or product. Finally, the integrated approach integrates both previous approaches (behavior and attitude) and creates its own loyalty concept (Chang et al., 2009).

246 Fatima Al Ali et al.

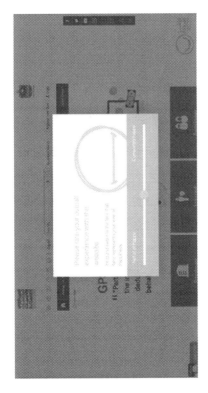

Users receive weekly auto-generated reports based on access levels.

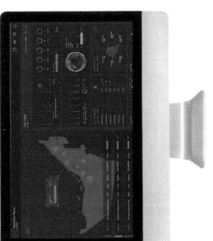

Central real-time reporting dashboards showing country heatmap with drill down capabilities.

FIGURE 16.3 Happiness Meter Dashboard.

Source: Government Experience, 2019.

In a government context, many studies emphasize the importance of examining government websites related sittings (Grimsley & Meehan, 2007). According to Sugandini, Feriyanto, Yuliansyah, Sukwadi, and Muafi (2018), websites are considered a very important element for organizations to maintain their customers. Loyalty in an e-government context means that customers return to use e-government services instead of using other channels providing the same services (such as service centers, mail or phone).

There are several definitions of customer loyalty in previous studies. E-loyalty is defined as a preferred attitude that a customer exerts toward an e-business that makes the customer repeat the purchasing behavior (Anderson & Srinivasan, 2003). Perera, Nayak, and Long (2019, p. 86) define e-loyalty as "the consumers' favorable attitude towards an electronic business resulting in buying behavior." Neal's (1999, p. 21) definition is

> the proportion of times a purchaser chooses the same product or service in a specific category compared to the total number of purchases made by the purchaser in that category, under the condition that other acceptable products or services are conveniently available in that category.

Most of the previous studies investigated the factors that affect customer loyalty in the e-service context. For example, Cristobal, Flavia'n, and Guinalı´u (2007) investigated the influence of perceived service quality on customer satisfaction and website loyalty. Their study revealed that customer satisfaction influences website loyalty and plays a mediating role in perceived service quality and loyalty. In another study, Chang, Wang, and Yang (2009) targeted online shoppers to examine the relationship between e-service quality, customer satisfaction, customer loyalty, and perceived value. The study showed a positive association between customer satisfaction and customer loyalty and a mediating influence of perceived value on the relationship between satisfaction and loyalty

Castañeda (2011) investigated the relationship between customer satisfaction and loyalty on the Internet. After using telephone interviews and surveys, the authors claimed that the effect of customer satisfaction and loyalty is high when customer involvement moderates this effect and is partially mediated by trust. They argue that for customers who are highly involved with the product, customer satisfaction is a good indicator of their loyalty.

Khan, Zubair, and Malik (2019) investigated e-loyalty and the constructs that have an impact on it, such as e-service quality. The aim of the study was to examine the correlation between e-service quality and e-loyalty in online shopping in Pakistan. The results show that e-service quality positively influences e-loyalty. Thus, to maintain customer e-loyalty, e-service quality should be considered. It can be noticed that a limited number of studies have investigated the role of customer loyalty in the e-government context (Gupta, Singh & Bhaskar, 2016) as most of the previous studies examined loyalty from an e-commerce context.

Conclusions: Business in an e-Government Context

As the chapter highlights, the role of business is to help the government achieve its objectives. In the case of UAE, the government is very agile and forward-looking, which means they are willing to work with the latest technologies. More important as the reputation of UAE is highly focused on the global market, there is a need to ensure that the services and products being offered are of the highest international quality. There are several areas of future study. For example, the impact of the international diaspora on future business opportunities in the UAR and its economic growth is yet to be determined. The relationship between the diaspora and soft power or reputation is another area that needs deeper study. The role of e-service quality and e-loyalty, especially in an environment of uncertainty, fake news, and geo-political tensions, is another area for research.

References

Aberbach, J., 2005. Citizens and consumers. *Public Management Review*, 7 (2), 225–246.

ai.UAE (2021). World Leaders in AI by 2031, Available: https://ai.gov.ae/about-us/

Al Bastaki, M. 2006. Dubai e-Government Achievements & Upcoming Challenges.

Al Dari, T., Jabeen, F. and Papastathopoulos, A., 2018. Examining the role of leadership inspiration, rewards and its relationship with contribution to knowledge sharing. *Journal of Workplace Learning*. 30(6), 488–512.

Alford, J. and Hughes, O., 2008. Public value pragmatism as the next phase of public management. *The American Review of Public Administration*, 38(2), 130–148.

Aljneibi, N. M., 2018. Well-being in the United Arab Emirates: How Findings from Positive Psychology Can Inform Government Programs and Research. Master of Applied Positive Psychology (MAPP) Capstone Projects. 147.

Al-Khouri, A. M., 2012. Customer relationship management: Proposed framework from a government perspective times. *Journal of Management and Strategy*, 3(4), 34.

Alzahrani, L., Al-Karaghouli, W., & Weerakkody, V. (2017). Analysing the critical factors influencing trust in e-government adoption from citizens' perspective: A systematic review and a conceptual framework. *International Business Review*, 26(1), 164–175.

Anderson, R. E., and Srinivasan, S. S., 2003. E-satisfaction and e-loyalty: A contingency framework. *Psychology & Marketing*, 20(2), 123–138.

Anholt, S., 2005. *Brand new justice: How branding places and products can help the developing world*. Routledge.

Anthopolous, L. G. 2017. Understanding smart cities: A tool for smart government or an industrial trick? http://dx.doi.org/10.1007/978-3-319-57015-0_2 Available: https://www.oecd.org/mena/governance/36279733.pdf

Awamleh, Stephens and Salem, 2021.

Bansal, H. S., McDougall, G. H., Dikolli, S. S. and Sedatole, K. L., 2004. Relating e-satisfaction to behavioral outcomes: An empirical study. *Journal of Services Marketing*, 18(4), 290–302.

Barnes, B. R., Fox, M. T. and Morris, D. S., 2004. Exploring the linkage between internal marketing, relationship marketing and service quality: A case study of a consulting organization. *Total Quality Management & Business Excellence*, 15(5–6), 593–601.

Barzelay, M., 1992. *Breaking through bureaucracy: A new vision for managing in government*, Berkeley: University of California Press.

Beeri, I., Uster, A. and Vigoda-Gadot, E., 2019. Does performance management relate to good governance? A study of its relationship with citizens' satisfaction with and trust in Israeli local government. *Public Performance & Management Review*, 42(2), 241–279.

Bouckaert, G., and Van de Walle, S., 2003. Comparing measures of citizen trust and user satisfaction as indicators of 'good governance': Difficulties in linking trust and satisfaction indicators. *International Review of Administrative Sciences*, 69(3), 329–343.

Carter, L and Bélanger, F. 2005. The utilization of e-government services: Citizen trust, innovation and acceptance factors. *Information Systems Journal*, 15, 5–25.

Carter, L., Schaupp, L. C., Hobbs, J., & Campbell, R. (2012). E-government utilization: Understanding the impact of reputation and risk. *International Journal of Electronic Government Research*, 8(1), 83–97.

Castañeda, J. A., 2011. Relationship between customer satisfaction and loyalty on the internet. *Journal of Business and Psychology*, 26(3), 371–383.

Chang, H., Wang, Y. and Yang, W., 2009. The impact of e-service quality, customer satisfaction and loyalty on e-marketing: Moderating effect of perceived value. *Total Quality Management & Business Excellence*, 20(4), 423–443.

Chun, S., Shulman, S., Sandoval, R., & Hovy, E. (2010). Government 2.0: Making connections between citizens, data, and government. *Information Polity*, 15(1, 2), 1–9.

Cristobal, E., Flavián, C. and Guinalíu, M., 2007. Perceived e-service quality (PeSQ): Measurement validation and effects on consumer satisfaction and web site loyalty. *Managing Service Quality: An International Journal*, 17(3), 317–340.

Da Silva, R. and Batista, L., 2007. Boosting government reputation through CRM. *International Journal of Public Sector Management*, 20(7), 588–607.

Danila, R. and Abdullah, A., 2014. User's satisfaction on e-government services: An integrated model. *Procedia-Social and Behavioral Sciences*, 164, 575–582.

deLeon, L. and Denhardt, R., 2000. The political theory of reinvention. *Public Administration Review*, 60(2), 89–97.

Denhardt, R., and Denhardt, J. 2003. *The new public service*. Armonk, NY: M.E. Sharpe.

Digital McKinsey (2016). Digital Middle East: Transforming the region into a leading digital economy Available: https://www.mckinsey.com/~/media/mckinsey/featured%20insights/middle%20east%20and%20africa/digital%20middle%20east%20transforming%20the%20region%20into%20a%20leading%20digital%20economy/digital-middle-east-final-updated.ashx

Dilulio, J., Garvey, G., and Kettl, D. 1993. *Improving government performance: An owner's manual.* Washington, DC: Brookings Institution.

Evans, D. and Yen, D. 2006. E-Government: Evolving relationship of citizens and government, domestic, and international development, *Government Information Quarterly*, 23(2), 207–235.

Evanschitzky, H., Iyer, G. R., Hesse, J. and Ahlert, D., 2004. E-satisfaction: A re-examination. *Journal of Retailing*, 80(3), 239–247.

Fcsa. 2019. *Home*. [online] Available at: https://fcsa.gov.ae/en-us [Accessed 24 December, 2019].

Ferrari, P., and Manzi, G., 2014. Citizens evaluate public services: A critical overview of statistical methods for analysing user satisfaction. *Journal of Economic Policy Reform*, 17(3), 236–252.

Fullerton, J. and Holtzhausen, D., 2012. Americans' attitudes toward South Africa: A study of country reputation and the 2010 FIFA World Cup. *Place Branding*, 8(4), 269–283.

GCR (2018). https://www.globalconstructionreview.com/news/what-about-carillions-middle-east-projects/

Grimsley, M. and Meehan, A., 2007. e-Government information systems: Evaluation-led design for public value and client trust. *European Journal of Information Systems*, 16(2), 134–148.

Gupta, K. P., Singh, S. and Bhaskar, P., 2016. Citizen adoption of e-government: A literature review and conceptual framework. *Electronic Government, an International Journal*, 12(2), 160–185.

Ha, H. and Janda, S., 2008. An empirical test of a proposed customer satisfaction model in e-services. *Journal of Services Marketing*, 22(5), 399–408.

Hirschman, A. 1970. *Exit, voice, and loyalty*, Cambridge, Mass: Harvard University Press.

Institute of Government 2018. Government Procurement. https://www.instituteforgovernment.org.uk/publications/government-procurement [19 May, 2021].

Johnson, M. D., Anderson, E. W. and Fornell, C., 1995. Rational and adaptive performance expectations in a customer satisfaction framework. *Journal of Consumer Research*, 21(4), 695–707.

Johnson, M. D., Gustafsson, A., Andreassen, T. W., Lervik, L. and Cha, J., 2001. The evolution and future of national customer satisfaction index models. *Journal of Economic Psychology*, 22(2), 217–245.

Jung, T. 2010 Citizens, co-producers, customers, clients, captives? A critical review of consumerism and public services. *Public Management Review*, 12(3), 439–446.

Kachwamba M. and Sæbø Ø. 2011. E-government in marketing a country: A strategy for reducing transaction cost of doing business in Tanzania. *International Journal of Marketing Studies*, 3(4), 2–16.

Khaleej Times, 2013. *Govt of future is innovative: Shaikh Mohammed*. [online] Available at: https://www.khaleejtimes.com/nation/government/govt-of-future-is-innovative-shaikh-mohammed [Accessed 26 January, 2018].

Khan, M. A., Zubair, S. S., and Malik, M. 2019. An assessment of e-service quality, e-satisfaction and e-loyalty. *South Asian Journal of Business Studies*, 8(3), 283–302.

Khan, S. M., 2014. United Arab Emirates Leading Competitiveness. *Defence Journal*, 18(2), 41–43.

King, S., 2007. Citizens as customers: Exploring the future of CRM in UK local government. *Government Information Quarterly*, 24(1), 47–63.

Kishnani, P. K., Manstof, J., Eggers, W. D. & Barroca, J. (2021). Seven pivots for the government's digital transformation. *Deloitte Insights*, dated 3 May. Available: https://www2.deloitte.com/us/en/insights/industry/public-sector/government-digital-transformation-strategy.html

Krepapa, A. B. P., Webb, D., and Pitt, L. 2003. Mind the gap: An analysis of service provider versus customer perceptions of market orientation and the impact on satisfaction. *European Journal of Marketing*, 1(4), 21–201.

López-López, V., Iglesias-Antelo, S., Vázquez-Sanmartín, A., Connolly, R., & Bannister, F. (2018). E-Government, transparency & reputation: An empirical study of Spanish local government. *Information Systems Management*, 35(4), 276–293.

Lu, Z., Fang, R. and Feng, Y., 2012. Empirical research on service satisfaction in e-government environment. *International Journal of Digital Content Technology and its Applications*, 6(14), 164–171.

Lucio, J., 2009. Customers, citizens, and residents: The semantics of public service recipients. *Administration & Society*, 41(7), 878–899.

Ma, L. and Zheng, Y., 2019. National e-government performance and citizen satisfaction: A multilevel analysis across European countries. *International Review of Administrative Sciences*, 85(3), 506–526.

Majeed, B., Niazi, H. A. K. and Sabahat, N., 2019. E-Government in developed and developing countries: A systematic literature review. In *2019 International Conference on Computing, Electronics & Communications Engineering (iCCECE)* (pp. 112–117). IEEE.

MarketsAndMarkets 2021, https://www.marketsandmarkets.com/Market-Reports/smart-government-market-60917358.html

Meijer A, Koops B, Pieterson W, Overman S and ten Tije S, 2012. Government 2.0: Key challenges to its realization. *Electronic Journal of e-Government*, 10(1), 59–69. Available at: www.ejeg.com

Mergel 2018, A timeline of national digital service team start-ups. Available at: https://inesmergel.wordpress.com/2018/03/12/a-timeline-of-national-digital-service-team-start-ups/

Moca.gov.ae, 2013. RESOURCE LIBRARY | Ministry of Cabinet Affairs. [online] Available at: http://www.moca.gov.ae/?page_id=685&lang=en [Accessed 1 April 2015].

Mocaf., 2020. [online] Available at: https://www.mocaf.gov.ae/en/media/news/national-wellbeing-strategy-2031-introduces-anew-approach-for-government-work [Accessed 27 May, 2020].

MoHAP 2020, MoHAP launches virtual clinics to further strengthen its telemedicine system, Available: https://www.mohap.gov.ae/en/MediaCenter/News/Pages/2407.aspx [Accessed 6 July, 2021].

Morgeson, F., 2014. *Citizen satisfaction improving government performance, efficiency, and citizen trust*, New York: Palgrave Macmillan.

Neal, W. D., 1999. Satisfaction is nice, but value drives loyalty. *Marketing Research*, 11(1), 21–23.

OECD 2011. *Government outsourcing, in Government at a Glance 2011*. Paris: OECD Publishing. https://doi.org/10.1787/gov_glance-2011-54-en

OECD (2020), Future of e-government: An agenda. https://www.oecd.org/governance/eleaders/43340370.pdf

Oh, H. C., 1998. An empirical study of the relationship between restaurant images and patronage behavior toward alternative restaurant chains. *Asia Pacific Journal of Tourism Research*, 2(2), 15–28.

Osborne, D., and Gaebler, T., 1992. *Reinventing government: How the rntrepreneurial spirit is transforming the public sector*. Addison-Wesley Publ. Co.

Pegnato, J., 1997. Is a citizen a customer? *Public Productivity & Management Review*, 20(4), 397–404.

Perera, C. H., Nayak, R. and Long, N. V. T., 2019. The impact of electronic-word-of mouth on e-loyalty and consumers' e-purchase decision making process: A social media perspective. *International Journal of Trade, Economics and Finance*, 10(4).

Pierre, J., 1998, Public consultation and citizen participation: Dilemmas of policy advice, in B. G. Peters and D. J. Savoie (eds) *Taking stock: Assessing public sector reforms*. Montreal & Kingston: McGill University Press.

Ribbink, D., Van Riel, A. C., Liljander, V. and Streukens, S., 2004. Comfort your online customer: Quality, trust and loyalty on the internet. *Managing Service Quality: An International Journal*, 14(6), 446–456.

Schmit, M. J. and Allscheid, S. P., 1995. Employee attitudes and customer satisfaction: Making theoretical and empirical connections. *Personnel Psychology*, 48(3), 521–536.

Shankar, V., Smith, A. K. and Rangaswamy, A., 2003. Customer satisfaction and loyalty in online and offline environments. *International Journal of Research in Marketing*, 20(2), 153–175.

Sharbat, O., and Amir, E., 2008, Design of a model for assessment of customer satisfaction in developmental banking industry and assessing the customer satisfaction of the Bank Sanat-va-Maadan on its basis. *Danesh Modiriat Quarterly*, 21, 57–74.

Sharma, G., Shakya, S. and Kharel, P., 2014. Technology acceptance perspectives on user satisfaction and trust of e-government adoption. *Journal of Applied Sciences*, 14(9), 860–872.

Sugandini, D., Feriyanto, N., Yuliansyah, Y., Sukwadi, R., and Muafi, M., 2018. Web quality, satisfaction, trust and its effects on government website loyalty. *International Journal for Quality Research*, 12(4), 885–904.

Tapscott, D., Williams, A. D., & Herman, D. 2008. Government 2.0: Transforming government and governance for the twenty-first century. *New Paradigm*, 1, 15.

The National (2019). Sheikh Mohammed issues eight principles of governance to strengthen growth and tolerance, dated 5 January, Available: https://www.thenationalnews.com/uae/sheikh-mohammed-issues-eight-principles-of-governance-to-strengthen-growth-and-tolerance-1.809562

Thomas, J., 2013. "Citizen, customer, partner: Rethinking the place of the public in public management," *Public Administration Review*, 73(6), 786–796.

Tra. 2018. The UAE Is Ranked Sixth Globally in Online Services Index According To The UN EDGI Report Covering 193 Countries - TRA Media - Media Hub - Telecommunications Regulatory Authority (TRA). [online] Available at: https://www.tra.gov.ae/en/media-hub/press-releases/2018/7/19/الإمارات-السادسة-عالمياً-في-المؤشر-العالمي-للخدمات-الذكية-وفقاً-لتقرير-الأمم-المتحدة-الذي-شمل-193-دولة.aspx [Accessed 24 March, 2018].

UAE, 2019. *UAE's happiness meter delivering government services innovation through data analytics* (pp. 1–19). Dubai: Government Experience.

UAE, 2021. Global star rating system for services. Available: https://u.ae/en/about-the-uae/the-uae-government/global-star-rating-system-for-services [Accessed 6 July, 2021].

UAE, 2022. Satisfaction with online mobile services Available: https://u.ae/en/about-the-uae/the-uae-government/global-star-rating-system-for-services [Accessed 20 May, 2022].

UAE PPP, 2021. Public Private Partnership (PPP). Available: https://u.ae/en/information-and-services/business/public-private-people-partnership/public-private-partnership [Accessed 6 July, 2021].

Ulbrich, F., Christensen, T. and Stankus, L., 2010. Gender-specific on-line shopping preferences. *Electronic Commerce Research*, 11(2), 181–199.

Valvi, A. C., and Fragkos, K. C. 2012. Critical review of the e-loyalty literature: A purchase-centred framework. *Electronic Commerce Research*, 12(3), 331–378.

Vision2021, 2020. UAE Vision | UAE Vision 2021. [online] Available at: http://www.vision2021.ae/en/our-vision [Accessed 26 May. 2020].

Vision2021.ae, 2015. UAE Vision | UAE Vision 2021. [online] Available at: http://www.vision2021.ae/en/our-vision [Accessed 1 April, 2015].

Wang, J., 2006. Managing national reputation and international relations in the global era: Public diplomacy revisite. *Public Relations Review*, 32(2), 91–96.

Woodruff, R. B., 1997. Customer value: The next source for competitive advantage. *Journal of the Academy of Marketing Science*, 25(2), 139–153.

World Happiness Report. 2020. World happiness report 2020. [online] Available at: https://worldhappiness.report/ed/2020/ [Accessed 12 June, 2020].

Yang, Z. and Peterson, R. T., 2004. Customer perceived value, satisfaction, and loyalty: The role of switching costs. *Psychology & Marketing*, 21(10), 799–822.

Zeithaml, V. A., 2002. Service excellence in electronic channels. *Managing Service Quality: An International Journal*, 12(3), 135–139.

Zeng, F., Hu, Z., Chen, R. and Yang, Z., 2009. Determinants of online service satisfaction and their impacts on behavioural intentions. *Total Quality Management*, 20(9), 953–969.

INDEX

Pages in *italics* refer figures and pages in **bold** refer tables.

accounting 139–142; challenges facing governments and MNCs 140–142; history of 139; Islamic rules 139–140; lack of consistency among systems 141; systems in Middle Eastern countries 139–140; Zakat 140
accounting and taxation systems 131–145; influencing factors 131
Arab Spring 16; Egypt, and 27

banking and financial institutions 116–130; Bahrain **123**; central banks operating in GCC 120–123; different national legal systems, effect 118–120; different types in Kuwait and Oman **125**; Dubai Financial Market 125–126; emerging equity market, and 125–126; financial crises 126–*127*; Fintech 120–122; history of doing business in Middle East 120; home bias 116; implications of difference in legal systems 119–120; institutions supervised by central banks 122–125; Islamic banking 120–122; Kuwait **125**; Oman **125**; role of central banks in GCC 120–122; Saudi Arabia **124**; source of asymmetric difference in knowledge 117; UAE **123**; universal regulatory framework 117–118; usage of English law in DIFC 118–119; vulnerability to crises 126–127; websites linking central banks 121

conflict management and negotiation in the workplace 161–175; aggression and loudness 172; aspirations 161; conflict resolution styles 171–172; contextual sources of power 170–171; cultural confluence 170; families of expats 166; foreign nationals 163, 166; free zones, and 163; gender participation 163; head of state 163; immigrants, and 162; individual differences 166–169; informational sources of power 162–166; interests 161; labour nationalization policies 166; legislative systems **164**–165; legitimate power 163; managing cultural differences 173; networks 169–171; nonverbal communication 171–172; orientation towards time 172; paradox of appraisal 170–171; personality differences 166–169; power based on position in organization 163–166; referent power 169–171; skilled human capital, need for 161; sources of power and influence 162; trust and relationship 172–173; way forward 173–174

economic diversification 15–20
economic environment 10–22; absence of markets 16; Arab Spring 16; corruption 16; diversification 16–18; Ease of Doing Business Index 18–20; educational reforms 19; literature 10; public bodies 15;

renewable energy projects 18; RQI 16, 17; steps toward changing 18; uncertainties of growth 19; unemployment 12–15; variable measures 14–15; varying degrees of development 10–11

Egypt 27–29; advantages and benefits of political and economic environment 28–29; Arab Spring, and 27; constraints and disadvantages of political and economic environment 29; economic reform 28–29; investor incentives 33; LLC manager 34; political system 27–28; regulations 33–34; terrorist attacks 29

employment relations 98–115; collective 103; collective bargaining 107–109; collective organisation 98; dismantling of independent unions 107; exclusions 100–102; freedom to associate 105–107; ILO conventions 104–105; Kuwaitization 100; labour markets and regulation 99–102; labour protection 110–112; legislative frameworks 104–105; localization programmes 99; management in practice 102–103; MENA 98–115; Qatar 111–112; right to strike 109–110; social dialogue 107–109; trade union membership 112–113; trade unions 105–107; variations 99; violent attacks on workers 107

expatriate management 191–206; administrative aspect 198; citizen care and resident welfare 196; climate 194; compensation packages 200; cost of hiring 199; cultural adaptability and flexibility 200; cultural factors 201; dependent 192–193; economic context of host country 194–196; efforts to attract expats 195; etiquette 201; expact.com 200; family owned businesses 195–196; female employees, and 193; financial and economic policies of state, and 195; footprints of international forums 197; free trade zones 196; GCC, and 192; government regulations 199; GPCI 200; hospitality 194; international relations of host country 197; Islamic banking and finance 195; key contractual considerations 192–197; law and order 201; lifestyles 202; person-environment fit 201; political context of host country 196–197; recommendation for excellence 197–202; recommendation for experts 200–202; recommendations for human resource professionals 198–199; recruitment and selection practices 198; resources for evaluating economic context **204**; resources for evaluating political context **205**; resources for evaluating sociocultural context **203**; safety and security levels 201; significance 192; social life 202; sociocultural context of host country 193–194; statistics 191; technology, use of 199; training and development interventions 198–199; Westernisation, and 193–194; workforce nationalisation, and 196–197; working 192–193; youth base, and 193

FAHR 187
free trade zones 88

GCC countries 38–61; challenges for investment 51; changing commercial company law structure to host 100% FDI 46–47; changing legal framework 38–61; ease of doing business 39–42; economic diversification 39–42; extending reform to ownership structure of public joint stock companies 49–50; FDI flows to 39–42; improving governance in public joint stock companies 47–49; indications of state of oil dependency **59**–60; liberalization of FDI law allowing 100% participation 42–44; minimum capital requirement in LLC and Private Joint Stock Company structure **48**; National Vision 2021 55; non-oil diversification strategy 39–**41**; positive and negative lists for 100% FDI participation **56**–**58**; protecting composition scheme 47–49; reform in legal framework 52, **53**

GDP: sectors of economy, across 17; per capita 11–12

gender issues 209–221; employment in feminine fields 213; invisible inequalities 212–214; networking 216; patriarchal structures 211–212; recommendations to promote gender equality 215–217; Saudi Arabia 214–215; Saudi Aramco 217; social-institutional challenges 211–212; subtle exclusion of women 214; targeted mentorship 216; tribal and Bedouin traditions 212; underrepresentation of women in senior leadership roles 213–214; visible inequalities 212–214 government e-services and reputation 235–252; citizen-centric approach 241–243; citizens as customers 242–243; citizens' dissatisfaction 242; citizens' satisfaction 239; conceptualization of customer satisfaction 243, 244; customer-centric approach 241–243; e-service loyalty 245–247; e-service satisfaction 243–245; failures 239; global cross-border flows 2005–2015 *238*; Government 2.0 237; happiness meter dashboard *246*; importance of digital transformation 235–237; NPM 242; reputation; UAE e-government 239–241; UAE government practices 244–245; use of e-government 237

human resources management 146–160; Arab culture and values, influence of 149; Arab management styles 150; challenges 152–155; changing mindset of top managers 153; competence or merit based approach 153; country-specific overview 147; definition 146; delegation of authority 149; developments 147–152; diversity management 154; emerging literature 151; high unemployment, and 154; increasing populations, and 154; issues for research 154; local culture, politics and people 149; localization programmes 150–151; major changes 152–153; more research, need for 154; pro-environmental 148–149; role in organizational development 151; studies covering specific aspects 147–148; UAE and technology 152; variation across countries 150; women in management-related issues 148

innovation 222–234; background 224–231; digital economy and public sector response *236*; Egypt 225–226; Egypt's innovation ecosystem **227**; GII 2021 rankings overall and by pillar, Saudi Arabia **228**; Global Innovation Index (GII) 224–225; Saudi Arabia 226–229; Saudi Arabia's innovation ecosystem 229; UAE 230–231; UAE's innovation ecosystem **231**

Iraq 29–31; advantages and benefits of political and economic environment 30; constraints and disadvantages of political and economic environment 30–31; corruption 30; decrease in violence 30; disadvantages of regulations 34; free trade zones 34; oil, dependence on 31; political instability 31; political system 29–30; regulations 34; taxation 34

Kafala: dismantling 111–112

market entry in GCC 85–97; broad mechanisms 86; civil law 87; commercial risk 91; common law 88; cultural and religious sensitivities 91; foreign direct investment 89; free trade zones 88; human capital 89–90; institutional risk 90–91; international treaties and membership 87; investment promotion policies 88–90; legal frameworks 86–88; mixed common and civil law 87; outward foreign direct investment 93; political risk 91; promoting responsible conduct 91–92; property ownership 94; renewable energy sources 92–93; risk mitigation 90–91; sector-related concerns for investors 92–94; Sharia law 87; smart cities, development of 93; sovereign wealth funds 93–94; theoretical lens 90; trade routes 89

Mars: acquisition of 100% ownership in onshore business 45

MENA **132**; compositions 98–99; employment relations 98–115

Middle East: accounting and taxation systems 7; banking and financial institutions 7; challenges for investment 51; changing legal framework in GCC countries 6; commonalities 3; conflict management 7–8; context 3–9; definition 3; economic environment 5–6; economic growth 4; employment relations 7; entry modes to GCC markets 7; e-services 8–9; evolution of business context 4–5; expatriate management 8; foreign direct investment, GDP per capita **11**; net inflows **40**; gender issues in the workplace 8; human resource and organisational development 5; human resources 7; innovation 8; performance management 8; political environment 6; regional disturbances 4; religions 3–4; terminology 3; wasta 6 performance management 176–190; annual appraisal outcome 184; collectivism 178; evaluation tool 176; factors affecting **177**; FAHR 187; family-owned enterprises 181; features of performance appraisal 185–186; foreign invested enterprises 181–182; impact of external factors 178–179; institutional factors 179–182; internal factors 182–183; leadership 183; legal uses of performance management 184–185; nepotism 178–179; performance appraisal 183–186; power distance 179; state-owned enterprises 180; sub-factors affecting 177; technology 182; wasta 178–179

political environment 23–37; Egypt 27–29; Iraq 29–31; UAE 25–27

taxation 132–139; challenges for foreign investors and MNCs 138–139; corporate tax rates 135; economic development, and 137; history 133–134; income distribution, and 136–137; low rates 135; MENA 132–133; Middle East 132–133; Middle East vs global comparison **134**; oil prices, and 125–137; overview 134–138; types 133–134

technology transfer 222–224; indigenous technological capability 223–224; innovation, and 222–224; meaning 222; reality 222–223

trade unions 105–107

UAE 25–27; advantages of political and economic environment 25–26; changing nominee shareholder arrangement 44–45; constraints and disadvantages of political and economic environment 26–27; dependence on oil 26; free trade zones 32; location in unstable region 26–27; natural resources 25–26; ownership of LLC 32; political and economic environment 25–26; political system 25; regulations 32–33; tax regime 32

unemployment 12–15; female 14; information 14; rates **13**; young people 13–15

wasta 6, 62–81; absence of social justice, and 70–71; act of charity, as 69–70; advice to international businesses 77–78; belief that essential in labor market 68–71; business, and 64–65; case study 78–79; changing institution, as 64; confirmatory factor analysis 75; corruption or opportunity 62–81; cultural-cognitive legitimacy 70–71; data analysis 74; deep-rooted cultural connection 167–168; effectiveness 64; enhancing relationships with supplies 72–73; expert opinion 73; exploratory factor analysis 75; family members, and 68–69; friendship expectations, and 69; getting best offers 67; hiring family members 67–68; increased use 62; ineffective bureaucracy 66; IT companies, and 66; legitimacy 65–66; meaning 62–63; measurement model for scale 76; moral legitimacy 73; nature of 169; nature of IT businesses, and 72; nepotism 167–168; networking 167–168; normative legitimacy 68–70; pragmatic legitimacy 66–68; protection and power, and 70; rates **63**; recruitment of employees, and 66–67; scale development 65; scale testing **74**; scale validation 73–74; shafa'a, and 69; social capital, and 62; social esteem, and 70; status, and 70; tenders, and 67

women's employment 209–211; nationalization programs 211; participation rates **210**; skills management 210

Printed in the United States
by Baker & Taylor Publisher Services